The Writings of
James Fenimore C

With the cooperation of
Cooper family, the present
Cooper's *Writings* was init
1960s under the sponsorship or Clark
University and the American Antiquarian
Society in response to a long-felt need for
responsibly edited texts of Cooper's fiction
and non-fiction.  An astute student of men,
society, and politics, Cooper was the first
distinguished American writer to publish
his observations of Europe in a multi-
volume series.  These five books, most of
them out-of-print for a century and a half,
examine European civilizations with much
the care and exactness Tocqueville was
employing at about the same time in his
study of the United States.

The Historical Introduction and
Explanatory Notes in this volume were
prepared by Thomas Philbrick, Professor of
English at the University of Pittsburgh.
He is author of *James Fenimore Cooper
and the Development of American Sea
Fiction* and editor of Cooper's *The Crater*
and Richard Henry Dana's *Two Years
Before the Mast*.  The text of *France* was
established by Professor Philbrick in
collaboration with Constance Ayers Denne,
Professor of English at Baruch College of
The City University of New York.

Editorial work on this volume was
funded (in part) by the Program for
Editions of the National Endowment for
the Humanities.  The text was approved by
the Committee on Scholarly Editions of the
Modern Language Association.

# Gleanings in Europe: France

# The Writings of
# James Fenimore Cooper

Gleanings in Europe

# France

**James Fenimore Cooper**

Historical Introduction and
Explanatory Notes
by Thomas Philbrick
Text Established by
Thomas Philbrick and Constance Ayers Denne

State University of New York Press, Albany

*The preparation of this volume was made possible (in part) by a grant from the Program for Editions of the National Endowment for the Humanities, an independent Federal agency.*

CENTER FOR
SCHOLARLY EDITIONS
*AN APPROVED EDITION*
MODERN LANGUAGE
ASSOCIATION OF AMERICA

*The Center emblem means that one of a panel of textual experts serving the Center has reviewed the text and textual apparatus of the printer's copy by thorough and scrupulous sampling, and has approved them for sound and consistent editorial principles employed and maximum accuracy attained. The accuracy of the text has been guarded by careful and repeated proofreading according to standards set by the Center.*

*Published by*
*State University of New York Press, Albany*

*©1983 State University of New York*

Library of Congress Cataloging in Publication Data

Cooper, James Fenimore, 1789-1851
  Gleanings in Europe, France.


(The Writings of James Fenimore Cooper)
Includes index.
   1. France—Description and travel.   2. France—Social life and customs—19th century.   3. Cooper, James Fenimore, 1789-1851.
I. Philbrick, Thomas.   II. Denne, Constance Ayers.   III. Title.
IV. Series: Cooper, James Fenimore, 1789-1851. Works. 1981.
Writings of James Fenimore Cooper.
DC27.C76 1983            944.06            82-669
ISBN 0-87395-368-1                         AACR2
ISBN 0-87395-599-4 (pbk.)

# Contents

# Acknowledgements

For institutional support in the preparation of this volume, the editors wish to thank Marcus McCorison, Director and Librarian of the American Antiquarian Society; President Mortimer H. Appley of Clark University; and Martin Stevens, Dean of the School of Liberal Arts and Sciences, Baruch College, The City University of New York. Assistance from the National Endowment for the Humanities ensured the completion of this and other volumes.

Among the many librarians and curators who helped in the preparation of this book, the editors wish especially to thank Charles E. Aston and George M. Jones of the University of Pittsburgh Library; Maud D. Cole, Faye Simkin, and Lola Szladits of the New York Public Library; and Frank G. White of Old Sturbridge Village. Further aid and information were provided by the staffs of the American Antiquarian Society, the Bibliothèque Nationale, the Boston Public Library, the Brown University Library, the Carnegie Library of Pittsburgh, the Harvard University Library, the Holy Cross College Library, and the Yale University Library.

For permission to use and publish manuscript material, the editors are deeply grateful to Dr. Paul Fenimore Cooper, Jr.

Constance Denne wishes to thank Professor C. J. Denne, Jr., and Frank A. Perone for their assistance with the collations. Thomas Philbrick is grateful for the advice and help given him by Professors James F. Beard, James P. Elliott, Kay S. House, Wayne R. Kime, and Edwin W. Marrs. The hard work and good judgment of Marianne Philbrick contributed to every phase of the preparation of this book and is here acknowledged with the deepest thanks.

# Illustrations

The engravings reproduced in this edition of *Gleanings in Europe: France* are selected from Jacques Antoine Dulaure's *Histoire civile, physique et morale de Paris*, first published in Paris in 1825, and *Histoire physique, civile et morale des environs de Paris*, first published in Paris in 1825-28. Cooper's several significant borrowings from Dulaure suggest that the volumes of *Paris* and the *Environs* were at his elbow as he wrote *France*. The illustrations thus not only offer contemporaneous visual renderings of scenes that Cooper describes in his book, but they may well have contributed to its composition by refreshing his memory of places which, in some instances, he had not seen for ten years.

The engravings were made from drawings by the French artist Christophe Civeton (1796-1831), whose chief work was the eighty-five illustrations that he supplied for *Paris* and the ninety-two that he furnished for the *Environs*. The illustrations reproduced here are taken from the fourth edition of *Paris*, published in ten volumes by Guillaume in 1829, and from the first edition of the *Environs*, also published by Guillaume, in seven volumes.

*Following page 114*

# HISTORICAL INTRODUCTION

*Gleanings in Europe: France,* the third of Cooper's European travel books in the sequence of publication, was the first volume in the chronology of travels recorded in this series. Its relative position, together with the variant titles under which it originally appeared, is indicated in the following chart:

| Chronology | Title in Cooper Edition | Title in American First Edition | Title in British First Edition |
|---|---|---|---|
| 14 July-15 Oct. 1828 | *Gleanings in Europe: Switzerland* | *Sketches of Switzerland* (1836) | *Excursions in Switzerland* (1836) |
| 20 Aug. 1830-17 July 1832 passim 18 July-11 Oct. 1832 | *Gleanings in Europe: The Rhine* | *Sketches of Switzerland, Part Second* (1836) | *A Residence in France: with an Excursion up the Rhine, and a Second Visit to Switzerland* (1836) |
| 1 June 1826-27 Feb. 1828 | *Gleanings in Europe: France* | *Gleanings in Europe* (1837) | *Recollections of Europe* (1837) |
| 28 Feb.-29 May 1828 | *Gleanings in Europe: England* | *Gleanings in Europe: England* (1837) | *England, With Sketches of Society in the Metropolis* (1837) |
| 16 Oct. 1828-11 May 1830 | *Gleanings in Europe: Italy* | *Gleanings in Europe: Italy* (1838) | *Excursions in Italy* (1838) |

# Historical Introduction

*Gleanings in Europe: France* records Cooper's first encounter with the Old World since his boyhood voyage before the mast to England and the Mediterranean in 1806-07. Beginning with the departure of the Coopers from New York on 1 June 1826, *France* carries the family across the Atlantic, pauses for their two-week stay in England, sets them in motion again on their journey by steamboat across the Channel to Le Havre and up the Seine to Rouen, and then transports them by carriage to Paris where, once they are comfortably quartered, the book can get down to its true concern, the leisurely exploration of French society and its culture in the waning years of the Bourbon Restoration. There are excursions into the environs—visits to Compiègne, Versailles, and Lafayette's La Grange—and there is a pleasant suburban summer in a thirty-room house in Saint-Ouen, but the focus is on the capital itself: its abattoirs and salons, its private gossip and public display, indeed, the whole "strange medley of finery[,] dirt and magnificence" that Cooper found in this "city turned inside out, with its elegance a little spoiled by the weather."[1] In the final letter of the book, the Coopers resume their travels as, in late February 1828, they set out for England by way of Calais.

The actual inception of Cooper's European travels antedated by far the June day in 1826 when he and his family embarked from Whitehall Wharf. Beset by debt and ill-health, he made plans for the trip as early as 1823, when the family began French lessons. By the fall of 1825, his intentions were taking definite shape, as he wrote to a young European acquaintance:

> Mrs. C—— and myself, talk very seriously of making an effort to get to France for a year or two—Nothing but poverty prevents—I wish you would make a few enquiries as to what a plain man, like myself, might live on [in] Paris—and also near a provincial town—say Orleans—...
>
> If I had influence enough to get a good consulate, or some such thing, my mind would be relieved, and I do think I would

venture—As it is, I feel afraid to take a wife and five children, the former well born and all tenderly educated, to a strange land— mais, nous verrons—[2]

Cooper's researches yielded encouraging results. One could live well in Europe as cheaply as in America, and the facilities there for continuing the education of his son and four daughters were unequalled. Besides, once upon the European scene, he might be able to negotiate better terms for his next book, *The Prairie*, and to extract some return from the French publishers who regularly pirated his novels. In February 1826, he informed John Miller, his English publisher, that he intended "to sail from here, some time in the month of June, either for France or Italy, which I have not yet determined," for a stay of "a year or two—My object, is my own health and the instruction of my children in the French and Italian languages—Perhaps there is, also, a little pleasure concealed, in the bottom of the Cup—"[3] In that same month, he asked De Witt Clinton, then governor of New York, to exert his influence with the federal government in securing "any Consulate, that would yield me a moderate sum," preferably a post on the Mediterranean, as a support for a projected European residence of "three or four years."[4] Acting on Clinton's recommendation, Henry Clay, the secretary of state, offered Cooper the post of minister to Sweden or, alternatively, proposed creating a consulate at Lyons for him. Unlucrative though the latter position would be, it carried with it no burdensome diplomatic responsibilities and it conferred upon the novelist an official identity in one of the two countries which he had in mind for his residence. Accordingly, he wrote to Clay in early May to request the post at Lyons and to announce that he would "sail for London on the first of June—My Stay in England will not exceed ten days, after which I shall proceed direct to Paris—"[5] John Quincy Adams promptly signed Cooper's commission, the Senate approved it, and, after attending an elaborate farewell banquet given by his club, the Bread and Cheese Lunch, on the evening of 29 May, he and his entourage—Mrs. Cooper, thirteen-year-old Susan Augusta Fenimore, ten-year-old Caroline Martha, nine-year-old Ann Charlotte, six-year-old Maria Frances, two-year-old Paul, and the novelist's nephew William Yeardley Cooper, sixteen, who was to act as his secretary and copyist—were ready to depart.

Casual though the choice of France as their destination may seem, Cooper's interest in that country and his acquaintance with her people were of long standing. The Cooperstown of his childhood provided sanctuary for a number of émigrés during the years of the Terror, among them M. Le Quoy, the former governor of Martinique who figures in *The Pioneers* as an amiable village storekeeper. Talleyrand, whom Cooper was soon to see attending his royal master at the Tuileries, had been the guest of Judge Cooper in 1795, but surely the most impressive visitor from France was Lafayette, whose American tour in 1824-25 Cooper followed with eager attention. "Though personally unknown to La Fayette," he told a correspondent soon after the General's visit, "I never felt so much interest, when a boy, in any foreigner as I did in him — It is a wonderful feeling, that binds us all, so strongly to that old man — "[6] Although Cooper could scarcely have anticipated the warmth of the reception that Lafayette was to extend to him in Paris or the extent of his own subsequent involvement in the old republican's political causes, it is significant that France, alone among the countries of Europe, possessed a citizen who inspired him with feelings so nearly filial. Perhaps he sensed what was indeed to come to pass — his gradual appropriation of France as a second home. Neither the thorny resentments that he brought to England nor the aesthetic eye with which he regarded Switzerland and Italy could be sustained by his experience in France; rather, he came to feel something of that admixture of affectionate concern and critical dismay which characterized his mature response to his own country.

But the principal magnet that drew the Coopers to Paris was the appeal of the city itself, which by the 1820s had once again assumed its role as the capital of Western culture. Although the physical appearance of Paris, still encircled by a toll wall at whose *barrières* the *octroi* was exacted, had not yet been transformed by Haussmann, the eighteenth-century city had acquired the new grandeur of its Napoleonic triumphal arches and bridges and, at the very time of Cooper's first residence there, was putting on the distinctive trappings of nineteenth-century civilization. The Bourse, Brogniart's elegant temple of capitalism, was opened in late 1826, a few sidewalks now provided pedestrians with some defense against the traffic and mire of the streets, and the first experiments in transportation by omnibus and street-lighting by gas were under way. The restaurants of Paris had already become famous, though Cooper thought that no well-bred woman should patronize them, and the first department stores were just then making their appearance.

As if to insulate themselves from these innovations, the members of the old aristocracy had taken their stand in the seclusion of the Faubourg Saint-Germain, on the Left Bank across the river from the Place de la Concorde and the Tuileries Gardens. On the Right Bank, many of the Napoleonic nobility and some of the wealthy bourgeoisie occupied the Faubourg Saint-Honoré, just north of the Champs-Élysées and the Place de la Concorde, but the stronghold of the bankers and industrialists lay a little to the east in the Chaussée d'Antin, the area immediately north of the Place Vendôme and the Palais Royal.

By and large, those territorial divisions reflected the major bands of the political spectrum of France during the Restoration. The center of support for Charles X, who had come to the throne upon the death of his brother, Louis XVIII, in 1824, and for the reactionary administration of the Comte de Villèle, which had been in power since 1822, was among the royalists of the Faubourg Saint-Germain. Among the inhabitants of the Faubourg Saint-Honoré and the Chausée d'Antin, on the other hand, were those who, for a variety of reasons, advocated a change in the existing order of things—Doctrinaires, who looked to England as the exemplar of constitutional monarchy; Orleanists, who supported Louis Philippe as a means of promoting the interests of the bourgeoisie; Bonapartists, who harked back to the glories of the Empire; and republicans, who rallied around Lafayette and sought an end to monarchy itself.

As *France* demonstrates, this intensely political atmosphere was to interest Cooper deeply, for it sustained a prolonged and searching debate on the most fundamental principles of government. It engaged the minds and pens of men who, like Chateaubriand and Benjamin Constant, were far more than politicians, and it supplied a theme, and sometimes a *raison d'être*, for the salons that still formed the basis of Parisian social life. In the Faubourg Saint-Germain, the salon of the Princesse de la Trémoille was the mecca of the Ultra-Royalists, while that of the Duchesse de Duras attracted a wider representation of the political right. More liberal than most of her neighbors, the Duchesse de Broglie, whose mother, the celebrated Madame de Staël, had once sought Judge Cooper's assistance in the management of her American land holdings, presided over the gatherings of the Doctrinaires. On the Right Bank, the liberals met at the houses of the banker Lafitte and the manufacturer Ternaux, while the Bonapartists attended the soirees of the Comtesse Baraguay d'Hilliers.

But not all of the soirees were so pointedly political. Some, like those held in the modest apartments of the lovely Madame de Mirbel, were more concerned with the arts and sciences than with government, and at such gatherings one might encounter poets like Lamartine, scientists like Cuvier, or composers like Rossini, who directed the Théâtre des Italiens. As Cooper observed to his old friend Mrs. Jay, "Talent is, or is thought to be every thing at Paris,"[7] and for good reason. It was a brilliant era in French culture, brought to a white heat by the struggle for supremacy between the forces of classicism and those of the new romanticism. Like the clash between reaction and reform in the political arena, the conflict in the arts pitted the apostles of new ideas and new modes against the upholders of the old order—in literature, Hugo against Lemercier; in painting, Delacroix against David; in music, Berlioz against Cherubini. Observing and contributing to the ferment were a host of others: Vigny, Mérimée, Stendahl, Sainte-Beuve, Béranger, Dumas *père*, Villemain, Sue, Scribe, Cousin, Guizot, Fourier, and Balzac all lived and wrote in Cooper's Paris.

The city of 800,000 inhabitants that lay at the end of the Coopers' long journey thus presented a striking juxtaposition of the old and the new, poised in precarious balance in these last years of France's first experiment in constitutional monarchy and threatened by each slight change in the political atmosphere. "Nous dansons sur un volcan," as Salvandy said a month before the July Revolution of 1830, but it was a dazzling dance, indeed.

In its issue for 30 July 1826, the jaunty new satirical newspaper *Figaro* announced in typical fashion the presence of a distinguished visitor:

> Est-il à Paris? on le dit, on le croit; l'avez-vous vu?—Pas encore.—Dites-moi sous le secret s'il est vrai qu'il existe?—Oui et non. Ses ouvrages, ou du moins ceux qu'on lui attribue, sont là: *le Pilote, l'Espion, le Dernier des Mohicans, les Pionniers.*—M. Cooper, américain, est-il l'auteur de ces excellens romans? Demandez à Walter-Scott s'il connaît le Walter-Scott américain.

Cooper's arrival in the city eight days before clearly had not gone unnoticed. Thanks to the power of his literary reputation, he found that his consular appointment was of little value to him, and he resigned the office on 8 September 1828, "being tired of the high distinction, which is of just no use at all to me, except as a travelling name."[8] Similarly, his letters of introduction proved to be less a help than a hindrance, for their main service was to put the Coopers in touch with the pretentious Mrs. Robertson, Mrs. Jay's cousin: "Had she been a good motherly old woman, (for she is the latter in spite of all her efforts to the contrary) she might have won our hearts but we are, as you well know, neither to be caught nor to be aw'd by airs."[9] As Mrs. Cooper reported of her husband to her sister in November 1826, the Parisians "make quite a Lion of him, and Princesses write to him, and he has invitations from Lords and Ladies." At the head of the welcoming committee was the charming celebrity hunter the Princess Galitzin (or Golitsyn), the fifty-six-year-old widow of Prince Michael Andreevich Golitsyn and a Russian countess in her own right, who, at the urging of her former Paris neighbor Albert Gallatin, sought out the Coopers and, together with her children, befriended them until her death in 1828. Cooper "has so many notes from the Princess Galitzin," his wife wrote, "that I should be absolutely jealous, were it not that she is a Grandmother."[10] By March 1827, any doubts that the novelist might have had about his reception in Paris were dispelled. So pervasive was the "perfect mania" of the French for literature that instead "of seeking for society, I am compelled to draw back from it, on account of my health and my pursuits."[11]

Cooper was apparently unaware of the fact that the romantic excitement which was sweeping over France had installed him among those foreign writers whom the literary salons of Paris most admired—Scott, Byron, Goethe, and Schiller. Scott, who put Mrs. Cooper "in mind of one of our country Presbyterian Parsons,"[12] met Cooper in Paris in November 1826, and the two created a sensation when, as the Great Unknown noted in his journal, "the Scotch and American lions took the field together" at a soiree given by the Princess Galitzin.[13] Although *France* makes little reference to its author's celebrity, Cooper himself was rapidly becoming one of those Parisian monuments which the writers of travel books and memoirs felt compelled to notice. George Washington Greene recalled his impressions upon first meeting Cooper in Paris when, as a sixteen-year-old Brown University student, he was a guest at Lafayette's reception for a touring party of Osage Indians in the summer of 1827:

> I saw a gentleman enter, whose appearance immediately called off the General's attention from the special guests of the hour. He was evidently in the prime of life, and of that vigor which air and

manly exercise give, and with something in all his movements which awakened in you an instantaneous conviction that the mind and will which governed them were of no ordinary energy and measure. I could not withdraw my eyes: I had seen heads of great men, and there were some great men close to me at the very moment—but there was none with such a full, expansive forehead, such strong, massive features, a mouth so firm without harshness, and an eye whose clear grey seemed to read you at a glance, while it met yours with the unflinching look of one that fears not to let you read him in turn. "Who is he?" I whispered to a grand-daughter of the General's, who stood near me. "Mr. Cooper: do you not know Mr. Cooper?—let me introduce you to him." "Cooper," said I to myself, "can it be that I am within five paces of Cooper, and that there, too, are the feeble representatives of the race around which his genius has shed a halo like that of Homer's own heroes!" I was fresh from the "Mohicans," and my hand trembled as it met the cordial grasp of the man to whom I owed so many pleasing hours . . . .

A day or two afterwards I met him in the General's bedroom, and I mention it here, as it offered me an opportunity of witnessing his first interview with Béranger, and seeing how warmly the great poet welcomed him.[14]

William Hazlitt, who saw Cooper in Paris in March 1827, was less entranced, remarking that he "strutted through the streets with a very consequential air; and in company held up his head, screwed up his features, and placed himself on a sort of pedestal to be observed and admired, as if he never relaxed in the assumption nor wished it to be forgotten by others, that he was the American Sir Walter Scott."[15] Apparently it made a difference whether the observer was American or English. Nathaniel Parker Willis, encountering Cooper on a Paris street "with the blue surtout buttoned up to his throat, and his hat over his eyes," described the novelist as "dark and corsair-looking, with his brows down over his eyes, and his strongly lined mouth fixed in an expression of moodiness and reserve." Despite Cooper's seeming Byronic remoteness, Willis found him to be extraordinarily generous in his support of worthy causes—perhaps because he lent Willis $150—and unfailingly loyal to his country, a quality that surely did not endear him to Hazlitt. The French, Willis reported, "idolize Cooper," and the rest of the Continent goes so far as to prefer him to Scott.[16]

*France* gives little indication of the steady professional labor by which Cooper maintained his international reputation while in Paris. When he sailed for Europe, the uncompleted manuscript of *The Prairie* was among his baggage, and the writing and publication of that novel occupied him heavily during his early months abroad. His quick excursion to London in July 1826 led to no satisfactory arrangement with his English publisher, John Miller, and in October he opened negotiations with Henry Colburn through Colburn's agent in Paris, Francis Moore. Although he began sending sheets of the first volume to Carey and Lea, his American publishers, at the end of that month, much of the book still remained unwritten. Not until April 1827 was *The Prairie* off his hands, but by then he was dickering with his publishers over the terms for his next book, *The Red Rover*. In October, the writing and printing of that novel were completed, and he could devote his attention to still another work, already "a good deal advanced."[17] Undertaken at the request of Lafayette, the new project was Cooper's first extended experiment in nonfiction, *Notions of the Americans*, an attempt to correct the misrepresentations of the United States by foreign observers. Since the book required the use of accurate statistical data, the work proceeded slowly, for Cooper was separated by the Atlantic from his best sources of information. By late February 1828, when he left Paris for England, *Notions* was still only half written. Meanwhile, there were smaller professional chores to do—the supervision of the translation of his novels into French, the composition of an account of the *grand couvert* of Charles X for the *New-York Commercial Advertiser*, and a protracted and finally futile effort to aid Scott by securing him some return from the American editions of his works.

But Cooper was a husband and a father as well as a writer, and the residence in France imposed additional burdens on him by complicating his domestic arrangements. Upon his arrival in Paris on 22 July 1826, he installed his family in temporary quarters in the Hôtel de Montmorency, a small public establishment in the Chausée d'Antin on the Rue Saint-Marc, around the corner from the fashionable cafés and shops of the Passage des Panoramas. In early August, the Coopers moved across the Seine to the Faubourg Saint-Germain, where they rented the third floor of the Hôtel de Jumilhac at 12 Rue Saint-Maur, a street that ran south from the Rue de Sèvres to the Rue du Cherche-Midi and that now, as the Rue de l'Abbé-Grégoire, continues south to

the Rue de Vaugirard. There, conveniently situated above the school
of Mmes. Trigant de la Tour and Kautz, the family established its first
home in Europe, as Cooper informed his friend Luther Bradish:

> We are rather comfortably lodged for Paris—Dirt, Bugs and Fleas
> of course, but still a good deal of comfort—There is a large salle à
> manger, (that is large for lodgings) a Petit et Grand Salon—deux
> chambres à coucher, a cabinet, and a cuisine—For these furnished,
> pretty well, I pay f2600 per an. The girls are all in the school
> below, at the rate of f700 each, with I suppose some extra charges
> where they will learn to speak French, to dance, to read—to write,
> and special little else I fancy—They sleep in our apartment,
> though they eat below, for the price I pay, includes every thing—[18]

A few days after this new arrangement was made, Cooper's second
daughter, Caroline, was severely stricken with scarlet fever and was
confined to her bed for two months. Mrs. Cooper, Charlotte, Frances,
and Paul had the disease in milder form, and Cooper himself suffered
a succession of "wretched colds, which have made him thin and pale"[19]
and which kept him in his room for the first six weeks of 1827. Work
and illness severely restricted the family's social activities until March
of that year, when they quickly made up for lost time. In that single
month, Cooper and his wife attended a large evening party given by
Mrs. Brown, the wife of the American minister to France; took their
brood to a children's party given by the Marquise de Terzi, the Princess
Galitzin's daughter; dined with the American banker Samuel Welles
and with Mrs. Brown; and attended a soiree at Lafayette's apartment
on the Rue d'Anjou. In the same month, Cooper, leaving his wife at
home, escorted the Princess Galitzin to a great ball given by Pozzo di
Borgo, the Russian ambassador; joined the five or six hundred guests
at a party of Madame Thuret, wife of an influential French banker;
dined with the Duchesse de Broglie; went to a soiree of Madame de
Mirbel; and spent a week with Lafayette at La Grange.

Meanwhile, there were plans for the summer to be made. Lafayette
was negotiating with a Madame Bigottini for the rental of her country
house near La Grange for the Coopers, but they decided instead on the
house on the Seine in Saint-Ouen, apparently on the advice of Welles,
who had rented it previously. Giving up their apartment on the Rue
Saint-Maur, the family moved to Saint-Ouen on 1 June 1827. "The
country is doing Uncle James a great deal of good," young William

Cooper wrote to his cousin Hannah Pomeroy on 12 June,[20] and the strenuousness of the novelist's activities during the summer and early fall confirms that judgment: expeditions to Saint-Denis, Senlis, Compiègne, Soissons, and Montmorency; excursions by cabriolet and on horseback through the region about Saint-Ouen; and a circuit on foot of the walls surrounding Paris. Cooper had some thoughts of spending the winter in the South of France, but the requirements of his daughters' education and the demands of his own work kept him in Paris. Accordingly, the four girls boarded at their old school, while the rest of the family took up quarters across the river in a small apartment on the Rue des Champs-Élysées in the Faubourg Saint-Honoré, on the site of the present 10 Rue Boissy-d'Anglas. Cooper planned a short visit to England, where he intended to publish *Notions of the Americans*, but the slow progress of the book evidently delayed him past his expected date of departure and, it would seem, past the expiration of his lease. At any rate, in early January 1828, he, his wife, William, and Paul moved once more, this time to the Hôtel Chatham on the Rue Neuve-Saint-Augustin in the Chausée d'Antin, and it was from there that the four set out for England on 25 February.

Paris was to serve as Cooper's principal place of residence throughout his subsequent years in Europe. He returned to 12 Rue Saint-Maur from 9 June to 14 July 1828 before leaving for Switzerland, Italy, and Germany. Then in August 1830, he and his family once again settled down in Paris, where, except for a three-month tour of the Rhine and Switzerland in 1832, they remained until their departure for the United States in September 1833. Indeed, of Cooper's seven years in Europe, four and half were spent in the French capital. When he turned to the composition of *France* in 1836, he thus could enrich his account of his first experience of Paris with the insights and perceptions that he had gathered over those later years of acquaintance with her people and their culture. The scheme of *France* would require the perspective of a newcomer, but its judgments and conclusions were in fact to be those of a seasoned observer.

Cooper had formed the intention to write a series of European travel books as early as March 1828, immediately after his first residence in Paris. In that month, he described to his American publisher a scheme which would begin with an account of his projected tour of northern Europe and then would take up France and the other countries of the

Continent: "I have no idea of boring mankind with statistics, and dry essays on Politics, but to give only, rapid sketches of what I shall see, with *American* eyes."[21] In preparation for the project, he began keeping journals of his travels, intending to publish a book on Holland and Switzerland in the spring of 1829.[22] Although nothing came of that intention, the project was still on his mind on 2 January 1832, when he described to Peter Augustus Jay a series of four travel volumes, the first of which—to be dedicated "to a short visit in England, and to my first residence in France"—precisely anticipated the scope of *Gleanings in Europe: France.*[23] Not until the spring of 1835, more than a year and a half after his return to America, did he initiate definite negotiations with his publishers for the travel books. Even then, the plan of the series was still fluid, for he apparently contemplated a sequential narrative of his European travels in two or three volumes, the first of which would contain the matter of *France.*[24] But that summer, when Cooper actually started writing, he turned first not to *France* but to *Switzerland* and *The Rhine*, perhaps because his journals provided him with fairly full and detailed accounts of the excursions with which those books deal, whereas no such materials existed for *France.*

On 21 July 1836, when Cooper had just finished seeing *The Rhine* through the press, he offered a third travel book to his British publisher, Richard Bentley; it was to be "a condensed account of my visit to Europe—extracts, like the scenes with La Fayette, the affair of the two day[s] &c—containing glimpses of different countries—"[25] This vague and inaccurate description of *France* suggests that he had not yet worked out the plan of the book, let alone begun its composition. Once started, however, the writing evidently proceeded rapidly. Established now in Otsego Hall, the family mansion which Cooper had retrieved from alien hands and renovated upon his return from Europe, he was so far along in October that he was correcting the proofs of the first volume by mail.[26] On 5 November, he arrived in Philadelphia to see the second volume through the press, and by 19 November, the work was done.[27]

It would seem that Cooper's one great resource in the composition of *France* was his powerfully retentive memory, helped out, one can be sure, by the recollections of Mrs. Cooper and the children. Although a few passages in *France*, like the description of the *grand couvert* in Letter IX and the account of Pozzo's ball in Letter XVIII, parallel letters that he wrote at the time of his first residence in Paris, small factual discrepancies between the two suggest that he wrote the book without reference to his earlier letters and without benefit of journal entries that might have refreshed his memory.[28] No true prototypes of the twenty-three "letters" of *France* have turned up among Cooper's surviving correspondence; indeed, there is no evidence that he wrote at all during his first stay in Paris to some of the people whom he addresses in the book, and even the few actual letters which contain parallels to *France* are addressed to correspondents different from those he names there.

With one notable exception, Cooper apparently made little use of guidebooks and other published materials as sources for *France*. He did borrow significantly from the historian Jacques Antoine Dulaure, whose massive *Histoire physique, civile et morale des environs de Paris* in seven volumes (Paris: Guillaume, 1825-28) and *Histoire civile, physique et morale de Paris* in ten volumes (Paris: Baudoin Frères, 1825) helped him to fill out the historical detail of *France*. Cooper evidently purchased the histories during his first residence in Paris, for he cites Dulaure in his journal entry for 10 August 1828 during his first tour of Switzerland.[29] In the summer and fall of 1836, when he was writing *France*, Dulaure's volumes were at his elbow, as his occasional citation and unacknowledged paraphrasing of them indicate. A comparison of the description of the ruins of Vivier in Letter XX of *France* with that of Dulaure in the *Environs* will illustrate Cooper's use of his source:

> The third day of our visit, we all drove three or four leagues across the country, to see an old ruin of a royal castle called Vivier. This name implies a pond, and sure enough we found the remains of the buildings in the midst of two or three pools of water. This has been a considerable house, the ruins being still quite extensive and rather pretty. It was originally the property of a great noble, but the kings of France were in possession of it, as early as the year 1300. Charles V. had a great affection for Vivier, and very materially increased its establishment. His son, Charles VI., who was at times deranged, was often confined here, and it was after his reign, and by means of the long wars that ravaged France, that the place came to be finally abandoned as a royal abode . . . .
>
> There are the ruins of a fine chapel and of two towers of considerable interest, beside extensive fragments of more vulgar buildings. One of these towers, being very high and very slender, is a striking object; but, from its form and position, it was one of

those narrow wells that were attached to larger towers, and which contained nothing but the stairs. (*France*, p. 245)

Le nom du Vivier, commun à plusiers autres lieux en France, indique la présence d'un étang ou vivier; et cette indication est ici très-juste, car on y voit plus d'un étang. (*Environs*, VI, 213)

Dans la suite, un des seigneurs de ce château le vendit, on ne sait à quelle époque, à un roi de France. Il est certain que Phillipe-le-Long en était propriétaire, et qu'en 1319 il y rendit une ordonnance relative à la chambre des comptes.

Le roi qui montra le plus de prédilection pour ce château fut Charles V. Lorsqui'il n'était encore que Dauphin, il entreprit de donner de l'importance à ce lieu. (*Environs*, VI, 215)

Charles VI, son fils, lors de ses trop fréquens accès de démence, fut souvent relégué au château du Vivier. (*Environs*, VI, 217)

Les rois cessèrent d'habiter le château du Vivier, qui resta sans réparations, sans doute par suite des longues guerres qui, sous les règnes de Charles VI et de Charles VII, désolèrent la France. (*Environs*, VI, 217-18)

L'objet le plus imposant de ces ruines, et qui attire principalement les regards, est une tour encore debout. Elle est d'une hauteur considérable, et semble avoir, du haut en bas, été partagée. On croirait qu'une moitié s'en est détachée, tandis que l'autre est restée intacte; mais, en examinant de près, en reconnaît que ce qui subsiste était un accessoire, et contenait l'esalier d'une tour beaucoup plus volumineuse qui ne subsiste plus. (*Environs*, VI, 221)

Not all of Cooper's other borrowings from Dulaure are as substantial as this one, but their frequency testifies to the fact that the depth of historical reference in *France* is almost entirely owing to information supplied by the *Environs* and *Paris*.[30] The present edition enlarges that debt by taking its illustrations from those of Dulaure's two histories.

Since no manuscript drafts, printer's copy, or revised proof sheets for *France* have survived, it is impossible to retrace the process by which the book took shape in Cooper's hands. Among the Cooper family papers, however, are eight pages of manuscript on French domestic customs that appear to constitute a rejected letter of *France*. Conceivably the pages are a fragment of some unfinished work, perhaps the second "and far more elaborate book on France" that Cooper at one time planned and abandoned for lack of encouragement from his publishers,[31] but all the evidence suggests that the manuscript, transcribed in Appendix B of this edition, was part of the first draft of *France*. Surely the aborted second book would have dealt with the last three years of Cooper's residence in Paris and not gone over the ground of *France* again, his first eighteen months in that city. But the time frame of the manuscript letter is precisely that of *France*. Charles X, not Louis Philippe, is on the throne, and the uproar over the Austrian ambassador's refusal to acknowledge the Napoleonic military titles, an event of early 1827, is referred to as "a recent occurrence." Indeed, everything about the manuscript letter—its content, tone, and format—is consistent with the twenty-three letters which Cooper did incorporate in *France*.

Why, then, did he reject this letter? Its chronology and subject matter suggest that it was designed to follow Letter XXI, a ranging consideration of the influence of French political institutions on social relations. The manuscript letter would deal with the more intimate sectors of French life—marriage and funeral customs, the education of young women, and attitudes within the family. But if this was indeed Cooper's design, then the manuscript letter would have occupied the crucial penultimate position in the sequence of letters. In that place, its rambling structure—trailing off, as it does, with the entirely unrelated matter of a visit to Marshal Soult's collection of Spanish paintings—and its primary concern with subjects of more interest to the father of four marriageable daughters than to the general public may have struck him as anticlimactic. It would seem that he discarded the manuscript letter and substituted in its place the present Letter XXII, the most anecdotal and entertaining of all the letters of *France*.

Letter XXII, the narrative of Cooper's encounters with a Parisian mesmerist, is an anomaly in that it is the only letter in *France* that deals with experiences which belong not to his residence of 1826-28 but to a considerably later period. He in fact became interested in animal magnetism in early 1833 at the prompting of his young American friend Albert Brisbane, and his visits to the practitioner and his *somnambule* were evidently made in January and February of that year.[32] Conceivably the substitution was a last-minute decision, for Letter XXII—unlike the manuscript letter, which quotes from the collection of cards and announcements that the Coopers had brought with them from Europe—is in no way dependent on documentation and could have been written in the hotel in Philadelphia during the two weeks in November 1836 when Cooper was seeing the last sections of *France* through the press. In any event, he could have contrived no more attractive conclusion to his observations on Paris than Letter XXII. It proved to be a favorite of the reviewers, as it undoubtedly did with readers generally, appearing as it did when the popular interest in hypnotism was at its height in America and England.

But the appeal of Letter XXII was not sufficient to make *France* a commercial success. From the beginning, Cooper's publishers had not been encouraging about the prospects of his series of travel books, and *France* did little to change their minds. Carey, Lea and Blanchard, who had paid him $750 for a printing of 2,000 copies,[33] delayed the publication of *France* until 4 March 1837, because of the slow sales of *Switzerland* and *The Rhine*.[34] By then, however, the country was in the grip of a financial panic so severe that food riots had broken out in New York City in mid-February. On 5 April 1837, Cooper reported to his wife from Philadelphia that *France* was selling "a little better than its predecessors, but nothing sells well, just now. Indeed you can hardly imagine the gravity of the moment, for those who have heavy engagements."[35] Carey, Lea and Blanchard were fortunate enough to survive the crisis, but not by the help of *France*, which, like the two earlier travel books, proved to be a losing proposition.[36] The book fared no better in England. With some reluctance, Richard Bentley had accepted Cooper's offer of *France* for £200, the same payment that he had made for *Switzerland* and *The Rhine*,[37] and had published an edition of 1250 copies on 24 January 1837.[38] Like his American counterpart, however, Bentley found that the publication of *France* was "unattended by profit."[39] The publishers of the Paris editions in English and in French translation and those of the three German translations presumably were more successful, for their costs did not include a payment to the author.[40]

The publication of *France* attracted only a modest response from the press. Both Bentley and Carey, Lea and Blanchard tried to prepare the ground by arranging for the printing of samples of the new book shortly before it went on sale, and the editors of a few literary magazines and papers were not reluctant to provide themselves with attractive free copy by printing copious extracts from it in the weeks following its publication.[41] But American newspapers, by and large, ignored the book, for Cooper's relations with the press, though not yet as violent as the controversy over *Home As Found* was to make them, were already at the stage of mutual suspicion and accusation. The *New-York American*, edited by Cooper's former friend and present enemy Charles King, was the only important paper to notice the appearance of the new work, contenting itself with the observation that anything from the novelist's pen "must possess more or less interest," though he "seems to carry with him everywhere, an arrow in his side, shot from the press."[42]

The reviewers for the American literary magazines paid *France* more attention, but much of it was unfavorable. Some, like the writers for the *Southern Literary Messenger* and the *American Quarterly Review*, thought the book trivial and urged its author to return to those fictional fields from which his reputation sprang, an opinion echoed by Francis Bowen, whose lengthy and admiring survey in the *North American Review* of Cooper's corpus to date ended anticlimactically with a disenchanted examination of *France*. The *Knickerbocker*, however, brought its usual geniality to Cooper's new book, finding it "one of the most interesting and instructive books of travels that we remember to have read for many a long year," commending it for its sturdy patriotism, and hoping that further volumes of Cooper's travels would soon appear. The *American Monthly Magazine* agreed, recommending *France* as "a useful book" and pointing to its "flowing and natural" style as the means by which Cooper made the "instructiveness" of the book "exceedingly readable and entertaining." Applying its own peculiar standard to the style of *France*, the *Southern Literary Journal* discovered the book to be "a less elegant work than the Rev. Mr. Dewey's 'Old World and New'" but still deserving of praise for its interest and "manly good sense."[43]

If the reception of *France* in the United States was lukewarm, the British reviewers, not yet provoked by Cooper's ungracious treatment of their country in *England*, generally gave the book a responsible reading and a favorable judgment. The *Atheneum* was alone in its dislike of *France*; declaring that never, "even in the most frivolous of fashionable novels, were we so pestered with popinjay philosophy about mere manners," the *Atheneum* suggested "that selections might be profitably made from it, and published as 'The American Manual of Gentility; or, Every Man his own Chesterfield.'" But the other English journals found no such matter for complaint. The *Literary Examiner* delighted in Cooper's courageous strictures against his own countrymen, while the *Literary Gazette*, viewing the book as a whole and not only in one of its several aspects, praised the intelligence and originality of its observation of the European scene. The most comprehensive and perceptive consideration of *France* appeared in the *Spectator*. Unlike any of the other reviewers, English or American, the writer for the *Spectator* attempted to place the new book in its proper relation to Cooper's two preceding travel books. Finding *France* "unquestionably the best" of the lot, he accurately noted its stronger narrative continuity and, as a record of France in the last years of the Bourbon dynasty, its greater historical interest. Only the critical tone of the book annoyed the reviewer, and even on this sensitive subject, he maintained his balance:

> Two personal points stand out, — a morbid dislike to England — an unwillingness to allow her any sort of merit, even down to those miracles in the eyes of all Americans, her horses and stagecoaches; a disagreeable shrewdness, which looks at the bad side of things, and is not the less offensive because it is not easy to confute it.

But these reviews all appeared in weekly journals. With the exception of the *Monthly Review*, which accorded *France* a review blatantly cribbed from those that had appeared in the *Literary Gazette* and the *Spectator*, the more prestigious monthly and quarterly magazines ignored the new book.[44] All in all, the reception of *France*, like that of the other travel books, provided Cooper with little encouragement. To an admirer who had assured him in 1841 that "the Series of Gleanings are the choicest *morceaux* in the travelling way I ever met with," Cooper could only point out that "Your estimate of The Gleanings in Europe is very different from that of the public. I much question if my publishers would incur the risk of paper and print, were I disposed to write out another member of the series."[45]

Surely those reviewers who regretted Cooper's apparent abandonment of the novel for such nonfictional forms as the travel books were justified in their sense of loss. *The Spy, The Pilot, The Red Rover,* and the first three Leatherstocking tales were stunningly original works of the imagination, novels that impressed his contemporaries as major contributions to Western literature. As Cooper himself confessed in the Preface to *France*, however, its two volumes were "the gleanings of a harvest already gathered," published at a time when the literary marketplace was overstocked with books of European travels. France and its capital were especially hackneyed subjects, already worked over by, among others, the bubbling Lady Morgan in her *France in 1829-30* (1830), by N. P. Willis with his puppy-dog excitement in *Pencillings by the Way* (1832-36), and, most recently, by Sir Henry Bulwer's solidly statistical *France: Social, Literary, Political* (1834-36) and by Cooper's *bête noire,* the acerb Frances Trollope, in her *Paris and the Parisians in 1835* (1836). If Cooper's book had special merit, it was largely owing to the access his reputation gave him to the inner circles of Parisian society or to such notables as Scott and Lafayette, areas denied to a Willis or a Mrs. Trollope.

For the modern reader, however, *France* assumes considerably greater interest and importance. Most obviously, its extensive image of France under the Bourbons is no longer a slightly faded picture of the recent past but a richly various recovery of a long-gone era, a time when dinosaurs like Charles X struggled for dominance with more recent species, fattened by factories and banking houses. And we have learned in the last nearly one hundred and fifty years to value the rigor and sweep of Cooper's political intelligence as it plays over that scene, always driving for the principles which underlie the minutiae of manners and customs and evoking the modes of England and America as a means of illumination by contrast. We have learned, too, to listen to the message which, explicitly or implicitly, is conveyed in everything that Cooper wrote: all of his works are "letters to his countrymen," intended to hold them to their democratic course by warning and encouragement, and *France* is no exception. Just behind the screen of its surface, a morality play of temptation and potential fall is in performance. On the level of individual reference, Cooper himself is the protagonist, as he moves through the often bewildering paths of Paris, clinging fast to his American identity and his American principles and resisting the errors and absurdities that call out to him in the name of European sophistication. On the level of society, France becomes the central actor as, in this time of transition, she struggles between reaction and reform, in imminent danger of turning to the privileged complacency of the English system as a model rather than to the republican virtue of Lafayette, forged in the furnace of the American Revolution. On both levels, the book preaches the necessity for discrimination between the false and the true and of unfaltering loyalty to the truth, once discerned. Seen in this light, *France* becomes a book about America, or, more accurately, a book about being American, the theme that Cooper was soon to develop directly and at length in *The American Democrat* of 1838.

For the student of Cooper's art, *France* has still other values. Together with his other writings of the mid-1830s, it provides the necessary connecting link between his great romances of the 1820s and the more subdued fiction of his last decade. The defining characteristics of many of the later novels — the diminished glamor and greater realism, the overt interest in specific social and political issues, and the more somber view of human possibility — are all evident in *France*. One can see, too, Cooper working out the techniques of first-person narration, primarily the use of an observer within the scene as the vehicle of description and interpretation, that were to reach their full development in *Afloat and Ashore* and *Miles Wallingford* and in the Littlepage trilogy. In smaller ways as well *France* anticipates Cooper's later work. The many snatches of conversation that the book reports are, in their relative naturalness and ease, in sharp contrast to the stilted dialogue of the romances of the 1820s and look forward to that of novels like *Wyandotté* and *Satanstoe*. The descriptive style of *France* is also more restrained and lucid than it was in much of his earlier work, striving less for grand effects than for an economical precision and immediacy. The design of *France*, it is true, rarely calls upon his powers of panoramic description, but when it does, there is a new crispness, as when in Letter V we survey Paris from Montmartre and see the domes of the city spring up "through the mist, like starting balloons."

*France* holds out yet another reward for the reader whose interest in Cooper extends to his personality. More apparently than his other travel books, it bears out George Washington Greene's observation that the series was "written exactly as he talked."[46] No other of Cooper's works, perhaps, brings us closer to his speaking voice or puts us more directly in contact with the man himself, with all his idiosyncratic preoccupations, his quick resentments, his restless curiosity, his surprising humor, and his nobility of principle. The most interesting of the many notables to whom *France* introduces us is, beyond question, Mr. Cooper.

## NOTES

1. Cooper to Luther Bradish, [10-20? August 1826], *The Letters and Journals of James Fenimore Cooper*, ed. James Franklin Beard, 6 vols. (Cambridge: Harvard University Press, Belknap Press, 1960-68), I, 154-55 (hereafter cited as *Letters and Journals*).

2. Cooper to F. Alphonse de Syon, 23 September 1825, *Letters and Journals*, I, 125.
3. Cooper to John Miller, [7-12? February 1826], *Letters and Journals*, I, 127.
4. Cooper to De Witt Clinton, 9 [February] 1826, *Letters and Journals*, I, 129.
5. Cooper to Henry Clay, 3 May 1826, *Letters and Journals*, I, 136.
6. Cooper to de Syon, 23 September 1825, *Letters and Journals*, I, 126.
7. Cooper to Mrs. Peter Augustus Jay, 26 March 1827, *Letters and Journals*, I, 202.
8. Cooper to Bradish, 16-21 August 1828, *Letters and Journals*, I, 290.
9. Cooper to Mrs. Jay, [1-15? October 1826], *Letters and Journals*, I, 158.
10. Mrs. Cooper to her sister, 28 November 1826, *Correspondence of James Fenimore-Cooper*, ed. James Fenimore Cooper, 2 vols. (1922; rpt. Freeport, N.Y.: Books for Libraries Press, 1971), I, 111 (hereafter cited as *Correspondence*).
11. Cooper to Mrs. Jay, 26 March 1827, *Letters and Journals*, I, 209.
12. Mrs. Cooper to her sister, 28 November 1826, *Correspondence*, I, 112.
13. *The Journal of Sir Walter Scott*, ed. John Guthrie Tait (Edinburgh: Oliver & Boyd, 1950), p. 269.
14. George Washington Greene, *Biographical Studies* (New York: G. P. Putnam, 1860), pp. 52-53.
15. *Conversations of James Northcote, Esq., R. A.* in *The Complete Works of William Hazlitt*, ed. P. P. Howe (London: J. M. Dent, 1932), XI, 276.
16. *Pencillings by the Way* in *The Prose Works of N. P. Willis* (Philadelphia: Henry C. Baird, 1850), pp. 12-13, 22, 33-34. For the novelist's aid to Willis in Paris, see Cooper to Peter Augustus Jay, 17 October 1832, *Letters and Journals*, VI, 317. For other reports of Cooper in Paris, see Julia Mayo Cabell, *An Odd Volume of Facts and Fiction* (Richmond: Nash & Woodhouse, 1852), p. 71; Vincent Nolte, *Fifty Years in Both Hemispheres* (New York: Redfield, 1854), p. 353; and *Letters of Henry Brevoort to Washington Irving* (New York: G. P. Putnam's Sons, 1916), pp. 74-75.
17. Cooper to Francis Moore, 20 October 182[7], *Letters and Journals*, I, 228.
18. Cooper to Bradish, [10-20? August 1826], *Letters and Journals*, I, 154.
19. Mrs. Cooper to her sister, 28 November 1826, *Correspondence*, I, 111.
20. *Voices Out of the Past*, ed. Clare Benedict (London: Ellis, 1929), p. 27.
21. Cooper to Carey, Lea and Carey, 11 March 1828, *Letters and Journals*, I, 258.
22. See Cooper to Bradish, 16 August 1828, *Letters and Journals*, I, 289, and to Mrs. Jay, [January-February 1829?], *Letters and Journals*, I, 359.
23. Cooper to Jay, 2 January 1832, *Letters and Journals*, II, 175.
24. See Cooper to Richard Bentley, 14 April 1835, *Letters and Journals*, III, 149; 30 April 1835, *Letters and Journals*, III, 150; 5 May 1835, *Letters and Journals*, III, 152; and 27 May 1835, *Letters and Journals*, III, 155-56.
25. *Letters and Journals*, III, 221. The date of 21 June which Cooper gave this letter is in error. The letter was sent from New York, though the novelist was in Cooperstown on 21 June. The letter, moreover, states that the printing of *The Rhine* has been completed, though the work was not in fact finished until 19 July. Finally, the letter bears a British postmark dated 20 August 1836, which indicates a trans-Atlantic passage of two months, double the time of a normal midsummer crossing from west to east in the 1830s. Beyond any doubt, Cooper mistakenly wrote "June 21st" for "July 21st," for his postscript dated 19 July to his letter of 18 July to Mrs. Cooper from Philadelphia reports that "I have just seen the last proof [of *The Rhine*], and shall leave here to-morrow, New-York Thursday [21 July], and be home, Friday or Saturday" *(Letters and Journals*, III, 230).
26. See Cooper to Mrs. Cooper, 12 October 1836, *Letters and Journals*, III, 240.

27. See Cooper to Mrs. Cooper, 4 November [1836], *Letters and Journals*, III, 248, and to Bentley, 19 November 1836, *Letters and Journals*, III, 249.

28. See the Explanatory Notes for specific indications of the relation of *France* to Cooper's letters of 1826-28.

29. See *Letters and Journals*, I, 283.

30. Important details of Cooper's treatment of the following subjects in *France* were apparently obtained from Dulaure:

| | |
|---|---|
| Letter IV: | Vernon and its tower (*France*, p. 61; cf. *Environs*, II, 270-78, and VII, 604). |
| | Rosny and Sully (*France*, p. 62; cf. *Environs*, II, 252-53, and VII, 561). |
| | The Bourbon palace at Saint-Germain-en-Laye (*France*, p. 62; cf. *Environs*, II, 160-64, and VII, 433-34). |
| Letter V: | The legend of St. Denis (*France*, p. 67; cf. *Environs*, II, 389-90, and *Paris*, I 180-81). |
| Letter IX: | The origin of *"dauphin"* (*France*, p. 119; cf. *Paris*, II, 385). |
| | The Sires de Coucy (*France*, pp. 119-120; cf. *Environs*, V, 205-35). |
| Letter X: | Versailles (*France*, pp. 128-29; cf. *Environs*, I, 180-88). |
| | The catacombs of Paris (*France*, p. 135; cf. *Paris*, IX, 211-13). |
| | Pierrefonds (*France*, p. 136; cf. *Environs*, IV, 404-11). |
| Letter XVI: | Saint-Ouen (*France*, pp. 190-91; cf. *Environs*, II, 370-79, and VII. 536-39). |
| | Anne de Montmorency (*France*, p. 191; cf. *Environs*, III, 20, and *Paris*, IV, 410). |
| | The Montmorency family (*France*, pp. 196-97; cf. *Environs*, III, 14-19, and *Paris*, II, 130-31). |
| Letter XX: | Vincennes (*France*, pp. 238-39; cf. *Environs*, V, 402-25). |
| | La Grange (*France*, pp. 240-45; cf. *Environs*, VI, 213-24). |
| | Vivier (*France*, pp. 245-46; cf. *Environs*, VI, 213-24). |
| | The Palais des Thermes (*France*, p. 246; cf. *Paris*, 99-103). |

31. See Cooper to Bentley, 6 March 1837, *Letters and Journals*, III, 258, and to Thomas Baldwin, 24 November 1841, *Letters and Journals*, IV, 194.

32. See Cooper to Horatio Greenough, 1 March 1833, *Letters and Journals*, II, 371.

33. See *The Cost Book of Carey and Lea, 1825-1838*, ed. David Kaser (Philadelphia: University of Pennsylvania Press, 1963), p. 213.

34. See Robert E. Spiller and Philip C. Blackburn, *A Descriptive Bibliography of the Writings of James Fenimore Cooper* (New York: R. R. Bowker & Company, 1934), p. 89, and Cooper to Mrs. Cooper, 25 January 1837, *Letters and Journals*, III, 253.

35. Cooper to Mrs. Cooper, [5 April 1837], *Letters and Journals*, III, 260.

36. See Carey, Lea and Blanchard to Cooper, 13 September 1837, quoted in *Letters and Journals*, III, 289-90, n. 1.

37. See Cooper to Bentley, [20 March] 1836, *Letters and Journals*, III, 207, and Bentley to Cooper, 19 September 1836, quoted in *Letters and Journals*, III, 222, n. 3.

38. See *The Lists of the Publications of Richard Bentley & Son. 1829-1898* (Bishops Stortford: Chadwyck-Healey, 1975), microfiche 5, folio 207.

39. Bentley to Cooper, 13 May 1837, quoted in *Letters and Journals*, III, 262, n. 3.

40. For the Continental editions of *France*, see Spiller and Blackburn, p. 90.

41. Bentley printed a long extract from Letter XVIII in his *Miscellany*, 1 (January 1837), 80-87. It was reprinted in whole or in part in the United States in the *Albion*, 25

March 1837; the *New-Yorker*, 1 April 1837; and the *Pittsburgh Saturday Evening Visiter*, 15 April 1837. The Carey firm supplied the *National Gazette and Literary Register* with extracts from Letter VI for its issue of 15 February 1837 and from Letter XXII for that of 3 March 1837. Other extracts from *France* appeared in the *New-York Mirror*, 4 March 1837; the *Ladies' Companion*, 6 (April 1837), 307; and the *Baltimore Monument*, 13 May 1837.

42. *New-York American*, 14 March 1837.

43. The reviewer's reference is to *The Old World and the New*, a travel book written by the Unitarian minister Orville Dewey and published by the Harpers in 1836. The following citations locate the American reviews mentioned or quoted in this paragraph: *Southern Literary Messenger*, 3 (April 1837), 272; *American Quarterly Review*, 21 (June 1837), 522-23; *North American Review*, 46 (January 1838), 1-19; *Knickerbocker*, 9 (April 1837), 421-22; *American Monthly Magazine*, NS 3 (April 1837), 401-5; and *Southern Literary Journal*, NS 1 (April 1837), 187-90.

44. The British reviews mentioned or quoted are located as follows: *Atheneum*, 28 January 1837; *Literary Examiner*, 29 January 1837; *Literary Gazette*, 28 January 1837; *Spectator*, 28 January 1837; and *Monthly Review*, 1 (March 1837), 321-30.

45. Thomas Baldwin to Cooper, 10 November 1841, *Correspondence*, II, 456; Cooper to Baldwin, 24 November 1841, *Letters and Journals*, IV, 194.

46. *Biographical Studies*, p. 32.

# Gleanings in Europe: France

# Preface

I T may seem to be late in the day, to give an account of the more ordinary characteristics of Europe. But the mass of all nations can form their opinions of others through the medium of testimony only; and as no two travellers see precisely the same things, or, when seen, view them with precisely the same eyes, this is a species of writing, after all, that is not likely to pall, or cease to be useful. The changes, that are constantly going on every where, call for as constant repetitions of the descriptions; and although the pictures may not always be drawn and coloured equally well, so long as they are taken in good faith, they will not be without their value.

It is not a very difficult task to make what is commonly called an amusing book of travels. Any one who will tell, with a reasonable degree of graphic effect, what he has seen, will not fail to carry the reader with him; for the interest we all feel in personal adventure is, of itself, almost success. But it is much more difficult to give an honest and a discriminating summary of what one has seen. The mind so naturally turns to exceptions, that an observer has great need of self-distrust, of the powers of analysis, and, most of all, of a knowledge of the world, to be what the lawyers call a safe witness.

I have no excuse of haste, or of a want of time, to offer for the defects of these volumes. All I ask is that they may be viewed as no more than they profess to be. They are the *gleanings* of *a harvest already gathered,* thrown together in a desultory manner and, without the slightest, or at least a very small, pretension to any of those arithmetical and statistical accounts, that properly belong to works of a graver character. They contain the passing remarks of one who has certainly seen something of the world, whether it has been to his advantage or not, who had reasonably good opportunities to examine what he saw, and who is not conscious of being, in the slightest degree, influenced "by fear, favour, or the hope of reward." His *compte rendu* must pass for what it is worth.

# Letter I

## To Captain Shubrick, U.S.N.

M Y DEAR SHUBRICK ——

"Passengers by the Liverpool, London and Havre packets, are informed that a steam-boat will leave the White Hall wharf precisely at 11, A.M. to-morrow, June 1st." If to this notice be added the year, 1826, you have the very hour and place of our embarkation. We were nominally of the London party, it being our intention, however, to land at Cowes, from which place we proposed crossing the channel to Havre. The reason for making this variation from the direct route was the superior comfort of the London ship; that of the French line for the 1st June, though a good vessel and well commanded, being actually the least commodious packet that plied between the two hemispheres.

We were punctual to the hour, and found one of the smaller steamers crowded with those who, like ourselves, were bound to the "old world," and the friends who had come to take the last look at them. We had our leave-takings too, which are sufficiently painful when it is known that years must intervene before there is another meeting. As is always done by good Manhattanese, the town house had been given up on the first of May, since which time, we had resided at a hotel. The furniture had been principally sold at auction, and the entire month had passed in what I believed to be very ample preparations. It may be questioned if there is any such thing as being completely prepared for so material a change; at all events, we found a dozen essentials neglected at the last moment, and as many oversights to be repaired in the same instant.

On quitting the hotel, some fifty or a hundred volumes and pamphlets lay on the floor of my bed-room. Luckily you were to sail on a cruise, in a day or two, and as you promised not only to give them a berth, but to read them one and all, they were transferred forthwith to the Lexington. They were a dear gift, if you kept your word! John was sent with a note, with orders to be at the wharf in half an hour. I have not seen him since. Then Abigail was to be discharged. We had long debated whether this excellent woman should, or should not, be taken. She was an American, and, like most of her country-women, who will consent to serve in a household, a most valuable domestic. She wished much to go, but, on the other side, was the conviction that a woman who had never been at sea, would be useless during the passage, and then we were told so many fine things of the European servants, that the odds were unfortunately against her. The principal objection, however, was her forms of speech. Foreign servants would of themselves be a great aid in acquiring the different languages, and poor Abigail, at the best, spoke that least desirable of all corruptions of the English tongue, the country dialect of New England. Her New England morals and New England sense, in this instance, were put in the balance against her "bens," "*an*-gels," "doozes," "nawthings," "noans," and even her "virtooes," (in a family of children, no immaterial considerations,) and the latter prevailed. We had occasion to regret this decision. A few years later, I met in Florence, an Italian family of high rank, which had brought with them from Philadelphia, two female domestics, whom they prized above all the other servants of a large establishment. Italy was not good enough for them, however, and after resisting a great deal of persuasion, they were sent back. What was Florence or Rome to Philadelphia! But then these people spoke good English, better, perhaps, than common English nursery maids, the greatest of their abuses in orthoepy, being merely to teach a child to call its mother a "mare."

It was a flat calm, and the packets were all dropping down the bay with the ebb. The day was lovely, and the view of the harbour, which *has* so many, while it *wants* so many of the elements of first rate scenery, was rarely finer. All estuaries are most beautiful, viewed in the calm; but this is peculiarly true of the Bay of New York — neither the colour of the water, nor its depth, nor the height of the surrounding land being favourable to the grander efforts of nature. There is little that is sublime in either the Hudson, or its mouth, but there is the very extreme of landscape beauty.

Experience will teach every one, that without returning to scenes that have made early impressions, after long absences, and many occasions to examine similar objects elsewhere, our means of comparison are of no great value. My acquaintance with the Hudson has been long and very intimate; for to say that I have gone up and down its waters a hundred times, would be literally much within the truth. During that journey, whose observations and events are about to fill these volumes, I retained a lively impression of its scenery, and, on returning to the country, its current was ascended with a little apprehension, that an eye which had got to be practised in the lights and shades of the Alps and Apennines, might prove too fastidious for our own river. What is usually termed the grandeur of the Highlands was certainly much impaired; but other parts of the scenery gained in proportion, and, on the whole, I found the passage between New York and Albany to be even finer than it had been painted by memory. I should think, there can be little doubt that, if not positively the most beautiful river, the Hudson possesses some of the most beautiful river scenery, of the known world.

Our ship was named after this noble stream. We got on board of her, off Bedlow's, and dropped quietly down as far as the quarantine ground, before we were met by the flood. Here we came-to, to wait for a wind, more passengers, and that important personage, whom man-of-war's men term the master, and landsmen the captain. In the course of the afternoon, we had all assembled, and began to reconnoitre each other, and to attend to our comforts.

To get accustomed to the smell of the ship, with its confined air, and especially to get all their little comforts about them in smooth water, is a good beginning for your novices. If to this be added, moderation in food, and especially in drink; as much exercise as one can obtain; refraining from reading and writing until accustomed to one's situation, and paying great attention to the use of aperients, I believe all is said, that an old traveller and an old sailor, too, can communicate on a subject so important to those who are unaccustomed to the sea. Can your experience suggest any thing more?

We lay that night at the quarantine ground; but early on the morning of the 2nd, all hands were called to heave-up. The wind came in puffs over the heights of Staten, and there was every prospect of our being able to get to sea, in two or three hours. We hove short, and sheeted home and hoisted the three topsails; but the anchor hung, and the people were ordered to get their breakfasts, leaving the ship to tug at her ground tackle with a view to loosen her hold of the bottom.

Every thing was now in motion. The little Don Quixote, the Havre ship just mentioned, was laying through the narrows, with a fresh breeze from the south-west. The Liverpool ship was out of sight, and six or seven sail were turning down with the ebb, under every stitch of canvass that would draw. One fine vessel tacked directly on our quarter. As she passed quite near our stern, some one cried from her deck—"A good run to you, Mr. [Cooper]." After thanking this well-wisher, I inquired his name. He gave me that of an Englishman who resided in Cuba, whither he was bound. "How long do you mean to be absent?" "Five years." "You will never come back." With this raven-like prediction we parted; the wind sweeping his vessel beyond the reach of the voice.

These words, "you will never come back!" were literally the last that I heard on quitting my country. They were uttered in a prophetic tone, and under circumstances that were of a nature to produce an impression. I thought of them often, when standing on the western verge of Europe, and following the course of the sun toward the land in which I was born; I remembered them from the peaks of the Alps, when the subtle mind, outstripping the senses, would make its mysterious flight westward across seas and oceans, to recur to the past, and to conjecture the future; and when the allotted five years were up, and found us still wanderers, I really began to think, what probably every man thinks, in some moment of weakness, that this call from the passing ship, was meant to prepare me for the future. The result proved in my case, however, as it has probably proved in those of most men, that Providence did not consider me of sufficient importance to give me audible information of what was about to happen. So strong was this impression to the last, notwithstanding, that on our return, when the vessel passed the spot where the evil-omened prediction was uttered, I caught myself muttering involuntarily, "——— is a false prophet; I *have* come back!"

We got our anchor as soon as the people were ready, and, the wind drawing fresh through the narrows, were not long turning into the lower bay. The ship was deep, and had not a sufficient spread of canvass for a summer passage, but she was well commanded, and exceedingly comfortable.

The wind became light in the lower bay. The Liverpool ship had got to sea the evening before, and the Don Quixote was passing the Hook, just as we opened the mouth of the Raritan. A light English bark was making a fair wind of it, by laying out across the swash, and it now became questionable whether the ebb would last long enough to sweep us round the south-west spit, a *détour* that our heavier draught rendered necessary.

By paying great attention to the ship, however, the pilot, who was of the dilatory school, succeeded, about 3 P.M. in getting us round that awkward but very necessary buoy, which makes so many foul winds of fair ones, when the ship's head was laid to the eastward, with square yards. In half an hour the vessel had 'slapped' past the low sandy spit of land, that you have so often regarded with philosophical eyes, and we fairly entered the Atlantic, at a point where nothing but water lay between us and the rock of Lisbon. We discharged the pilot on the bar.

By this time the wind had entirely left us, the flood was making strong, and there was a prospect of our being compelled to anchor. The bark was nearly hull-down in the offing, and the top-gallant-sails of the Don Quixote were just settling into the water. All this was very provoking, for there might be a good breeze to seaward, while we had it calm in-shore. The suspense was short, for a fresh-looking line along the sea to the southward, gave notice of the approach of wind, the yards were braced forward, and in half an hour we were standing east southerly, with strong head-way. About sunset we passed the light-vessel which then lay moored several leagues from land, in the open ocean, an experiment that has since failed. The highlands of Navesink disappeared with the day.

The other passengers were driven below, before evening. The first mate, a straight-forward Kennebunk-man, gave me a wink, (he had detected my sea education by a single expression, that of "send it an-end," while mounting the side of the ship,) and said, "a clear quarter-deck! a good time to take a walk, sir." I had it all to myself, sure enough, for the first two or three days, after which our land-birds came crawling up, one by one; but, long before the end of the passage, nothing short of a double-reefed-top-sail breeze, could send the greater part of them below. There was one man, however, who, the mate affirmed, wore the heel of a spare top-mast smooth, by seating himself on it, as the precise spot where the motion of the ship excited the least nausea. I got into my berth at nine, but hearing a movement over head, about midnight, I turned out again, with a sense of uneasiness I had rarely before experienced at sea. The responsibility of a large family, acted, in some measure, like the responsibility of command. The captain was at his post, shortening sail, for it blew fresher; there was some rain; and thunder and lightning were at work in the heavens, in the direction of the adjacent continent; the air was full of wild, unnatural lucidity, as if the frequent flashes left a sort of twilight behind them; and objects were discernible at a distance of two or three leagues. We had been busy in the first watch, as the omens denoted easterly weather; the English bark was struggling along the troubled waters, already quite a league on our lee-quarter.

I remained on deck half an hour, watching the movements of the master. He was a mild, reasoning, Connecticut man, whose manner of ministering to the wants of the female passengers, had given me already a good opinion of his kindness and forethought, while it left some doubts of his ability to manage the rude elements of drunkenness and insubordination which existed among the crew, quite one half of whom were Europeans. He was now on deck in a south-wester,* giving his orders in a way effectually to shake all that was left of the "horrors" out of the ship's company. I went below, satisfied that we were in good hands, and before the end of the passage, I was at a loss to say whether nature had most fitted this truly worthy man to be a ship-master, or a child's-nurse, for he really appeared to me to be equally skilful in both capacities.

Such a temperament is admirably suited to the command of a packet, a station in which so many different dispositions, habits, and prejudices are to be soothed, at the same time that a proper regard is to be had to the safety of their persons. If any proof is wanting, that the characters of seamen in general, have been formed under adverse circumstances, and without sufficient attention, or, indeed, any attention to their real interests, it is afforded in the fact, that the officers of the packet-ships, men usually trained like other mariners, so easily adapt their habits to their new situation, and become more mild, reflecting, and humane. It is very rare to hear a complaint against an officer of one of these vessels; yet it is not easy to appreciate the embarrassments they have frequently to encounter from whimsical, irritable, ignorant, and exacting passengers. As a rule, the eastern men of this country, make the best packet-officers. They are less accustomed to sail with foreigners than those who have been trained in the other ports, but acquire habits of thought and justice, by commanding their country-men; for, of all the seamen of the known world, I take it the most subordinate, the least troublesome, and the easiest to govern, so long as he is not oppressed, is the native American. This, indeed, is true, both ashore and afloat, for very obvious reasons: they who are accustomed to reason themselves, being the most likely to submit to reasonable regulations; and they who are habituated to plenty, are the least likely to be injured by prosperity, which causes quite as much trouble in this world as adversity. It is this prosperity, too suddenly acquired, which spoils most of the labouring Europeans who emigrate, while they seldom acquire the real, frank, independence of feeling which charac-

* Doric—*sow*-wester.

terizes the natives. They adopt an insolent and rude manner as its substitute, mistaking the shadow for the substance. This opinion of the American seamen is precisely the converse of what is generally believed in Europe, however, and more particularly in England; for, following out the one-sided political theories, in which they have been nurtured, disorganization, in the minds of the inhabitants of the old world, is inseparable from popular institutions.

The early part of the season of 1826, was remarkable for the quantities of ice that had drifted from the north into the track of European and American ships. The Crisis, a London packet, had been missing nearly three months, when we sailed. She was known to have been full of passengers, and the worst fears were felt for her safety; ten years have since elapsed, and no vestige of this unhappy ship has ever been found!

Our master prudently decided that safety was of much more importance than speed, and he kept the Hudson well to the southward. Instead of crossing the banks, we were as low as 40°, when in their meridian; and although we had some of the usual signs, in distant piles of fog, and exceedingly chilly and disagreeable weather, for a day or two, we saw no ice. About the fifteenth, the wind got round to the southward and eastward, and we began to fall-off more than we wished even, to the northward.

All the charts for the last fifty years, have three rocks laid down, to the west-ward of Ireland, which are known as the "Three Chimneys." Most American mariners have little faith in their existence, and yet, I fancy, no seaman draws near the spot where they are said to be, without keeping a good look-out for the danger. The master of the Hudson, once carried a lieutenant of the English navy, as a passenger, who assured him that he had actually seen these "Three Chimneys." He may have been mistaken, and he may not. Our course lay far to the southward of them, but the wind gradually hauled ahead, in such a way as to bring us as near as might be to the very spot where they ought to appear, if properly laid down. The look-outs of a merchant ship are of no great value, except in serious cases, and I passed nearly a whole night on deck, quite as much incited by my precious charge, as by curiosity, in order to ascertain all that eyes could ascertain, under the circumstances. No signs of these rocks, however, were seen from the Hudson.

It is surprising in the present state of commerce, and with the vast

interests which are at stake, that any facts affecting the ordinary navigation between the two hemispheres, should be left in doubt. There is a
shoal, and I believe a reef, laid down near the tail of the Great Bank,
whose existence is still uncertain. Seamen respect this danger more
than that of the "Three Chimneys," for it lies very much in the track of
ships between Liverpool and New York; still, while tacking, or giving it
a berth, they do not know whether they are not losing a wind for a
groundless apprehension! Our own government would do well to
employ a light cruiser, or two, in ascertaining just these facts (many
more might be added to the list,) during the summer months. Our own
brief naval history is pregnant with instances of the calamities that
befall ships. No man can say when, or how, the Insurgente, the
Pickering, the Wasp, the Epervier, the Lynx, and the Hornet, disappeared. We know that they are gone, and of all the brave spirits they
held, not one has been left to relate the histories of the different
disasters. We have some plausible conjectures, concerning the manner
in which the two latter were wrecked; but an impenetrable mystery
conceals the fate of the four others. They may have run on unknown
reefs. These reefs may be constantly heaving up from the depths of the
ocean, by subterranean efforts; for a marine rock is merely the summit
of a sub-marine mountain.*

* There is a touching incident connected with the fortunes of two young officers of the
navy, that is not generally known. When the Essex frigate was captured in the Pacific, by
the Phoebe and Cherub, two of the officers of the former were left in the ship, in order to
make certain affidavits that were necessary to the condemnation. The remainder were
paroled and returned to America. After a considerable interval, some uneasiness was
felt at the protracted absence of those who had been left in the Essex. On inquiry, it was
found, that, after accompanying the ship to Rio Janeiro, they had been exchanged,
according to agreement, and suffered to go where they pleased. After some delay, they
took passage in a Swedish brig bound to Norway, as the only means which offered to get
to Europe, whence they intended to return home. About this time, great interest was
also felt for the sloop Wasp. She had sailed for the mouth of the British channel, where
she fell-in with, and took the Reindeer, carrying her prisoners into France. Shortly
after, she had an action with, and took the Avon, but was compelled to abandon her
prize by others of the enemy's cruisers, one of which (the Castilian,) actually came up
with her and gave her a broadside. About twenty days after the latter action, she took a
merchant brig, near the Western Islands, and sent her into Philadelphia. This was the
last that had been heard of her. Months and even years went by, and no farther
intelligence was obtained. All this time, too, the gentlemen of the Essex were missing.
Government ordered inquiries to be made in Sweden, for the master of the brig in
which they had embarked. He was absent on a long voyage, and a weary period elapsed

We were eighteen days out, when, early one morning, we made an American ship, on our weather quarter. Both vessels had every thing set that would draw, and were going about five knots, close on the wind. The stranger made a signal to speak us, and, on the Hudson's main-topsail being laid to the mast, he came down under our stern, and ranged up along-side to leeward. He proved to be a ship called the "London Packet," from Charleston, bound to Havre, and his chronometer having stopped, he wanted to get the longitude.

When we had given him our meridian, a trial of sailing commenced, which continued without intermission for three entire days. During this time, we had the wind from all quarters, and of every degree of force from the lightest air to a double-reefed-topsail breeze. We were never a mile separated, and frequently we were for hours within a cable's length of each other. One night the two ships nearly got foul, in a very light air. The result showed, that they sailed as nearly alike, one being deep and the other light, as might well happen to two vessels. On the third day, both ships being under reefed topsails, with the wind at east, and in thick weather, after holding her own with us for two watches, the London Packet edged a little off the wind, while the Hudson still hugged it, and we soon lost sight of our consort in the mist.

We were ten days longer struggling with adverse winds. During this time, the ship made all possible traverses, our vigilant master resorting to every expedient of an experienced seaman to get to the eastward. We were driven up as high as fifty-four, where we fell into the track of the St. Lawrence traders. The sea seemed covered with them, and I believe we made more than a hundred, most of which were brigs. All these we passed without difficulty. At length a stiff breeze came from the southwest, and we laid our course for the mouth of the British Channel under studding-sails.

On the 28th, we got the bottom in about sixty fathoms water. The 29th was thick weather, with a very light, but a fair wind; we were now quite sensibly within the influence of the tides. Towards evening the horizon brightened a little, and we made the Bill of Portland, resem-

---

before he could be found. When this did happen he was required to give an account of his passengers. By producing his log book and proper receipts, he proved that he had fallen in with the Wasp, near the line, about a fortnight after she had taken the merchant brig, named, when the young officers in question, availed themselves of the occasion to return to their flag. Since that time, a period of twenty-one years, the Wasp has not been heard of.

bling a faint bluish cloud. It was soon obscured, and most of the landsmen were incredulous about its having been seen at all. In the course of the night, however, we got a good view of the Eddystone.

Going on deck early, on the morning of the 30th, a glorious view presented itself. The day was fine, clear, and exhilarating, and the wind was blowing fresh from the westward. Ninety-seven sail, which had come into the channel, like ourselves, during the thick weather, were in plain sight. The majority were English, but we recognised the build of half the maritime nations of Christendom in the brilliant fleet. Every body was busy, and the blue waters were glittering with canvass. A frigate was in the midst of us, walking through the crowd like a giant stepping among pigmies. Our own good vessel left every thing behind her, also, with the exception of two or three other bright-sided ships, which happened to be as fast as herself.

I found the master busy with the glass, and soon as he caught my eye, he made a sign for me to come forward. "Look at that ship directly ahead of us." The vessel alluded to, led the fleet, being nearly hull down to the eastward. It was the Don Quixote, which had left the port of New York, one month before, about the same distance in our advance. "Now look here, in-shore of us," added the master. "It is an American, but I cannot make her out." "Look again: she has a new cloth in her main-top-gallant-sail." This was true enough, and by that sign, the vessel was our late competitor, the London Packet!

As respects the Don Quixote, we had made a journey of some five thousand miles, and not varied our distance, on arriving, a league. There was probably, some accident in this; for the Don Quixote had the reputation of a fast ship, while the Hudson was merely a pretty fair sailer. We had probably got the best of the winds. But a hard and close trial of three days had shown that neither the Hudson nor the London Packet, in their present trims, could go ahead of the other, in any wind. And yet, here, after a separation of ten days, during which time our ship had tacked and wore fifty times, had calms, foul winds and fair, and had run fully a thousand miles, there was not a league's difference between the two vessels!

I have related these circumstances, because I think they are connected with causes that have a great influence on the success of American navigation. On passing several of the British ships to-day, I observed that their officers were below, or at least out of sight; and in one instance, a vessel of a very fair mould, and with every appearance of a good sailer, actually lay with some of her light sails aback, long enough to permit us to come up with, and pass her. The Hudson probably went with this wind some fifteen or twenty miles farther than this loiterer, while I much question if she could have gone as far, had the latter been well attended to. The secret is to be found in the fact, that so large a portion of American ship-masters are also ship-owners, as to have erected a standard of activity and vigilance, below which few are permitted to fall. These men work for themselves, and, like all their countrymen, are looking out for something more than a mere support.

About noon we got a Cowes pilot. He brought no news, but told us the English vessel, I have just named, was sixty days from Leghorn, and that she had been once a privateer. We were just thirty from New York.

We had distant glimpses of the land all day, and several of the passengers determined to make their way to the shore, in the pilot boat. These channel craft are sloops of about thirty or forty tons, and are rather picturesque and pretty boats, more especially when under low sail. They are usually fitted to take passengers, frequently earning more in this way than by their pilotage. They have the long sliding bowsprit, a short lower mast, very long cross-trees, with a taunt top-mast, and, though not so "wicked" to the eye, I think them prettier objects at sea, than our own schooners. The party from the Hudson had scarcely got on board their new vessel when it fell calm, and the master and myself paid them a visit. They looked like a set of smugglers waiting for the darkness to run in. On our return we rowed round the ship. One cannot approach a vessel at sea, in this manner, without being struck with the boldness of the experiment, which launched such massive and complicated fabrics on the ocean. The pure water is a medium almost as transparent as the atmosphere, and the very keel is seen, usually, so near the surface, in consequence of refraction, as to give us but a very indifferent opinion of the security of the whole machine. I do not remember ever looking at my own vessel, when at sea, from a boat, without wondering at my own folly in seeking such a home.

In the afternoon, the breeze sprang up again, and we soon lost sight of our friends, who were hauling in for the still distant land. All that afternoon and night, we had a fresh and a favourable wind. The next day, I went on deck, while the people were washing the ship. It was Sunday, and there was a flat calm. The entire scene admirably suited a day of rest. The channel was like a mirror, unruffled by a breath of air, and some twenty or thirty vessels lay scattered about the view, with their sails festooned and drooping, thrown into as many picturesque positions by the eddying waters. Our own ship had got close in with the land; so near, indeed, as to render a horse, or a man, on the shore distinctly visible. We were on the coast of Dorsetshire. A range of low cliffs lay directly abeam of us, and as the land rose to a ridge behind them, we had a distinct view of a fair expanse of nearly houseless fields. We had left America verdant and smiling; but we found England brown and parched, there having been a long continuance of dry easterly winds.

The cliffs terminated suddenly, a little way ahead of the ship, and the land retired inward, with a wide sweep, forming a large, though not a very deep bay, that was bounded by rather low shores. It was under these very cliffs, on which we were looking with so much pleasure and security, and at so short a distance, that the well known and terrible wreck of an Indiaman occurred, when the master, with his two daughters, and hundreds of other lives, were lost. The pilot pointed out the precise spot where that ill-fated vessel went to pieces. But the sea in its anger, and the sea at rest, are very different powers. The place had no terrors for us.

Ahead of us, near twenty miles distant, lay a high hazy bluff, that was just visible. This was the western extremity of the Isle of Wight, and the end of our passage in the Hudson. A sloop of war was pointing her head in towards this bluff, and all the vessels in sight now began to take new forms, varying and increasing the picturesque character of the view. We soon got a light air ourselves, and succeeded in laying the ship's head off shore, towards which we had been gradually drifting nearer than was desirable. The wind came fresh and fair about ten, when we directed our course towards the distant bluff. Every thing was again in motion. The cliffs behind us gradually sunk, as those before us rose, and lost their indistinctness; the blue of the latter soon became gray, and ere long white as chalk; this being the material of which they are, in truth, composed.

We saw a small whale, (it might have been a large grampus) floundering ahead of us, and acting as an extra pilot, for he appeared to be steering, like ourselves, for the Needles. These Needles, are fragments of the chalk cliffs, that have been pointed and rendered picturesque, by the action of the weather, and our course lay directly past them. They form a line from the extremity of the Isle of Wight, and are awkwardly placed for vessels that come this way in thick weather, or in the dark. The sloop of war got round them first, and we were not far behind her. When fairly within the Needles the ship was embayed, our course now lying between Hampshire and the Isle of Wight, through a channel of no great width. The country was not particularly beautiful, and still looked parched, though we got a distant view of one pretty town, Lymington, in Hampshire. This place, in the distance, appeared not unlike a large New England village, though there was less glare to the houses. The cliffs, however, were very fine, without being of any extraordinary elevation. Though much inferior to the shores of the Mediterranean, they as much surpass any thing I remember to have seen on our own coast, between Cape Anne and Cape Florida; which, for its extent, a part of India, perhaps, excepted, is, I take it, just the flattest, and tamest, and least interesting coast in the entire world.

The master pointed out a mass of dark herbage, on a distant height, which resembled a copse of wood that had been studiously clipped into square forms, at its different angles. It was visible only for a few moments, through a vista in the hills. This was Carisbrooke Castle, buried in ivy.

There was another little castle, on a low point of land, which was erected by Henry VIII., as a part of a system of marine defence. It would scarcely serve to scale the guns of a modern twenty-four pounder frigate, judging of its means of resistance and annoyance by the eye. These things are by-gones for England, a country that has little need of marine batteries.

About three, we reached a broad basin, the land retiring on each side of us. The estuary to the northward is called Southampton Water, the town of that name, being seated on its margin. The opening in the Isle of Wight is little more than a very wide mouth to a very diminutive river, or creek, and Cowes, divided into East and West, lines its shores. The anchorage, in the arm of the sea off this little haven, was well filled with vessels, chiefly the yachts of amateur seamen, and the port itself contained little more than pilot boats and crafts of a smaller size. The Hudson brought up among the former. Hauling up the fore-course of a merchant ship, is like lifting the curtain again on the drama of the land. These vessels rarely furl this sail; and they who have not experienced it, cannot imagine what a change it produces on those who have lived a month, or six weeks, beneath its shadow. The sound of the chain running out was very grateful, and I believe, though well satisfied with the ship as such, that every body was glad to get a nearer view of our great mother earth.

It was Sunday, but we were soon visited by boats from the town. Some came to carry us ashore, others to see that we carried nothing off with us. At first, the officer of the customs manifested a desire to make us all go without the smallest article of dress, or any thing belonging to our most ordinary comforts; but he listened to remonstrances, and we were eventually allowed to depart with our night bags. As the Hudson was to sail immediately for London, all our effects were sent within the hour to the custom house. At 3 P.M. July 2nd, 1826, we put foot in Europe, after a passage of thirty-one days from the quarantine ground.

# Letter II
To Mrs. Pomeroy, Cooperstown, New York.

We were no sooner on English ground, than we hurried to one of the two or three small inns of West Cowes, or the principal quarter of the place, and got rooms at the Fountain. Mr. and Mrs. [Pedersen] had preceded us, and were already in possession of a parlour adjoining our own. On casting an eye out at the street, I found them, one at each window of their own room, already engaged in a lively discussion of the comparative merits of Cowes and Philadelphia! This propensity to exaggerate the value of whatever is our own, and to depreciate that which is our neighbours', a principle that is connected with the very ground-work of poor human nature, forms a material portion of the travelling equipage of nearly every one who quits the scenes of his own youth, to visit those of other people. A comparison between Cowes and Philadelphia, is even more absurd than a comparison between New York and London, and yet, in this instance, it answered the purpose of raising a lively controversy, between an American wife and a European husband.

The consul at Cowes had been an old acquaintance at school, some five and twenty years before, and an inquiry was set on foot for his residence. He was absent in France, but his deputy soon presented himself with an offer of services. We wished for our trunks, and it was soon arranged that there should be an immediate examination. Within an hour, we were summoned to the store-house, where an officer attended on behalf of the customs. Every thing was done in a very expeditious and civil manner, not only for us, but for a few steerage passengers, and this, too, without the least necessity for a *douceur*, the usual *passe-partout* of England. America sends no manufactures to Europe; and, a little smuggling in tobacco excepted, there is probably less of the contraband in our commercial connexion with England, than ever before occurred between two nations that have so large a trade. This, however, is only in reference to what goes eastward, for immense amounts of the smaller manufactured articles of all Europe, find their way, duty free, into the United States. There is also a regular system of smuggling through the Canadas, I have been told.

While the ladies were enjoying the negative luxury of being liberated from a ship, at the Fountain Inn, I strolled about the place. You know that I had twice visited England, professionally, before I was eighteen; and, on one occasion, the ship I was in, anchored off this very island, though not at this precise spot. I now thought the people altered. There had certainly been so many important changes in myself, during the same period, that it becomes me to speak with hesitation on this point; but even the common class seemed less peculiar, less English, *less provincial*, if one might use such an expression, as applied to so great a nation; in short, more like the rest of the world, than formerly. Twenty years before, England was engaged in a war, by which she was, in a degree, isolated from most of Christendom. This insulated condition, sustained by a consciousness of wealth, knowledge, and power, had served to produce a decided peculiarity of manners, and even of appearance. In the article of dress, I could not be mistaken. In 1806, I had seen all the lower classes of the English, clad in something like *costumes*. The channel waterman wore the short dowlas petticoat; the Thames waterman, a jacket and breeches of velveteen, and a badge; the gentleman and gentlewoman, attire such as was certainly to be seen in no other part of the Christian world, the English colonies excepted. Something of this still remained, but it existed rather as the exception, than as the rule. I then felt, at every turn, that I was in a foreign country; whereas, now, the idea did not obtrude itself, unless I was brought in immediate contact with the people.

America, in my time, at least, has always had an active and swift communication with the rest of the world. As a people, we are, beyond a question, decidedly provincial, but our provincialism is not exactly one of external appearance. The men are negligent of dress, for they are much occupied, have few servants, and clothes are expensive, but the women dress remarkably near the Parisian *modes*. We have not sufficient confidence in ourselves to set fashions. All our departures from the usages of the rest of mankind, are the results of circumstances, and not of calculation, unless, indeed, it be one that is pecuniary. Those, whose interest it is to produce changes, cause fashions to travel fast, and there is not so much difficulty, or more cost, in transporting any thing from Havre to New York, than there is in transporting the same thing from Calais to London; and far less difficulty in causing a new *mode* to be introduced, since, as a young people, we are essentially imitative. An example or two, will better illustrate what I mean.

When I visited London, with a part of my family, in 1828, after passing near two years on the continent of Europe, Mrs. [Cooper] was compelled to change her dress—at all times simple, but then, as a matter of course, Parisian—in order not to be the subject of unpleasant observation. She might have gone in a carriage attired as a French woman, for they who ride in England, are not much like those who walk. But to walk in the streets, and look at objects, it was far pleasanter to seem English than to seem French. Five years later, we took London on our way to America, and even then, something of the same necessity was felt. On reaching home, with dresses fresh from Paris, the same party was only in the *mode;* with *toilettes* a little, and but very little, better arranged, it is true, but in surprising conformity with those of all around them. On visiting our own little retired mountain-village, these Parisian-made dresses were scarcely the subject of remark to any but to your *connoisseurs.* My family struck me as being much less peculiar, in the streets of C[ooperstown], than they had been, a few months before, in the streets of London. All this must be explained by the activity of the intercourse between France and America, and by the greater facility of the Americans, in submitting to the despotism of foreign fashions.

Another fact will show you another side of the subject. While at Paris, a book of travels in America, written by an Englishman, (Mr. Vigne,) fell into my hands. The writer, apparently a well-disposed and sensible man, states that he was dancing *dos-à-dos* in a *quadrille,* in New York, when he found, by the embarrassment of the rest of the set, he had done something wrong. Some one kindly told him that they no longer danced *dos-à-dos.* In commenting on this trifling circumstance, the writer ascribes the whole affair to the false delicacy of our women! Unable to see the connexion between the cause and the effect, I pointed out the paragraph to one of my family, who was then in the daily practice of dancing, and that too in Paris, itself, the very court of Terpsichore. She laughed, and told me that the practice of dancing *dos-à-dos, had gone out at Paris a year or two before,* and that doubtless the newer *mode* had reached New York before it reached Mr. Vigne! These are trifles, but they are the trifles that make up the sum of national peculiarities, ignorance of which leads us into a thousand fruitless and absurd conjectures. In this little anecdote we learn the great rapidity with which new fashions penetrate American usages, and the greater ductility of American society in visible and tangible things, at least; and the heedless manner with which even those who write in a good spirit of America, jump to their conclusions. Had Capt. Hall, or Mrs. Trollope, encountered this unlucky *quadrille*, they would probably have found some clever means of imputing, the *nez-à-nez* tendencies of our dances, to the spirit of democracy! The latter, for instance, is greatly outraged by the practice of wearing hats in Congress, and of placing the legs on tables; and, yet, both have been practised in Parliament from time immemorial! She had never seen her own Legislature, and having a set of theories cut and dried for Congress, every thing that struck her as novel, was referred to one of her preconceived notions. In this manner are books manufactured, and by such means are nations made acquainted with each other!

Cowes resembles a toy-town. The houses are tiny, the streets, in the main, are narrow and not particularly straight, while every thing is neat as wax. Some new avenues, however, are well planned, and long ere this, are probably occupied: and there were several small marine villas in, or near, the place. One was shown me, that belonged to the Duke of Norfolk. It had the outward appearance of a medium-sized American country-house. The bluff King Hal caused another castle to be built here, also, which I understood was inhabited at the time, by the family of the Marquis of Anglesey, who was said to be its governor. A part of the system of the English government-patronage is connected with these useless castles, and nominally fortified places. Salaries are attached to the governments, and the situations are usually bestowed on military men. This is a good, or a bad, regulation, as the patronage is used. In a nation of extensive military operations, it might prove a commendable and a delicate way of rewarding services; but, as the tendency of mankind is to defer to intrigue, and to augment power rather than to reward merit, the probability is that these places are rarely bestowed, except in the way of political *quids pro quos*.

I was, with one striking exception, greatly disappointed in the general appearance of the females that I met in the streets. While strolling in the skirts of the town, I came across a group of girls and boys, in which a laughable scene of nautical gallantry was going on. The boys, lads of fourteen or fifteen, were young sailors, and among the girls, who were of the same age and class, was one of bewitching beauty. There had been some very palpable passages of coquetry between the two parties, when one of the young sailors, a tight lad of thirteen or fourteen, rushed into the bevy of petticoats, and, borne away by an ecstasy of admiration, but certainly guided by an excellent taste, he seized the young Venus round the neck, and dealt out some as hearty smacks as I remember to have heard. The working of emotion in the face of the girl was a perfect study. Confusion and shame came first; indignation followed; and, darting out from among her companions, she dealt her robust young admirer such a slap in the face, that it sounded like the report of a pocket pistol. The blow was well meant, and admirably administered. It left the mark of every finger on the cheek of the sturdy little fellow. The lad clenched his fist, seemed much disposed to retort in kind, and ended by telling his beautiful antagonist that it was very fortunate for her she was not a boy. But it was the face of the girl herself that drew my attention. It was like a mirror which reflected every passing thought. When she gave the blow, it was red with indignation. This feeling instantly gave way to a kinder sentiment, and her colour softened to a flush of surprise at the boldness of her own act. Then came a laugh, and a look about her, as if to inquire if she had been very wrong; the whole terminating in an expression of regret in the prettiest blue eyes in the world, which might have satisfied any one that an offence occasioned by her own sweet face, was not unpardonable. The sweetness, the ingenuousness, the spirit mingled with softness, exhibited in the countenance of this girl, are, I think, all characteristic of the English female countenance, when it has not been marble-ized by the over-wrought polish of high breeding. Similar countenances occur in America, though, I think, less frequently than here, and I believe them to be quite peculiar to the Anglo-Saxon race. The workings of such a countenance are like the play of lights and shades in a southern sky.

From the windows of the inn we had a very good view of a small castellated dwelling that one of the King's architects had caused to be erected for himself. The effect of gray towers seen over the tree-tops, with glimpses of the lawn, visible through vistas in the copses, was exceedingly pretty, though the indescribable influence of association prevented us from paying that homage to turrets and walls of the nineteenth, that we were ready so devotedly to pay to any thing of the thirteenth, or fourteenth, centuries.

We broke bread, for the first time in Europe, that evening, having made an early and a hurried dinner on board the ship. The Isle of Wight is celebrated for its butter, and yet we found it difficult to eat it! The English, and many other European nations, put no salt in their table butter, and we, who had been accustomed to the American usage, exclaimed with one voice against its insipidity. A near relation of [Susan]'s, who once served in the British army, used to relate an anecdote on the subject of tastes, that is quite in point. A brother officer, who had gone safely through the celebrated siege of Gibraltar, landed at Portsmouth, on his return home. Among the other privations of his recent service, he had been compelled to eat butter whose fragrance scented the whole Rock. Before retiring for the night, he gave particular orders to have hot rolls and Isle of Wight butter served for breakfast. The first mouthful disappointed him, and of course the unlucky waiter suffered. The latter protested that he had executed the order to the letter. "Then, take away your Isle of Wight butter," growled the officer, "and bring me some that *has a taste.*"

Like him of Gibraltar, we were ready to exclaim, "take away your Isle of Wight butter, and bring us some from the good ship Hudson," which, though not quite as fragrant as that which had obtained its odour in a siege, was not entirely without a taste. This little event, homely as it may appear, is connected with the principle that influences the decisions of more than half of those who visit foreign nations. Usages are condemned because they are not our own; practices are denounced if their connexion with fitness is not self-apparent to our inexperience; and men and things are judged by rules that are of local origin and local application. The moral will be complete when I add, that we, who were so fastidious about the butter at Cowes, after an absence of nearly eight years from America, had the salt regularly worked out of all we ate, for months after our return home, protesting there was no such thing as good butter in America. Had Mrs. [Pedersen] introduced the Philadelphia butter, however, I think her husband must have succumbed, for I believe it to be the best in the world, not even excepting that of Leyden.

Towards evening, the Hudson, having landed all her cabin passengers, and the most of those who were in the steerage, went round the eastern point of the little port, on her way to London.

After taking an early breakfast, we all got into a carriage called a sociable, which is very like a larger sort of American coachee, and went to Newport, the principal town of the island. The road ran between hedges, and the scenery was strictly English. Small enclosures, copses, a sward clipped close as velvet, and trees (of no great size or beauty, however) scattered in the fields, with an effect nearly equal to landscape gardening, were the predominant features. The drought had less influence on the verdure here than in Dorsetshire. The road was narrow and winding, the very *beau idéal* of a highway; for, in this particular, the general rule obtains that what is agreeable is the least useful. Thanks to the practical good sense and perseverance of Mr. McAdam, not only the road in question, but nearly all the roads of Great Britain have been made, within the last five-and-twenty years, to resemble, in appearance, but really to exceed in solidity and strength, the roads one formerly saw in the grounds of private gentlemen. These roads are almost flat, and when they have been properly constructed the wheel rolls over them as if passing along a bed of iron. Apart from the levels, which, of course, are not so rigidly observed, there is not, in fact, any very sensible difference between the draft on a really good McAdamized road and on a rail-road. We have a few roads in America that are nearly as good as most one meets with, but we have nothing that deserves to be termed a real imitation of the system of Mr. McAdam.

The distance to Newport was only four or five miles. The town itself, a borough, but otherwise of little note, lies in a very sweet vale, and is neat but plain, resembling, in all but its greater appearance of antiquity and the greater size of its churches, one of our own provincial towns of the same size. [Susan] and myself took a fly, and went, by a very rural road, to Carisbrooke, a distance of about a mile, in quest of lodgings. Carisbrooke is a mere village, but the whole valley in this part of the island is so highly cultivated, and so many pretty cottages meet the eye—not cottages of the poor, but cottages of the rich—that it has an air of finish and high cultivation that we are accustomed to see only in the immediate vicinity of large towns, and not always even there.

On reaching the hamlet of Carisbrooke we found ourselves immediately beneath the castle. There was a fine old village church, one of those picturesque rustic edifices which abound in England, a building that time had warped and twisted in such a way as to leave few parallel lines, or straight edges, or even regular angles, in any part of it. They told us, also, that the remains of a ruined priory were at hand. We have often laughed since at the eagerness and delight with which we hurried off to look at these venerable objects. It was soon decided, however, that it was a pleasure too exquisite to be niggardly enjoyed alone, and the carriage was sent back with orders to bring up the whole party.

While the fly—a Liliputian coach, drawn by a single horse; a sort of diminutive buggy—was absent, we went in quest of the priory. The people were very civil, and quite readily pointed out the way. We found the ruin in a farm yard. There was literally nothing but a very small fragment of a blind wall, but with these materials we went to work with the imagination, and soon completed the whole edifice. We might even have peopled it, had not Carisbrooke, with its keep, its gate-way, and its ivy-clad ramparts, lain in full view, inviting us to something less ideal. The church, too, the rude, old, humpbacked church was already opened, waiting to be inspected.

The interior of this building was as ancient, in appearance at least, and quite as little in harmony with right lines and regular angles, as its exterior. All the wood work was of unpainted oak, a colour, however, that was scarcely dark enough to be rich; a circumstance which, to American eyes, at least, eyes on whose lenses paint is ever present, gave it an unfinished look. Had we seen this old building five years later, we might have thought differently. As for the English oak, of which one has heard so much, it is no great matter; our own common oaks are much prettier, and did we understand their beauty, there would not be a village church in America, that, in this particular, would not excel the finest English cathedral. I saw nothing, in all Europe, of this nature, that equalled the common oaken doors of the hall at C[ooperstown], which you know so well.

A movement in the church-yard called us out, and we became pained witnesses of the interment of two of the "unhonoured dead." The air, manner, and conduct of these funerals, made a deep impression on us both. The dead were a woman and a child, but of different families. There were three or four mourners belonging to each party. Both the bodies were brought in the same horse-cart, and they were buried by the same service. The coffins were of some coarse wood stained with black, in a way to betray poverty. It was literally *le convoi du pauvre*. Deference to their superiors, and the struggle to maintain appearances, for there was a semblance of the pomp of wo, even in these extraordinary groups, of which all were in deep mourning, contrasted strangely with the extreme poverty of the parties, the niggardly administration of the sacred offices, and the business-like manner of the whole *transaction*. The mourners evidently struggled between natural grief and the bewilderment of their situation. The clergyman was a good-looking young man, in a dirty surplice. Most probably he was a curate. He read the service in a strong voice, but without reverence, and as if he were doing it by the job. In every way, short-measure was dealt out to the poor mourners. When the solemn words of "dust to dust, ashes to ashes," were uttered, he bowed hastily towards each grave, — he stood between them, — and the assistants met his wholesale administration of the rites with a wholesale sympathy.

The ceremony was no sooner over, than the clergyman and his clerk retired into the church. One or two of the men cast wistful eyes toward the graves, neither of which was half filled, and reluctantly followed. I could scarcely believe my senses, and ventured to approach the door. Here I met such a view as I had never before seen, and hope never to witness again. On one side of me two men were filling the graves; on the opposite, two others were actually paying the funeral fees. In one ear was the hollow sound of the clod on the coffin; in the other the chinking of silver on the altar! Yea, literally on the altar! We are certainly far behind this great people in many essential particulars; our manners are less formed; our civilization is less perfect; but thanks to the spirit which led our ancestors into the wilderness, such mockery of the Almighty and his worship, such a mingling of God and Mammon, never yet disgraced the temple within the wide reach of the American borders.

We were joined by the whole party before the sods were laid on the graves of the poor, but some time after the silver had been given for the consolations of religion. With melancholy reflections we mounted to the castle. [Susan] had been educated in opinions peculiarly favourable to England, but I saw, as we walked mournfully away from the spot, that one fact like this, did more to remove the film from her eyes, than volumes of reading.

Carisbrooke has been too often described to need many words. Externally, it is a pile of high battlemented wall, completely buried in ivy, forming within a large area, that was once subdivided into courts, of which, however, there are, at present, scarcely any remains. We found an old woman as warder, who occupied a room or two, in a sort of cottage that had been made out of the ruins. The part of the edifice which had been the prison of Charles I. was a total ruin, resembling any ordinary house without roof, floors, or chimneys. The aperture of the window, through which he attempted to escape, is still visible. It is in the outer wall, against which the principal apartments had been erected. The whole work stands on a high irregular ridge of a rocky hill, the keep being much the most elevated. We ascended to the sort of bastion which its summit forms, whence the view was charming. The whole vale, which contains Carisbrooke and Newport, with a multitude of cottages, villas, farm-houses, and orchards, with meads, lawns, and shrubberies, lay in full view, and we had distant glimpses of the water. The setting of this sweet picture, or the adjacent hills, was as naked and brown, as the vale itself was crowded with objects and verdant. The Isle of Wight, as a whole, did not strike me as being either particularly fertile, or particularly beautiful, while it contains certain spots that are eminently both. I have sailed entirely round it, more than once, and judging from the appearance of its coasts, and from what was visible in this little excursion, I should think that it had more than a usual amount of waste, treeless land. The sea-views are fine, as a matter of course, and the air is pure and bracing. It is consequently much frequented in summer. It were better to call it the "watering place," than to call it the "garden of England."

We had come in quest of a house where the family might be left, for a few days, while I went up to London. But the whole party was anxious to put their feet in *bonâ fide* old England, before they crossed the channel, and the plan was changed to meet their wishes. We slept that night at Newport, therefore, and returned in the morning to Cowes, early enough to get on board a steamboat for Southampton. This town lies several miles up an estuary that receives one or two small streams. There are a few dwellings on the banks of the latter, that are about the size and of the appearance of the better sort of country-houses on the Hudson, although more attention appears to have been generally paid to the grounds. There were two more of Henry VIIIth's forts, and we caught a glimpse of a fine, ruined, Gothic window, in passing Netley Abbey.

We landed on the pier at Southampton about one, and found ourselves truly in England. "Boat, sir, boat?" "Coach, sir, coach?" "London, sir, London?" — "No—we have need of neither!" — "Thank 'ee, sir— thank 'ee, sir." These few words, in one sense, are an epitome of England. They rang in our ears for the first five minutes after landing. Pressing forward for a livelihood, a multitude of conveniences, a choice of amusements, and a trained, but a heartless and unmeaning civility. "No, I do not want a boat." "Thank 'ee, sir." You are just as much "thank'ee" if you do not employ the man, as if you did. You are thanked for condescending to give an order, for declining, for listening. It is plain to see that such thanks dwell only on the lips. And yet we so easily get to be sophisticated; words can be so readily made to supplant things; deference, however unmeaning, is usually so grateful, that one soon becomes accustomed to all this, and even begins to complain that he is not imposed on.

We turned into the first clean-looking inn that offered. It was called the Vine, and though a second-rate house, for Southampton even, we were sufficiently well served. Every thing was neat, and the waiter, an old man with a powdered head, was as methodical as a clock, and a most busy servitor to human wants. He told me he had been twenty-eight years doing exactly the same things daily, and in precisely the same place. Think of a man crying "coming, sir," and setting table, for a whole life, within an area of forty feet square! Truly, this was not America.

The principal street in Southampton, though making a sweep, is a broad, clean avenue, that is lined with houses having, with very few exceptions, bow-windows, as far as an ancient gate, a part of the old defences of the town. Here the High Street is divided into "Above-bar" and "Below-bar." The former is much the most modern, and promises to be an exceedingly pretty place, when a little more advanced. "Below-bar" is neat and agreeable too. The people appeared singularly well dressed, after New York. The women, though less fashionably attired than our own, taking the Paris modes for the criterion, were in beautiful English chintzes, spotlessly neat, and the men all looked as if they had been born with hat-brushes and clothes-brushes in their hands, and yet every one was in a sort of sea-shore *costume*. I saw many men whom my nautical instinct detected at once to be naval officers, — some of whom must have been captains— in round-abouts; but it was quite impossible to criticise toilettes that were so faultessly neat, and so perfectly well arranged.

We ordered dinner, and sallied forth in quest of lodgings. Southampton is said to be peculiar for "long passages, bow-windows, and old maids." I can vouch that it merits the two first distinctions. The season had scarcely commenced, and we had little difficulty in obtaining rooms, the bow-window and long passage included. These lodgings comprise one or more drawing-rooms, the requisite number of bed-rooms, and the use of the kitchen. The people of the house, ordinarily trades-people, do the cooking and furnish the necessary attendance. We engaged an extra servant, and prepared to take possession that evening.

When we returned to the Vine, we found a visiter, in this land of strangers. Mrs. R[omaine], of New York, a relative and an old friend, had heard that Americans of our name, were there, and she came doubting, and hoping, to the Vine. We found that the windows of our own drawing-room looked directly into those of hers. A few doors below us, dwelt Mrs. L[aight], a still nearer relative, and a few days later, we had *vis-à-vis*, Mrs. McA[dam], a sister of [Susan]'s, on whom we all laid eyes for the first time in our lives! Such little incidents recall to mind the close consanguinity of the two nations, although for myself, I have always felt as a stranger in England. This has not been so much from the want of kindness and a community of opinion on many subjects, as from a consciousness, that in the whole of that great nation, there is not a single individual, with whom I could claim affinity. And yet, with a slight exception, we are purely of English extraction. Our father was the great-great-grand-son of an Englishman. I once met with a man, (an Englishman,) who bore so strong a resemblance to him, in stature, form, walk, features, and expression, that I actually took the trouble to ascertain his name. He even had our own. I had no means of tracing the matter any farther, but here was physical evidence to show the affinity between the two people. On the other hand, [Susan] comes of the Huguenots. She is purely American by every intermarriage, from the time of Louis XIVth, down, and yet she found cousins, in England, at every turn, and even a child of the same parents, who was as much of an English woman, as she herself was an American.

We drunk to the happiness of America, at dinner. That day, fifty years, she declared herself a nation; that very day, and nearly, at that hour, two of the co-labourers in the great work we celebrated, departed in company for the world of spirits!

A day or two was necessary to become familiarized to the novel objects around us, and my departure for London was postponed. We profited by the delay, to visit Netley Abbey, a ruin of some note, at no great distance from Southampton. The road was circuitous, and we passed several pretty country houses, few of which exceeded in size or embellishments, shrubbery excepted, similar dwellings at home. There was one, however, of an architecture much more ancient than we had been accustomed to see, it being, by all appearance, of the time of Elizabeth or James. It had turrets and battlements, but was otherwise plain.

The Abbey was a fine, without being a very imposing, ruin, standing in the midst of a field of English neatness, prettily relieved by woods. The window already mentioned, formed the finest part. The effect of these ruins on us proved the wonderful power of association. The greater force of the past than of the future on the mind, can only be the result of questionable causes. Our real concern with the future is incalculably the greatest, and yet we are dreaming over our own graves, on the events and scenes which throw a charm around the graves of those who have gone before us! Had we seen Netley Abbey, just as far advanced towards completion, as it was, in fact, advanced towards decay, our speculations would have been limited by a few conjectures on its probable appearance, but gazing at it, as we did, we peopled its passages, imagined Benedictines stalking along its galleries, and fancied that we heard the voices of the choir, pealing among its arches.

Our fresh American feelings were strangely interrupted by the sounds of junketting. A party of Southampton cockneys, (there are cockneys even in New York,) having established themselves on the grass, in one of the courts, were lighting a fire, and were deliberately proceeding to make tea! "To tea, and ruins," the invitations most probably run. We retreated into a little battery of the bluff King Hal, that was near by, a work that sufficiently proved the state of nautical warfare in the sixteenth century.

# Letter III

To R. Cooper, Esq., Cooperstown.

A t a very early hour, one of the London coaches stopped at the door. I had secured a seat by the side of the coachman, and we went through the "bar" at a round trot. The distance was about sixty miles, and I had paid a guinea for my place. There were four or five other passengers, all on the outside.

The road between Southampton and London, is one of little interest; even the high-way itself is not as good as usual, for the first twenty or thirty miles, being made chiefly of gravel, instead of broken stones. The soil for a long distance was thirsty, and the verdure was nearly gone. England feels a drought sooner than most countries, probably from the circumstance of its vegetation being so little accustomed to the absence of moisture, and to the comparative lightness of the dews. The wind, until just before the arrival of the Hudson, had been blowing from the eastward for several weeks, and in England this is usually a dry wind. The roads were dusty, the hedges were brown, and the fields had nothing to boast of over our own verdure. Indeed, it is unusual to see the grasses of New York so much discoloured, so early in the season.

I soon established amicable relations with my companion on the box. He had been ordered at the Vine to stop for an American, and he soon began to converse about the new world. "Is America any where near Van Dieman's Land?" was one of his first questions. I satisfied him on this head, and he apologized for the mistake, by explaining that he had a sister settled in Van Dieman's Land, and he had a natural desire to know something about her welfare! We passed a house which had more the air of a considerable place than any I had yet seen, though of far less architectural pretensions than the miniature castle near Cowes. This my companion informed me, had once been occupied by George IVth, when Prince of Wales. "Here his Royal Highness enjoyed what I call the perfection of life, sir; women, wine, and fox-hunting!" added the professor of the whip, with the leer of a true amateur.

These coachmen are a class by themselves. They have no concern with grooming the horses, and keep the reins for a certain number of relays. They dress in a particular way, without being at all in livery or uniform, like the continental postillions, talk in a particular way, and act in a particular way. We changed this personage for another, about half the distance between Southampton and London. His successor proved to be even a still better specimen of his class. He was a thorough cockney, and altogether the superior of his country colleague; he was clearly the oracle of the boys, delivering his sentiments in the manner of one accustomed to dictate to all in and about the stables. In addition to this, there was an indescribable, but ludicrous salvo to his dignity, in the way of surliness. Some one had engaged him to carry a black-bird to town, and caused him to wait. On this subject he sang a Jeremiad in the true cockney key. "He didn't want to *take* the *bla-a-a-ck-bud*, but if the man wanted to *send* the *bla-a-a-ck-bud*, why didn't he *bring* the *bla-a-a-ck-bud?*" This is one of the hundred dialects of the lower classes of the English. One of the horses of the last team was restiff, and it became necessary to restrain him by an additional curb, before we ventured into the streets of London. I intimated that I had known such horses completely subdued in America, by filling their ears with cotton. This suggestion evidently gave offence, and he took occasion soon after to show it. He wrung the nose of the horse with a cord, attaching its end below, in the manner of a severe martingale. While going through this harsh process, which, by the way, effectually subdued the animal, he had leisure to tell him, that "he was an *English* horse, and not an *out-landish* horse, and *he* knew best what was good for him," with a great deal more similar sound nationality.

Winchester was the only town of any importance on the road. It is pleasantly seated in a valley, is of no great size, is but meanly built, though extremely neat, has a cathedral and a bishop, and is the shire-town of Hampshire. The assizes were sitting, and Southampton was full of troops that had been sent from Winchester, in order to comply with a custom which forbids the military to remain near the courts of justice. England is full of these political mystifications, and it is one of the reasons that she is so much in arrears in many of the great essentials. In carrying out the practice in this identical case, a serious private wrong was inflicted, in order, that, in form, an abstract and perfectly useless principle might be maintained. The inns at South- ampton were filled with troops, who were billeted on the publicans, will ye, nill ye, and not only the masters of the different houses, but travellers were subjected to a great inconvenience, in order that this

abstraction might not be violated. There may be some small remuner-
ation, but no one can suppose, for a moment, that the keeper of a
genteel establishment of this nature, wishes to see his carriage-houses,
gate-ways, and halls, thronged with soldiers. Society oppresses him, to
maintain appearances! At the present day, the presence of soldiers
might be the means of sustaining justice, while there is not the smallest
probability that they would be used for contrary purposes, except in
cases in which this usage, or law—for I believe there is a statute for
it—would not be in the least respected. This is not an age, nor is
England the country, in which a judge is to be overawed by the roll of a
drum. All sacrifices of common sense, and all recourse to plausible
political combinations, whether of individuals, or of men, are uniformly made at the expense of the majority. The day is certainly
arrived when absurdities like these should be done away with.

The weather was oppressively hot, nor do I remember to have
suffered more from the sun, than during this little journey. Were I to
indulge in the traveller's propensity to refer every thing to his own
state of feeling, you might be told what a sultry place England is, in
July. But I was too old a sailor, not to understand the cause. The sea is
always more temperate than the land, being cooler in summer and
warmer in winter. After being thirty days at sea, we all feel this truth,
either in one way, or the other. I was quitting the coast, too, which is
uniformly cooler than the interior.

When some twelve or thirteen miles from town, the coachman
pointed to a wood enclosed by a wall, on our left. A rill trickled from
the thicket, and run beneath the road. I was told that Virginia Water
lay there, and that the evening before, a single foot-pad had robbed a
coach in that precise spot, or within a few hundred yards of the very
place where the King of England, at the moment, was amusing himself
with the fishing-rod. High-way robberies, however, are now of exceedingly rare occurrence, that in question being spoken of as the only one
within the knowledge of my informant, for many years.

Our rate of travelling was much the same as that of one of our own
better sort of stages. The distance was not materially less than that
between Albany and C[ooperstow]n, the roads were not so hilly, and
much better than our own road, and yet, at the same season, we usually
perform it, in about the same time, that we went the distance between
Southampton and London. The scenery was tame, nor, with the exception of Winchester, was there a single object of any interest visible,
until we got near London. We crossed the Thames, a stream of trifling

expanse, and at Kew we had a glimpse of an old German-looking edifice in yellow bricks, with towers, turrets, and battlements. This was one of the royal palaces. It stood on the opposite side of the river, in the midst of tolerably extensive grounds. Here a nearly incessant stream of vehicles commenced. I attempted to count the stage-coaches, and got as high as thirty-three, when we met a line of mail-coaches that caused me to stop, in despair. I think we met not less than fifty, within the last hour of our journey. There were seven belonging to the mail, in one group. They all leave London at the same hour, for different parts of the kingdom.

At Hyde Park corner, I began to recall objects known in my early visits to London. Apsley House had changed owners, and had become the property of one whose great name was still in the germ, when I had last seen his present dwelling. The Parks, a gate-way or two excepted, were unchanged. In the row of noble houses that line Piccadilly, in that hospital-looking edifice, Devonshire-house, in the dingy, mean, irregular, and yet interesting front of St. James', in Brooks', White's, the Thatched House, and various other historical *monuments*, I saw no change. Buckingham-house had disappeared, and an unintelligible pile was rising on its ruins. A noble *"palazzo-non-finito,"* stood at the angle between the Green and St. James' Parks, and, here and there, I discovered houses of better architecture than London was wont, of old, to boast. One of the very best of these, I was told, was raised in honour of Mercury, and probably out of his legitimate profits. It is called Crockford's.

Our *"bla-a-a-ck-bud"* pulled up, in the Strand, at the head of Adam-street, Adelphi, and I descended from my seat at his side. An extra shilling brought the glimmering of a surly smile athwart his blubber-cheeks, and we parted in good-humour. My fellow travellers were all men of no very high class, but they had been civil, and were sufficiently attentive to my wants, when they found I was a stranger, by pointing out objects on the road, and explaining the usages of the inns. One of them had been in America, and he boasted a little of his intimacy with General This, and Commodore That. At one time, too, he appeared somewhat disposed to institute comparisons between the two countries, a good deal at our expense, as you may suppose; but as I made no answers, I soon heard him settling it with his companions, that, after all, it was quite natural a man should not like to hear his own country abused; and so he gave the matter up. With this exception, I had no cause of complaint, but, on the contrary, good reason to be pleased.

I was set down at the Adam-street Hotel, a house much frequented by Americans. The respectable woman who has so long kept it, received me with quiet civility, saw that I had a room, and promised me a dinner in a few minutes. While the latter was preparing, having got rid of the dust, I went out into the streets. The lamps were just lighted, and I went swiftly along the Strand, recalling objects at every step. In this manner I passed, at a rapid pace, Somerset-house, St. Clement's-le-Dane, St. Mary-le-Strand, Temple-bar, Bridge-street, Ludgate Hill, pausing only before St. Paul's. Along the whole of this line, I saw but little change. A grand bridge, Waterloo, with a noble approach to it, had been thrown across the river just above Somerset-house, but nearly every thing else remained unaltered. I believe my manner, and the eagerness with which I gazed at long remembered objects, attracted attention, for I soon observed I was dogged around the church, by a suspicious-looking fellow. He either suspected me of evil, or, attracted by my want of a London air, he meditated evil himself. Knowing my own innocence, I determined to bring the matter to an issue. We were alone, in a retired part of the place, and, first making sure that my watch, wallet, and handkerchief had not already disappeared, I walked directly up to him, and looked him intently in the face, as if to recognise his features. He took the hint, and, turning on his heels, moved nimbly off. It is surprising how soon an accustomed eye will distinguish a stranger, in the streets of a large town. On mentioning this circumstance next day to ———, he said that the Londoners pretend to recognise a rustic air in a Countess, if she has been six months from town. Rusticity, in such cases, however, must merely mean a little behind the fashions.

I had suffered curiosity to draw me two miles from my dinner, and was as glad to get back, as just before I had been to run away from it. Still, the past, with the recollections which crowded on the mind, bringing with them a flood of all sorts of associations, prevented me from getting into a coach, which would, in a measure, have excluded objects from my sight. I went to bed that night with the strange sensation of being again in London, after an interval of twenty years.

The next day, I set about the business which had brought me to the English capital. Most of our passengers were in town, and we met, as a matter of course. I had calls from three or four Americans established here, some in one capacity, and some in others, for our country has long been giving back its increase to England, in the shape of Admirals,

Generals, Judges, Artists, Writers, and *notion-mongers*. But what is all
this, compared to the constant accessions of Europeans among ourselves? Eight years later, on returning home, I found New York, in
feeling, opinions, desires, (apart from profit,) and I might almost say,
in population, a foreign, rather than an American town.

I had passed months in London, when a boy, and yet had no
knowledge of Westminster Abbey! I cannot account for this oversight,
for I was a great devotee of Gothic architecture, of which, by the way, I
knew nothing except through the prints, and I could not reproach
myself with a want of proper curiosity on such subjects, for I had
devoted as much time to their examination as my duty to the ship
would at all allow. Still, all I could recall of the Abbey was an indistinct
image of two towers, with a glimpse in at a great door. Now that I was
master of my own movements, one of my first acts was to hurry to the
venerable church.

Westminster Abbey is built in the form of a cross, as is, I believe,
invariably the case with every catholic church of any pretension. At its
northern end, are two towers, and at its southern, is the celebrated
chapel of Henry VIIth. This chapel is an addition, which, allowing for
a vast difference in the scale, resembles, in its general appearance, a
school, or vestry room, attached to the end of one of our own churches.
A Gothic church is, indeed, seldom complete, without such a chapel. It
is not an easy matter to impress an American with a proper idea of
European architecture. Even while the edifice is before his eyes, he is
very apt to form an erroneous opinion of its comparative magnitude.
The proportions aid deception in the first place, and absence uniformly exaggerates the beauty and extent of familiar objects. None but
those who have disciplined the eye, and who have accustomed themselves to measure proportions by rules more definite than those of the
fancy, should trust to their judgments in descriptions of this sort.

Westminster Abbey is built in the forms of a cross, as is, I believe,
Paul's, and an ordinary parish church, called St. Margaret's, which
must be, I think, quite as large as Trinity, New York, and stands within
a hundred yards of the Abbey, is but a pigmy compared with Westminster. I took a position in St. Margaret's church-yard, at a point
where the whole of the eastern side of the edifice might be seen, and for
the first time in my life, gazed upon a truly Gothic structure of any
magnitude. It was near sunset, and the light was peculiarly suited to
the sombre architecture. The material was a gray stone, that time had

rendered dull, and which had broad shades of black about its angles and faces. That of the chapel was fresher, and of a warmer tint; a change well suited to the greater delicacy of the ornaments.

The principal building is in the severer style of the Gothic, without, however, being one of its best specimens. It is comparatively plain, nor are the proportions faultless. The towers are twins, are far from being high, and to me they have since seemed to have a crowded appearance, or to be too near each other, a defect that sensibly lessens the grandeur of the north front. A few feet, more or less, in such a case, may carry the architect too much without, or too much within, the just proportions. I lay claim to very little science on the subject, but I have frequently observed since, that, to my own eye, (and the uninitiated can have no other criterion,) these towers, as seen from the parks, above the tops of the trees, have a contracted and pinched air.

But while the Abbey church itself is as plain as almost any similar edifice I remember, its great extent, and the noble windows and doors, rendered it to me, deeply impressive. On the other hand, the chapel is an exquisite specimen of the most elaborated ornaments of the style. All sorts of monstrosities have, at one period or another, been pressed into the service of the Gothic, such as lizards, toads, frogs, serpents, dragons, spitfires, and salamanders. There is, I believe, some typical connexion between these offensive objects, and the different sins. When well carved, properly placed, and not viewed too near, their effect is far from bad. They help to give the edifice its fretted appearance, or a look resembling that of lace. Various other features, which have been taken from familiar objects, such as parts of castellated buildings, port-cullises, and armorial bearings, help to make up the sum of the detail. On Henry VIIth's chapel, toads, lizards, and the whole group of metaphorical sins are sufficiently numerous, without being offensively apparent, while miniature port-cullises, escutcheons, and other ornaments, give the whole the rich, and imaginative — almost fairy-like aspect, — which forms the distinctive feature of the most ornamented portions of the order. You have seen ivory work boxes from the east, that were cut and carved in a way to render them so very complicated, delicate and beautiful, that they please us without conveying any fixed forms to the mind. It would be no great departure from literal truth, were I to bid you fancy one of these boxes swelled to the dimensions of a church, the material changed to stone, and, after a due allowance for a difference in form, for the painted windows, and for the emblems, were I to add, that such a box would probably give you the best idea of a highly wrought Gothic edifice, that any comparison of the sort can furnish.

I stood gazing at the pile, until I felt the sensation we term "a creeping of the blood." I knew that Westminster, though remarkable for its chapel, was, by no means, a first-rate specimen of its own style of architecture; and, at that moment, a journey through Europe promised to be a gradation of enjoyments, each more exquisite than the other. All the architecture of America united, would not assemble a tithe of the grandeur, the fanciful, or of the beautiful, (a few imitations of Grecian temples excepted,) that were to be seen in this single edifice. If I were to enumerate the strong and excited feelings which are awakened by viewing novel objects, I should place this short visit to the Abbey as giving birth in me, to sensation No. 1. The emotion of a first landing in Europe had long passed; our recent "land-fall" had been like any other "land-fall," merely pleasant; and I even looked upon St. Paul's as an old and a rather familiar friend. This was absolutely my introduction to the Gothic, and it has proved to be an acquaintance pregnant of more pure satisfaction, than any other it has been my good fortune to make since youth.

It was too late to enter the church, and I turned away towards the adjoining public buildings. The English kings had a palace at Westminster, in the times of the Plantagenets. It was the ancient usage to assemble the parliament, which was little more than a *lit de justice* previously to the struggle which terminated in the commonwealth, in the royal residence, and, in this manner, Westminster Palace became, permanently, the place for holding the meetings of these bodies. The buildings, ancient and modern, form a cluster on the banks of the river, and are separated from the Abbey by a street. I believe their site was once an island.

Westminster Hall was built as the banqueting room of the palace. There is no uniformity to the architecture of the pile, which is exceedingly complicated and confused. My examination, at this time, was too hurried for details, and I shall refer you to a later visit to England, for a description. A vacant space at the Abbey end of the palace, is called Old Palace Yard, which sufficiently indicates the locality of the ancient royal residence; and a similar, but larger space, or square, at the entrance to the Hall, is known as New Palace Yard. Two sides of the latter are filled with the buildings of the pile; namely, the courts of law, the principal part of the hall, and certain houses that are occupied by some of the minor functionaries of the establishment, with buildings to contain records, &c. The latter are mean, and altogether unworthy of the neighbourhood. They were plaistered on the exterior, and observing a hole in the mortar, I approached and found to my surprise, that here, in the heart of the English capital, as a part of the legislative and judicial structures, in plain view, and on the most frequented square of the vicinity, were houses actually built of wood, and covered with lath and mortar!

The next morning I sent for a hair dresser. As he entered the room, I made him a sign, without speaking, to cut my hair. I was reading the morning paper, and my operator had got half through with his job, without a syllable being exchanged between us, when the man of the comb, suddenly demanded, "What is the reason, sir, that the Americans think every thing in their own country, so much better than it is every where else?" You will suppose that the *brusquerie* as well as the purport of this interrogatory, occasioned some surprise. How he knew I was an American, at all, I am unable to say, but the fellow had been fidgetting the whole time to break out upon me with this question.

I mention the anecdote, in order to show you how lively and general the feeling of jealousy has got to be among our transatlantic kinsmen. — There will be a better occasion to speak of this hereafter.

London was empty. The fashionable streets were actually without a soul, for minutes at a time, and, without seeing it, I could not have believed that a town which, at certain times, is so crowded as actually to render crossing its streets hazardous, was ever so like a mere wilderness of houses. During these recesses in dissipation and fashion, I believe that the meanest residents disappear for a few months.

Our fellow traveller, Mr. L[ynch], however, was in London, and we passed a day or two in company. As he is a votary of music, he took me to hear Madame Pasta. I was nearly as much struck with the extent and magnificence of the Opera-house, as I had been with the architecture of the Abbey. The brilliant manner in which it was lighted, in particular, excited my admiration, for want of light is a decided and a prominent fault of all scenic exhibitions at home, whether they are made in public, or in private. Madame Pasta played *Semiramide*. "How do you like her?" demanded L[ynch], at the close of the first act. "Extremely; I scarce know which to praise the most, the command and the range of her voice, or her powers as a mere actress. But, don't you

think her exceedingly like the *Signorina?*" The present Madame
Malibran was then singing in New York, under the name of Signorina
Garcia. L[ynch] laughed, and told me the remark was well enough, but
I had not put the question in exactly the proper form. "Do you not
think the Signorina exceedingly like Madame Pasta?" would have
been better. I had got the matter wrong end foremost.

L[ynch] reminded me of our having amused ourselves, on the
passage, with the nasal tones of the chorus at New York. He now
directed my attention to the same peculiarity here. In this particular, I
saw no difference; nor should there be any, for I believe nearly all who
are on the American stage, in any character, are foreigners, and chiefly
English.

The next day we went to old Drury, where we found a countryman
and townsman, Mr. Stephen Price, in the chair of Sheridan. The
season was over, but we were shown the whole of the interior. It is also a
magnificent structure in extent and internal embellishment, though a
very plain brick pile externally. It must have eight or ten times the
cubic contents of the largest American theatre. The rival building,
Covent Garden, is within a few hundred feet of it, and has much more
of architectural pretension, though neither can lay claim to much. The
taste of the latter is very well, but it is built of that penny-saving
material, stuccoed bricks.

We dined with Mr. Price, and on the table was some of our own justly
celebrated Madeira. L[ynch], who is an oracle on these subjects, pronounced it injured. He was told it was so lately arrived from New York,
that there had not been time to affect it. This fact, coupled with others
that have since come to my knowledge, induce me to believe that the
change of tastes, which is so often remarked in liquors, fruits, and other
eatables, is as much wrought on ourselves, as in the much abused
viands. Those delicate organs which are necessary to this particular
sense may readily undergo modifications by the varieties of temperature. We know that taste and its sister-sense, smelling, are both tempo-
rarily destroyed by colds. The voice is signally affected by temperature.
In cold climates it is clear and soft; in warm, harsh and deep. All these
facts would serve to sustain the probability of the theory that a large
portion of the strictures that are lavished on the products of different
countries, should be lavished on our own capricious organs. *Au reste*,
the consequence is much the same, let the cause be what it will.

Mr. M———, an Englishman, who has many business concerns with

America, came in, while we were still at table, and I quitted the house in his company. It was still broad day-light. As we were walking together, arm and arm, my companion suddenly placed a hand behind him, and said, "My fine fellow, you are there, are you?" A lad of about seventeen had a hand in one of his pockets, feeling for his handkerchief. The case was perfectly clear, for Mr. M——— had him still in his gripe, when I saw them. Instead of showing apprehension or shame, the fellow began to bluster and threaten. My companion, after a word or two of advice, hurried me from the spot. On expressing the surprise I felt, at his permitting such a hardened rogue to go at large, he said that our wisest course was to get away. The lad was evidently supported by a gang, and we might be beaten as well as robbed, for our pains. Besides, the handkerchief was not actually taken, attendance in the courts was both expensive and vexatious, and he would be bound over to prosecute. In England, the complainant is compelled to prosecute, which is, in effect, a premium on crime! We retain many of the absurdities of the common law, and among others, some which depend on a distinction between the intention and the commission of the act, but I do not know that any of our states is so unjust as to punish a citizen, in this way, because he has already been the victim of a rogue.

After all, I am not so certain our law is much better, but I believe more of the *onus* of obtaining justice falls on the injured party here, than it does with us; still we are both too much under the dominion of the common law.

The next day I was looking at a bronze statue of Achilles, at Hyde Park corner, which had been erected in honour of the Duke of Wellington. The place, like every other fashionable haunt at that season, was comparatively deserted. Still, there might have been fifty persons in sight. "Stop him! stop him!" cried a man, who was chasing another directly towards me. The chase, to use nautical terms, began to lighten ship, by throwing overboard, first one article and then another. As these objects were cast in different directions, he probably hoped that his pursuer, like Atalanta, might stop to pick them up. The last that appeared in the air was a hat, when finding himself hemmed in between three of us, the thief suffered himself to be taken. A young man had been sleeping on the grass, and this land-pirate had absolutely succeeded in getting his shoes, his handkerchief, and his hat; but an attempt to *take off his cravat* had awoke the sleeper. In this case, the prisoner was marched off under sundry severe threats of vengeance, for the *robbee* was heated with the run, and really looked so ridiculous that his anger was quite natural.

My business was now done, and I left London, in a night coach, for Southampton. The place of rendezvous was the White Horse Cellar, in Piccadilly, a spot almost as celebrated for those who are *in transitu*, as was the Isthmus of Suez, of old. I took an inside seat, this time, for the convenience of a nap. At first, I had but a single fellow-traveller. Venturing to ask him the names of one or two objects that we passed, and fearing he might think my curiosity impertinent, I apologized for it, by mentioning that I was a foreigner. "A foreigner!" he exclaimed, "why, you speak English, as well as I do myself!" I confess I had thought, until that moment, that the advantage, in this particular, was altogether on my side; but it seems I was mistaken. By way of relieving his mind, however, I told him I was an American. "An American!" and he seemed more puzzled than ever. After a few minutes of meditation, on what he had just heard, he civilly pointed to a bit of meadow, though which the Thames meanders, and good naturedly told me it was Runnymeade. I presume my manner denoted a proper interest, for he now took up the subject of the English Barons, and entered into a long account of their modern magnificence and wealth. This is a topic, that a large class in England, who only know their aristocracy by report, usually discuss with great unction. They appear to have the same pride in the superiority of their great families, that the American slave is known to feel in the importance of his master. I say this seriously, and not with a view to sneer, but to point out to you a state of feeling that, at first, struck me as very extraordinary. I suppose that the feelings of both *castes* depend on a very natural principle. The Englishman, however, as he is better educated, has one respectable feature in his deference. He exults, with reason, in the superiority of his betters over the betters of most other people: in this particular, he is fully borne out by the fact. Subsequent observation has given me occasion to observe, that the English gentleman, in appearance, attainments, manliness, and perhaps I might add principles, although this and deportment are points on which I should speak with less confidence, stands as a rule, at the head of his class, in christendom. This should not be, nor would it be, were the gentlemen of America equal to their fortunes, which, unhappily, they are not. Facts have so far preceded opinions, at home, as to leave but few minds capable of keeping in their company. But this is a subject, to which we may also, have occasion to return.

The coach stopped, and we took up a third inside. This man proved to be a radical. He soon began to make side hits, at the "nobility and gentry," and, mingled with some biting truths, he uttered a vast deal of nonsense. While he was in the midst of his denunciations, the coach again stopped, and one of the outsides was driven into it by the night air. He was evidently a gentleman, and the guard afterwards told me he was a Captain Somebody, and a nephew of a Lord Something, to whose country place he was going. The appearance of the captain checked the radical, for a little while, but, finding that the other was quiet, he soon returned to the attack. The aristocrat was silent, and the admirer of aristocracy evidently thought himself too good to enter into a dispute, with one of the mere people; for *to admire* aristocracy was, in his eyes, something like an *illustration*; but wincing under one of the other's home-pushes, he said, "These opinions may do very well for this gentleman," meaning me, who as yet had not uttered a syllable— "who is an American; but I must say, I think them out of place, in the mouth of an Englishman." The radical regarded me a moment, and inquired if what the other had just said was true. I answered that it was. He then began an eulogium on America; which, like his Jeremiad on England, had a good many truths blended with a great deal of nonsense. At length, he unfortunately referred to me, to corroborate one of his most capital errors. As this could not be done conscientiously, for his theory depended on the material misconstruction of giving the whole legislative power to Congress, I was obliged to explain the mistake into which he had fallen. The captain and the *toady*, were both evidently pleased; nor, can I say, I was sorry the appeal had been made, for it had the effect of silencing a commentator, who knew very little of his subject. The captain manifested his satisfaction, by commencing a conversation, which lasted until we all went to sleep. Both the captain and the radical quitted us in the night.

Men like the one just described, do the truth a great deal of harm. Their knowledge does not extend to first principles, and they are always for maintaining their positions by a citation of facts. One half of the latter are imagined; and even that which is true is so enveloped with collateral absurdities, that when pushed, they are invariably exposed. These are the travellers who come among us Liberals, and go back Tories. Finding that things fall short of the political Elysiums of their imaginations, they fly into the opposite extreme, as a sort of *amende honorable* to their own folly and ignorance.

At the distance of a few miles from Winchester, we passed an encampment of gipsies, by the way-side. They were better-looking than I had expected to see them, though their faces were hardly perceptible in the gray of the morning. They appeared well fed and very comfortably bivouacked. Why do not these people appear in America? or, do they come, and get absorbed like all the rest, by the humane and popular tendencies of the country. What a homage will it be to the institutions, if it be found that even a gipsy cease to be a gipsy, in such a country! Just as the sun rose, I got out to our lodgings and went to bed.

After a sound sleep of two or three hours, I rose and went to the drawing-room. A lady was in it, seated in a way to allow me to see no more than a small part of her side-face. In that little, I saw the countenance of your aunt's family. It was the sister whom we had never seen, and who had hastened out of Hertfordshire to meet us. There are obvious reasons why such a subject cannot be treated in this letter, but the study of two sisters who had been educated, the one in England and the other in America, who possessed so much in common, and yet, who were separated by so much that was not in common, was to me a matter of singular interest. It showed me, at a glance, the manner in which the distinctive moral and physical features of nations are formed; the points of resemblance being just sufficient to render the points of difference more obvious.

A new and nearer route to Netley, had been discovered during my absence, and our unpractised Americans had done little else than admire ruins, for the past week. The European who comes to America, plunges into the virgin forest with wonder and delight, while the American who goes to Europe finds his greatest pleasure, at first, in hunting up the memorials of the past. Each is in quest of novelty, and is burning with the desire to gaze at objects of which he has often read.

The steam-boat made but one or two voyages a week, between Southampton and Havre, and we were obliged to wait a day or two for the next trip. The intervening time was passed in the manner just named. Every place of any importance in England, has some work or other written on the subject of its history, its beauties, and its monuments. It is lucky to escape a folio. Our works on Southampton, (which are of moderate dimensions, however,) spoke of some Roman remains in the neighbourhood. The spot was found, and, although the imagination was of greater use than common in following the author's description, we stood on the spot with a species of antiquarian awe.

Southampton had formerly been a port of some importance. Many of the expeditions sent against France embarked here, and the town had once been well fortified, for the warfare of the period. A good deal of the old wall remains. All of this was industriously traced out, while the "bow-windows, long passages, and old maids," found no favour in our eyes.

One simple and touching memorial, I well remember. There is a ferry between the town and the grounds near Netley Abbey. A lady had caught a cold which terminated in death, in consequence of waiting on the shore, during a storm, for the arrival of a boat. To protect others from a similar calamity, she had ordered a very suitable defence against the weather, to be built on the fatal spot, and to be kept in repair for ever. The structure is entirely of stone, small and exceedingly simple and ingenious. The ground plan is that of a Greek cross. On this foundation are reared four walls, which, of course, cross each other in the centre, at right angles. A little above the height of a man, the whole is amply roofed. Let the wind blow which way it will, you perceive there is always shelter. There is no external wall, and the diameter of the whole does not exceed ten feet, if it be as much. This little work is exceedingly English, and it is just as unlike any thing American as possible. It has its origin in benevolence, is original in the idea, and it is picturesque. We might accomplish the benevolence, but it would be of a more public character: the picturesque is a thing of which we hardly know the meaning; and as for the originality, the dread of doing any thing different from his neighbour, would effectually prevent an American from erecting such a shelter; even charity, with us, being subject to the control of the general voice. On the other hand, what a clever expedient would have been devised, in the first instance, in America, to get across the ferry without taking cold! All these little peculiarities have an intimate connexion with national character and national habits. The desire to be independent and original, causes a multitude of silly things to be invented here, while the apprehension of doing any thing different from those around them, causes a multitude of silly things to be *perpetuated* in America, and yet, we are children of the same parents! When profit is in view, we have but one soul, and that is certainly inventive enough; but when money has been made, and is to be spent, we really do not seem to know how to set about it, except by routine.

# Letter IV
## To R. Cooper, Esq., Cooperstown.

On quitting England, we embarked from the very strand where Henry Vth embarked for the fruitless field of Agincourt. A fearful rumour had gone abroad, that the Camilla (the steam-boat,) had been shorn of a wing, and there were many rueful faces in the boat that took us off to the vessel. In plainer speech, one of the boilers was out of order, and the passage was to be made with just half the usual propelling power. At that season, or, indeed, at any season, the only probable consequence was loss of time. With a strong head wind, it is true, the Camilla might have been compelled to return, but this might also have happened with the use of both the boilers.

Our adventurers did not see things in this light. The division of employments, which produces prices so cheap and good, makes bad travellers. Our boat's cargo embarked with fear and trembling, and "she has but one boiler!" passed from mouth to mouth, amid ominous faces. A bachelor-looking personage of about fifty, with his person well swaddled in July, declared in a loud voice that we were "all going on board, to be drowned." This startled [Susan], who, having full faith in my nautical experience, asked what we were to think of it. It was a mere question between ten hours and fifteen, and so I told her. The females who had just before been trembling with alarm, brightened at this, and two or three of them civilly thanked me, for the information they had thus obtained incidentally! — "Boat, sir; boat?" — "Thank 'ee, sir; thank 'ee, sir."

We found two or three parties on board, of a higher condition than common. Apprehension cast a shade over the cold marble-like polish of even the English aristocrat; for if, as Mrs. Opie has well observed, there is nothing "so like a lord in a passion, as a commoner in a passion," "your fear" is also a sad leveller. The boat was soon under way, and gradually our cargo of mental apprehensions settled into the usual dolorous physical suffering of landsmen, in rough water. So much for excessive civilization. The want of a boiler, under similar circumstances, would have excited no feeling whatever, among a similar number of Americans, nineteen in twenty of whom, thanks to their rough-and-tumble habits, would know exactly what to think of it.

I was seated, during a part of the day, near a group of young men, who were conversing with a lady of some three or four and twenty. They expressed their surprise at meeting her on board. She told them it was a sudden whim; that no one knew of her movements; she meant only to be gone a fortnight, to take a run into Normandy. In the course of the conversation, I learned that she was single, and had a maid and a footman with her. In this guise she might go where she pleased, whereas, had she taken "an escort," in the American fashion, her character would have suffered. This usage, however, is English, rather than European. Single women on the continent, except in extraordinary cases, are obliged to maintain far greater reserve even than with us; and there, single or married, they cannot travel under the protection of any man, who is not very nearly connected with them, domestics and dependants excepted.

The debates about proceeding at all, had detained us so long, and the "one boiler" proved to be so powerless, that night set in, and we had not yet made the coast of France. The breeze had been fresh, but it lulled towards sunset, though not before we began to feel the influence of the tides. About midnight, however, I heard some one exclaim, "Land!" and we all hastened on deck, to take a first look at France.

The boat was running along beneath some cliffs. The moon was shining bright, and her rays lighted up the chalky sides of the high coast, giving them a ghostly hue. The towers of two light-houses, also, glittered on a head-land near by. Presently, a long sea-wall became visible, and rounding its end, we shot into smooth water. We entered the little port of Havre, between artificial works, on one of which stands a low, massive, circular tower, that tradition attributes to no less a personage than Julius Cæsar.

What a change, in so short a time! On the other side of the channel, beyond the usual demands for employment, which were made in a modest way, and the eternal "Thank 'ee, sir," there was a quiet in the people, that was not entirely free from a suspicion of surliness. Here, every man seemed to have two voices, both of which he used, as if with no other desire than to hear himself speak. Notwithstanding the hour, which was past midnight, the quay was well lined, and a dozen officials poured on board the boat to prevent our landing. Custom-house officers, *gendarmes*, with enormous hats, and female *commissionnaires*, were counteracting each other, at every turn. At length we were permitted to land, being ordered up to a building, near by. Here the females were taken into a separate room, where their persons were examined, by functionaries of their own sex, for contraband goods! This process has been described to me, as being, to the last degree, offensive and humiliating. My own person was respected, I know not why, for we were herded like sheep. As we were without spot, at least so far as smuggling was concerned, we were soon liberated. All our effects were left in the office, and we were turned into the streets, without even a rag, but what we had on. This was an inauspicious commencement, for a country so polished, and yet, when one comes to look at the causes, it is not easy to point out an alternative. It was our own fault that we came so late.

The streets were empty, and the tall gray houses, narrow avenues, and the unaccustomed objects, presented a strange spectacle, by the placid light of the moon. It appeared as if we had alighted in a different planet. Though fatigued and sleepy, the whole party would involuntarily stop to admire some novelty, and our march was straggling and irregular. One house refused us after another, and it soon became seriously a question whether the night was not to be passed in the open air. P[aul] was less than three years old, and as we had a regular gradation from that age upward, our *début* in France promised to be any thing but agreeable. The guide said his resources were exhausted, and hinted at the impossibility of getting in. Nothing, but the inns, was open, and at all these we were refused. At length I remembered that, in poring over an English guide-book, purchased in New York, a certain *Hôtel d'Angleterre* had been recommended as the best house in Havre. *"Savez-vous, mon ami, où est l'hôtel d'Angleterre?" "Ma foi, oui; c'est tout près."* This *"ma foi, oui,"* was ominous, and the *"c'est tout près,"* was more so still. Thither we went, however, and we were received. — Then commenced the process of climbing. We ascended several stories, by a narrow crooked stair-case, and were shown into rooms on the fifth floor.

The floors were of waxed tiles, without carpets or mats, and the furniture was tawdry. We got into our beds, which fatigue could scarcely render it possible to endure, on account of the bugs. A more infernal night I never passed, and I have often thought since, how hazardous it is to trust to first impressions. This night, and one or two more passed at Havre, and one other passed between Rouen and Paris, were among the most uncomfortable I can remember; and yet if I were to name a country in which one would be the most certain to get a good and a clean bed, I think I should name France!

The next morning I arose, and went down the ladder, for it was little better, to the lower world. The servant wished to know if we intended to use the *table d'hôte*, which he pronounced excellent. Curiosity induced me to look at the appliances. It was a dark, dirty and crowded room, and yet not without certain savory smells. French cookery can even get the better of French dirt. It was the only place about the house, the kitchen excepted, where a tolerable smell was to be found, and I mounted to the upper regions, in self-defence.

An hour or two afterwards, the consul did me the favour to call. I apologized for the necessity of causing him to clamber up so high. "It is not a misfortune here," was the answer, "for the higher one is, the purer is the atmosphere," and he was right enough. It was not necessary to explain that we were in an inferior house, and certainly every thing was extremely novel. At breakfast, however, there was a sensible improvement. The linen was white as snow; we were served with silver forks—it was a breakfast *à la fourchette*—spotlessly clean napkins, excellent rolls, and delicious butter, to say nothing of *côtelettes* that appeared to have been cooked by magic. Your aunt and myself looked at each other with ludicrous satisfaction when we came to taste the coffee, which happened to be precisely at the same instant. It was the first time either of us had ever tasted French coffee—it would scarcely be exaggeration to say, that either of us had ever tasted coffee, at all. I have had many French cooks since; have lived years in the capital of France itself, but I could never yet obtain a servant who understood the secret of making *café au lait*, as it is made in most of the inns and *cafés*, of that country. The discrepancy between the excellence of the table, and the abominations of the place, struck them all, so forcibly, that the rest of the party did little else but talk about it. As for myself, I wished to do nothing but eat.

I had now another specimen of national manners. It was necessary to get our luggage through the custom house. The consul recommended a *commissionnaire* to help me. "You are not to be surprised," he said, laughing, as he went away, "if I send you one in petticoats." In a few minutes, sure enough, one of the *beau sexe* presented herself. Her name was *Désirée*, and an abler negotiator was never employed. She scolded, coaxed, advised, wrangled, and uniformly triumphed. The officers were more civil, by day-light, than we had found them under the influence of the moon, and our business was soon effected.

W[illiam] had brought with him a spy-glass. It was old and of little value, but it was an heir-loom of the family. It came from the Hall at C[ooperstow]n, and had become historical for its service in detecting deer, in the lake, during the early years of the settlement. This glass had disappeared. No inquiry could recover it. "Send for *Désirée,*" said the consul. *Désirée* came, received her orders, and in half an hour the glass was restored. There was an oversight in not getting a passport, when we were about to quit Havre. The office hours were over, and the steam-boat could not wait. "Where is *Désirée?*" Désirée was made acquainted with the difficulty, and the passport was obtained. "*Désirée, où est Désirée?*" cried some one in the crowd, that had assembled to see the Camilla start for England, the day after our arrival. "Here is an Englishman who is too late to get his passport *viséd,*" said this person to Désirée, so near me that I heard it all, "the boat goes in ten minutes— what is to be done?" "*Ma foi—* it is too late!" "Try, *ma bonne—* it's a pity he should lose his passage—*voici.*" The Englishman gave his fee. Désirée looked about her, and then taking the idler by the arm, she hurried him through the crowd, this way and that way, ending by putting him aboard without any passport at all. "It is too late to get one," she said; "and they can but send you back." He passed undetected. France has a plenty of these managing females, though Désirée is one of the cleverest of them all. I understood this woman had passed a year or two in England, expressly to fit herself for her present occupation, by learning the language.

While engaged in taking our passages on board the steam-boat for Rouen, some one called me by name, in English. The sound of the most familiar words, in one's own language, soon gets to be startling in a foreign country. I remember, on returning to England, after an absence of five years, that it was more than a week before I could persuade myself I was not addressed, whenever a passer by spoke suddenly. On the present occasion, I was called to by an old school-boy acquaintance, Mr. H[unte]r, who was a consul in England, but who had taken a house on what is called the *Côte,* a hill-side, just above Ingouville, a village at no great distance from the town. We went out to his pretty little cottage, which enjoyed a charming view. Indeed I should particularize this spot, as the one which gave me the first idea of one species of distinctive European scenery. The houses cling to the declivity, rising above each other in a way that might literally enable one to toss a stone into his neighbour's chimney-top. They are of stone, but being white-washed, and very numerous, they give the whole mountain-side the appearance of a pretty hamlet, scattered without order in the midst of gardens. Italy abounds with such little scenes; nor are they unfrequent in France, especially in the vicinity of towns, though whitened edifices are far from being the prevailing taste of that country.

That evening we had an infernal clamour of drums in the principal street, which happened to be our own. There might have been fifty, unaccompanied by any wind instrument. The French do not use the fife, and when one is treated to the drum, it is generally in large potions, and nothing but drum. This is a relic of barbarism, and is quite unworthy of a musical age. There is more or less of it, in all the garrisoned towns of Europe. You may imagine the satisfaction with which one listens to a hundred or two of these plaintive instruments, beat between houses six or eight stories high, in a narrow street, and with desperate perseverance! The object is to recall the troops to their quarters.

Havre, is a tide-harbour. In America, where there is, on an average, not more than five feet of rise and fall to the water of the sea, such a haven would, of course, be impracticable for large vessels. But the majority of the ports on the British channel, are of this character, and indeed, a large portion of the harbours of Great Britain. Calais, Boulogne, Havre and Dieppe, are all inaccessible at low water. The cliffs are broken by a large ravine, a creek makes up the gorge, or a small stream flows outward into the sea, a basin is excavated, the entrance is rendered safe by moles which project into deep water, and the town is crowded around this semi-artificial port, as well as circumstances will allow. Such is, more or less, the history of them all. Havre, however, is, in some measure, an exception. It stands on a plain, that I should think had once been a marsh. The cliffs are near it, seaward, and towards the interior there are fine receding hills, leaving a sufficient site, notwithstanding, for a town of large dimensions.

The port of Havre has been much improved of late years. Large basins have been excavated, and formed into regular wet-docks. They are nearly in the centre of the town. The mole stretches out several hundred yards, on that side of the entrance of the port which is next the sea. Here signals are regularly made to acquaint vessels in the offing with the precise number of feet that can be brought into the port. These signals are changed at the rise or fall of every foot, according to a graduated scale which is near the signal pole. At dead low water the entrance to the harbour, and the outer-harbour itself, are merely beds of soft mud. Machines are kept constantly at work, to deepen them.

The ship from sea makes the lights, and judges of the state of the tide by the signals. She rounds the Mole-Head at the distance of fifty or sixty yards, and sails along a passage too narrow to admit another vessel, at the same moment, into the harbor. Here she finds from eighteen to twenty, or, even twenty-four feet of water, according to circumstances. She is hauled up to the gates of a dock, which are opened at high water only. As the water falls, one gate is shut, and the entrance to the dock becomes a lock: vessels can enter, therefore, as long as there remains sufficient water in the outer harbour for a ship to float. If caught outside, however, she must lie in the mud until the ensuing tide.

Havre is the sea-port of Paris, and is rapidly increasing in importance. There is a project for connecting the latter with the sea, by a ship-channel. Such a project is hardly suited to the French impulses, which imagine a thousand grand projects, but hardly ever convert any of them to much practical good. The opinions of the people are formed on habits of great saving, and it requires older calculations, greater familiarity with risks, and more liberal notions of industry, and, possibly, more capital than is commonly found in their enterprises, to induce the people to encounter the extra charges of these improvements, when they can have recourse to what, in their eyes, are simpler and safer means of making money. The government employs men of science, who conceive well; but their conceptions are but indifferently sustained by the average practical intellect of the country. In this particular, France is the very converse of America.

The project of making a sea-port of Paris, is founded on a principle that is radically wrong. It is easier to build a house on the sea-side, than to carry the sea into the interior. But the political economy of France, like that of nearly all the continental nations, is based on a false principle, that of forcing improvements. The intellects of the mass should first be acted on, and when the public mind is sufficiently improved to benefit by innovations, the public sentiment might be trusted to decide the questions of locality and usefulness. The French system looks to a concentration of every thing in Paris. The political organization of the country favours such a scheme, and in a project of this sort, the interests of all the northern and western departments would be sacrificed to the interests of Paris. As for the departments east and south of Paris, they would in no degree be benefited by making a port of Paris, as goods would still have to be transhipped to reach them. A system of canals and rail-roads is much wanted in France, and most of all a system of general instruction, to prepare the minds of the operatives to profit by such advantages. When I say that we are behind our facts in America, I do not mean in a physical, but in a moral, sense. All that is visible and tangible is led by opinion; in all that is purely moral, the facts precede the notions of the people.

I found, at a later day, many droll theories broached in France, more especially in the Chamber of Deputies, on the subject of our own great success in the useful enterprises. As is usual, in such cases, any reason but the true one was given. At the period of our arrival in Europe, the plan of connecting the great lakes with the Atlantic had just been completed, and the vast results were beginning to attract attention in Europe. At first, it was thought, as a matter of course, that engineers from the old world had been employed. This was disproved, and it was shown that they who laid out the work, however skilful they may have since become by practice, were at first little more than common American surveyors. Then the trifling cost was a stumbling-block, for labour was known to be far better paid in America than in Europe; and lastly, the results created astonishment. Several deputies affirmed that the cause of the great success, was owing to the fact, that in America, we trusted such things to private competition, whereas, in France, the government meddled with every thing. But it was the state governments, (which indeed alone possess the necessary means and authority) that had caused most of the American canals to be constructed. These political economists knew too little of other systems to apply a clever saying of their own — *il y a de la Rochefoucauld, et de la Rochefoucauld.* All governments do not wither what they touch.

Some Americans have introduced steam-boats on the rivers of France, and on the lakes of Switzerland and Italy. We embarked in one, after passing two delectable nights at the *Hôtel d'Angleterre.* The boat was a frail-looking thing, and so loaded with passengers that it appeared actually to stagger under its freight. The Seine has a wide mouth, and a long ground-swell was setting in from the channel. Our Parisian cockneys, of whom there were several on board, stood aghast. *Nous voici en pleine mer!* one muttered to the other, and the annals of that eventful voyage are still related, I make no question, to admiring auditors in the interior of France. The French make excellent seamen when properly trained; but, I think, on the whole, they are more thoroughly landsmen than any people of my acquaintance, who possess a coast. There has been too much sympathy with the army to permit the mariners to receive a proper share of the public favour.

The boat shaped her course diagonally across the broad current, directly for Honfleur. Here we first began to get an idea of the true points of difference between our own scenery and that of the continent of Europe, and chiefly of that of France. The general characteristics of England are not essentially different from those of America, after allowing for a much higher finish in the former, substituting hedges for fences, and stripping the earth of its forests. These, you may think, are, in themselves, grand points of difference, but they fall far short of those which render the continent of Europe altogether of a different nature. Of forest, there is vastly more in France than in England. But, with few exceptions, the fields are not separated by enclosures. The houses are of stone, or of wood, rough-cast. Honfleur, as we approached, had a gray distinctness that is difficult to describe. The atmosphere seemed visible, around the angles of the buildings, as in certain Flemish pictures, bringing out the fine old sombre piles from the depth of the view, in a way to leave little concealed, while nothing was meretricious or gaudy. At first, though we found these hues imposing, and even beautiful, we thought the view would have been gayer and more agreeable, had the tints been livelier; but a little use taught us that our tastes had been corrupted. On our return home every structure appeared flaring and tawdry. Even those of stone had a recent and mushroom air, besides being in colours equally ill-suited to architecture or a landscape. The only thing of the sort in America which appeared venerable and of a suitable hue, after an absence of eight years, was our own family abode, and this the despoiler, paint, had not defiled for near forty years.

We discharged part of our cargo at Honfleur, but the boat was still greatly crowded. Fatigue and ill health rendered standing painful to [Susan], and all the benches were crowded. She approached a young girl of about eighteen, who occupied *three* chairs. On one she was seated; on another she had her feet; and the third held her *reticule*. Apologizing for the liberty, [Susan] asked leave to put the *reticule* on the second chair, and to take the third for her own use. This request was refused! The selfishness created by sophistication and a factitious state of things renders such acts quite frequent, for it is more my wish to offer you distinctive traits of character than exceptions. This case of selfishness might have been a little stronger than usual, it is true, but similar acts are of daily occurrence, *out of society*, in France. *In society*, the utmost respect to the wants and feelings of others is paid, vastly more than with us; while, with us, it is scarcely too strong to say that such an instance of unfeeling selfishness could scarcely have occurred at all. We may have occasion to inquire into the causes of this difference in national manners hereafter.

The Seine narrows at *Quillebeuf*, about thirty miles from Havre, to the width of an ordinary European tide river. On a high bluff we passed a ruin called *Tancarville*, which was formerly a castle of the *de Montmorencies*. This place was the cradle of one of William's barons; and an English descendant, I believe, has been ennobled by the title of Earl of Tankerville.

Above *Quillebeuf* the river becomes exceedingly pretty. It is crooked, a charm in itself, has many willowy islands, and here and there a gray venerable town is seated in the opening of the high hills which contract the view, with crumbling towers, and walls that did good service in the times of the old English and French wars. There were fewer seats than might have been expected, though we passed three or four. One near the water-side, of some size, was in the ancient French style, with avenues cut in formal lines, mutilated statues, precise and treeless terraces, and other elaborated monstrosities. These places are not entirely without a pretension to magnificence; but, considered in reference to what is desirable in landscape gardening, they are the very *laid idéal* of deformity. After winding our way for eight or ten hours amid such scenes, the towers of Rouen came in view. They had a dark ebony-coloured look, which did great violence to our Manhattan-ese notions, but which harmonized gloriously with a bluish sky, the gray walls beneath, and a back-ground of hanging fields.

Rouen is a sea-port; vessels of two hundred, or two hundred and fifty tons burden, lying at its quays. Here is also a custom-house, and our baggage was again opened for examination. This was done amid a great deal of noise and confusion, and yet so cursorily as to be of no real service. At Havre, landing as we did in the night, and committing all to Désirée the next day, I escaped collision with subordinates. But, not having a servant, I was now compelled to look after our effects in person. W[illiam] protested that we had fallen among barbarians; what, between brawls, contests for the trunks, cries, oaths and snatching, the scene was equally provoking and comic.

Without schooling, without training of any sort, little checked by morals, pressed upon by society, with nearly every necessary of life highly taxed, and yet entirely loosened from the deference of feudal manners, the Frenchmen of this class have, in general, become what they who wish to ride upon their fellow mortals love to represent them as being: truculent, violent, greedy of gain, and but too much disposed to exaction. There is great *bonhomie* and many touches of chivalry in the national character; but it is asking too much to suppose that men who are placed in the situation I have named, should not exhibit some of the most unpleasant traits of human infirmity. Our trunks were put into a hand-barrow and wheeled by two men a few hundred yards, the whole occupying half an hour of time. For this service ten francs were demanded. I offered five, or double what would have been required by a dray-man in New York, a place where labour is proverbially dear. This was disdainfully refused, and I was threatened with the law. Of the latter I knew nothing, but, determined not to be bullied into what I felt persuaded was an imposition, I threw down the five francs and walked away. These fellows kept prowling about the hotel the whole day, alternately wheedling and menacing, without success. Towards night one of them appeared and returned the five francs, saying that he gave me his services for nothing. I thanked him, and put the money in my pocket. This fit of dignity lasted about five minutes, when, as a *finale*, I received a proposal to pay the money again, and bring the matter to a close, which was done accordingly.

An Englishman of the same class would have done his work in silence, with a respect approaching to servility, and with a system that any little *contretemps* would derange. He would ask enough, take his money with a "thankee, sir," and go off looking as surly as if he were dissatisfied. An American would do his work silently, but independently as to manner—but a fact will best illustrate the conduct of the American. The day after we landed at New York, I returned to the ship for the light articles. They made a troublesome load, and filled a horse cart. "What do you think I *ought* to get for carrying this load, squire?" asked the cartman, as he looked at the baskets, umbrellas, band boxes, valises, secretaries, trunks, &c. &c., "it is quite two miles to Carroll Place." "It is, indeed; what is your fare?" "Only thirty-seven and a half cents;" (about two francs;) "and it is justly worth seventy-five, there is so much trumpery." "I will give you a dollar." "No more need be said, sir; you shall have every thing safe." I was so much struck with this straight-forward manner of proceeding, after all I had undergone in Europe, that I made a note of it the same day.

The Hotel de l'Europe, at Rouen, was not a first rate inn, for France, but it effectually removed the disagreeable impression left by the Hotel d'Angleterre at Havre. We were well lodged, well fed, and otherwise well treated. After ordering dinner, all of a suitable age hurried off to the cathedral.

Rouen is an old, and by no means a well built town. Some improvements along the river are on a large scale, and promise well; but the heart of the city is composed principally of houses of wooden frames, with the interstices filled-in with cement. Work of this kind is very common in all the northern provincial towns of France. It gives a place a singular, and not altogether an unpicturesque air; the short dark studs that time has imbrowned, forming a sort of visible ribs to the houses.

When we reached the little square in front of the cathedral, verily Henry VIIth's chapel sunk into insignificance. I can only compare the effect of the chiseling on the quaint Gothic of this edifice, to that of an enormous skreen of dark lace, thrown into the form of a church. This was the first building of the kind that my companions had ever seen; and they had, in-so-much, the advantage over me, as I had, in a degree, taken off the edge of wonder by the visit, already mentioned, to Westminster. The first look at this pile was one of inextricable details. It was not difficult to distinguish the vast and magnificent doors, and the beautiful oriel windows, buried as they were in ornament, but an examination was absolutely necessary to trace the little towers, pinnacles, and the crowds of pointed arches, amid such a scene of architectural confusion. "It is worth crossing the Atlantic, were it only to see this!" was the common feeling among us.

It was some time before we discovered that divers dwellings had actually been built between the buttresses of the church, for their comparative diminutiveness, quaint style, and close incorporation with the pile, caused us to think them, at first, a part of the edifice itself. This desecration of the Gothic is of very frequent occurrence on the continent of Europe, taking its rise in the straitened limits of fortified towns, the cupidity of churchmen, and the general indifference to knowledge, and, consequently, to taste, which depressed the ages that immediately followed the construction of most of these cathedrals.

We were less struck by the interior, than by the exterior of this building. It is vast, has some fine windows, and is purely Gothic; but after the richness of the external details, the aisles and the choir appeared rather plain. It possessed, however, in some of its monuments, subjects of great interest to those who had never stood over a grave of more than two centuries, and rarely even over one of half that age. Among other objects of this nature, is the heart of *Cœur de Lion*, for the church was commenced in the reign of one of his predecessors, Normandy at that time belonging to the English kings, and claiming to be the depository of the "lion heart."

Rouen has many more memorials of the past. We visited the square in which Joan of Arc was burned; a small irregular area in front of her prison; the prison itself, and the hall in which she had been condemned. All these edifices are Gothic, quaint, and some of them sufficiently dilapidated.

I had forgotten to relate, in its place, a fact, as an offset to the truculent garrulity of the porters. We were shown round the cathedral by a respectable-looking old man in a red scarf, a cocked hat, and a livery, one of the officers of the place. He was respectful, modest, and well instructed in his tale. The tone of this good old *cicerone* was so much superior to any thing I had seen in England — in America such a functionary is nearly unknown — that, under the influence of our national manners, I had awkward doubts as to the propriety of offering him money. At length the five francs rescued from the cupidity of the half-civilized peasants of *la basse Normandie* were put into his hand. A look of indecision caused me to repent the indiscretion. I thought his feelings had been wounded. *"Est-ce-que Monsieur, compte me présenter tout ceci?"* I told him I hoped he would do me the favour to accept it. I had only given *more* than was usual, and the honesty of the worthy cicerone hesitated about taking it. To know when to pay, and what to pay is a useful attainment of the experienced traveller.

Paris lay before us, and, although Rouen is a venerable and historical town, we were impatient to reach the French capital. A carriage was procured, and, on the afternoon of the second day, we proceeded.

After quitting Rouen, the road runs, for several miles, at the foot of high hills, and immediately on the banks of the Seine. At length we were compelled to climb the mountain which terminates near the city, and offers one of the noblest views in France, from a point called St. Catherine's Hill. We did not obtain so fine a prospect from the road, but the view far surpassed any thing we had yet seen in Europe. Putting my head out the window, when about half way up the ascent, I saw an object booming down upon us, at the rate of six or eight miles the hour, that resembled in magnitude, at least, a moving house. It was a *diligence*, and being the first we had met, it caused a general sensation in our party. Our heads were in each other's way, and finding it impossible to get a good view in any other manner, we fairly alighted in the highway, old and young, to look at the monster, unincumbered. Our admiration and eagerness, caused as much amusement to the travellers it held, as their extraordinary equipage gave rise to among us; and two merrier parties did not encounter each other, on the public road, that day.

A proper *diligence* is formed of a chariot-body, and two coach-bodies placed one before the other, the first in front. These are all on a large scale, and the wheels and train are in proportion. On the roof, (the three bodies are closely united) is a *cabriolet*, or covered seat, and baggage is frequently piled there, many feet in height. A large leathern apron covers the latter. An ordinary load of hay, though wider, is scarcely of more bulk than one of these vehicles, which sometimes carries twenty-five or thirty passengers, and two or three tons of luggage. The usual team is composed of five horses, two of which go on the pole, and three on the lead, the latter turning their heads outwards, as W[illiam] remarked, so as to resemble a spread eagle. Notwithstanding the weight, these carriages usually go down a hill faster than when travelling on the plain. A bar of wood is brought, by means of a winch that is controlled by a person called the *conducteur*, one who has charge of both ship and cargo, to bear on the hind wheels, with a greater or less force, according to circumstances, so that all the pressure is taken off the wheel horses. A similar invention has latterly been applied to rail-road cars. I have since gone over this very road with ten horses, two on the wheel, and eight in two lines on the lead. On that occasion, we came down this very hill, at the rate of nine miles the hour.

After amusing ourselves with the spectacle of the diligence, we found the scenery too beautiful to re-enter the carriage immediately, and we walked to the top of the mountain. The view from the summit was truly admirable. The Seine comes winding its way, through a broad rich valley, from the southward, having just before run east, and, a league or two beyond, due west, our own Susquehanna being less crooked. The stream was not broad, but its numerous isles, willowy banks, and verdant meadows, formed a line for the eye to follow. Rouen, in the distance, with its ebony towers, fantastic roofs, and straggling suburbs, lines its shores, at a curvature where the stream swept away west again, bearing craft of the sea on its bosom. These dark old towers have a sombre, mysterious air, which harmonizes admirably with the recollections that crowd the mind, at such a moment! Scarce an isolated dwelling was to be seen, but the dense population is compressed into villages and *bourgs*, that dot the view, looking brown and teeming, like the nests of wasps. Some of these places have still remains of walls, and most of them are so compact and well defined that they appear more like vast castles, than like the villages of England or America. All are gray, sombre, and without glare, rising from the back ground of pale verdure, so many appropriate *bas reliefs*.

The road was strewed with peasants of both sexes, wending their way homeward, from the market of Rouen. One, a tawny woman, with no other protection for her head than a high but perfectly clean cap, was going past us, driving an ass, with the panniers loaded with manure. We were about six miles from the town, and the poor beast, after staggering some eight or ten miles to the market in the morning, was staggering back with this heavy freight, at even. I asked the woman, who, under the circumstances, could not but be a resident of one of the neighbouring villages, the name of a considerable *bourg*, that lay about a gun-shot distant in plain view, on the other side of the river. "*Monsieur, je ne saurais pas vous dire, parce que, voyez-vous, je ne suis pas de ce pays-là,*" was the answer!

Knowledge is the parent of knowledge. He who possesses most of the information of his age, will not quietly submit to neglect its current acquisitions, but will go on improving as long as means and opportunities offer; while he who finds himself ignorant of most things, is only too apt to shrink from a labour which becomes Herculean. In this manner, ambition is stifled, the mind gets to be inactive, and finally sinks into unresisting apathy. Such is the case with a large portion of the European peasantry. The multitude of objects that surround them, becomes a reason of indifference; and they pass, from day to day, for a whole life, in full view of a town, without sufficient curiosity in its history to inquire its name, or, if told by accident, sufficient interest to remember it. We see this principle exemplified daily in cities. One seldom thinks of asking the name of a passer by, though he may be seen constantly, whereas, in the country, such objects being comparatively rare, the stranger is not often permitted to appear, without some question touching his character.*

I once inquired of a servant girl at a French inn, who might be the owner of a *château* near by, the gate of which was within a hundred feet of the house we were in. She was unable to say, urging, as an apology, that she had only been six weeks in her present place! This, too, was in a small country hamlet. I think every one must have remarked, *coeteris paribus*, how much more activity and curiosity of mind is displayed by a countryman, who first visits a town, than by the dweller in a city, who first visits the country. The first wishes to learn every thing, since he has been accustomed to understand every thing he has hitherto seen; while the last, accustomed to a crowd of objects, usually regards most of the novel things he now sees for the first time, with indifference.

The road, for the rest of the afternoon, led us over hills, and plains, from one reach of the river to another, for we crossed the latter repeatedly before reaching Paris. The appearance of the country was extraordinary, in our eyes. Isolated houses were rare, but villages dotted the whole expanse. No obtrusive colours, but the eye had frequently to search against the hill-side, or in the valley, and, first detecting a mass, it gradually took in the picturesque angles, roofs, towers and walls of the little *bourg*. Not a fence, or visible boundary of any sort, to mark the limits of possessions. Not a hoof in the fields grazing, and occasionally, a sweep of mountain land resembled a pattern card, with its stripes of green and yellow and other hues, the narrow fields of the small proprietors. The play of light and shade on these gay upland patches, though not strictly in conformity with the laws of taste, certainly was attractive. When they fell entirely into shadow, the harvest being over, and their gaudy colours lessened, they resembled the melancholy and wasted vestiges of a festival.

At Louviers we dined, and there we found a new object of wonder in the church. It was of the Gothic of the *bourgs*, less elaborated and more rudely wrought than that of the larger towns, but quaint, and, the population considered, vast. Ugly dragons thrust out their grinning heads at us from the buttresses. The most agreeable monstrosities imaginable, were crawling along the gray old stones. After passing this

---

* When in London, two years later, I saw a gentleman of rather striking appearance pass my door for two months, five or six times of a morning. Remembering the apathy of the Norman peasant, I at length asked who it was— "Sir Francis Burdett," was the answer.

place, the scenery lost a good deal of the pastoral appearance, which renders Normandy rather remarkable in France, and took still more of the starched pattern-card look, just mentioned. Still it was sombre, the villages were to be extracted by the eye from their setting of fields, and, here and there, one of those "silent fingers pointing to the skies," raised itself into the air like a needle, to prick the consciences of the thoughtless. The dusky hues of all the villages, contrasted oddly, and not unpleasantly, with the carnival colours of the grains.

We slept at Vernon, and before retiring for the night, passed half an hour in a fruitless attempt to carry by storm a large old circular tower, that is imputed to the inexhaustible industry of Caesar. This was the third of his reputed works that we had seen, since landing in France. In this part of Europe, Caesar has the credit of every thing for which no one else is willing to apply, as is the case with Virgil, at Naples.

It was a sensation to rise in the morning with the rational prospect of seeing Paris, for the first time in one's life, before night. In my catalogue it stands numbered as sensation the 5th; Westminster, the night arrival in France, and the Cathedral of Rouen giving birth to No's. 1, 2, and 4. Though accustomed to the tattoo, and the evening bugle of a man-of-war, the drums of Havre had the honour of No. 3. Alas! how soon we cease to feel those agreeable excitements at all, even a drum coming in time to pall on the ear.

Near Vernon we passed a village, which gave us the first idea of one feature in the old *régime*. The place was gray, sombre, and picturesque, as usual, in the distance; but crowded, dirty, inconvenient, and mean, when the eye got too near. Just without the limits of its nuisances, stood the *château*, a regular pile of hewn stone, with formal *allées*, abundance of windows, extensive stables, and broken vases. The ancient *seigneur* probably retained no more of this ancient possession than its name, while some Monsieur Le Blanc, or Monsieur Le Noir filled his place in the house, and *"Personne dans la seigneurie."*

A few leagues farther brought us to an eminence, whence we got a beautiful glimpse of the sweeping river, and of a wide expanse of fertile country less formally striped, and more picturesque than the preceding. Another gray castellated town lay on the verge of the river, with towers that seemed even darker than ever. How different was all this from the glare of our own objects! As we wound round the brow of the height, extensive park grounds, a village more modern, less picturesque, and less dirty than common, with a large *château* in red bricks was brought in sight, in the valley. This was *Rosny*, the place that gave his hereditary title to the celebrated *Sully*, as *Baron* and *Marquis de Rosny: Sully*, a man, who, like Bacon, almost deserves the character so justly given of the latter by Pope, that of "The wisest, greatest, *meanest*, of mankind." The house and grounds were now the property of *Madame*, as it is the etiquette to term the *Duchesse de Berri*. The town in the distance, with the dark towers, was Mantes, a place well known in the history of Normandy. We breakfasted at *le Cheval Blanc*. The church drew us all out, but it was less monstrous than that of Louviers, and, as a cathedral, unworthy to be named with those of the larger places.

The next stage brought us to *St. Germain en Laye*, or to the verge of the circle of low mountains, that surround the plains of Paris. Here we got within the influence of royal magnificence and the capital. The Bourbons, down to the period of the revolution, were indeed kings, and they have left physical and moral impressions of their dynasty of seven hundred years, that will require as long a period to eradicate. Nearly every foot of the entire semicircle of hills, to the west of Paris, is historical, and garnished by palaces, pavilions, forests, parks, aqueducts, gardens or chases. A carriage terrace, of a mile in length, and on a most magnificent scale in other respects, overlooks the river, at an elevation of several hundred feet above its bed. The palace itself, a quaint old edifice of the time of Francis 1st., who seems to have had an architecture not unlike that of Elizabeth of England, has long been abandoned as a royal abode. I believe its last royal occupant was the dethroned James II. It is said to have been deserted by its owners, because it commands a distant view of that silent monitor, the sombre but beautiful spire of St. Denis, whose walls shadow the vaults of the Bourbons; they who sat on a throne not choosing to be thus constantly reminded of the time, when they must descend to the common fate and crumbling equality of the grave.

An aqueduct, worthy of the Romans, gave an imposing idea of the scale on which these royal works were conducted. It appeared, at the distance of a league or two, a vast succession of arches, displaying a broader range of masonry than I had ever before seen. So many years had passed since I was last in Europe, that I gazed, in wonder at its vastness.

From St. Germain we plunged into the valley, and took our way towards Paris, by a broad paved avenue, that was bordered with trees. The road now began to show an approach to a capital, being crowded with all sorts of uncouth looking vehicles, used as public conveyances. Still it was on a Liliputian scale as compared to London, and semi-barbarous even, as compared to one of our towns. *Marly-la-Machine* was passed; an hydraulic invention to force water up the mountains to supply the different princely dwellings of the neighbourhood. Then came a house of no great pretension, buried in trees, at the foot of the hill. This was the celebrated consular abode, *Malmaison*. After this we mounted to a hamlet, and the road stretched away before us, with the river between, to the unfinished *arc de l'Etoile*, or the barrier of the capital. The evening was soft, and there had been a passing shower. As the mist drove away, a mass rose like a glittering beacon, beyond the nearest hill, proclaiming Paris. It was the dome of the Hotel of the Invalids!

Though Paris possesses better points of view, from its immediate vicinity, than most capitals, it is little seen from any of its ordinary approaches, until fairly entered. We descended to the river, by a gentle declivity. The *château* and grounds of *Neuilly*, a private possession of the Duke of Orleans, lay on our left; the *Bois de Boulogne*, the carriage promenade of the capital, on our right. We passed one of those abortions, a *magnificent* village (*Neuilly*,) and ascended gently towards the unfinished arch of the star. Bending around this imposing memorial of — Heaven knows what! for it has had as many destinations as France has had governors — we entered the iron gate of the barrier, and found ourselves within the walls of Paris.

We were in the *avenue de Neuilly*. The *Champs-Elysées*, without verdure, a grove divided by the broad approach, and moderately peopled by a well-dressed crowd, lay on each side. In front, at the distance of a mile, was a mass of foliage that looked more like a rich copse in a park, than an embellishment of a town garden, and above this, again, peered the pointed roofs of two or three large and high members of some vast structure, sombre in colour and quaint in form. They were the pavilions of the *Tuileries*.* A line of hotels became visible through trees and shrubbery on the left, and on the right we soon got evidence that we were again near the river. We had just left it behind us, and after a *détour* of several leagues, here it was again flowing in our front, cutting in twain the capital.

* Tuileries is derived from *Tuile,* or tile; the site of the present gardens having been a tile yard.

Objects now grew confused, for they came fast. We entered and crossed a paved area, that lay between the Seine, the *Champs-Elysées*, the garden of the *Tuileries*, and two little palaces of extraordinary beauty of architecture. This was the place where Louis XVIth, and his unfortunate wife, were beheaded. Passing between the two edifices last named, we came upon the *Boulevards*, and plunged at once into the street-gaiety and movement of this remarkable town.

# Letter V

## To R. Cooper, Esquire, Cooperstown.

W e were not a fortnight in Paris, before we were quietly estab-lished, *en bourgeois,* in the *Faubourg St. Germain.* Then fol-lowed the long and wearying toil of sight-seeing. Happily, our time was not limited, and we took months for that which is usually performed in a few days. This labor is connected with objects that de-scription has already rendered familiar, and I shall say nothing of them, except as they may incidentally belong to such parts of my sub-ject as I believe worthy to be noticed.

Paris was empty in the month of August, 1826. The court was at St. Cloud; the *Duchesse de Berri* at her favourite Dieppe; and the fashion-able world was scattered abroad over the face of Europe. Our own minister was at the baths of Aix, in Savoy.

One of the first things was to obtain precise and accurate ideas of the position and *entourage* of the place. In addition to those enjoyed from its towers, there are noble views of Paris from Montmartre and Père la Chaise. The former has the best look-out, and thither we proceeded. This little mountain is entirely isolated, forming no part of the exte-rior circle of heights which environ the town. It lies north of the walls, which cross its base. The ascent is so steep, as to require a winding road, and the summit, a table of a hundred acres, is crowned by a crowded village, a church, and divers wind-mills. There was formerly a convent or two, and small country houses still cling to its sides, buried in the shrubbery that clothe their terraces.

We were fortunate in our sky, which was well veiled in clouds, and occasionally darkened by mists. A bright sun may suit particular scenes, and peculiar moods of the mind, but every connoisseur in the beauties of nature will allow that, as a rule, clouds, and very frequently a partial obscurity, greatly aid a landscape. This is yet more true of a bird's-eye view of a grey old mass of walls, which give up their con-fused and dusky objects all the better for the absence of glare. I love to study a place teeming with historical recollections, under this light; leaving the sites of memorable scenes to issue, one by one, out of the grey mass of gloom, as time gives up its facts from the obscurity of ages.

Unlike English and American towns, Paris has scarcely any suburbs. Those parts which are called its *Faubourgs* are in truth integral parts of the city, and, with the exception of a few clusters of wine-houses and *guinguettes*, which have collected near its gates to escape the city duties, the continuity of houses ceases suddenly with the *barrières*, and, at the distance of half a mile from the latter, one is as effectually in the country, so far as the eye is concerned, as if a hundred leagues in the provinces. The unfenced meadows, vineyards, lucerne, oats, wheat, and vegetables, in many places, literally reach the walls. These walls are not intended for defence, but are merely a financial *enceinte*, created for offensive operations against the pockets of the inhabitants. Every town in France that has two thousand inhabitants, is entitled to set up an *octroi* on its articles of consumption, and something like four millions of dollars are taken, annually, at the gates of Paris, in duties on this internal trade. It is merely the old expedient to tax the poor, by laying impositions on food and necessaries.

From the windmills of Montmartre, the day we ascended, the eye took in the whole vast capital, at a glance. The domes sprung up through the mist, like starting balloons; and, here and there, the meandering stream threw back a gleam of silvery light. Enormous roofs denoted the sites of the palaces, churches, or theatres. The summits of columns, the crosses of the minor churches, and the pyramids of pavilion-tops, seemed struggling to rear their heads from out the plain of edifices. A better idea of the vastness of the principal structures was obtained here, in one hour, than could be got from the streets in a twelvemonth. Taking the roofs of the palace, for instance, the eye followed its field of slate and lead, through a parallelogram, for quite a mile. The sheet of the French opera resembled a blue pond, and the aisles of Notre-Dame, and St. Eustache, with their slender ribs and massive buttresses, towered so much above the lofty houses around them, as to seem to stand on their ridges. The church of *St. Geneviève*, the Pantheon of the revolution, faced us, on the swelling land of the opposite side of the town, but surrounded still with crowded lines of dwellings; the Observatory limiting, equally, the view, and the vast field of houses, in that direction.

Owing to the state of the atmosphere, and the varying light, the picture before us was not that simply of a town, but, from the multiplicity and variety of its objects, it was a vast and magnificent view. I have frequently looked at Paris since from the same spot, or from its church towers, when the strong sun-light reduced it to the appearance of confused glittering piles, on which the eye almost refused to dwell; but, on a clouded day, all the peculiarities stand out sombre and distinct, resembling the grey accessaries of the ordinary French landscape.

From the town we turned to the heights which surround it. East and south-east, after crossing the Seine, the country lay in the waste-like unfenced fields which characterize the scenery of this part of Europe. Roads stretched away in the direction of Orleans, marked by the usual lines of clipped and branchless trees. More to the west commence the abrupt heights, which, washed by the river, enclose nearly half the wide plain, like an amphitheatre. This has been the favorite region of the kings of France, from the time of Louis XIIIth, down to the present day. The palaces of Versailles, St. Germain, St. Cloud, and Meudon, all lie in this direction, within short distances of the capital, and the royal forests, avenues, and chases, intersect it in every direction, as mentioned before.

Farther north, the hills rise to be low mountains, though a wide and perfectly level plain spreads itself between the town and their bases, varying in breadth from two to four leagues. On the whole of this expanse of cultivated fields, there was hardly such a thing as an isolated house. Though not literally true, this fact was so nearly so, as to render the effect oddly peculiar, when one stood on the eastern extremity of Montmartre, where, by turning southward, he looked down upon the affluence, and heard the din of a vast capital, and by turning northward, he beheld a country with all the appliances of rural life, and dotted by grey villages. Two places, however, were in sight, in this direction, that might aspire to be termed towns. One was *St. Denis*, from time immemorial, the burying place of the French kings, and the other was *Montmorency*, the *bourg* which gives its name to, or receives it from, the illustrious family that is so styled, for I am unable to say which is the fact. The church spire of the former, is one of the most beautiful objects in view from Montmartre, the church itself, which was desecrated in the revolution, having been restored by Napoleon. St. Denis is celebrated, in the Catholic annals, by the fact of the martyr, from whom the name is derived, having walked, after decapitation, with his head under his arm, all the way from Paris to this very spot.

Montmorency is a town of no great size or importance, but lying on the side of a respectable mountain, in a way to give the spectator more than a profile, it appears to be larger than it actually is. This place is scarcely distinguishable from Paris, under the ordinary light, but on a day like that which we had chosen, it stood out in fine relief from the surrounding fields, even the grey mass of its church being plainly visible.

If Paris is so beautiful and striking, when seen from the surrounding heights, there are many singularly fine pictures, in the bosom of the place itself. We rarely crossed the Pont Royal, during the first month or two of our residence, without stopping the carriage to gaze at the two remarkable views it offers. One is up the reach of the Seine which stretches through the heart of the town, separated by the island, and the other, in an opposite direction, looks down the reach by which the stream flows into the meadows, on its way to the sea. The first is a look into the avenues of a large town, the eye resting on the quaint outlines and endless mazes of walls, towers, and roofs, while the last is a prospect, in which the front of the picture is a collection of some of the finest objects of a high state of civilization, and the back ground a beautiful termination of wooded and decorated heights.

At first, one who is accustomed to the forms and movements of a sea-port, feels a little disappointment at seeing a river that bears nothing but dingy barges loaded with charcoal and wine casks. The magnificence of the quays seems disproportioned to the trifling character of the commerce they are destined to receive. But familiarity with the town soon changes all these notions, and while we admit that Paris is altogether secondary so far as trade is concerned, we come to feel the magnificence of her public works, and to find something that is pleasing and picturesque, even in her huge and unwieldy wood and coal barges. Trade is a good thing in its way, but its agents rarely contribute to the taste, learning, manners, or morals of a nation.

The sight of the different interesting objects that encircle Paris stimulated our curiosity to nearer views, and we proceeded, immediately, to visit the environs. These little excursions occupied more than a month, and they not only made us familiar with the adjacent country, but, by compelling us to pass out at nearly every one of the twenty, or thirty, different gates, or barriers, as they are called, with a large portion of the town also. This capital has been too often described to render any further account of the principal objects necessary, and in speaking of it, I shall endeavour to confine my remarks to things that I think may still interest you by their novelty.

The royal residences in Paris, at this time, are, strictly speaking, but two, the Tuileries and the Palais Royal. The Louvre is connected with the first, and it has no finished apartments that are occupied by any of princely rank, most of its better rooms being unfinished, and are occupied as cabinets or museums. A small palace, called the *Elysée Bourbon*, is fitted up as a residence for the heir presumptive, the Duc de Bordeaux; but, though it contains his princely toys, such as miniature batteries of artillery, &c., he is much too young to maintain a separate establishment. This little scion of royalty only completed his seventh year not long after our arrival in France, on which occasion one of those silly ceremonies, which some of the present age appear to think inseparable from sound principles, was observed. The child was solemnly and formally transferred from the care of the women to that of the men. Up to this period, Madame la Vicomtesse de Gontaut-Biron had been his governess, and she now resigned her charge into the hands of the Baron de Damas, who had lately been Minister of Foreign Affairs. Madame de Gontaut was raised to the rank of Duchess on the occasion. The boy himself is said to have passed from the hands of the one party, to those of the other, in presence of the whole court, *absolutely naked.* Some such absurdity was observed at the reception of *Marie-Antoinette*, it being a part of regal etiquette that a royal bride, on entering France, should leave her old wardrobe, even to the last garment, behind her. You will be amused to hear that there are people in Europe, who still attach great importance to a rigid adherence to all the old etiquette, at similar ceremonies. These are the men who believe it to be essential that judges and advocates should wear wigs, in an age when, their use being rejected by the rest of the world, their presence cannot fail, if it excite any feeling, to excite that of inconvenience and absurdity. There is such a thing as leaving society too naked, I admit, but a *chemise* at least, could not have injured the little Duke of Bordeaux, at this ceremony. Whenever a usage that is poetical in itself, and which awakens a sentiment without doing violence to decency, or comfort, or common sense, can be preserved, I would rigidly adhere to it, if it were only for antiquity's sake; but, surely, it would be far more rational for judges to wear false beards, because formerly Bacon and Coke did not shave their chins, than it is for a magistrate to appear on the bench with a cumbrous, hot, and inconvenient cloud of powdered flax, or whatever may be the material, on his poll, because our ancestors, a century or two since, were so silly as to violate nature in the same extraordinary manner.

Speaking of the Duke of Bordeaux, reminds me of an odd, and, indeed, in some degree, a painful scene, of which I was accidentally a witness, a short time before the ceremony just mentioned. The *émigrés* have brought back with them into France, a taste for horse-racing, and, supported by a few of the English who are here, there are regular races, spring and autumn, in the *Champ de Mars*. The course is one of the finest imaginable, being more than a mile in circumference, and surrounded by mounds of earth, raised expressly with that object, which permit the spectators to overlook the entire field. The result is a species of amphitheatric arena, in which any of the dramatic exhibitions, that are so pleasing to this spectacle-loving nation, may be enacted. Pavilions are permanently erected at the starting-post, and one or two of these are usually fitted up for the use of the court, whenever it is the pleasure of the royal family to attend, as was the case at the time the little occurrence, I am about to relate, took place.

On this occasion, Charles Xth came in royal state, from St. Cloud, accompanied by detachments of his guards, many carriages, several of which were drawn by eight horses, and a cloud of mounted footmen. Most of the dignitaries of the kingdom were present, in the different pavilions, or stands, and nearly or quite all the ministers, together with the whole diplomatic corps. There could not have been less than a hundred thousand spectators on the mounds.

The racing itself was no great matter, being neither within time, nor well contested. The horses were all French, the trial being intended for the encouragement of the French breeders, and the sports were yet too recent to have produced much influence on the stock of the country. During the heats, accompanied by a young American friend, I had strolled among the royal equipages, in order to examine their magnificence, and returning towards the course, we came out unexpectedly at a little open space, immediately at one end of the pavilion in which the royal family was seated. There were not a dozen people near us, and one of these was a sturdy Englishman, evidently a tradesman, who betrayed a keen and a truly national desire to get a look at the king. The head of a little girl was just visible above the side of the pavilion, and my companion, who, by a singular accident, not long before, had been thrown into company with *les enfans de France*, as the royal children are called, informed me that it was *Mademoiselle d'Artois*, the sister of the heir presumptive. He had given me a favorable account of the children, whom he represented as both lively and intelligent, and I changed my position a little, to get a better look of the face of this little personage, who was not twenty feet from the spot where we stood. My movement attracted her attention, and, after looking down a moment into the small area in which we were enclosed, she disappeared. Presently a lady looked over the balustrade, and our Englishman seemed to be on tenter-hooks. Some thirty or forty French gathered round us immediately, and I presume it was thought none but loyal subjects could manifest so much desire to gaze at the family, especially as one or two of the French clapped the little princess, whose head now appeared and disappeared again, as if she were earnestly pressing something on the attention of those within the pavilion. In a moment, the form of a pale and sickly looking boy was seen, the little girl, who was a year or two older, keeping her place at his side. The boy was raised on the knee of a melancholy-looking and rather hard-featured female of fifty, who removed his straw hat, in order to salute us. "These are the *Dauphine* and the *Duc de Bordeaux*," whispered my companion, who knew the person of the former by sight. The Dauphine looked anxiously, and I thought mournfully, at the little cluster we formed directly before her, as if waiting to observe in what manner her nephew would be received. Of course my friend and myself, who were in the foreground, stood uncovered; as gentlemen we could not do less, nor as *foreign* gentlemen could we very well do more. Not a Frenchman, however, even touched his hat! On the other hand, the Englishman, straddled his legs, gave a wide sweep with his beaver, and uttered as hearty a hurrah as if he had been cheering a member of Parliament who gave gin in his beer. The effect of this single, unaccompanied, unanswered cheer, was both ludicrous and painful. The poor fellow himself seemed startled at hearing his own voice amid so profound a stillness, and checking his zeal as unexpectedly as he had commenced its exhibition, he looked furiously around him, and walked surlily away. The *Dauphine* followed him with her eyes. There was no mistaking his gaitered limbs, dogged mien, and florid countenance; he clearly was not French, and those that were, as clearly turned his enthusiasm into ridicule. I felt sorry for her, as with a saddened face, she set down the boy, and withdrew her own head within the covering of the pavilion. The little *Mademoiselle d'Artois* kept her bright looks, in a sort of wonder, on us, until the circumspection of those around her, gave her a hint to disappear.

This was the first direct and near view I got of the true state of popular feeling in Paris, towards the reigning family. According to the journals in the interest of the court, enthusiasm was invariably exhibited whenever any of their princes appeared in public; but the journals in every country, our own dear and shrewd republic not excepted, are very unsafe guides for those who desire truth.

I am told that the style of this court has been materially altered, and perhaps improved, by the impetuous character of Napoleon. The king rarely appears in public with less than eight horses, which are usually in a foam. His liveries are not showy, neither are the carriages as neat and elegant as one would expect. The former are blue and white, with a few slight ornaments of white and red lace, and the vehicles are showy, large and even magnificent, but, I think, without good taste. You will be surprised to hear that he drives with what, in America, we call "Dutch collars." Six of the horses are held in hand, and the leaders are managed by a postillion. There is always one or more empty carriages, according to the number of the royal personages present, equipped in every respect like those which are filled, and which are held in reserve against accidents; a provision, by the way, that is not at all unreasonable in those who scamper over the broken pavements, in and about Paris, as fast as leg can be put to the ground.

Notwithstanding the present magnificence of the court, royalty is shorn of much of its splendor in France, since the days of Louis XVIth. Then a city of a hundred thousand souls, (Versailles) was a mere dependant of the crown; lodgings for many hundred *abbés*, it is said, were provided in the palace alone, and a simple representation at the palace opera, cost a fortune.

It is not an easy matter to come at the real cost of the kingly office in this country, all the expenditures of the European governments being mystified in such a way, as to require a very intimate knowledge of the details, to give a perfectly clear account of them. But, so far as I have been able to ascertain, the charges that arise from this feature of the system do not fall much short, if indeed they do any, of eight millions of dollars, annually. Out of this sum, however, the king pays the extra allowances of his guards, the war office taking the same view of all classes of soldiers, after distinguishing between foot and cavalry. You will get an idea of the luxury of royalty, by a short account of the *gardes du corps*. These troops are all officers, the privates having the rank, and receiving the pay, of lieutenants. Their duty, as the name implies, is to have the royal person in their especial care, and there is always a guard of them, in an ante-chamber of the royal apartments. They are heavy cavalry, and when they mount guard in the palaces, their arm is a carabine. A party of them, always appear near the carriage of the king, or indeed near that of any of the reigning branch of the family. There are said to be four regiments or companies of them, of four hundred men each; but it strikes me the number must be exaggerated. I should think, however, that there are fully a thousand of them. In addition to these selected troops, there are three hundred Swiss, of the Swiss and royal guards; of the latter, including all arms, there must be many thousands. These are the troops that usually mount guard, in and about all the palaces. The annual budget of France appears in the estimates, at about a *milliard*, or a thousand millions of francs, but the usual mystifications are resorted to, and the truth will give the annual central expenses of the country, at not less, I think, than two hundred millions of dollars. This sum, however, covers many items of expenditure, that we are accustomed to consider purely local. The clergy, for instance, are paid out of it, as is a portion of the cost of maintaining the roads. On the other hand, much money is collected, as a general regulation, that does not appear in the budget. Few or no churches are built, and there are charges for masses, interments, christenings, and fees for a hundred things, of which no account is taken, in making out the sum total of the cost of government.

It was the policy of Napoleon to create a system of centralization, that should cause every thing to emanate from himself. The whole organization of government had this end in view, and all the details of the departments have been framed expressly to further this object. The prefects are no more than so many political *aides*, whose duty it is to carry into effect the orders that emanate from the great head, and lines of telegraphs, are established all over France, in such a way that a communication may be sent from the Tuileries, to the remotest corner of the kingdom, in the course of a few hours. It has been said that one of the first steps towards effecting a revolution, ought to be to seize the telegraphs at Paris, by means of which such information and orders could be sent into the provinces, as the emergency might seem to require.

This system of centralization has almost neutralized the advancement of the nation, in a knowledge of the usages and objects of the political liberty that the French have obtained, by bitter experience, from other sources. It is the constant aim of that portion of the community which understands the action of free institutions, to increase the powers of the municipalities, and to lessen the functions of the central government; but their efforts are resisted with a jealous distrust of every thing like popular dictation. Their municipal privileges are, rightly enough, thought to be the entering wedges of real liberty. The people ought to manage their own affairs, just as far as they can do so without sacrificing their interests for want of a proper care, and here is the starting point of representation. So far from France enjoying such a system, however, half the time a bell cannot be hung in a parish church, or a bridge repaired, without communications with, and orders from, Paris.

# Letter VI
## To Mrs. Pomeroy, Cooperstown, New York.

I quitted America with some twenty letters of introduction, that had been pressed upon me by different friends, but which were carefully locked up in a secretary, where they still remain, and are likely to remain for ever, or until they are destroyed. As this may appear a singular resolution for one who left his own country to be absent for years, I shall endeavour to explain it. In the first place, I have a strong repugnance to pushing myself on the acquaintance of any man; this feeling may, in fact, proceed from pride, but I have a disposition to believe, that it proceeds, in part, also, from a better motive. These letters of introduction, like verbal introductions, are so much abused in America, that the latter feeling, perhaps I might say both feelings, are increased by the fact. Of all the people in the world we are the most prodigal of these favors, when self-respect and propriety would teach us we ought to be among the most reserved, simply because the character of the nation is so low, that the European, more than half the time, fancies he is condescending when he bestows attentions on our people at all. Other travellers may give you a different account of the matter, but let every one be responsible for his own opinions and facts. Then, a friend, who, just as we left home, returned from Europe after an absence of five years, assured me that he found his letters of but little use; that nearly every agreeable acquaintance he made was the result of accident, and that the Europeans, in general, were much more cautious in giving and receiving letters of this nature, than ourselves.

The usages of all Europe, those of the English excepted, differ from our own on the subject of visits. There the stranger, or the latest arrival, is expected to make the first visit, and an inquiry for your address, is always taken for an intimation that your acquaintance would be acceptable. Many, perhaps most, Americans lose a great deal through their provincial breeding, in this respect, in waiting for attentions that it is their duty to invite, by putting themselves in the way of receiving them. The European usage is not only the most rational, but it is the most delicate. It is the most rational, as there is a manifest absurdity in supposing, for instance, that the inhabitant of a town is to know whenever a visiter from the country arrives, and it is the most delicate, as it leaves the new-comer, who is supposed to know his own wishes best, to decide, for himself, whether he wishes to make acquaintances, or not. In short, our own practices are provincial and rustic, and cannot exist when the society of the country shall have taken the usual phases of an advanced civilization. Even in England, in the higher classes, the cases of distinguished men excepted, it is usual for the stranger to seek the introduction.

Under such circumstances, coupled with the utter insignificance of an ordinary individual in a town like Paris, you will easily understand that we had the first months of our residence, entirely to ourselves. As a matter of course, we called on our own minister and his wife, and as a matter of course, we have been included in the dinners and parties, that they are accustomed to give at this season of the year. This, however, has merely brought us in contact with a chance-medley of our own countrymen, these diplomatic entertainments being quite obviously a matter of accident, so far as the set is concerned. The dinners of your banker, however, are still worse, since with them the visiting list is usually a mere extract from the leger.

Our privacy has not been without its advantages. It has enabled us to visit all the visible objects without the incumbrance of engagements, and given me leisure to note and to comment on things, that might otherwise, have been overlooked. For several months we have had nothing to do, but to see sights, get familiarized with a situation, that, at first, we found singularly novel, and to brush up our French.

I never had sufficient faith in the popular accounts of the usages of other countries, to believe one half of what I have heard. I distrusted, from the first, the fact of ladies, I mean real *bonâ fide* ladies, women of sentiment, delicacy, taste, and condition, frequenting public eating-houses, and habitually living, without the retirement and reserve, that is so necessary, to all *women*, not to say *men*, of the *caste*. I found it difficult, therefore, to imagine I should meet with many females of condition in *restaurants* and *cafés*. Such a thing might happen on an emergency, but it was assailing too much all those feelings and tastes which become inherent in refinement, to suppose that the tables of even the best house of the sort, in Paris, could be honored by the presence of such persons, except under particular circumstances. My own observation corroborated this opinion, and, in order to make sure of the fact, I have put the question to nearly every French woman of

rank, it has since been my good fortune to become sufficiently acquainted with, to take the liberty. The answer has been uniform. Such
things are sometimes done, but rarely; and even then it is usual to have
the service in a private room. One old lady, a woman perfectly competent to decide on such a point, told me frankly, "We never do it, except
by way of a frolick, or when in a humour which induces people to do
many other silly and unbecoming things. Why should we go to the
*restaurateurs* to eat? We have our own houses and servants, as well as the
English, or even you Americans"—it may be supposed I laughed—
"and certainly the French are not so devoid of good taste as not to
understand that the mixed society of a public house, is not the best
possible company for a woman."

It is, moreover, a great mistake to imagine that the French are not
hospitable, and that they do not entertain as freely, and as often as any
other people. The only difference between them and the English, in
this respect, or between them and ourselves, is in the better taste and
ease which regulate their intercourse of this nature. While there is a
great deal of true elegance, there is no fuss, at a French entertainment;
and all that you have heard of the superiority of the kitchen, in this
country, is certainly true. Society is divided into *castes*, in Paris, as it is
every where else; and the degrees of elegance and refinement increase
as one ascends, as a matter of course, but there is less of effort, in every
class, than is usual with us. One of the best-bred Englishmen of my
acquaintance, and one, too, who had long been in the world, has
frankly admitted to me, that the highest tone of English society, is
merely an imitation of that which existed in Paris, previously to the
revolution, and of which, though modified as to usages and forms, a
good deal still remains. By the highest tone, however, you are not to
suppose I mean that labored, frigid, heartless manner, that so many, in
England especially, mistake for high breeding, merely because they do
not know how to unite with the finish which constant intercourse with
the world creates, the graceful semblance of living less for one's self
than for others, and to express, as it were, their feelings and wishes,
rather than to permit one's own to escape him, a habit, that, like the
reflection of a mirror, produces the truest and most pleasing images,
when thrown back from surfaces the most highly polished. But I am
anticipating, rather than giving you a history of what I have seen.

In consequence of our not having brought any letters, as has just
been mentioned, and of not having sought society, no one gave them-

selves any trouble on our account, for the first three or four months of our residence in Paris. At the end of that period, however, I made my *début*, at probably as brilliant an entertainment, as one usually sees, here, in the course of a whole winter. Mr. Canning, then Secretary of State for Foreign Affairs, came to Paris on a visit, and, as is usual on such occasions, diplomacy was a good deal mixed up with eating and drinking. Report says, that the etiquette of the court was a good deal deranged by this visit, the Bourbons not having adopted the hail-fellow hospitality of the English kings. *M. de Villèle*, or *M. de Damas*, would be invited to dine at Windsor, almost as a matter of course; but the descendant of Hugh Capet hesitated about breaking bread with an English commoner. The matter is understood to have been gotten over, by giving the entertainment at St. Cloud; where, it would seem, the royal person has fewer immunities than at the Tuileries. But, among other attentions that were bestowed on the English statesman, Mr. Brown determined to give him a great diplomatic dinner; and, our own legations having a great poverty of subordinates, except in the way of travelling *attachés*, I was invited to occupy one end of the table, while the regular Secretary took his seat at the other. Before I attempt a short description of this entertainment, it may help to enliven the solitude of your mountain residence, and serve to give you more distinct ideas of the matter, than can be obtained from novels, if I commence with a summary of the appliances and modes of polite intercourse in this part of the world, as they are to be distinguished from our own.

In the first place, you are to discard from your mind, all images of two rooms and folding-doors, with a passage six feet wide, a narrow carpeted flight of steps, and a bed-room prepared for the ladies to uncloak in, and another in which the men can brush their hair, and hide their hats. Some such snuggeries, very possibly exist in England among the middling classes; but I believe all over the continent of Europe, style is never attempted, without more suitable means to carry out the intention.

In Paris every one, who mingles with the world, lives in a hotel, or a house that has a court and an outer gate. Usually, the building surrounds three sides of this court, and sometimes, the whole four; though small hotels are to be found, in which the court is encircled on two, or even on three of its sides, merely by high walls. The gate is always in the keeping of a regular porter, who is an important personage about the establishment, taking in letters, tickets, &c., ejecting blackguards and all other suspicious persons, carrying messages, besides levying contributions on all the inmates of the house, in the way of wood and coal. In short, he is, in some measure, held to be responsible for the *exits* and entrances, being a sort of domestic *gendarme*. In the larger hotels, there are two courts, the great and *la basse-cour*, the latter being connected with the offices and stables.

Of course, these hotels vary in size and magnificence. Some are not larger than our own largest town-dwellings, while others, again, are palaces. As these buildings were originally constructed to lodge a single establishment, they have their principal and their inferior apartments; some have their summer and their winter apartments. As is, and always must be the case, where every thing like state and magnificence are affected, the reception rooms are *en suite*; the mode of building which prevails in America, being derived from the secondary class of English houses. It is true, that in London, many men of rank, perhaps of the nobility, do not live in houses any larger, or much better, than the best of our own; though I think, that one oftener sees rooms of a good size and proper elevation, even in these dwellings, than it is usual to see in America. But the great houses of London, such as Burlington-house, Northumberland-house, Devonshire-house, Lansdowne-house, Sutherland-house, (the most magnificent of all,) &c. &c., are, more or less, on the continental plan, though not generally built around courts. This plan eschews passages of all descriptions, except among the private parts of the dwelling. In this respect, an American house, is the very opposite of a European house. We are nothing without passages, it being indispensable that every room should open on one; whereas, here, the great point is to have as little to do with them as possible. Thus you quit the great stair-case, by a principal door, and find yourself in an ante-chamber; this communicates with one or two more rooms of the same character, gradually improving in ornaments and fixtures, until you enter a *salon*. Then comes a succession of apartments, of greater or less magnificence, according to circumstances, until you are led entirely round the edifice, quitting it by a door on the great stair-case, again, opposite to the one by which you entered. In those cases in which there are courts, the principal rooms are ranged, in this manner, *en suite*, on the exterior range, usually looking out on the gardens, while those within them, which look into the court, contain the bed-rooms, boudoir, eating-rooms, and perhaps the library. So tenacious are those, who lay any claim to gentility here, of the use of ante-chambers, that I scarcely recollect a lodging of any sort, beyond the solitary chamber of some student, without, at least, one. They seem indispensable, and I think rightly, to all ideas of style, or even of comfort. I remember to have seen an amusing instance of the strength of this feeling, in the case of the wife of a former French Minister, at Washington. The building she inhabited, was one of the ordinary American double-houses, as they are called, with a passage through the centre, the stairs in the passage, and a short corridore, to communicate with the bed-rooms, above. Off the end of this upper corridore, if, indeed, so short a transverse passage deserves the name, was partitioned a room, of some eight feet by ten, as a bed-room. A room adjoining this, was converted into a boudoir and bed-room, for Madame de ———, by means of a silk screen. The usual door of the latter opened, of course, on the passage. In a morning call one day, I was received in the *boudoir*. Surprised to be carried up stairs, on such an occasion, I was still more so to find myself taken through a small room, before I was admitted to the larger. The amount of it all was, that Madame de ———, accustomed to have many rooms, and to think it vulgar to receive in her great drawing-room of a morning, believing *au premier*, or up one pair of stairs, more genteel than the *rez de chaussée*, or the ground floor, and feeling the necessity of an *ante-chamber*, as there was an abruptness in being at once admitted into the presence of a lady from a stair-case, a sort of local *brusquerie*, that would suit her cook, better than the wife of an envoy extraordinary, had contrived to introduce her guests through the little bed-room, at the end of the up-stairs entry!

From all this you will be prepared to understand some of the essential differences between a reception in Paris, and one at New-York, or even at Washington. The footman, or footmen, if there are two, ascend to the inner ante-chamber, with their masters and mistresses, where they receive the cloaks, shawls, over-coats, or whatever else has been used for the sake of mere warmth, and withdraw. If they are sent home, as is usually the case at dinners and evening parties, they return with the things at the hour ordered, but if the call be merely a passing one, or the guest means to go early to some other house, they either wait in the ante-chamber, or in a room provided for that purpose. The French are kind to their servants; much kinder than either the English, or their humble imitators, ourselves; and it is quite common to see, not only a good warm room, but refreshments, provided for the servants at a French party. In England, they either crowd the narrow passages and the door-way, or throng the street, as with us. In both countries, the poor coachmen sit for hours on their carriage-boxes, like so many ducks, in the drizzle and rain.

The footman gives the names of his party to the *maître d'hôtel*, or the groom of the chambers, who, as he throws open the door of the first drawing-room, announces them in a loud voice. Announcing by means of a line of servants, is rarely, if ever, practised in France, though it is still done in England, at large parties, and in the great houses. Every one has heard the story of the attempt at Philadelphia, some forty years ago, to introduce the latter custom, when, by the awkwardness of a servant, a party was announced as "Master and Mistress, and the young ladies;" but you will smile when I tell you that the latter part of this style is precisely that which is most in vogue at Paris. A young lady here, may be admired, she may be danced with, and she may even look and be looked at; but in society she talks little, is never loud or *belleish*, is always neat and simple in her attire, using very little jewelry, and has scarcely any other name than *Mademoiselle*. The usual mode of announcing is, "*Monsieur le Comte, et Madame la Comtesse d'une telle, avec leurs demoiselles:*" or, in plain English, "The Count and Countess Such-a-one, *with their daughters.*" This you will perceive is not so far, after all, from "Master and Mistress, and the young ladies." The English, more simple in some respects, and less so in others, usually give every name, though, in the use of titles, the utmost good taste is observed. Thus every nobleman below a Duke, is almost uniformly addressed and styled Lord A———, Lord B———, &c., and their wives, Ladies A——— and B———. Thus the Marquess of Lansdowne would, I think, always be addressed and spoken of, and even announced, merely as Lord Lansdowne. This, you will observe, is using the simplest possible style, and it appears to me that there is rather an affectation of simplicity in their ordinary intercourse, the term "My Lord" being hardly ever used, except by the tradesmen and domestics. The safest rule for an American, and certainly the one that good taste would dictate, is to be very sparing in his use of every thing of this sort, since he cannot be always certain of the proper usages of the different countries he visits, and, so long as he avoids unnecessary affectations of republicanisms, and, if a gentleman, this he will do without any effort, simplicity is his cue. When I say *avoids the affectations of republicanisms*, I do not mean the points connected with principles, but those vulgar and under-bred pretensions of ultra equality and liberalism, which, while they mark neither manliness nor a real appreciation of equal rights, almost uniformly betray a want of proper training and great ignorance of the world. Whenever, however, any attempt is made to identify equality of rights and democratical institutions with vulgarity and truculency, as is sometimes attempted here, in the presence of Americans, and even in good company, it is the part of every *gentleman* of our country to improve the opportunity that is thus afforded him, to show it is a source of pride, with him, to belong to a nation in which a hundred men are not depressed politically, in order that one may be great; and also to show how much advantage, after all, he who is right in substance has over him who is substantially wrong, even in the forms of society, and in that true politeness which depends on natural justice. Such a principle, acted on systematically, would soon place the gentlemen of America where they ought to be, and the gentlemen of other countries where, sooner or later, they must be content to descend, or to change their systems. That these things are not so, must be ascribed to our provincial habits, our remote situation, comparative insignificance, and chiefly to the circumstance that men's minds, trained under a different state of things, cannot keep even pace with the wonderful progress of the facts of the country.

But all this time, I have only got you into the outer *salon* of a French hotel. In order that we may proceed more regularly, we will return to the dinner given by our minister to Mr. Canning. Mr. Brown has an apartment in the *Hôtel Monaco*, one of the best houses in Paris. The Prince of Monaco is the sovereign of a little territory of the same name, on the Gulf of Nice, at the foot of the maritime Alps. His states may be some six or eight miles square, and the population some six or eight thousand. The ancient name of the family is Grimaldi, but by some intermarriage or other, the Duke of Valentinois, a Frenchman, has become the prince. This little state is still independent, though under the especial protection of the king of Sardinia, and without foreign relations. It was formerly a common thing for the petty princes of Europe to own hotels at Paris. Thus the present hotel of the Legion of Honour, was built by a Prince of Salm, and the Princes of Monaco had two, one of which is occupied by the Austrian ambassador, and, in the other, our own minister, just at this moment, has an apartment. As I had been pressed especially to be early, I went a little before six, and finding no one in the drawing-room, I strolled into the bureau, where I found Mr. Sheldon, the Secretary of Legation, who lived in the family, dressed for dinner. We chatted a little, and, on my admiring the magnificence of the rooms, he gave me the history of the hotel, as you have just heard it, with an additional anecdote that may be worth relating.

"This hotel," said the Secretary, "was once owned by M. de Talleyrand, and this bureau was probably the receptacle of state secrets of far greater importance than any that are connected with our own simple and unsupported claims for justice." He then went on to say, that the citizens of Hamburgh, understanding it was the intention of Napoleon to incorporate their town with the empire, had recourse to a *douceur*, in order to prevent an act, that, by destroying their neutrality, would annihilate their commerce. Four millions of francs were administered on this occasion, and of these a large proportion, it is said, went to pay for the hotel Monaco, which was a recent purchase of M. de Talleyrand. To the horror of the *Hambourgeois*, the money was scarcely paid, when the deprecated decree appeared, and every man of them was converted into a Frenchman, by the stroke of a pen. The worthy burghers were accustomed to receive a *quid pro quo*, for every florin they bestowed, failing of which, on the present occasion, they sent a deputation forthwith to Napoleon, to reveal the facts, and to make their complaints. That great man little liked that any one but himself should peculate in his dominions, and, in the end, M. de Talleyrand, was obliged to quit the hotel Monaco. By some means, with which I am unacquainted, most probably by purchase, however, the house is now the property of Madame Adelaide of Orleans.

The rolling of a coach into the court was a signal for us to be at our posts, and we abandoned the bureau, so lately occupied by the great father of diplomacy, for the drawing-room. I have already told you that this dinner was in honor of Mr. Canning, and, although diplomatic in one sense, it was not so strictly confined to the corps as to prevent a selection. This selection, in honor of the principal guest, had been made from the representatives of the great powers, Spain being the least important nation represented on the occasion, the republic of Switzerland excepted. I do not know whether the presence of the Swiss *Chargé d'Affaires* was so intended or not, but it struck me as pointed, and in good taste, for all the other foreign agents were ambassadors, with the exception of the Prussian, who was an Envoy Extraordinary.

Diplomacy has its honorary gradations as well as a military corps, and as you can know but little of such matters, I will explain them *en passant*. First in rank comes the ambassador. This functionary is supposed to represent the personal dignity of the state that sends him. If a king, there is a room in his house that has a throne, and it is usual to see the chair reversed, in respect for its sanctity, and it appears to be etiquette to suspend the portrait of the sovereign beneath the canopy. The Envoy Extraordinary comes next, and then the Minister Plenipotentiary. Ordinarily, these two functions are united in the same individual. Such is the rank of Mr. Brown. The Minister Resident is a lower grade, and the *Chargé d'Affaires* the lowest of all. *Inter se*, these personages take rank according to this scale. Previously to the peace of 1814, the representative of one monarch laid claim to precede the representative of another, always admitting, however, of the validity of the foregoing rule. This pretension gave rise to a good deal of heartburning and contention. Nothing can, in itself, be of greater indifference, whether A. or B. walk into the reception-room, or to the dinner-table, first, but when the idea of general superiority is associated with the act, the aspect of the thing is entirely changed. Under the old system, the ambassador of the Emperor claimed precedence over all other ambassadors, and, I believe, the representatives of the kings of France had high pretensions also. Now there are great mutations in states. Spain, once the most important kingdom of Europe, has much less influence to-day than Prussia, a power of yesterday. Then the minister of the most insignificant prince claimed precedency over the representative of the most potent republic. This might have passed while republics were insignificant and dependent, but no one can believe that a minister of America, for instance, representing a state of fifty millions, as will be the case before long, would submit to such an extravagant pretension on the part of a minister of Wurtemburg, or Sardinia, or Portugal. He would not submit to such a pretension on the part of the minister of any power on earth.

I do not believe that the Congress of Vienna had sufficient foresight, or sufficient knowledge of the actual condition of the United States, to foresee this difficulty, but there were embarrassing points to be settled among the European states themselves, and the whole affair was disposed of, on a very discreet and equitable principle. It was decided that priority of standing at a particular court, should regulate the rank between the different classes of agents at that particular court. Thus the ambassador longest at Paris, precedes all the other ambassadors at Paris, and the same rule prevails with the ministers and *chargés*, according to their respective gradations of rank. A provision, however, was made in favor of the representative of the Pope, who, if of the rank of a Nuncio, precedes all ambassadors. This concession has been made in honor of the church, which, as you must know, or ought to be told, is an interest much protected in all monarchies, statesmen being notoriously of tender consciences.

The constant habit of meeting, drills the diplomatic corps so well, that they go through the evolutions of etiquette as dexterously as a corps of regular troops perform their wheelings and counter-marches. The first great point with them is punctuality, for to people who sacrifice so much of it to forms, time gets to be precious. The roll of wheels was incessant in the court of the hotel Monaco, from the time the first carriage entered, until the last had set down its company. I know, as every man who reflects must know, that it is inherently ill-bred to be late any where, but I never before felt how completely it was high-breeding to be as punctual as possible. The *maître d'hôtel* had as much as he could do to announce the company, who entered as closely after each other as decorum and dignity would permit. I presume one party waited a little for the others in the outer drawing-room, the reception being altogether in the inner room.

The Americans very properly came first. We were Mr. Gallatin, who was absent from London on leave, his wife and daughter, and a clergyman and his wife, and myself; Mrs. [Cooper] having declined the invitation, on account of ill-health. The announcing and the entrance of most of the company, especially as every body was in high dinner dress, the women in jewels and the men wearing all their orders, had something of the air of a scenic display. The effect was heightened by the magnificence of the hotel, the drawing-room in which we were collected being almost regal.

The first person who appeared, was a handsome, compact, well-built, gentleman-like little man, who was announced as the Duke of Villa Hermosa, the Spanish Ambassador. He was dressed with great simplicity and beauty, having, however, the breast of his coat covered with stars, among which I recognised, with historical reverence, that of the Golden Fleece. He came alone, his wife, pleading indisposition for her absence. The Prussian Minister and his wife came next. Then followed Lord and Lady Granville, the representatives of England.

He was a large well-looking man, but wanted the perfect command of movement and manner that so much distinguish his brethren in diplomacy; as for mere physical stuff, he and our own minister, who stands six feet four in his stockings, would make material enough for all the rest of the corps. He wore the star of the Bath. The Austrian ambassador and ambassadress followed, a couple of singularly high air and a good tone of manner. He is a Hungarian, and very handsome; she a Veronese, I believe, and certainly a woman admirably adapted for her station. They had hardly made their salutations, before *M. le Comte, et Mad. la Comtesse de Villèle* were announced. Here, then, we had the French prime minister. As the women precede the men into a drawing-room, here, knowing how to walk and to curtsey, alone, I did not, at first, perceive the great man, who followed so close to his wife's skirts as to be nearly hid. But he was soon flying about the room, at large, and betrayed himself, immediately, to be a fidget. Instead of remaining stationary, or nearly so, as became his high quality, he took the *initiative* in compliments, and had nearly every diplomatic man, walking apart in the adjoining room, in a political aside, in less than twenty minutes. He had a countenance of shrewdness, and I make little doubt is a better man in a bureau than in a drawing-room. His colleague, the foreign minister, M. de Damas and his wife came next. He was a large, heavy-looking personage, that I suspect throws no small part of the diplomacy on the shoulders of the Premier, though he had more the manner of good society than his colleague. He has already exchanged his office for that of Governor of the Heir Pre-sumptive, as I have already stated. There was a pause, when a quiet, even-paced, classical-looking man, in the attire of an ecclesiastic, appeared in the door, and was announced as "My Lord the Nuncio." He was then an Arch-bishop, and wore the usual dress of his rank; but I have since met him at an evening party, with a red hat under his arm, the Pope having recalled him and raised him to that dignity. He is now Cardinal Macchi. He was a priestly and an intellectual-looking per-sonage, and, externals considered, well suited to his station. He wore a decoration, or two, as well as most of the others.

"My Lord Clanricarde and Mr. Canning" came next, and the great man, followed by his son-in-law, made his appearance. He walked into the room with the quiet *aplomb* of a man accustomed to being *lionized*, and, certainly, without being of striking, he was of very pleasing appearance. His size was ordinary, but his frame was compact and well built, neither too heavy nor too light for his years, but of just the proportions to give one the idea of a perfect management of the machine. His face was agreeable, and his eye steady and searching. He and M. de Villele were the very opposites in demeanour, though, after all, it was easy to see that the Englishman had the most latent force about him. One was fidgety, and the other humorous; for with all his command of limb and gesture, nothing could be more natural than the expression of Mr. Canning. I may have imagined that I detected some of his wit, from a knowledge of the character of his mind. He left the impression, however, of a man whose natural powers were checked by a trained and factitious deference to the rank of those with whom he associated. Lord Granville, I thought, treated him with a sort of affectionate deference, and, right or wrong, I jumped to the conclusion, that the English ambassador was a straight-forward good fellow, at the bottom, and one very likely to badger the fidgety premier, by his steady determination to do what was right. I thought M. de Damas, too, looked like an honest man. God forgive me, if I do injustice to any of these gentlemen!

All this time, I have forgotten Count Pozzo di Borgo, the Russian ambassador. Being a bachelor, he came alone. It might have been fancy, but I thought he appeared more at his ease, under the American roof, than any of his colleagues. The perfect good understanding between our own government and that of Russia, extends to their representatives, and, policy or not, we are better treated by them, than by any other foreign ministers. This fact should be known and appreciated, for as one citizen of the republic, however insignificant, I have no notion of being blackguarded and vituperated half a century, and then cajoled into forgetfulness, at the suggestions of fear and expediency, as circumstances render our good will of importance. Let us at least show that we are not mannikins to be pulled about for the convenience and humours of others, but that we know what honest words are, understand the difference between civility and abuse, and have pride enough to resent contumely, when, at least, we feel it to be unmerited. M. Pozzo is a handsome man, of good size and a fine dark eye, and has a greater reputation for talents, than any other member of the diplomatic corps now at Paris. He is, by birth, a Corsican, and I have heard it said, distantly related to Bonaparte. This may be true, Corsica being so small a country; just as some of us are related to every body in West Jersey. Our party now consisted of the prime minister, the secretary of foreign affairs, the Austrian and English ambassadors, and the Prussian minister, with their wives, the Nuncio, the Russian and Spanish ambassadors, the Swiss Chargé d'Affaires, Mr. Canning, Lord Clanricarde, Mr., Mrs., and Miss Gallatin, and the other Americans already mentioned, or twenty-five in all.

If I had been struck with the rapid and business-like manner in which the company entered, I was amused with the readiness with which they paired off when dinner was announced. It was like a *coup de théâtre*, every man and every woman knowing his or her exact rank and precedency, and the time when to move. This business of getting out of a drawing-room to a dinner table is often one of difficulty, though less frequently in France, than in most other European countries, on account of the admirable tact of the women, who seldom suffer a knotty point to get the ascendency, but, by choosing the gentleman for themselves, settle the affair off hand. From their decision, of course, there is no appeal. In order that in your simplicity, you may not mistake the importance of this moment, I will relate an anecdote of what lately occurred, at a dinner given by an English functionary in Holland.

When William invaded England, in 1688, he took with him many Dutch nobles, some of whom remained, and became English peers. Among others, he created one of his followers an Irish Earl; but choosing to return to Holland, this person was afterwards known as the Count de [Reede-Ginckel], although his Irish rank was always acknowledged. It happened that the wife of the descendant of this person was present at the entertainment in question. When dinner was announced, the company remarked that the master of the house was in a dilemma. There was much consultation, and a delay of near half an hour before the matter was decided. The debated point was, whether Mad. de [Reede-Ginckel] was to be considered as a Dutch or an Irish Countess. If the latter, there were English ladies present who were entitled to precede her; if the former, as a stranger, she might get that advantage herself. Luckily for the rights of hospitality, the Dutch lady got the best of it.

These things sound absurd, and sometimes they are so, but this social drilling, unless carried to extremes, is not without its use. In America, I have always understood that, on such occasions, silent laws of etiquette exist, in all good company, which are founded on propriety and tact. The young give way to the old, the undistinguished to the distinguished, and he who is at home to the stranger. These rules are certainly the most rational, and in the best taste, when they can be observed, and, on the whole, they lead perhaps to the fewest embarrassments; always so, if there happen to be none but the well bred present, since seats become of little consideration where no importance is attached to them. I confess to some manoeuvering in my time, to get near, or away from a fire, out of a draught, or next some agreeable woman; but the idea whether I was at the head or the foot of the table never crossed my mind: and yet here, where they do mean the salt to come into the account, I begin to take care that they do not "bite their thumbs" at me. Two or three little things have occurred in my presence, which show that all our people do not even understand the ways of their own good society. A very young man lately, under the impression that gallantry required it, led one of the most distinguished women in the room, to the table, merely because he happened to be next her, at the moment dinner was announced. This was certainly a failure even in American etiquette, every woman being more disposed to appreciate the delicacy and respect which should have induced such a person to give place to one of higher claims, than to prize the head-over-heels assiduity that caused the boy to forget himself. Sentiment should be the guide on such occasions, and no man is a gentleman until his habits are brought completely in subjection to its dictates, in all matters of this sort.

There was very little sentiment, however, in marshalling the company at the dinner given to Mr. Canning. I will not undertake to say that all the guests were invited to meet this gentleman, and that he had been asked to name a day, as is usual when it is intended to pay an especial compliment; but I was asked to meet him, and I understood that the dinner was in his honour. Diplomatic etiquette made short work of the matter, notwithstanding, for the doors were hardly thrown open, before all the privileged vanished, with a quickness that was surprising. The minister took Mad. de Villele; M. de Villele, Mrs. Brown; M. de Damas, the wife of the oldest ambassador, and the Nuncio, Mad. de Damas; after which, the ambassadors and ministers took each other's wives in due order, and with a promptitude that denoted great practice. Even the chargé disappeared, leaving the rest of us to settle matters among ourselves as well as we could. Mr. Canning, Mr. Gallatin, Lord Clanricarde, the divine, the secretary and myself, were left with only the wife of the clergyman and Miss Gallatin. As a matter of course, the Americans, feeling themselves at home, made signs for the two Englishmen to precede them, and Mr. Canning offered his arm to Mrs. [Jarvis], and Lord Clanricarde, his, to Miss Gallatin. Here occurred a touch of character that is worthy to be mentioned, as showing of how very little account an American, male or female, is in the estimation of a European, and how very arbitrary are the laws of etiquette among our English cousins. Mr. Canning actually gave way to his son-in-law, leaving the oldest of the two ladies to come after the youngest, because, as a Marquis, his son-in-law took precedence of a commoner! This was out of place in America, at least, where the parties were, by a fiction in law, if not in politeness, and it greatly scandalized all our Yankee notions of propriety. Mrs. [Jarvis] afterwards told me that he apologized for the circumstance, giving Lord Clanricarde's rank as the reason. *"Semper eadem,"* or "worse and worse" as my old friend O[gde]n used to translate it. What became of the precedency of the married lady all this time, you will be ready to ask? Alas! she was an American, and had no precedency. The twelve millions may not settle this matter as it should be, but, take my word for it the "fifty millions" will. Insignificant as all this is, or rather ought to be, your grandchildren and mine will live to see the mistake rectified. How much better would it be for those who cannot stop the progress of events, by vain wishes and idle regrets, to concede the point gracefully, and on just principles, than to have their cherished prejudices broken down by dint of sheer numbers and power?

The dinner, itself, was like every dinner that is given at Paris, beautiful in decoration, admirable in its order, and excellent in viands, or rather, in its dishes; for it is the cookery and not the staple articles that form the boast of the French kitchen. As you are notable in your own region, for understanding these matters, I must say a word, touching the gastric science as it is understood here. A general error exists in America on the subject of French cookery, which is not highly seasoned, but whose merit consists in blending flavors and in arranging compounds, in such a manner as to produce, at the same time, the lightest and most agreeable food. A lady who, from her public situation, receives once a week, for the entire year, and whose table has a reputation, assured me, lately, that all the spices consumed annually in her kitchen did not cost her a franc! The *effect* of a French dinner is its principal charm. One of reasonably moderate habits, rises from the table with a sense of enjoyment, that, to a stranger, at least, is sometimes startling. I have, on several occasions, been afraid I was relaxing into the vices of a *gourmet*, if, indeed, vices they can be called. The *gourmand* is a beast, and there is nothing to be said in his favour, but, after all, I incline to the opinion that no one is the worse for a knowledge of what is agreeable to the palate. Perhaps no one of either sex is thoroughly trained, or properly bred, without being *tant soit peu de gourmet*. The difference between sheer eating, and eating with tact and intelligence, is so apparent as to need no explanation. A dinner here does not oppress one. The wine neither intoxicates nor heats, and the frame of mind and body in which one is left, is precisely that best suited to intellectual and social pleasures. I make no doubt, that one of the chief causes of the French being so agreeable as companions, is, in a considerable degree, owing to the admirable qualities of their table. A national character may emanate from a kitchen. Roast beef, bacon, pudding, and beer, and port, will make a different man, in time, from Château Margau, *côtelettes, consommés* and *soufflés*. The very name of *vol-au-vent* is enough to make one walk on air!

Seriously, these things have more influence than may be, at a glance, imagined. The first great change I could wish to make in America, would be to see a juster appreciation of the substance, and less importance attached to outward forms, in moral things. The second, would be to create a standard of greatness and distinction, that should be independent, or nearly independent, of money. The next, a more reasoning and original tone of thought, as respects our own distinctive principles and *distinctive situation*, with a total indifference to the theories that have been broached to sustain an alien and an antagonist system, in England; and the last, (the climax) a total reform in the kitchen! If I were to reverse the order of these improvements, I am not certain the three last might not follow as a consequence of the first. After our people have been taught to cook a dinner, they ought also to be taught how to eat it.

Our entertainment lasted the usual hour and a half, and, as one is all this time eating, and there are limits to the capacity of a stomach, a part of the lightness and gaiety with which one rises from a French dinner ought to be attributed to the time that is consumed at the table. The different ingredients have opportunity to dispose of themselves, in their new abode, and are not crowded together pell mell, or like papers and books in ———— ———— library, as I think they must be after a transatlantic meal. As for the point of a mere consumption of food, I take it, the palm must be given to your Frenchman. I had some amusement to-day in watching the different countries. The Americans were nearly all through their dinner, by the time the first course was removed. All that was eaten afterwards, was literally with them, pure make-weight, though they kept a hungry look, to the last. The English seemed fed even before the dinner was begun, and, although the continental powers in general, had the art of picking till they got to the finger-bowls, none really kept up the ball but the Frenchmen. It happened to be Friday, and I was a little curious to discover whether the Nuncio came to these places with a dispensation in his pocket. He sat next to Mad. de Damas, as good a Catholic as himself, and I observed them helping themselves to several suspicious-looking dishes, during the first course. I ought to have told you before, that one rarely, almost never, helps his neighbour, at a French entertainment. The dishes are usually put on the table, removed by the servants to be carved, in succession, and handed to the guests to help themselves. When the service is perfect, every dish is handed to each guest. In the great houses, servants out of livery help the guests to the different *plats*, servants in livery holding the dishes, sauces, &c., and changing the plates. I believe it is strictly *haut ton* for the servants in livery, to do nothing but assist those out of livery. In America it is thought stylish to give liveries; in Europe those who keep most servants out of livery, are in the highest mode, since these are always a superior class of menials. The habits of this quarter of the world give servants a very different estimation from that which they hold with us. Nobles of high rank are employed about the persons of princes, and, although, in this age, they perform no strictly menial offices, or only on great occasions, they are, in theory, the servitors of the body. Nobles have been even employed by nobles, and it is still considered an honor for the child of a physician, or a clergyman, or a shop-keeper, in some parts of Europe, to fill a high place in the household of a great noble. The body servant, or the *gentleman* as he is sometimes called even in England, of a man of rank, looks down upon a mechanic, as his inferior. Contrary to all our notions as all this is, it is strictly reasonable, when the relative conditions, information, habits, and characters of the people, are considered. But servants here, are divided into many classes; for some are scullions, and some are intrusted with the keys. It follows that those who maintain most of the higher class, who are never in livery, maintain the highest style. To say he keeps a servant out of livery, means that he keeps a better sort of domestic. Mere footmen always wear it, the *maître d'hôtel*, or groom of the chambers, and the valet, never.

But to return to the dispensation, I made it a point to taste every dish that had been partaken of by the Nuncio and his neighbor, and I found that they were all fish; but fish, so treated, that they could hardly know what to think of themselves. You may remember, however, that an Archbishop of Paris was sufficiently complaisant to declare a particular duck, of which one of Louis XVIth's aunts was fond, to be fish, and, of course, fit to be eaten on fast-days.

The fasting of these people would strike you as singular, for I verily believe they eat more of a fast-day, than on any other. We engaged a governess for the girls, not long after our arrival, and she proved to be a bigoted Catholic, a furious royalist, and as ignorant as a calf. She had been but a few weeks in the house, when I detected her teaching her *élèves* to think Washington an unpardonable rebel, La Fayette a monster, Louis XVIth a martyr, and all heretics in the high road to damnation. There remained no alternative but to give her a quarter's salary, and to get rid of her. By the way, this woman was of a noble family, and, as such, received a small pension from the court. But I kept her fully a month longer, than I think I otherwise should, to see her eat on fast-days. Your sister-in-law had the consideration, invariably, to order fish for her, and she made as much havoc among them as a pike. She always commenced the Friday, with an extra allowance of fruit, which she was eating all the morning; and, at dinner, she contrived to eat half the vegetables, and all the fish. One day, by mistake, the soup happened to be *gras* instead of *maigre*, and, after she had swallowed a large plate-full, I was malicious enough to express my regrets at the mistake. I really thought the poor woman was about to disgorge on the spot, but by dint of consolation she managed to spare us this scene. So good an occasion offering, I ventured to ask her why she fasted at all, as I did not see it made any great difference in the sum total of her bodily nutriment. She assured me that I did not understand the matter. The fruit was merely *"rafraîchissante,"* and so counted for nothing; and as for the fish and vegetables, I might possibly think them very good eating, and for that matter, so did she, on Thursdays and Saturdays, but no sooner did Friday come than she longed for meat. The merit of the thing consisted, therefore, more in denying her appetite than in going without food. I tried hard to persuade her to take a *côtelette* with me, but the proposition made her shudder, though she admitted that she envied me every mouthful I swallowed. The knowledge of this craving did not take away my appetite.

Lest you should suppose that I am indulging in the vulgar English slang against French governesses, I will add that our own was the very worst, in every respect, I ever saw in, or out, of France, and that I have met with ladies in this situation, every way qualified, by principles, attainments, manners and antecedents, to be received with pleasure, in the best company of Europe.

Our *convives* in the Hotel Monaco, soon disappeared after the *chasse-café*, leaving none but the Americans behind them. Men and women retired as they came; the latter, however, taking leave, as is always required by the punctilios of your sex, except at very large and crowded parties, and even then properly, and the former, if alone, getting away as quietly as possible. The whole affair was over before nine o'clock, at which hour the diplomatick corps was scattered all through Paris.

Previously to this dispersion, however, Mr. Gallatin did me the favor to present me to Mr. Canning. The conversation was short, and was chiefly on America. There was a sore spot in his feelings, in consequence of a recent negotiation, and he betrayed it. He clearly does not love us, but what Englishman does? You will be amused to hear that unimportant in other respects, as this little conversation was, it has been the means of affecting the happiness of two individuals of high station in Great Britain. It would be improper for me to say more, but of the fact I can entertain no manner of doubt, and I mention it here, merely as a curious instance of the manner in which "tall oaks from little acorns grow."

I ought to have said that two, instead of one event, followed this dinner. The second was our own introduction into European society. The how and wherefore it is unnecessary to explain, but some of the cleverest and best-bred people of this well-bred and clever capital took us by the hand, all "unlettered" as we were, and from that moment, taking into consideration our tastes and my health, the question has been not how to get into, but how to keep out of, the great world. You know enough of these matters, to understand that, the ice once broken, any one can float in the current of society.

This little footing has not been obtained without some *contretemps*, and I have learned early to understand that wherever there is an Englishman in the question, it behoves an American to be reserved, punctilious and sometimes stubborn. There is a strange mixture of kind feeling, prejudice and ill nature, as respects us, wrought into the national character of that people, that will not admit of much mystification. That they should not like us may be natural enough; but if they seek the intercourse, they ought, on all occasions, to be made to conduct it equally without annoyance and condescension, and on terms of perfect equality; conditions, by the way, that are scarcely agreeable to their present* notions of superiority.

In order to understand why I mention any other than the French, in the capital of France, you will remember that there are many thousands of foreigners established here, for longer or shorter periods, who, by means of their money (a necessary that, relatively, is less abundant with the French) materially affect society, contriving to penetrate it, in all directions, in some way or other.

---

* The change in this respect, during the last ten years is *patent*. No European nation has, probably, just at this moment as much real respect for America, as the English, though it is still mixed with great ignorance, and a very sincere dislike. Still, the enterprise, activity, and growing power of the country are forcing themselves on the attention of our kinsmen; and if the government understood its foreign relations as well as it does its domestic, and made a proper exhibition of maritime preparation and of maritime force, this people would hold the balance in many of the grave questions that are now only in abeyance, in European politics. Hitherto we have been influenced by every vacillation in English interests, and it is quite time to think of turning the tables, and of placing, as far as practicable, American interests above the vicissitudes of those of other people. The thing is more easily done, than is commonly imagined, but a party politician is rarely a statesman, the subordinate management necessary to the one, being death to the comprehensive views that belong to the other. The peculiar nature of the American institutions, and the peculiar geographical situation of the country, moreover, render higher qualities necessary, perhaps, to make a statesman here, than elsewhere.

# Letter VII
## To Jacob Sutherland, Esq., New York.

Your legal pursuits, will naturally give you an interest in the subject of the state of justice in this part of the world. A correspondence like mine would not admit of any very profound analysis of the subject, did I possess the necessary learning, which I do not, but I may present a few general facts and notions, that will give you some idea of the state of this important feature of society. The forms and modes of English jurisprudence are so much like our own, as to create the impression that the administration of justice is equally free from venality and favor. As a whole, and when the points at issue reach the higher functionaries of the law, I should think this opinion true; but, taking those facts that appear in the daily prints, through the police reports and in the form of personal narratives, as guides, I should think that there is much more oppression, many more abuses, and far more outrages on the intention of the law, in the purlieus of the courts in England, through the agency of subordinates, than with us. The delays and charges of a suit in chancery, almost amount to a denial of justice. Quite lately, I saw a statement, which went to show that a legacy to a charity of about £1000, with the interest of some fourteen years, had been consumed in this court, with the exception of rather more than £100. This is an intolerable state of things, and goes to prove, I think, that, in some of its features at least, English jurisprudence is behind that of every other free country.

But I have been much impressed, lately, by a case that would be likely to escape the attention of more regular commentators. A peer of the realm having struck a constable on a race course, is proceeded against, in the civil action. The jury found for the plaintiff, damages £50. In summing up, the judge reasoned exactly contrary to what I am inclined to think would have been the case, had the matter been tried before you. He gave it as his opinion that the action was frivolous and ought never to have been brought, that the affair should have been settled out of court, and, in short, left the impression that it was not, as such, so great a hardship for a constable to be struck by a peer, that his honor might not be satisfied with the offering of a guinea or two. The jury thought differently; from which I infer that the facts did not sustain the judge in his notions. Now, the reasoning at home, would, I think, have been just the other way. The English judge said, in substance, a man of Lord ———'s dignity ought not to have been exposed to this action; you would have said, a senator is a law-maker, and owes even a higher example of order than common to the community; *he* insinuated that a small reparation ought to suffice, while *you* would have made some strong hints at smart-money.

I mention this case, for I think it rather illustrative of English justice. Indeed, it is not easy to see how it well can be otherwise: when society is divided into castes, the weak must go to the wall. I know that the theory, here, is quite different, and that one of the boasts of England is the equality of its justice, but I am dealing in *facts* and not in theories. In America it is thought, and with proper limitations, I dare say, justly, that the bias of juries, in the very lowest courts, is in favour of the poor against the rich, but the right of appeal restores the balance, and, in a great degree, secures justice. In each case, it is the controlling power that does the wrong; in England the few, in America the many.

In France, as you probably know, juries are confined to criminal cases. The consequence is a continuance of the old practice of soliciting justice. The judge virtually decides in chambers, and he hears the parties in chambers, or, in other words, wherever he may choose to receive them. The client depends as much on external influence and his own solicitations, as on the law and the justice of his case. He visits the judge officially, and works upon his mind, by all the means in his power. You and I have been acquainted intimately from boyhood, and it has been my bad luck to have had more to do with the courts than I could wish, and yet, in all the freedom of an otherwise unfettered intercourse, I have never dared to introduce the subject of any suit, in which I have been a party. I have been afraid of wounding your sense of right, to say nothing of my own, and of forfeiting your esteem, or at least of losing your society. Now had we been Frenchmen you would have expected me to *solicit* you, you would probably have heard me with the bias of an old friend, and my adversary must have been a singularly lucky fellow, or you a very honest one, if he did not get the worst of it, supposing the case to admit of doubt. Formerly, it was known that influence prevailed; bribes were offered and received, and a suit was a contest of money and favoritism, rather than one of facts and principles.

I asked Gen. La Fayette, not long since, what he thought of the actual condition of France, as respects the administration of justice. In most political cases he accused the government of the grossest injustice, illegality and oppression. In the ordinary criminal cases, he believed the intentions of the courts and juries perfectly fair, as, indeed, it is difficult to believe they should not be. In the civil suits he thought a great improvement had taken place, nor did he believe that there now exists much of the ancient corruption. The civil code of Napoleon had worked well, and all he complained of was a want of fitness between the subordinate provisions of a system invented by a military despot for his own support, and the system of *quasi* liberty that had been adopted at the restoration; for the Bourbons had gladly availed themselves of all the machinery of power, that Napoleon bequeathed to France.

A gentleman who heard the conversation, afterwards told me the following anecdote. A friend of his had long been an unsuccessful suitor in one of the higher courts of the kingdom. They met one day in the street, when the other told him that an unsealed letter which he held in his hand, contained an offer of a pair of carriage-horses, to the wife of the judge who had the control of his affair. On being told he dare not take so strong a step, M. de ———, my informant, was requested to read the letter, to seal it, and to put it in the *boîte aux lettres* with his own hands, in order to satisfy himself of the actual state of justice in France. All this was done, and "I can only add," continued M. de ———, "that I afterwards saw the horses in the carriage of Mad. ———, and that my friend gained his cause." To this anecdote, I can only say, I tell it exactly as I heard it, and that M. de ——— is a deputy, and one of the honestest and simplest-minded men of my acquaintance. It is but proper to add, that the judge in question has a bad name, and is little esteemed by the bar, but the above-mentioned fact would go to show that too much of the old system remains.

In Germany justice bears a better name, though the absence of juries generally, must subject the suitor to the assaults of personal influence. Farther south report speaks still less favourably of the manner in which the laws are interpreted, and, indeed, it would seem to be an inevitable consequence of despotism, that justice should be abused. One hears, occasionally, of some signal act of moderation and equity, on the part of monarchies, but the merits of systems are to be proved, not by these brilliant *coups de justice*, but by the steady, quiet, and regular working of the machine, on which men know how to calculate, in which they have faith, and which as seldom deceives them as comports with human fallibility, rather than by *scenes* in which the blind goddess is made to play a part in a *melo-drama*.

On the whole, it is fair to presume that, while public opinion, and that intelligence which acts virtually as a bill of rights, even in the most despotic governments of Europe, not even excepting Turkey perhaps, have produced a beneficial influence on the courts, the secrecy of their proceedings, the irresponsible nature of their trusts (responsible to power, and irresponsible to the nation) and the absence of publicity, produce precisely the effects that a common-sense view of the facts, would lead one, who understands human nature, to expect.

I am no great admirer of the compromising verdicts of juries, in civil suits that admit of a question as to amounts. They are an admirable invention to settle questions of guilty or not guilty, but an enlightened court would, nine times in ten, do more justice in the cases just named. Would it not be an improvement to alter the present powers of juries, by letting them simply find for or against the suitor, leaving the damages to be assessed by regular officers, that might resemble masters in chancery? At all events, juries or some active substitute, cannot be safely dispensed with, until a people have made great progress in the science of publicity, and in a knowledge of the general principles connected with jurisprudence.

This latter feature is quite peculiar to America. Nothing has struck me more in Europe, than the ignorance which every where exists on such subjects, even among educated people. No one appears to have any distinct notions of legal principles, or even of general law, beyond a few prominent facts, but the professional men. Chance threw me, not long since, into the company of three of four exceedingly clever young Englishmen. They were all elder sons, and two were the heirs of peers. Something was said on the subject of a claim of a gentleman, with whom I am connected, to a large Irish estate. The grandfather of this gentleman was the next brother to the incumbent, who died intestate. The grandson, however, was defeated in his claim in consequence of its being proved, that the ancestor, through whom he derived his claim, was of the half-blood. My English companions did not understand the principle, and when I explained by adding that the grandfather of the claimant was born of a different mother from the last holder in fee, and that he could never inherit at law (unless by devise), the estate going to a hundredth cousin of the whole blood in preference, or even escheating to the king, they one and all protested England had no such law! They were evidently struck with the injustice of transferring property that had been acquired by the common ancestor of two brothers, to a remote cousin, merely because the affinity between the sons was only on the father's side, although that very father may have accumulated the estate, and they could not believe that what struck them as so grievous a wrong, could be the law of descents under which they lived. Luckily for me, one learned in the profession happened to be present, and corroborated the fact. Now all these gentlemen were members of parliament, but they were accustomed to leave legal questions of this nature to the management of professional men.*

I mentioned this conversation to another Englishman, who thought the difficulty well disposed of, by saying that if property ever escheated in this manner, I ought to remember that the crown invariably bestowed it on the natural heir. This struck me as singular reasoning to be used by a people who profess to cherish liberty, inasmuch as, to a certain degree, it places all the land in the kingdom, at the mercy of the sovereign. I need not tell you moreover, that this answer was insufficient, as it did not meet the contigency of a remote cousin's inheriting, to the prejudice of the children of him who earned the estate. But habit is all in all, with the English in such matters, and that which they are accustomed to see and hear, they are accustomed to think right.

The bar is rising greatly in public consideration in France. Before the revolution there were certain legal families of great distinction, but these could scarcely be considered as forming a portion of the regular practitioners. Now, many of the most distinguished statesmen, peers, and politicians of France, commenced their careers as advocates. The practice of public speaking gives them an immense advantage in the chambers, and fully half of the most popular debaters, are members who belong to the profession. New candidates for public favor appear every day, and the time is at hand when the fortunes of France, so lately controlled by soldiers, will be more influenced by men of this profession, than by those of all the others. This is a great step in moral civilization, for the country that most feels the ascendency of the law, and that least feels that of arms, is nearest to the summit of human

---

* This absurd and unaccountable provision of the common law, has since been superseded by a statute regulating descents on a more intelligible and just provision. England has made greater advances in common sense and in the right, in all such matters, within the last five years, than during the previous hundred.

perfection. When asked which profession takes rank, in America, I tell them the law in influence, and the church in deference. Some of my *moustachoed* auditors stare at this reply, for, here, the sword has precedence of all others, and the law, with few exceptions, is deemed a calling for none but those who are in the secondary ranks of society. But, as I have told you, opinion is undergoing a great change, in this particular. I believe that every efficient man in the present ministry is or has been a lawyer.

# Letter VIII
## To Col. Bankhead, U.S. Artillery.

The army of France obtained so high a reputation, during the wars of the revolution and of the empire, that you may feel some curiosity to know its actual condition. As the Bourbons understand that they have been restored to the throne, by the great powers of Europe, if not in opposition to the wishes of a majority of Frenchmen, certainly in opposition to the wishes of the active portion of the population, and consequently to that part of the nation which would be the most likely to oppose their interests, they have been accused of endeavouring to keep the establishments of France so low as to put her at the mercy of any new combination of the allies. I should think this accusation, in a great degree, certainly, unmerited; for France, at this moment, has a large and, so far as I can judge, a well appointed army, and one that is charged by the liberal party with being a heavy expense to the nation, and that, too, chiefly with the intention of keeping the people in subjection to tyranny. But these contradictions are common in party politics. It is not easy here to get at statistical facts, accurately, especially those which are connected with expenditure. Nominally, the army is about 200,000 men, but it is whispered, that numerous *congés* are given, in order to divert the funds that are thus saved, to other objects. Admitting all this to be true, and it probably is so in part, I should think France must have fully 150,000 men embodied, without including the National Guards. Paris is pretty well garrisoned, and the *casernes* in the vicinity of the capital are always occupied. It appears to me there cannot be less than 20,000 men, within a day's march of the Tuileries, and there may be half as many more.*

Since our arrival there have been several great military displays, and I have made it a point to be present at them all. The first was a *petite guerre*,† on the plains of Issy, or within a mile of the walls of the town.

---

* The sudden disbandment of the guards and other troops in 1830, greatly diminished the actual force of the country.
† Sham-fight.

There may have been 15,000 men assembled for the occasion, including troops of all arms.

One of the first things that struck me at Paris, was the careless militia-like manner in which the French troops marched about the streets. The disorder, irregularity, careless and indifferent style of moving, were all exactly such as I have heard laughed at, a thousand times, in our own great body of national defenders. But this is only one of many similar instances, in which I have discovered that what has been deemed a peculiarity in ourselves, arising from the institutions perhaps, is a very general quality belonging rather to man than to any particular set of men. Our notions, you will excuse the freedom of the remark, are apt to be a little provincial, and every one knows that fashions, opinions and tastes, only become the more exaggerated, the farther we remove from the centre of light. In this way, we come to think of things in an exaggerated sense, until, like the boy who is disappointed at finding a king a man, we form notions of life that are any thing but natural and true.

I was still so new to all this, however, that I confess I went to the plain of Issy, expecting to see a new style of manœuvring, or, at least, one very different from that which I had so often witnessed at home, nor, can I say that, in this instance, there was so much disappointment. The plan of the day did not embrace two parties, but was merely an attack on an imaginary position, against which the assailants were regularly and scientifically brought up, the victory being a matter of convention. The movements were very beautiful, and were made with astonishing spirit and accuracy. All idea of disorder, or the want of regularity, was lost, here, for entire battalions advanced to the charges without the slightest apparent deviation from perfectly mathematical lines.

When we reached the acclivity that overlooked the field, a new line was forming directly beneath us, it being supposed that the advance of the enemy had already been driven in upon his main body, and the great attack was just on the point of commencing.

A long line of infantry of the French guards, formed the centre of the assailants. Several batteries of artillery were at hand, and divers strong columns of horse and foot were held in reserve. A regiment of lancers was on the nearest flank, and another of cuirassiers was stationed at the opposite. All the men of the royal family were in the field, surrounded by a brilliant staff. A gun was fired near them, by way of signal, I suppose, when two brigades of artillery galloped through the intervals of the line, unlimbered, and went to work as if they were in downright earnest. The cannonade continued a short time, when the infantry advanced in line, and delivered its fire by companies, or battalions, I could not discern which, in the smoke. This lasted some ten minutes, when I observed a strong column of troops dressed in scarlet, moving up, with great steadiness and regularity, from the rear. These were the Swiss guards, and there might have been fifteen hundred, or two thousand of them. The column divided into two, as it approached the rear of the line, which broke into column, in turn, and for a minute there was a confused crowd of red and blue coats, in the smoke, that quite set my nautical instinct at defiance. The cuirassiers chose this moment to make a rapid and menacing movement in advance, but without opening their column, and some of the artillery reappeared and commenced firing, at the unoccupied intervals. This lasted a very little while, for the Swiss displayed into line like clock-work, and then made a quick charge, with beautiful precision. Halting, they threw in a heavy fire, by battalions; the French guard rallied and formed upon their flanks; the whole reserve came up; the cuirassiers and lancers charged, by turning the position assailed, and for ten or fifteen minutes there was a succession of quick evolutions, which, like the *finale* of a grand piece of music, appeared confused even while it was the most scientific, and then there was a sudden pause. The position, whose centre was a copse, had been carried, and we soon saw the guards formed on the ground that was supposed to have been held by the enemy. The artillery still fired, occasionally, as on a retreating foe, and the lancers and cuirassiers were charging and manœuvring, half a mile farther in advance, as if following up their advantage.

Altogether, this was much the prettiest field exercise I ever witnessed. There was a unity of plan, a perfection of evolution, and a division of *matériel* about it, that rendered it to my eyes, as nearly perfect as might be. The troops were the best of France, and the management of the whole had been confided to some one accustomed to the field. It contained all the poetry, without any of the horrors of a battle. It could not possess the heart-stirring interest of a real conflict, and yet it was not without great excitement.

Some time after the *petite guerre* of Issy, the capital celebrated the *fête* of the Trocadero. The Trocadero, you may remember, was the fortress of Cadiz, carried by assault, under the order of the *Dauphin*, in the war of the late Spanish revolution. This government, which has destroyed all the statues of the Emperor, proscribed his family, and obliterated every visible mark of his reign in their power, has had the unaccountable folly of endeavouring to supplant the military glory acquired under Napoleon, by that of Louis Antoine, Dauphin of France! A necessary consequence of the attempt, is a concentration of all the military *souvenirs* of the day, in this affair of the Trocadero. Bold as all this will appear to one who has not the advantage of taking a near view of what is going on here, it has even been exceeded, through the abject spirit of subserviency in those who have the care of public instruction, by an attempt to exclude even the name of the Bonaparte from French history. My girls have shown me an abridgment of the history of France, that has been officially prepared for the ordinary schools, in which there is no sort of allusion to him. The wags here, say that a work has been especially prepared for the heir presumptive, however, in which the emperor is a little better treated; being spoken of as "a certain *Marquis de Bonaparte*, who commanded the armies of the king."

The mimic attack on the Trocadero, like its great original, was at night. The troops assembled in the *Champ de Mars*, and the assault was made, across the beautiful bridge of Jena, on a sharp acclivity near Passy, which was the imaginary fortress. The result was a pretty good effect of night-firing, some smoke, not a little noise, with a very pretty movement of masses. I could make nothing of it, of much interest, for the obscurity prevented the eyes from helping the imagination.

Not long since, the king held a great review of regular troops and of the entire body of the National Guards of Paris and its environs. This review also took place in the *Champ de Mars*, and it was said that nearly a hundred thousand men were under arms, for the occasion. I think there might have been quite seventy thousand. These mere reviews have little interest, the evolutions being limited to marching by regiments on and off the ground. In doing the latter, the troops defile before the king. Previously to this, the royal cortége passed along the several lines, receiving the usual honours.

On this occasion, the *Dauphine* and the *Duchesse de Berri*, followed the king in open carriages, accompanied by the little *Duc de Bordeaux* and his sister. I happened to be at an angle of the field, as the royal party, surrounded by a showy group of marshals and generals, passed, and when there seemed to be a little confusion. As a matter of course, the cry of *vive le roi* had passed along with the procession, for, popular or not, it is always easy for a sovereign to procure this sign of affection, or, for others to procure it for him. You will readily understand that *employés* of the government, are especially directed to betray the proper enthusiasm on such occasions. There was, however, a cry at this corner of the area, that did not seem so unequivocally loyal, and, on inquiry, I was told that some of the National Guards had cried *à bas les ministres*. The affair passed off without much notice, however, and I believe it was generally forgotten by the population, within an hour. The desire to get rid of *M. de Villèle*, and his set, was so general in Paris, that most people considered the interruption quite as a matter of course.

The next day the capital was electrified by a royal ordinance disbanding all the National Guards of Paris! A more infatuated, or if it were intended to punish the disaffected, a more unjust decree, could not easily have been issued. It was telling the great majority of the very class which forms the true force of every government, that their rulers could not confide in them. As confidence, by awakening pride, begets a spirit in favour of those who depend on it, so does obvious distrust engender disaffection. But the certainty that Louis XVIth, lost his throne and his life for the want of decision, has created one of those sweeping opinions, here, of the virtue of energy, that constantly leads the rulers into false measures. An act that might have restrained the France of 1792, would be certain to throw the France of 1827, into open revolt. The present generation of Frenchmen, in a political sense, have little in common with even the French of 1814, and measures must be suited to the times in which we live. As well might one think of using the birch on the man, that had been found profitable with the boy, as to suppose these people can be treated like their ancestors.

As might have been expected, a deep, and what is likely to prove a lasting discontent, has been the consequence of the blunder. It is pretended that the shop-keepers of Paris are glad to be rid of the trouble of occasionally mounting guard, and that the affair will be forgotten in a short time. All this may be true enough, in part, and it would also be true in the whole, were there not a press to keep disaffection alive, and to inflame the feelings of those who have been treated so cavalierly, for he knows little of human nature who does not understand that, while bodies of men commit flagrant wrongs without the responsibility being kept in view by their individual members, an affront to the whole is pretty certain to be received as an affront to each of those who make an integral part.

The immediate demonstrations of dissatisfaction have not amounted to much, though the law and medical students paraded the streets, and shouted, beneath the windows of the ministers, the very cry that gave rise to the disbandment of the guards. But, if no other consequence has followed this exercise of arbitrary power, I, at least, have learned how to disperse a crowd. As you may have occasion, some day, in your military capacity, to perform this unpleasant duty, it may be worth while to give you a hint concerning the *modus operandi*.

Happening to pass through the *Place Vendôme*, I found the foot of the celebrated column, which stands directly in the centre of the square, surrounded by several hundred students. They were clustered together like bees, close to the iron railing which encloses the base of the pillar, or around an area of some fifty or sixty feet, square. From time to time, they raised a shout, evidently directed against the ministers, of whom one resided at no great distance from the column. As the hotel of the *Etat-Major*, of Paris, is in this square, and there is always a post at it, it soon became apparent there was no intention quietly to submit to this insult. I was attracted by a demonstration on the part of the *corps de garde*, and, taking a station at no great distance from the students, I awaited the issue.

The guard, some thirty foot soldiers, came swiftly out of the court of the hotel, and drew up in a line before its gate. This happened as I reached their own side of the square, which I had just crossed. Presently, a party of fifteen or twenty *gendarmes à cheval*, came up, and wheeled into line. The students raised another shout, as it might be, in defiance. The infantry shouldered arms, and filing off singly, headed by an officer, they marched, in what we call Indian file, towards the crowd. All this was done in the most quiet manner possible, but promptly, and with an air of great decision and determination. On reaching the crowd, they penetrated it, in the same order, quite up to the railing. Nothing was said, nor was any thing done, for it would have been going farther than the students were prepared to proceed, had they attempted to seize and disarm the soldiers. This appeared to be understood, and instead of wasting the moments, and exasperating his enemies by a parley, the officer, as has just been said, went directly through them, until he reached the railing. Once there, he began to encircle it, followed in the same order by his men. The first turn loosened the crowd, necessarily, and then I observed that the muskets, which hitherto had been kept at a "carry," were inclined a little outwards. Two turns, enabled the men to throw their pieces to a charge, and, by this time, they had opened their order so far, as to occupy the four sides of the area. Facing outwards, they advanced very slowly, but giving time for the crowd to recede. This manoeuvre rendered the throng less and less dense, when, watching their time, the mounted *gendarmes* rode into it, in a body, and, making a circuit, on a trot, without the line of infantry, they got the mass so loosened and scattered, that, unarmed as the students were, had they been disposed to resist, they would now have been completely at the mercy of the troops. Every step that was gained, of course, weakened the crowd, and, in ten minutes, the square was empty; some being driven out of it in one direction, and some in another, without a blow being struck, or, even an angry word used. The force of the old saying, that "the king's name is a tower of strength," or, the law being on the side of the troops, probably was of some avail; but a mob of fiery young Frenchmen is not too apt to look at the law, with reverence.

I stood near the hotels, but still in the square, when a *gendarme*, sweeping his sabre as one would use a stick in driving sheep, came near me. He told me to go away. I smiled, and said I was a stranger, who was looking at the scene purely from curiosity. "I see you are, sir," he answered, "but you had better fall back into the *Rue de la Paix.*" We exchanged friendly nods, and I did as he told me, without further hesitation. In truth, there remained no more to be seen.

Certainly, nothing could have been done in better temper, more effectually, nor more steadily than this dispersion of the students. There is no want of spirit in these young men, you must know, but the reverse is rather the case. The troops were under fifty in number, and the mob was between six hundred and a thousand; resolute, active, sturdy young fellows, who had plenty of fight in them, but who wanted the unity of purpose that a single leader can give to soldiers. I thought this little campaign of the column of the Place Vendôme, quite as good in its way, as the *petite guerre* of the plains of Issy.

I do not know whether you have fallen into the same error as myself, in relation to the comparative merits of the cavalry of this part of the world, though I think it is one common to most Americans. From the excellence of their horses, as well as from that general deference for the character and prowess of the nation, which exists at home, I had been led to believe that the superior qualities of the British cavalry were admitted in Europe. This is any thing but true; military men, so far as I can learn, giving the palm to the Austrian artillery, the British infantry, and the French cavalry. The Russians are said to be generally good for the purposes of defence, and in the same degree deficient for those of attack. Some shrewd observers, however, think the Prussian army, once more, the best in Europe.

The French cavalry is usually mounted on small, clumsy, but sturdy beasts, that do not show a particle of blood. Their movement is awkward, and their powers, for a short effort, certainly are very much inferior to those of either England or America. Their superiority must consist in their powers of endurance, for the blooded animal soon falls off, on scanty fare and bad grooming. I have heard the moral qualities of the men, given as a reason why the French cavalry should be superior to that of England. The system of conscription secures to an army the best materials, while that of enlistment necessarily includes the worst. In this fact is to be found the real moral superiority of the French and Prussian armies. Here, service, even in the ranks, is deemed honorable; whereas with us, or in England, it would be certain degradation to a man of the smallest pretension to enlist as a soldier, except in moments that made stronger appeals than usual to patriotism. In short, it is *primâ facie* evidence of a degraded condition, for a man to carry a musket in a regular battalion. Not so here. I have frequently seen common soldiers copying in the gallery of the Louvre, or otherwise engaged in examining works of science, or of taste; not ignorantly and with vulgar wonder, but like men who had been regularly instructed. I have been told that a work on artillery practice lately appeared in France which excited so much surprise by its cleverness, that an inquiry was set on foot for its author. He was found seated in a *cabriolet*, in the streets; his vocation being that of a driver. What renders his knowledge more surprising, is the fact, that the man was never a soldier at all, but, having a great deal of leisure, while waiting for his fares, he had turned his attention to this subject, and had obtained all he knew by means of books. Nothing is more common than to see the drivers of *cabriolets* and *fiacres* reading in their seats, and I have even seen market women, under their umbrellas, *à la Robinson*, with books in their hands. You are not, however, to be misled by these facts, which merely show the influence of the peculiar literature of the country, so attractive and amusing, for a very great majority of the French can neither read nor write. It is only in the north that such things are seen at all, except among the soldiers, and a large proportion of even the French army are entirely without schooling.

To return to the cavalry, I have heard the superiority of the French ascribed also to their dexterity in the use of the sabre, or, as it is termed here, *l'arme blanche*. After all, this is rather a poetical conclusion; for charges of cavalry rarely result in regular, hand to hand, conflicts. Like the bayonet, the sabre is seldom used, except on an unresisting enemy. Still the consciousness of such a manual superiority might induce a squadron, less expert, to wheel away, or to break, without waiting for orders.

I have made the acquaintance, here, of an old, English General, who has passed all his life in the dragoons, and who commanded brigades of cavalry in Spain and at Waterloo. As he is a sensible old man, of great frankness and simplicity of character, perfect good-breeding and good nature, and, moreover, so far as I can discover, absolutely without prejudice against America, he has quite won my heart, and I have availed myself of his kindness to see a good deal of him. We walk together, frequently, and chat of all things in heaven and earth, just as they come uppermost. The other day I asked him to explain the details of a charge of his own particular arm to me, of which I confessed a proper ignorance. "This is soon done," said the old gentleman, taking my arm with a sort of sly humour, as if he were about to relate something facetious — "against foot, a charge is a menace; if they break, we profit by it; if they stand, we get out of the scrape as well as we can. When foot are in disorder, cavalry does the most, and it is always active in securing a victory, usually taking most of the prisoners. But as against cavalry, there is much misconception. When two regiments assault each other, it is in compact line — ." "How," I interrupted him, "do not you open, so as to leave room to swing a sabre?" "Not at all. The theory is knee to knee; but this is easier said than done, in actual service. I will suppose an unsuccessful charge. We start, knee to knee, on a trot. This loosens the ranks, and, as we increase the speed, they become still looser. We are under the fire of artillery, or perhaps, of infantry, all the time, and the enemy won't run. At this moment, a clever officer will command a retreat to be sounded. If he should not, some officer is opportunely killed, or some leading man loses command of his horse, which is wounded and wheels, the squadron follows, and we get away as well as we can. The enemy follows, and if he catches us, we are cut up. Other charges do occur, but this is the common history of cavalry against cavalry, and, in unsuccessful attacks of cavalry, against infantry, too. A knowledge of the use of the sword is necessary, for did your enemy believe you ignorant of it, he would not fly; but the weapon itself is rarely used on such occasions. Very few men are slain, in their ranks, by the bayonet, or the sabre."

I was once told, though not directly by an officer, that the English dragoon neglected his horse in the field, selling the provender for liquor, and that, as a consequence, the corps became inefficient; whereas the French dragoon, being usually a sober man, was less exposed to this temptation. This may, or may not, be true; but drunkenness is now quite common in the French army, though I think much less so in the cavalry, than in the foot. The former are generally selected with some care, and the common regiments of the line, as a matter of course, receive the refuse of the conscription.

This conscription is, after all, extremely oppressive and unjust, though it has the appearance of an equal tax. Napoleon had made it so unpopular, by the inordinate nature of his demands for men, that Louis XVIIIth caused an article to be inserted in the charter, by which it was to be altogether abolished. But a *law* being necessary to carry out this constitutional provision, the clause remains a perfect dead letter, it being no uncommon thing for the law to be stronger than the constitution, even in America, and quite a common thing here. I will give you an instance of the injustice of the system. An old servant of mine has been drafted for the cavalry. I paid this man seven hundred francs a year, gave him coffee, butter, and wine, with his food, and he fell heir to a good portion of my old clothes. The other day he came to see me, and I inquired into his present situation. His arms and clothes were found him. He got neither coffee, wine, nor butter, and his other food, as a matter of course, was much inferior to that he had been accustomed to receive with me. His pay, after deducting the necessary demands on it, in the shape of regular contributions, amounts to about two sous a day, instead of the two francs he got in my service.

Now, necessity, in such matters, is clearly the primary law. If a country cannot exist without a large standing army, and the men are not to be had by voluntary enlistments, a draft is probably the wisest and best regulation for its security. But, taking this principle as the basis of the national defence, a just and a paternal government would occupy itself in equalizing the effects of the burden, as far as circumstances would in any manner admit. The most obvious and efficient means would be by raising the rate of pay to the level, at least, of a scale that should admit of substitutes being obtained at reasonable rates. This is done with us, where a soldier receives a full ration, all his clothes, and sixty dollars a year.* It is true, that this would make an army very costly, and, to bear the charge, it might be necessary to curtail some of the useless magnificence and prodigality of the other branches of the government, and herein is just the point of difference between the expenditures of America and those of France. It must be remembered, too, that a really free government, by enlisting the popular feeling in its behalf through its justice, escapes all the charges that are incident to the necessity of maintaining power by force, wanting soldiers for its enemies without, and not for its enemies within. We have no need of a large standing army on account of our geographical position, it is true, but had we the government of France, we should not find that our geographical position exempted us from the charge.

You have heard a great deal of the celebrated soldiers who surrounded Napoleon, and whose names have become almost as familiar to us as his own. I do not find that the French consider the marshals men of singular talents. Most of them reached their high stations, on account of their cleverness in some particular branch of their duties, and by their strong devotion, in the earlier parts of their career, to their master. *Maréchal Soult* has a reputation for skill in managing the civil details of service. As a soldier, he is also distinguished for manoeuvring in the face of his enemy, and under fire. Some such excitement appears necessary to arouse his dormant talents. *Suchet* is said to have had capacity, but, I think, to *Masséna*, and to the present king of Sweden, the French usually yield the palm, in this respect. *Davoust* was a man of terrible military energy, and suited to certain circumstances, but scarcely a man of talents. It was to him Napoleon said, "Remember, you have but a single friend in France—myself; take care you do not lose him." *Lannes* seems to have stood better than most of them as a soldier, and *Macdonald* as a man. But, on the whole, I think it quite apparent there was scarcely one among them all, calculated to have carried out a very high fortune for himself, without the aid of the directing genius of his master. Many of them had ambition enough for any thing, but it was an ambition stimulated by example, rather than by a consciousness of superiority.

In nothing have I been more disappointed than in the appearance of these men. There is more or less of character about the exterior and physiognomy of them all, it is true, but scarcely one has what we are

* He now receives seventy-two.

accustomed to think the carriage of a soldier. It may be known to you that *Moreau* had very little of this, and really one is apt to fancy he can see the civic origin in nearly all of them. While the common French soldiers have a good deal of military coquetry, the higher officers appear to be nearly destitute of it. *Maréchal Molitor* is a fine man; *Maréchal Marmont* neat, compact, and soldierly looking; *Maréchal Mortier* a grenadier, without grace; *Maréchal Oudinot* much the same, and so on, to the end of the chapter. *Lamarque* is a little swarthy man, with good features and a keen eye, but he is military in neither carriage nor mien.

Crossing the Pont Royal, shortly after my arrival, in company with a friend, the latter pointed out to me a stranger, on the opposite sidewalk, and desired me to guess who and what he might be. The subject of my examination was a compact solidly built man, with a plodding rustic air, and who walked a little lame. After looking at him a minute, I guessed he was some substantial grazier, who had come to Paris on business connected with the supplies of the town. My friend laughed, and told me it was Marshal Soult. To my inexperienced eye, he had not a bit of the exterior of a soldier, and was as unlike the engravings we see of the French heroes as possible. But here, art is art, and, like the man who was accused of betraying another into a profitless speculation by drawing streams on his map, when the land was without any, and who defended himself by declaring no one ever saw a *map* without streams, the French artists appear to think every one should be represented in his ideal character, let him be as *bourgeois* as he may, in truth. I have seen Marshal Soult in company, and his face has much character. The head is good, and the eye searching, the whole physiognomy possessing those latent fires that one would be apt to think would require the noise and excitement of a battle to awaken. La Fayette looks more like an old soldier than any of them. Gérard, however, is both a handsome man, and of a military mien.

Now and then we see a *vieux moustache* in the guards, but, on the whole, I have been much surprised at finding how completely the army of this country is composed of young soldiers. The campaigns of Russia, of 1813, 1814, and of 1815, left few besides conscripts beneath the eagles of Napoleon. My old servant *Charles* tells me that the guard-house is obliged to listen to tales of the campaign of Spain, and of the glories of the Trocadero!

The army of France is understood to be very generally disaffected.

The restoration has introduced into it, in the capacity of general officers, many who followed the fortunes of the Bourbons into exile, and some, I believe, who actually fought against this country, in the ranks of her enemies. This may be, in some measure, necessary, but it is singularly unfortunate.

I have been told, on good authority, that, since the restoration of 1815, several occasions have occurred, when the court thought itself menaced with a revolution. On all these occasions, the army, as a matter of course, has been looked to, with hope, or with distrust. Investigation is said to have always discovered so bad a spirit, that little reliance is placed on its support.

The traditions of the service are all against the Bourbons. It is true, that very few of the men who fought at Marengo and Austerlitz still remain, but then the recollection of their deeds forms the great delight of most Frenchmen. There is but one power that can counteract this feeling, and it is the power of money. By throwing itself into the arms of the industrious classes, the court might possibly obtain an ally, sufficiently strong to quell the martial spirit of the nation; but, so far from pursuing such a policy, it has all the commercial and manufacturing interests marshalled against it, because it wishes to return to the *bon vieux temps* of the old system.

After all, I much question if any government in France, will have the army cordially with it, that does not find it better employment than mock-fights on the plain of Issy, and night attacks on the mimic Trocadero.

1.    The City and Port of Rouen

II. The Cathedral of Rouen

III.    The Château of Rosny

IV.    The Champ de Mars and the Military College

# Letter IX
To Mrs. Samuel W. Beall, Green Bay.

W e have lately witnessed a ceremony that may have some interest for one who, like yourself, dwells in the retirement of a remote frontier post. It is etiquette for the Kings of France to dine in public twice in the year, viz.: the first of January, and the day that is set apart for the *fête* of the king. Having some idle curiosity to be present on one of these occasions, I wrote the usual note to the lord in waiting, or, as he is called here, *"le premier gentilhomme de la chambre du roi, de service,"* and we got the customary answer, enclosing us tickets of admission. There are two sorts of permissions granted on these occasions; by one you are allowed to remain in the room during the dinner, and by the other you are obliged to walk slowly through the *salle,* in at one side, and out at the other, without, however, being suffered to pause even for a moment. Ours were of the former description.

The King of France having the laudable custom of being punctual, and as every one dines in Paris at six, that best of all hours for a town life, we were obliged to order our own dinner an hour earlier than common, for looking at others eating on an empty stomach, is, of all amusements, the least satisfactory. Having taken this wise precaution, we drove to the *château,* at half after five, it not being seemly to enter the room after the king, and, as we discovered, for females impossible.

Magnificence and comfort seldom have much in common. We were struck with this truth on entering the palace of the King of France. The room into which we were first admitted, was filled with tall lounging foot-soldiers, richly attired, but who lolled about the place, with their caps on, and with a barrack-like air, that seemed to us singularly in contrast with the prompt and respectful civility with which one is received in the ante-chamber of a private hotel. It is true that we had nothing to do with the soldiers and lackies who thronged the place; but if their presence was intended to impress visiters with the importance of their master, I think a more private entrance would have been most likely to produce that effect, for I confess, that it appeared to me as a mark of poverty, that, troops being necessary to the state and security of the monarch, he was obliged to keep them in the vestibule, by which his guests entered. But this is royal state. Formerly, the executioner was present, and in the semi-barbarous courts of the east, such is the fact even now. The soldiers were a party of the hundred Swiss, men chosen for their great stature, and remarkable for the perfection of their musket. Two of them were posted as sentinels at the foot of the great staircase, by which we ascended, and we passed several more on the landings.

We were soon in the *salle des gardes*, or the room which the *gardes du corps*, on service, occupied. Two of these quasi soldiers, were also acting as sentinels here, while others lounged about the room. Their apartment communicated with the *salle de Diane*, the hall or gallery prepared for the entertainment. I had no other means but the eye, of judging of the dimensions of this room, but its length considerably exceeds a hundred feet and its breadth is probably forty, or more. It is of the proper height, and the ceiling is painted in imitation of those of the celebrated Farnese palace at Rome.

We found this noble room divided, by a low railing, into three compartments. The centre, an area of some thirty feet by forty, contained the table, and was otherwise prepared for the reception of the court. On one side of it, were raised benches for the ladies, who were allowed to be seated; and, on the other, a vacant space for the gentlemen, who stood. All these, you will understand, were considered merely as spectators, not being supposed to be in the presence of the king. The mere spectators were dressed as usual, or in common evening dress, and not all the women even in that; while those within the railings, being deemed to be in the royal presence, were in high court dresses. Thus, I stood for an hour, within five-and-twenty feet of the king, and part of the time much nearer, while, by a fiction of etiquette, I was not understood to be there at all. I was a good while within ten feet of the *Duchesse de Berri*, while, by convention, I was no where. There was abundance of room in our area, and every facility of moving about, many coming and going, as they saw fit. Behind us, but at a little distance, were other rows of raised seats, filled with the best instrumental musicians of Paris. Along the wall, facing the table, was a narrow, raised platform, wide enough to allow of two or three to walk abreast, separated from the rest of the room by a railing, and extending from a door at one end of the gallery, to a door at the other. This was the place designed for the passage of the public during the dinner, no one, however, being admitted, even here, without a ticket.

A gentleman of the court led your aunt to the seats reserved for the female spectators, which were also without the railing, and I took my post among the men. Although the court of the Tuileries, was, when we entered the palace, filled with a throng of those who were waiting to pass through the gallery of Diana, to my surprise the number of persons who were to remain in the room was very small. I account for the circumstance by supposing that it is not etiquette for any who have been presented to attend, unless they are among the court, and, as some reserve was necessary in issuing these tickets, the number was necessarily limited. I do not think there were fifty men on our side, which might have held several hundred, and the seats of the ladies were not half filled. Boxes were fitted up in the enormous windows, which were closed and curtained, a family of fine children occupying that nearest to me. Some one said they were the princes of the house of Orleans, for none of the members of the royal family have seats at the *Grands Couverts,* as these dinners are called, unless they belong to the reigning branch. There is but one Bourbon prince more remote from the crown* than the *Duc d'Orléans,* and this is the *Prince de Condé,* or as he is more familiarly termed here, the *Duc de Bourbon,* the father of the unfortunate *Duc d'Enghien.* So broad are the distinctions made between the sovereign and the other members of his family, in these govern- ments, that it was the duty of the *Prince de Condé* to appear, to-day, behind the king's chair, as the highest dignitary of his household; though it was understood that he was excused on account of his age and infirmities. These broad distinctions, you will readily imagine, how- ever, are only maintained on solemn and great state occasions; for, in their ordinary intercourse, kings, now-a-days, dispense with most of the ancient formalities of their rank. It would have been curious, however, to see one descendant of St. Louis standing behind the chair of another, as a servitor, and, more especially, to see the Prince de Condé standing behind the chair of Charles Xth, for when *Comte d'Artois* and *Duc de Bourbon,* some fifty years since, they actually fought a duel, on account of some slight neglect of the wife of the latter, by the former.

The crown of France, as you know, passes only in the male line. The Duke of Orleans is descended from Louis XIII. and the Prince de Condé from Louis IX. In the male line, the Duke of Orleans is only the

* 1827.

fourth cousin, once removed, of the King, and the Prince de Condé the eighth or ninth. The latter would be even much more remotely related to the crown, but for the accession of his own branch of the family in the person of Henry IV., who was a near cousin of his ancestor. Thus you perceive, while royalty is always held in reverence, for any member of the family may possibly become the king, still there are broad distinctions made between the near, and the more distant branches, of the line. The Duke of Orleans fills that equivocal position in the family, which is rather common in the history of this species of government. He is a liberal, and is regarded with distrust by the reigning branch, and with hope by that portion of the people who think seriously of the actual state of the country. A saying of M. de Talleyrand, however, is circulated at his expense, which, if true, would go to show that this wary prince is not disposed to risk his immense fortune in a crusade for liberty. "*Ce n'est pas assez, d'être quelqu'un; il faut être quelque chose,*" are the words attributed to the witty and wily politician; but, usually, men have neither half the wit nor half the cunning that popular accounts ascribe to them, when it becomes the fashion to record their acts and sayings. I believe the Duke of Orleans holds no situation about the court, although the King has given him the title of *Royal* Highness, his birth entitling him to be styled no more than *Serene* Highness. This act of grace is much spoken of by the Bourbonists, who consider it a favour that for ever secures the loyalty and gratitude of the Duke. The Duchess, being the daughter of a King, had this rank from her birth.

The orchestra was playing when we entered the Gallery of Diana, and, throughout the whole evening it gave us, from time to time, such music as can only be found in a few of the great capitals of Europe.

The covers were laid, and every preparation was made within the railing, for the reception of the *convives*. The table was in the shape of a young moon, with the horns towards the spectators, or from the wall. It was of some length, and as there were but four covers, the guests were obliged to be seated several feet from each other. In the centre was an arm-chair, covered with crimson velvet, and ornamented with a crown; this was for the king. A chair without arms, on his right, was intended for the *Dauphin*; another on his left, for the *Dauphine*; and the fourth, which was still further on the right of the *Dauphin*, was intended for *Madame*, as she is called, or the Duchess of Berri. These are the old and favourite appellations of the monarchy, and, absurd as some of them are, they excite reverence and respect from their antiquity. Your

*Wolverines,* and *Suckers,* and *Buckeyes,* and *Hooziers* would look amazed to hear an executive styled the *White Fish of Michigan,* or the *Sturgeon of Wisconsin*; and yet there is nothing more absurd in it, in the abstract, than the titles that were formerly given in Europe, some of which have descended to our times. The name of the country, as well as the title of the sovereign, in the case of *Dauphiné,* was derived from the same source. Thus, in homely English, the Dolphin of Dolphinstown, renders *le Dauphin de Dauphiné,* perfectly well. The last independent Dauphin, in bequeathing his states to the King of France of the day, (the unfortunate John, the prisoner of the Black Prince,) made a condition that the heir-apparent of the kingdom, should always be known by his own title, and consequently, ever since, the appellation has been continued. You will understand that none but an *heir-apparent* is called the *Dauphin,* and not an *heir-presumptive.* Thus, should the present Dauphin and the Duc de Bordeaux die, the Duke of Orleans, according to a treaty of the time of Louis XIV., though not according to the ancient laws of the monarchy, would become *heir-presumptive,* but he could never be the *Dauphin,* since, should the King marry again, and have another son, his rights would be superseded. None but the *heir-apparent,* or the *inevitable* heir, bears this title. There were formerly *Bears* in Belgium, who were of the rank of Counts. These appellations were derived from the arms, the *Dauphin* now bearing Dolphins with the lilies of France. The Boar of Ardennes got his *soubriquet* from bearing the head of a wild-boar in his arms. There were formerly many titles in France that are now extinct, such as *Captal, Vidame* and *Castellan,* all of which were general, I believe, and referred to official duties. There was, however, formerly, a singular proof of how even simplicity can exalt a man when the fashion runs into the opposite extremes. In the thirteenth and fourteenth centuries, there existed in France, powerful noblemen, the owners and lords of the castle and lands of *Coucy* or *Couci,* who were content to bear the appellation of Sire, a word from which our own "Sir" is derived, and which means, like Sir, the simplest term of courtesy that could be used. These *Sires de Coucy* were so powerful as to make royal alliances; they waged war with their sovereign, and maintained a state nearly royal. Their pride lay in their antiquity, independence and power, and they showed their contempt for titles by their device, which is said to have been derived from the answer of one of the family to the sovereign, who, struck with the splendour of his appearance and the number of his attendants, had demanded "What King has come to my court?" This motto, which is still to be seen on the ancient monuments of the family, reads—

"Je ne suis roi, ne prince, ne duc, ne comte aussi;
Je suis le Sire de Coucy."*

This greatly beats Coke of Holkam, of whom it is said that George IV., who had been a liberal in his youth, and the friend of the great Norfolk commoner, vexed by his bringing up so many liberal addresses, threatened—"If Coke comes to me with any more of his Whig petitions *I'll Knight him.*"

I have often thought that this simplicity of the *Sires de Couci*, furnishes an excellent example for our own ministers and citizens when abroad. Instead of attempting to imitate the gorgeous attire of their colleagues, whose magnificence, for the want of stars and similar conventional decorations, they can never equal, they should go to court as they go to the President's House, in the simple attire of American gentlemen. If any prince should inquire—"Who is this that approaches me, clad so simply that I may mistake him for a butler, or a groom of the chambers?" let him answer, "*Je ne suis roi, ne prince, ne duc, ne comte aussi*—I am the minister of the United States of Ameri*key*," and leave the rest to the millions at home. My life for it, the question would not be asked twice. Indeed no man who is truly fit to represent the republic would ever have any concern about the matter. But all this time the dinner of the King of France is getting cold.

We might have been in the gallery fifteen minutes, when there was a stir at a door on the side where the females were seated, and a *huissier* cried out—"*Madame la Dauphine!*" and sure enough, the *Dauphine* appeared, followed by two *dames d'honneur*. She walked quite through the gallery, across the area reserved for the court, and passed out at the little gate in the railing which communicated with our side of the room, leaving the place by the same door at which we had entered. She was in high court dress, with diamonds and lappets, and was proceeding from her own apartments, in the other wing of the palace, to those of the king. As she went within six feet of me, I observed her hard and yet saddened countenance with interest; for she has the reputation of dwelling on her early fortunes, and of constantly anticipating evil. Of course she was saluted by all in passing, but she hardly raised her

* "I am neither king, nor prince, nor duke, nor even a count: I am M. de Coucy."

eyes from the floor; though, favoured by my position, I got a slight, melancholy smile, in return for my own bow.

The *Dauphine* had scarcely disappeared, when *Her Royal Highness, Madame,* was announced, and the Duchess of Berri went through in a similar manner. Her air was altogether less constrained, and she had smiles and inclinations for all she passed. She is a slight, delicate, little woman, with large blue eyes, a fair complexion, and light hair. She struck me as being less a Bourbon than an Austrian, and though wanting in *embonpoint* she would be quite pretty, but for a cast in one of her eyes.

A minute or two later, we had *Monseigneur le Dauphin,* who passed through the gallery, in the same manner as his wife and sister-in-law. He had been reviewing some troops, and was in the uniform of a colonel of the guards; booted to the knees, and carrying a military hat in his hand. He is not of commanding presence, though I think he has the countenance of an amiable man, and his face is decidedly Bourbon. We were indebted to the same lantern-like construction of the palace, for this preliminary glimpse at so many of the actors in the coming scene.

After the passage of the Dauphin, a few courtiers and superior officers of the household began to appear within the railed space. Among them were five or six duchesses. Women of this rank have the privilege of being seated in the presence of the king, on state occasions, and *tabourets* were provided for them accordingly. A *tabouret* is a stuffed stool, nearly of the form of the ancient curule chair, without its back, for a back would make it a chair at once, and, by the etiquette of courts, these are reserved for the blood-royal, ambassadors, &c. As none but duchesses could be seated at the *grand couvert,* you may be certain none below that rank appeared. There might have been a dozen present. They were all in high court dresses. One, of great personal charms and quite young, was seated near me, and my neighbour, an old *abbé,* carried away by enthusiasm, suddenly exclaimed to me—"*Quelle belle fortune! Monsieur, d'être jeune, jolie et duchesse!*" I dare say the lady had the same opinion of the matter.

Baron Louis, not the financier, but the king's physician, arrived. It was his duty to stand behind the king's chair, like Sancho's tormentor, and see that he did not over-eat himself. The ancient usages were very tender of the royal person. If he travelled, he had a spare litter, or a spare coach, to receive him, in the event of accident, a practice that is continued to this day; if he ate, there was one to taste his food, lest he might be poisoned; and when he lay down to sleep, armed sentinels watched at the door of his chamber. Most of these usages are still continued, in some form or other, and the ceremonies which are observed at these public dinners, are mere memorials of the olden time.

I was told the following anecdote by Mad. de ———, who was intimate with Louis XVIII. One day, in taking an airing, the king was thirsty, and sent a footman to a cottage for water. The peasants appeared with some grapes, which they offered, as the homage of their condition. The king took them and ate them, notwithstanding the remonstrances of his attendants. This little incident was spoken of at court, where all the monarch does and says becomes matter of interest, and the next time Mad. de ——— was admitted, she joined her remonstrances to those of the other courtiers. "We no longer live in an age when kings need dread assassins," said Louis, smiling. A month passed, and Mad. de ——— was again admitted. She was received with a melancholy shake of the head, and with tears. The Duc de Berri had been killed in the interval!

A few gentlemen, who did not strictly belong to the court, appeared among the duchesses, but, at the most, there were but six or eight. One of them, however, was the gayest-looking personage I ever saw, in the station of a gentleman, being nothing but lace and embroidery, even to the seams of his coat; a sort of genteel harlequin. The *abbé*, who seemed to understand himself, said he was a Spanish grandee.

I was near the little gate, when an old man, in a strictly court dress, but plain and matter of fact in air, made an application for admittance. In giving way for him to pass, my attention was drawn to his appearance. The long white hair that hung down his face, the *cordon bleu*, the lame foot, the imperturbable countenance, and the *unearthly aspect*, made me suspect the truth. On inquiring, I was right. It was *M. de Talleyrand!* He came as grand chamberlain, to officiate at the dinner of his master.

Everything, in a court, goes by clock-work. Your little great may be out of time, and affect a want of punctuality, but a rigid attention to appointments, is indispensable to those who are really in high situations. A failure in this respect, would produce the same impression on the affairs of men, that a delay in the rising of the sun, would produce on the day. The appearance of the different personages named, all so near each other, was the certain sign that one greater than all could not be far behind. They were the dawn of the royal presence. Accordingly, the door which communicated with the apartments of the king, and the only one within the railed space, opened with the announcement of "*le service du Roi,*" when a procession of footmen of the palace appeared, bearing the dishes of the first course. All the vessels, whether already on the table, or those in their hands, were of gold, richly wrought, or, at least, silver gilt, I had no means of knowing which; most probably they were of the former metal. The dishes were taken from the footmen, by pages of honor, in scarlet dresses, and by them placed in order on the table. The first course was no sooner ready, than we heard the welcome announcement of "*le Roi.*" The family immediately made their appearance, at the same door by which the service had entered. They were followed by a proper number of lords and ladies in waiting. Every one arose, as a matter of course, even to the "*jeunes, jolies, et duchesses;*" and the music, as became it, gave us a royal crash. The *huissier*, in announcing the king, spoke in a modest voice, and less loud, I observed, than in announcing the Dauphin and the ladies. It was, however, a different person, and it is probable one was a common *huissier,* and the other a gentleman acting in that character.

Charles X. is tall, without being of a too heavy frame, flexible of movement, and decidedly graceful. By remembering that he is a king, and the lineal chief of the ancient and powerful family of the Bourbons, by deferring properly to history and the illusions of the past, and by feeling *tant soit peu* more respect for those of the present day than is strictly philosophical, or perhaps wise, it is certainly possible to fancy that he has a good deal of that peculiar port and majesty, that the poetry of feeling is so apt to impute to sovereigns. I know not whether it is the fault of a cynical temperament, or of republican prejudices, but I can see no more about him than the easy grace of an old gentleman, accustomed all his life, to be a principal personage among the principal personages of the earth. This you may think was quite sufficient, — but it did not altogether satisfy the *exigence* of my unpoetical ideas. His countenance betrayed a species of vacant *bonhomie*, rather than of thought, or dignity of mind, and while he possessed, in a singular degree, the mere physical machinery of his rank, he was wanting in the majesty of character and expression, without which no man can act, well, the representation of royalty. Even a little more severity of aspect would have better suited the part, and rendered *le grand couvert, encore plus grand.*

The King seated himself, after receiving the salutations of the courtiers within the railing, taking no notice, however, of those who, by a fiction of etiquette, were not supposed to be in his presence. The rest of the family occupied their respective places in the order I have named, and the eating and drinking began, from the score. The different courses were taken off and served by footmen and pages, in the manner already described, which, after all, by substituting servants out of livery for pages, is very much the way great dinners are served, in great houses, all over Europe.

As soon as the King was seated, the north door of the gallery, or that on the side opposite to the place where I had taken post, was opened, and the public was admitted, passing slowly through the room without stopping. A droller *mélange* could not be imagined, than presented itself in the panoramic procession; and long before the *grand couvert* was over, I thought it much the most amusing part of the scene. Very respectable persons, gentlemen certainly, and I believe in a few instances ladies, came in this way, to catch a glimpse of the spectacle. I saw several men that I knew, and the women with them could have been no other than their friends. To these must be added, *cochers de fiacres*, in their glazed hats, *bonnes*, in their high Norman caps, peasants, soldiers, in their shakos, *épiciers* and *garçons* without number. The constant passage, for it lasted without intermission, for an hour and a half, of so many queer faces, reminded me strongly of one of those mechanical panoramas, that bring towns, streets and armies, before the spectator. One of the droll effects of this scene was produced by the faces, all of which turned, like sunflowers, towards the light of royalty, as the bodies moved steadily on. Thus, on entering, the eyes were a little inclined to the right; as they got nearer to the meridian, they became gradually bent more aside; when opposite the table, every face was *full*; and, in retiring, all were bent backwards over their owners' shoulders, constantly offering a dense crowd of faces, looking towards a common centre, while the bodies were coming on, or moving slowly off, the stage. This, you will see, resembled in some measure the revolutions of the moon around our orb, matter and a king possessing the same beneficent attraction. I make no doubt, these good people thought we presented a curious spectacle, but I am persuaded they presented one that was infinitely more so.

I had seen in America, in divers places, an Englishman, a colonel in the army. We had never been introduced, but had sat opposite to each other at *tables d'hôte*, jostled each other in the President's House, met in steamboats, in the streets, and in many other places, until it was evident our faces were perfectly familiar to both parties; and yet we never nodded, spoke, or gave any other sign of recognition, than by certain knowing expressions of the eyes. In Europe, the colonel re-appeared. We met in London, in Paris, in the public walks, in the sight-seeing places of resort, until we evidently began to think ourselves a couple of *Monsieur Tonsons*. To-night, as I was standing near the public platform, whose face should appear in the halo of countenances, but that of my colonel. The poor fellow had a wooden leg, and he was obliged to stump on in his orbit, as well as he could, while I kept my eye on him, determined to catch a look of recognition, if possible. When he got so far forward as to bring me in his line of sight, our eyes met, and he smiled involuntarily. Then he took a deliberate survey of my comfortable position, and he disappeared in the horizon, with some such expression on his features as must have belonged to Commodore Trunnion, when he called out to Hatchway, while the hunter was leaping over the lieutenant, "Oh! d−n you; you are well anchored!"

I do not think the dinner, in a culinary point of view, was anything extraordinary. The King eat and drank but little, for, unlike his two brothers and predecessors, he is said to be abstemious. The *Dauphin* played a better knife and fork, but, on the whole, the execution was by no means great for Frenchmen. The guests sat so far apart, and the music made so much noise, that conversation was nearly out of the question, though the King and the *Dauphin* exchanged a few words, in the course of the evening. Each of the gentlemen, also, spoke once or twice to his female neighbour, and that was pretty much the amount of the discourse. The whole party appeared greatly relieved by having something to do during the dessert, in admiring the service, which was of the beautiful *Sèvres* china. They all took up the plates, and examined them attentively, and really I was glad they had so rational an amusement, to relieve their *ennui*.

Once, early in the entertainment, *M. de Talleyrand* approached the king, and showed him the bill of fare! It was an odd spectacle to see this old *diplomate* descending to the pantomime of royalty, and acting the part of a *maître d'hôtel*. Had the duty fallen on *Cambacérès*, one would understand it, and fancy that it might be well done. The king smiled on him graciously, and, I presume, gave him leave to retire; for soon after this act of loyal servitude, the prince disappeared. As for *M. Louis*, he treated Charles better than his brother treated Sancho, for I did not observe the slightest interference on his part during the whole entertainment, though one of those near me said he had tasted a dish or two, by way of ceremony, an act of precaution that I did not myself observe. I asked my neighbour, the *abbé*, what he thought of *M. de Talleyrand*. After looking up in my face distrustfully, he whispered—"*Mais, Monsieur, c'est un chat qui tombe toujours sur ses pieds*," a remark that was literally true to-night, for the old man was kept on his feet longer than could have been agreeable to the owner of two such gouty legs.

The *Duchesse de Berri*, who sat quite near the place where I stood, was busy a good deal of the time *à lorgner* the public through her eye-glass. This she did with very little diffidence of manner, and quite as coolly as an English duchess would have stared at a late intimate, whom she was disposed to cut. It certainly was neither a graceful, nor a feminine, nor a princely occupation. The *Dauphine* played the Bourbon better, though when she turned her saddened, not to say *cruel* eyes, on the public, it was with an expression that almost amounted to reproach. I did not see her smile once during the whole time she was at table, and yet *I* thought there were many things to smile at.

At length the finger bowls appeared, and I was not sorry to see them. Contrary to what is commonly practised in very great houses, the pages placed them on the table, just as *Henri* puts them before us democrats every day. I ought to have said that the service was made altogether in front, or at the unoccupied side of the table, nothing but the bill of fare, in the hands of *M. de Talleyrand*, appearing in the rear. As soon as this part of the dinner was over, the King arose, and the whole party withdrew, by the door on the further side of the gallery. In passing the *gradins* of the ladies, he stopped to say a few kind words to an old woman, who was seated there, muffled in a cloak, and the light of royalty vanished.

The catastrophe is to come. The instant the King's back was turned, the gallery became a scene of confusion. The musicians ceased playing and began to chatter; the pages dashed about to remove the service, and every body was in motion. Observing that your [aunt] was standing, undecided what to do, I walked into the railed area, brushed past the gorgeous state-table, and gave her my arm. She laughed, and said it had all been very magnificent, and amusing, but that some one had stolen her shawl! A few years before, I had purchased for her a merino shawl of singular fineness, simplicity and beauty. It was now old, and she had worn it, on this occasion, because she distrusted the dirt of a palace, and laying it carelessly by her side, in the course of the evening, she had found in its place, a very common thing of the same colour. The thief was deceived by its appearance, your [aunt] being dressed for an evening party, and had probably mistaken it for a cashmere. So much for the company one meets at court! Too much importance, however, must not be attached to this little *contretemps*, as people of condition are apt to procure tickets for such places, and to give them to their *femmes de chambre*. Probably half the women present, the "*jeunes et jolies*" excepted, were of this class. But, mentioning this affair to the old *Princesse de*————, she edified me by an account of the manner in which *Madame la Comtesse de*———— had actually appropriated to the service of her own pretty person, the *cachemire* of Madame *la Baronne de* ———— in the royal presence; and how there was a famous quarrel, *à outrance*, about it; so I suspend my opinion, as to the quality of the thief.

# Letter X

To R. Cooper, Esq., Cooperstown, New York.

W e have been to Versailles, and although I have no intention to give a laboured description of a place about which men have written and talked these two centuries, it is impossible to pass over a spot of so much celebrity, in total silence. The road to Versailles lies between the park of St. Cloud and the village and manufactories of Sèvres. A little above the latter, is a small palace called Meudon, which, from its great elevation, commands a fine view of Paris. The palace of St. Cloud, of course, stands in the park; Versailles lies six or eight miles farther west; Compiègne is about fifty miles from Paris in one direction; Fontainebleau some thirty in another, and Rambouillet rather more remotely, in a third. All these palaces, except Versailles, are kept up, and, from time to time, are visited by the court. Versailles was stripped of its furniture, in the revolution, and even Napoleon, at a time when the French empire extended from Hamburgh to Rome, shrunk from the enormous charge of putting it in a habitable state. It is computed that the establishment at Versailles, first and last, in matters of construction merely, cost the French monarchy two hundred millions of dollars! This is almost an incredible sum, when we remember the low price of wages in France; but, on the other hand, when we consider the vastness of the place, how many natural difficulties were overcome, and the multitude of works from the hands of artists of the first order it contained, it scarcely seems sufficient.

Versailles originated as a hunting-seat, in the time of Louis XIII. In that age, most of the upland near Paris, in this direction, lay in forest, royal chases; and as hunting was truly a princely sport, numberless temporary residences of this nature, existed in the neighbourhood of the capital. There are still many remains of this barbarous magnificence, as in the wood of Vincennes, the forests of St. Germain, Compiègne, Fontainebleau, and divers others; but great inroads have been made in their limits, by the progress of civilization and the wants of society. So lately as the reign of Louis XV. they hunted quite near the town, and we are actually, at this moment, dwelling in a country house, at St. Ouen, in which tradition hath it, he was wont to take his refreshments.

The original building at Versailles was a small *château*, of a very ugly formation, and it was built of bricks. I believe it was enlarged, but not entirely constructed, by Louis XIII. A portion of this building is still visible, having been embraced in the subsequent structures, and, judging from its architecture, I should think it must be nearly as ancient as the time of Francis I. Around this modest nucleus was constructed, by a succession of monarchs, but chiefly by Louis XIV., the most regal residence of Europe, in magnificence and extent, if not in taste.

The present *château*, besides containing numberless wings and courts, has vast *casernes* for the quarters of the household troops, stables for many hundred horses, and is surrounded by a great many separate hotels, for the accommodation of the courtiers. It offers a front on the garden, in a single continuous line, that is broken only by a projection in the centre, of more than a third of a mile in length. This is the only complete part of the edifice that possesses uniformity; the rest of it being huge piles, grouped around irregular courts, or thrown forward in wings, that correspond to the huge body like those of the ostrich. There is on the front next the town, however, some attempt at simplicity and intelligibility of plan, for there is a vast open court lined by buildings, which have been commenced in the Grecian style. Napoleon, I believe, did something here, from which there is reason to suppose that he sometimes thought of inhabiting the palace. Indeed, so long as France has a king, it is impossible that such a truly royal abode can ever be wholly deserted. At present, it is the fashion to grant lodgings in it, to dependants and favourites. Nothing that I have seen gives me so just and so imposing an idea of the nature of the old French monarchy, as a visit to Versailles. Apart from the vastness and splendour of the palace, here is a town that actually contained, in former times, a hundred thousand souls, that entirely owed its existence to the presence of the court. Other monarchs lived in large towns, but here was a monarch whose presence created one. Figure to yourself the style of the prince, when a place more populous than Baltimore, and infinitely richer in externals, existed merely as an appendage to his abode!

The celebrated garden contains two or three hundred acres of land, besides the ground that is included in the gardens of the two Trianons. These Trianons are small palaces erected in the gardens, as if the occupants of the *château*, having reached the acmé of magnificence and splendour, in the principal residence, were seeking refuge against the effects of satiety, in these humbler abodes. They appear small and insignificant after the palace; but the great Trianon is a considerable house, and contains a fine suite of apartments, among which are some very good rooms. There are few English abodes of royalty that equal even this of *le Grand Trianon*. The *Petit Trianon* was the residence of Mad. de Maintenon; it afterwards was presented to the unfortunate *Marie-Antoinette*, who, in part, converted its grounds into an English garden, in addition to setting aside a portion into what is called *la petite Suisse*.

We went through this exceedingly pretty house and its gardens, with melancholy interest. The first is merely a pavilion in the Italian taste, though it is about half as large as the President's House at Washington. I should think the Great Trianon has quite twice the room of our own Executive residence, and, as you can well imagine from what has already been said, the capitol, itself, would be but a speck among the endless edifices of the *château*. The projection in the centre of the latter, is considerably larger than the capitol, and it materially exceeds that building in cubic contents. Now this projection is but a small part, indeed, of the long line of *façade*, it actually appearing too short for the ranges of wings.

*Marie-Antoinette* was much censured for the amusements in which she indulged, in the grounds of the Little Trianon, and vulgar rumour exaggerating their nature, no small portion of her personal unpopularity is attributable to this cause. The family of Louis XVI. appears to have suffered for the misdeeds of his predecessors, for it not being very easy to fancy anything much worse than the immoralities of Louis XV., the public were greatly disposed "to visit the sins of the fathers on the children."

*La petite Suisse* is merely a romantic portion of the garden in which has been built what is called the Swiss hamlet. It contains the miniature abodes of the Curé, the Farmer, the Dairy-Woman, the *Garde-Chasse* and the *Seigneur*, besides the mill. There is not much that is Swiss, however, about the place, with the exception of some resemblance in the exterior of the buildings. Here it is said the royal family used occasionally to meet and pass an afternoon in a silly representation of rural life, that must have proved to be a prodigious caricature. The King (at least so the guide affirmed) performed the part of the *Seigneur*, and occupied the proper abode; the Queen was the Dairy-Woman, and we were shown the marble tables that held her porcelain milk-pans; the present King, as became his notorious propensity to field-sports, was the *Garde-Chasse*, the late King was the Miller, and, *mirabile dictu*, the archbishop of Paris did not disdain to play the part of the *Curé*. There was probably a good deal of poetry in this account, though it is pretty certain that the Queen did indulge in some of these phantasies. There happened to be with me, the day I visited this spot, an American from our own mountains, who had come fresh from home, with all his provincial opinions and habits strong about him. As the guide explained these matters, I translated them literally into English for the benefit of my companion, adding that the fact rendered the Queen extremely unpopular, with her subjects. "Unpopular!" exclaimed my country neighbour; "why so, sir?" "I cannot say; perhaps they thought it was not a fit amusement for a Queen." My mountaineer stood a minute cogitating the affair in his American mind, and then nodding his head, he said—"I understand it, now. The people thought that a King and Queen, coming from yonder palace to amuse themselves in this toy hamlet, in the characters of poor people, *were making game of them!*" I do not know whether this inference will amuse you, as much as it did me at the time.

Of the gardens and the *jets d'eau*, so renowned, I shall say little. The former are in the old French style, formal and stiff, with long straight *allées*, but magnificent by their proportions and ornaments. The statuary and vases that are exposed to the open air, in this garden, must have cost an enormous sum. They are chiefly copies from the *antique*. As you stand on the great terrace, before the centre of the palace, the view is down the principal avenue, which terminates at the distance of two or three miles with a low naked hill, beyond which appears the void of the firmament. This conceit singularly helps the idea of vastness, though in effect it is certainly inferior to the pastoral prettiness, and rural thoughts of modern landscape gardening. Probably too much is attempted here, for if the mind cannot conceive of illimitable space, still less can it be represented by means of material substances.

We examined the interior of the palace with melancholy pleasure. The vast and gorgeous apartments were entirely without furniture, though many of the pictures still remain. The painted ceilings, and the gildings too, contribute to render the rooms less desolate than they would otherwise have been. I shall not stop to describe the saloons of Peace and War, and all the other celebrated apartments, that are so named from the subjects of their paintings, but merely add that the state apartments lie *en suite*, in the main body of the building, and that the principal room, or the great gallery, as it is termed, is in the centre, with the windows looking up the main avenue of the garden. This gallery greatly surpasses in richness and size any other room, intended for the ordinary purposes of a palace, that I have ever seen. Its length exceeds two hundred and thirty feet, its width is about thirty-five, and its height is rather more than forty. The walls are a complete succession of marbles, mirrors and gildings. I believe, the windows and doors excepted, that literally no part of the sides or ends of this room show any other material. Even some of the doors are loaded with these decorations. The ceiling is vaulted, and gorgeous with allegories and gildings; they are painted by the best artists of France. Here Louis XIV. moved among his courtiers, more like a god than a man, and here was exhibited that mixture of grace and moral fraud, of elegance and meanness, of hope and disappointment, of pleasure and mortification, that form the characters and compose the existence of courtiers.

I do not know the precise number of magnificent antechambers, and saloons through which we passed to reach this gallery, but there could not have been less than eight; one of which, as a specimen of the scale on which the palace is built, is near eighty feet long and sixty wide. Continuing our course along the *suite*, we passed, among others, a council room, that looked more like state than business, and then came to the apartments of the Queen. There were several drawing-rooms, and ball-rooms, and card-rooms, and ante-rooms, and the change from the gorgeousness of the state apartments, to the neat, tasteful, chaste, feminine, white and gold of this part of the palace was agreeable, for I had got to be tired of splendour, and was beginning to feel a disposition to "make game of the people," by descending to rusticity.

The bed-room of *Marie-Antoinette* is in the *suite*. It is a large chamber, in the same style of ornament as the rest of her rooms, and the dressing-rooms, bath, and other similar conveniences, were in that exquisite French taste, which can only be equalled by imitation. The chamber of the King looked upon the court, and was connected with that of the Queen, by a winding and intricate communication of some length. The door that entered the apartments of the latter, opened into a dressing-room, and, both this door and that which communicated with the bed-room, form a part of the regular wall, being tapestried as such, so as not to be immediately seen, a style of finish that is quite usual in French houses. It was owing to this circumstance that *Marie-Antoinette* made her escape, undetected, to the King's chamber, the night the palace was entered by the fish-women.

We saw the rooms in which Louis XIV. and Louis XV. died. The latter, you may remember, fell a victim to the small-pox, and the disgusting body, that had so lately been almost worshipped, was deserted, the moment he was dead. It was left for hours, without even the usual decent observances. It was on the same occasion, we have been told, that his grand-children, including the heir, were assembled in a private drawing-room, waiting the result, when they were startled by a hurried trampling of feet. It was the courtiers, rushing in a crowd, to pay their homage to the new monarch! All these things forced themselves painfully on our minds, as we walked through the state rooms. Indeed, there are few things that can be more usefully studied, or which awaken a greater source of profitable recollections, than a palace that has been occupied by a great and historical court. Still they are not poetical.

The balcony, in which La Fayette appeared with the Queen and her children, opens from one of these rooms. It overlooks the inner court; or that in which the carriages of none but the privileged entered, for all these things were regulated by arbitrary rules. No one, for instance, was permitted to ride in the King's coach, unless his nobility dated from a certain century, (the fourteenth, I believe,) and these were your *gentilshommes*; for the word implies more than a noble, meaning an ancient nobleman.

The writing cabinet, private dining-room, council room in ordinary, library, &c. of the King, came next; the circuit ending in the *salle des gardes*, and the apartments usually occupied by the officers and troops on service.

There was one room we got into, I scarce know how. It was a long, high gallery, plainly finished for a palace, and it seemed to be lighted from an interior court, or well; for one was completely caged, when in it. This was the celebrated Bull's Eye, *(oeil de boeuf)* where the courtiers danced attendance, before they were received. It got its name from an oval window, over the principal door.

We looked at no more than the state apartments, and those of the

King and Queen, and yet, we must have gone through some thirty or forty rooms, of which, the baths and dressing-room of the Queen excepted, the very smallest would be deemed a very large room, in America. Perhaps no private house contains any as large as the smallest of these rooms, with the exception of here and there a hall in a country house; and, no room at all, with ceilings nearly as high, and as noble, to say nothing of the permanent decorations, of which we have no knowledge whatever, if we omit the window glass, and the mantels, in both of which, size apart, we often beat even the French palaces.

We next proceeded to the *salle de spectacle*, which is a huge theatre. It may not be as large as the French Opera house at Paris, but its dimensions did not appear to me to be much less. It is true, the stage was open, and came into the view; but it is a very large house for dramatic representations. Now, neither this building, nor the Chapel, seen on the exterior of the palace, though additions that project from the regular line of wall, obtrudes itself on the eye, more than a *verandah* attached to a window, on one of our largest houses! In this place, the celebrated dinner was given to the officers of the guards.

The chapel is rich and beautiful. No catholic church has pews, or, at all events, they are very unusual, though the municipalities do sometimes occupy them in France, and, of course, the area was vacant. We were most struck with the paintings on the ceiling, in which the face of Louis XIV. was strangely and mystically blended with that of God the Father! Pictorial and carved representations of the Saviour, and of the Virgin abound in all catholic countries; nor do they much offend, unless when the crucifixion is represented with bleeding wounds; for, as both are known to have appeared in the human form, the mind is not shocked at seeing them in the semblance of humanity. But this was the first attempt to delineate the Deity we had yet seen; and it caused us all to shudder. He is represented in the person of an old man looking from the clouds, in the centre of the ceiling, and the King appears among the angels that encircle him. Flattery could not go much farther, without encroaching on omnipotence itself.

In returning from Versailles, to a tithe of the magnificence of which I have not alluded, I observed carts coming out of the side of a hill, loaded with the whitish stone, that composes the building material of Paris. We stopped the carriage, and went into the passage, where we found extensive excavations. A lane of fifteen or twenty feet was cut through the stone, and the material was carted away in heavy square blocks. Piers were left, at short intervals, to sustain the superincumbent earth; and, in the end, the place gets to be a succession of intricate passages, separated by these piers, which resemble so many small masses of houses among the streets of a town. The entire region around Paris lies on a substratum of this stone, which indurates by exposure to the air, and the whole secret of the celebrated catacombs of Paris, is just the same as that of this quarry, with the difference that this opens on a level with the upper world, lying in a hill, while one is compelled to descend to get to the level of the others. But enormous wheels, scattered about the fields in the vicinity of the town, show where shafts descend to new quarries on the plains, which are precisely the same as those under Paris. The history of these subterranean passages is very simple. The stone beneath, has been transferred to the surface, as a building material; and, the graves of the town, after centuries, were emptied into the vaults below. Any apprehensions of the caverns falling in, on a great scale, are absurd, as the constant recurrence of the piers, which are the living rock, must prevent such a calamity; though it is within the limits of possibility, that a house or two might disappear. Quite lately, it is said, a tree in the garden of the Luxembourg fell through, owing to the water working a passage down into the quarries, by following its roots. The top of the tree remained above ground, some distance; and, to prevent unnecessary panic, the police immediately caused the place to be concealed by a high and close board fence. The tree was cut away in the night, the hole was filled up, and few knew any thing about it. But it is scarcely possible, that any serious accident should occur, even to a single house, without a previous and gradual sinking of its walls giving notice of the event. The palace of the Luxembourg, one of the largest and finest edifices of Paris, stands quite near the spot where the tree fell through, and yet there is not the smallest danger of the structure's disappearing some dark night, the piers below always affording sufficient support. *Au reste*, the catacombs lie under no other part of Paris, than the *quartier St. Jacques*, not crossing the river, nor reaching even the *Faubourg St. Germain*.

I have taken you so unceremoniously out of the *château* of Versailles to put you into the catacombs, that some of the royal residences have not received the attention I intended. We have visited Compiègne this summer, including it in a little excursion of about a hundred miles, that we made in the vicinity of the capital, though it scarcely offered sufficient matter of interest to be the subject of an especial letter. We found the forest deserving of its name, and some parts of it almost as fine as an old American wood of the second class. We rode through it five or six miles, to see a celebrated ruin, called *Pierre-fond*, which was one of those baronial holds, out of which noble robbers used to issue, to plunder on the high-way, and commit all sort of acts of genteel violence. The castle, and the adjacent territory, formed one of the most ancient *seigneuries* of France. The place was often besieged and taken. In the time of Henry IV. that monarch, finding the castle had fallen into the hands of a set of desperadoes, who were ranked with the leaguers, sent the *Duc d'Epernon* against the place, but he was wounded and obliged to raise the siege. Marshal Biron was next despatched, with all the heavy artillery that could be spared, but he met with little better success. This roused Henry, who finally succeeded in getting possession of the place. In the reign of his son, Louis XIII., the robberies and excesses of those who occupied the castle became so intolerable, that the government seized it again, and ordered it to be destroyed. Now, you will remember, that this castle stood in the very heart of France, within fifty miles of the capital, and but two leagues from a royal residence, and all so lately as the year 1617, and that it was found necessary to destroy it, on account of the irregularities of its owners. What an opinion one is driven to form of the moral civilization of Europe, from a fact like this! Feudal grandeur loses greatly, in a comparison with modern law, and more humble honesty.

It was easier, however, to order the *château de Pierre-font* to be destroyed, than to effect that desirable object. Little more was achieved than to make cuts into the external parts of the towers and walls, and to unroof the different buildings, and, although this was done two hundred years since, time has made little impression on the ruins. We were shown a place where there had been an attempt to break into the walls for stones, but which had been abandoned, because it was found easier to quarry them from the living rock. The principal towers were more than a hundred feet high, and their angles and ornaments seemed to be as sharp and solid as ever. This was much the noblest French ruin we have seen, and it may be questioned if there are many finer, out of Italy, in Europe.

The palace of Compiègne after that of Versailles, hardly rewarded us for the trouble of examining it. Still it is large and in perfect repair. But the apartments are common-place, though there are a few that are good. A prince, however, is as well lodged even here, as is usual in the north of Europe. The present king is fond of resorting to this house, on account of the game of the neighbouring forest. We saw several roe-bucks bounding among the trees, in our drive to *Pierre-font*.*

I have dwelt on the palaces and the court so much, because one cannot get a correct idea of what France was, and perhaps I ought to say of what France, through the reaction, *will* be, if this point were overlooked. The monarch was all in all, in the nation; the centre of light, wealth and honour; letters, the arts and the sciences revolved around him, as the planets revolve around the sun, and if there ever was a civilized people whose example it would be fair to quote, for or against the effects of monarchy, I think it would be the people of France. I was surprised at my own ignorance on the subject of the magnificence of these kings, of which indeed it is not easy for an untravelled American to form any just notion, and it has struck me you might be glad to hear a little on these points.

After all I have said, I find I have entirely omitted the orangery at Versailles. But then I have said little or nothing of the canals, the *jets d'eau*, of the great and little parks, which united are fifty miles in circumference, and of a hundred other things. Still, as this orangery is on a truly royal scale, it deserves a word of notice, before I close my letter. The trees are housed in winter, in long vaulted galleries beneath the great terrace, and there is a sort of sub-court in front of them, where they are put into the sun, during the pleasant season. This place is really an orange grove, and, although every tree is in a box, and is nursed like a child, many of them are as large as it is usual to find in the orange groves of low latitudes. Several are very old; two or three dating from the fifteenth century, and one from the early part of it. What notions do you get of the magnificence of the place, when you are told that a palace, subterraneous it is true, is devoted to this single luxury, and that acres are covered with trees, in boxes?

* Pierre-fond, or Pierre-font.

# Letter XI
To James Stevenson, Esquire, Albany.

I intend this letter to be useful rather than entertaining. Living, as we Americans do, remote from the rest of the world, and possessing so many practices peculiar to ourselves, at the same time that we are altogether wanting in usages that are familiar to most other nations, it should not be matter of surprise that we commit some mistakes on this side of the water, in matters of taste and etiquette. A few words simply expressed, and a few explanations plainly made, may serve to remove some errors, and perhaps render your own contemplated visit to this part of the world more agreeable.

There is no essential difference in the leading rules of ordinary intercourse among the polished of all Christian nations. Though some of these rules may appear arbitrary, it will be found, on examination, that they are usually derived from very rational and sufficient motives. They may vary, in immaterial points, but even these variations arise from some valid circumstance.

The American towns are growing so rapidly, that they are getting to have the population of capitals without enjoying their commonest facilities. The exaggerated tone of our largest towns, for instance, forbids the exchange of visits by means of servants. It may suit the habits of provincial life to laugh at this, as an absurdity, but it may be taken pretty safely as a rule, that men and women of as much common sense as the rest of their fellow creatures, with the best opportunities of cultivating all those tastes that are dependant on society, and with no other possible motive than convenience, would not resort to such a practice without a suitable inducement. No one who has not lived in a large town that *does* possess these facilities, can justly appreciate their great advantages, or properly understand how much a place like New York, with its three hundred thousand inhabitants, loses by not adopting them. We have conventions for all sorts of things in America, some of which do good and others harm, but I cannot imagine anything that would contribute more to the comfort of society, than one which should settle the laws of intercourse, on principles better suited to the real condition of the country, than those which now exist. It is not unusual to read descriptions deriding the forms of Europe, written by travelling Americans, but I must think they have been the productions of very young travellers, or, at least, of such as have not had the proper means of appreciating the usages they ridicule. Taking my own experience as a guide, I have no hesitation in saying, that I know no people among whom the ordinary social intercourse is as uncomfortable, and as little likely to stand the test of a rational examination, as our own.

The first rule, all-important for an American to know, is that the latest arrival makes the first visit. England is, in some respects, an exception to this practice, but I believe it prevails in all the rest of Europe. I do not mean to say that departures are not made from this law, in particular instances; but they should always be taken as exceptions, and as pointed compliments. This rule has many conveniences, and I think it also shows a more delicate attention to sentiment and feeling. While the points of intrusion and of disagreeable acquaintances, are left just where they would be under our own rule, the stranger is made the judge of his own wishes. It is, moreover, impossible, in a large town, to know of every arrival. Many Americans, who come to Europe with every claim to attention, pass through it nearly unnoticed, from a hesitation about obtruding themselves on others, under the influence of the opinions in which they have been educated. This for a long time was my own case, and it was only when a more familiar acquaintance with the practices of this part of the world made me acquainted with their advantages, that I could consent freely to put myself forward.

You are not to understand that any stranger arriving in a place like Paris, or London, has a right to leave cards for whom he pleases. It is not the custom, except for those who, by birth, or official station, or a high reputation, may fairly deem themselves privileged, to assume this liberty, and even then, it is always better to take some preliminary step to assure one's self that the visit will be acceptable. The law of salutes, is very much the law of visits, in this part of the world. The ship arriving sends an officer to know if his salute will be returned gun for gun, and the whole affair, it is true, is conducted in rather a categorical manner, but the governing principles are the same in both cases, though more management may be required between two gentlemen, than between two men-of-war.

The Americans in Europe, on account of the country's having abjured all the old feudal distinctions that still so generally prevail here, labour under certain disadvantages, that require, on the one hand, much tact and discretion to overcome, and on the other, occasionally much firmness and decision.

The rule I have adopted, in my own case, is to defer to every usage, in matters of etiquette, so far as I have understood them, that belongs to the country in which I may happen to be. If, as has sometimes happened (but not in a solitary instance in France,) the claims of a stranger have been overlooked, I have satisfied myself by remembering, that, in this respect at least, the Americans are the superiors, for that is a point in which we seldom fail; and if they are remembered, to accept of just as much attention as shall be offered. In cases, in which those arbitrary distinctions are set up, that, by the nature of our institutions cannot, either in similar, or in any parallel cases exist in America, and the party making the pretension is on neutral ground, *if the claim be in any manner pressed*, I would say that it became an American to resist it promptly; neither to go out of his way to meet it, nor to defer to it, when it crosses his path. In really good society awkward cases of this nature are not very likely to occur; they are, however, more likely to occur as between our own people and the English, than between those of any other nation; for the latter, in mixed general associations, have scarcely yet learned to look upon, and treat us as the possessors of an independent country. It requires perfect self-possession, great tact, and some nerve for an American, who is brought much in contact with the English on the continent of Europe, to avoid a querulous and un-gentlemanlike disposition to raise objections on these points, and at the same time to maintain the position, and command the respect, with which he should never consent to dispense. From my own little experience, I should say we are better treated, and have less to overlook, in our intercourse with the higher than with the intermediate classes of the English.

You will have very different accounts of these points, from some of our travellers. I only give you the results of my own observation, under the necessary limitations of my own opportunities. Still I must be permitted to say that too many of our people, in their habitual deference to England, mistake offensive condescension for civility. Of the two, I will confess I would rather encounter direct arrogance, than the assumption of a right to be affable. The first may at least be resisted.

Of all sorts of superiority, that of a condescending quality is the least palatable.

I believe Washington is the only place in America, where it is permitted to send cards. In every other town, unless accompanied by an invitation, and even then the card is *supposed* to be left, it would be viewed as airs. It is even equivocal to leave a card in person, unless denied. Nothing can be worse adapted to the wants of American society than this rigid conformity to facts. Without porters; with dwellings in which the kitchens and servants' halls are placed just as far from the street-doors as the dimensions of the houses will allow; with large straggling towns that cover as much ground as the more populous capitals of Europe, and these towns not properly divided into quarters; with a society as ambitious of effect, in its way, as any I know; and with people more than usually occupied with business and the family cares, one is expected to comply rigidly with the most formal rules of village propriety. It is easy to trace these usages to their source, provincial habits and rustic manners, but towns with three hundred thousand inhabitants, ought to be free from both. Such rigid conditions cannot well be observed, and a consequence already to be traced is, that those forms of society, which tend to refine it, and to render it more human and graceful, are neglected from sheer necessity. Carelessness in the points of association connected with sentiment (and all personal civilities and attention have this root) grows upon one like carelessness in dress, until an entire community may get to be as ungracious in deportment, as it is unattractive in attire.

The etiquette of visits, here, is reduced to a sort of science. A card is sent by a servant, and returned by a servant. It is polite to return it, next day, though three, I believe, is the lawful limits, and it is politer still to return it the day it is received. There is no affectation about sending the card, as it is not at all unusual to put E.P. (*en personne*) on it, by way of expressing a greater degree of attention, even when the card is sent. When the call is really made in person, though the visiter does not ask to be admitted, it is also common to request the porter to say that the party was at the gate. All these niceties may seem absurd and supererogatory, but depend on it, they have a direct and powerful agency in refining and polishing intercourse, just as begging a man's pardon, when you tread on his toe, has an effect to humanize, though the parties know no offence was intended. Circumstances once rendered it proper that I should leave a card for a Russian *diplomate*, an act that I took care he should know, indirectly, I went out of my way to do, as an acknowledgment for the civilities his countrymen showed to us Americans. My name was left at the gate of his hotel, (it was not in Paris,) as I was taking a morning ride. On returning home, after an absence of an hour, I found his card lying on my table. Instead, however, of its containing the usual official titles, it was simply Prince ———. I was profoundly immerged in the study of this new feature in the forms of etiquette, when the friend, who had prepared the way for the visit, entered. I asked an explanation, and he told me that I had received a higher compliment than could be conveyed by a merely official card, this being a proffer of *personal* attention. "You will get an invitation to dinner soon;" and, sure enough, one came before he had quitted the house. Now, here was a delicate and flattering attention paid, and one that I felt, without trouble to either party; one that the occupations of the *diplomate* would scarcely permit him to pay, except in extraordinary cases, under rules more rigid.

There is no obligation on a stranger to make the first visit, certainly, but if he do not, he is not to be surprised if no one notices him. It is a matter of delicacy to obtrude on the privacy of such a person, it being presumed that he wishes to be retired. We have passed some time in a village near Paris, which contains six or eight visitable families. With one of these I had some acquaintance, and we exchanged civilities, but wishing to be undisturbed, I extended my visit no farther, and I never saw anything of the rest of my neighbours. They waited for me to make the advances.

A person in society, here, who is desirous of relieving himself, for a time, from the labour and care of maintaining the necessary intercourse, can easily do it, by leaving cards of P.P.C. It might be awkward to remain long in a place very publicly, after such a step, but I ventured on it once, to extricate myself from engagements that interfered with more important pursuits, with entire success. I met several acquaintances in the street, after the cards were sent, and we even talked together, but I got no more visits or invitations. When ready *to return to town*, all I had to do was to leave cards again, and things went on as if nothing had happened. I parried one or two allusions to my absence, and had no further difficulty. The only awkward part of it was, that I accepted an invitation to dine *en famille* with a literary friend, and one of the guests, of whom there were but three, happened to be a person whose invitation to dinner I had declined on account of quitting town!

As he was a sensible man, I told him the simple fact, and we laughed at the *contretemps*, and drank our wine in peace.

The Americans who come abroad frequently complain of a want of hospitality in the public agents. There is a strong disposition in every man, under institutions like our own, to mistake himself for a part of the government, in matters with which he has no proper connexion, while too many totally overlook those interests which it is their duty to watch. In the first place, the people of the United States do not give salaries to their ministers, of sufficient amount to authorize them to expect that any part of the money should be returned in the way of personal civilities. Fifty thousand francs a-year is the usual sum named by the French, as the money necessary to maintain a genteel town establishment, with moderate evening entertainments, and an occasional dinner. This is three thousand francs more than the salary of the minister, out of which he is moreover expected to maintain his regular diplomatic intercourse. It is impossible for any one to do much in the way of personal civilities, on such an allowance.

There is, moreover, on the part of too many of our people, an aptitude to betray a jealous sensitiveness on the subject of being presented at foreign courts. I have known some claim it *as a right*, when it is yielded to the minister himself, as an act of grace. The receptions of a sovereign are merely his particular mode of receiving visits. No one will pretend that the President of the United States is obliged to give levees and dinners, nor is a king any more compelled to receive strangers, or even his own subjects, unless it suit his policy and his taste. His palace is his house, and he is the master of it, the same as any other man is master of his own abode. It is true, the public expects something of him, and his allowance is probably regulated by this expectation, but the interference does not go so far as to point out his company. Some kings pass years without holding a court at all; others receive every week. The public obligation to open his door, is no more than an obligation of expediency, of which he, and he only, can be the judge. This being the rule, not only propriety but fair dealing requires that all who frequent a court, should comply with the conditions that are understood to be implied in the permission. While there exists an exaggerated opinion, on the part of some of our people, on the subject of the fastidiousness of princes, as respects their associates, there exists among others very confused notions on the other side of the question. A monarch usually cares very little about the quarterings and the nobility of the person he receives, but he always wishes his court to be frequented by people of education, accomplishments, and breeding. In Europe these qualities are confined to *castes*, and, beyond a question, as a general practice, every king would not only prefer, but were there a necessity for it, he would command that his doors should be closed against all others, unless they came in a character different from that of courtiers. This object has, in effect, been obtained, by establishing a rule, that no one who has not been presented at his own court, can claim to be presented at any foreign European court; thus leaving each sovereign to see that no one of his own subjects shall travel with this privilege, who would be likely to prove an unpleasant guest to any other prince. But we have neither any princes nor any court, and the minister is left to decide for himself who is, and who is not proper to be presented.

Let us suppose a case. A master and his servant make a simultaneous request to be presented to the King of France. Both are American citizens, and if *either* has any political *claim*, beyond mere courtesy, to have his request attended to, *both* have. The minister is left to decide for himself. He cannot so far abuse the courtesy that permits him to present his countrymen at all, as to present the domestic, and of course he declines doing it. In this case, perhaps, public opinion would sustain him, as, unluckily, the party of the domestics is small in America, the duties usually falling to the share of foreigners and blacks. But the principle may be carried upwards, until a point is attained where a minister might find it difficult to decide between that which his own sense of propriety should dictate, and that which others might be disposed to claim. All other ministers get rid of their responsibility by the acts of their own courts; but the minister of the republic, is left exposed to the calumny, abuse and misrepresentation of any disappointed individual, should he determine to do what is strictly right.

Under these circumstances, it appears to me, that there are but two courses left for any agent of our government to pursue; either to take *official* rank as his only guide, or to decline presenting any one. It is not his duty to act as a master of ceremonies; every court has a regular officer for this purpose, and any one who has been presented himself, is permitted on proper representations to present others. The trifling disadvantage will be amply compensated for, by the great and peculiar benefits that arise from our peculiar form of government.

These things will quite likely strike you as of little moment. They are, however, of more concern than one living in the simple society of America may at first suppose. The etiquette of visiting has of course an influence on the entire associations of a traveller, and may not be overlooked, while the single fact that one people were practically excluded from the European courts, would have the same effect on their other enjoyments here, that it has to exclude an individual from the most select circles of any particular town. Ordinary life is altogether coloured by things that, in themselves, may appear trifling, but which can no more be neglected with impunity, than one can neglect the varying fashions in dress.

The Americans are not a shoving people, like their cousins the English. Their fault in this particular lies in a morbid pride, with a stubbornness that is the result of a limited experience, and which is too apt to induce them to set up their own provincial notions, as the standard, and to throw them backward into the intrenchments, of self-esteem. This feeling is peculiarly fostered by the institutions. It is easy to err in this manner; and it is precisely the failing of the countryman, everywhere, when he first visits town. It is, in fact, the fault of ignorance of the world. By referring to what I have just told you, it will be seen that these are the very propensities which will be the most likely to make one uncomfortable in Europe, where so much of the *initiative* of intercourse is thrown upon the shoulders of the stranger.

I cannot conclude this letter, without touching on another point, that suggests itself at the moment. It is the fashion to decry the niggardliness of the American government on the subject of money, as compared with those of this hemisphere. Nothing can be more unjust. Our working men are paid better than even those of England, with the exception of a few who have high dignities to support. I do not see the least necessity for giving the President a dollar more than he gets to-day, since all he wants is enough to entertain handsomely, and to shield him from loss. Under our system, we never can have an *exclusive* court, nor is it desirable, for in this age a court is neither a school of manners, nor a school of anything else that is estimable. These facts are sufficiently proved by England, a country whose mental cultivation and manners never stood as high as they do to-day, and yet it has virtually been without a court for an entire generation. A court may certainly foster taste and elegance, but they may be quite as well fostered by other, and less exclusive, means. But while the President may receive enough, the heads of Departments, at home, and the Foreign Ministers of the country, are not more than half paid, *particularly the latter*. The present minister is childless, his establishment and his manner of living are both handsome, but not a bit more so than those of a thousand others, who inhabit this vast capital, and his intercourse with his colleagues is not greater than is necessary to the interests of his country. Now, I know from his own statement, that his expenses, without a family, exceed by one hundred per cent. his salary. With a personal income of eighty to a hundred thousand francs a year, he can bear this drain on his private fortune, but he is almost the only minister we ever had here, who could.

The actual position of our diplomatic agents in Europe is little understood at home. There are but two or three modes of maintaining the rights of a nation, to say nothing of procuring those concessions from others which enter into the commercial relations of states, and in some degree affect their interests. The best method, certainly, as respects the two first, is to manifest a determination to defend them by an appeal to force; but so many conflicting interests stand in the way of such a policy that it is exceedingly difficult, wisest and safest in the end though it be, to carry it out properly. At any rate, such a course has never yet been in the power of the American government, whatever it may be able to do hereafter, with its increasing numbers and growing wealth. But even strength is not always sufficient to obtain voluntary and friendly concessions, for principle must, in some degree, be respected by the most potent people, or they will be put to the ban of the world. Long diplomatic letters, although they may answer the purposes of ministerial *exposés*, and read well enough in the columns of a journal, do very little, in fact, as make weights in negotiations. I have been told here, *sub rosâ*, and I believe it, that some of our laboured efforts, in this way, to obtain redress in the protracted negotiation for indemnity, have actually lain months in the *bureaux*, unread by those who alone have the power to settle the question. Some *commis* perhaps may have cursorily related their contents to his superior, but the superior himself is usually too much occupied in procuring and maintaining ministerial majorities, or, in looking after the monopolising concerns of European politics, to wade through folios of elaborate argument in manuscript. The public ought to understand, that the point presents itself to him, in the security of his master's capital, and with little or no apprehension of its coming to an appeal to arms, very differently from what it occasionally presents itself, in the pages of a President's message, or in a debate in Congress. He has so many demands on his time, that it is even difficult to have a working interview with him at all, and when one is obtained, it is not usual to do more than to go over the preliminaries. The details are necessarily referred to subordinates.

Now, in such a state of things, any one accustomed to the world, can readily understand how much may be effected by the kind feelings that are engendered by daily, social, intercourse. A few words can be whispered in the ears of a minister, in the corner of a drawing-room, that would never reach him in his bureau. Then *all* the ministers are met in society, while the *diplomate*, properly speaking, can claim officially to see but *one*. In short, in saving, out of an overflowing treasury, a few thousand dollars a year, we trifle with our own interests, frequently embarrass our agents, and in some degree discredit the country. I am not one of your *sensitives* on the subject of parade and appearance, nor a member of the embroidery school; still I would substitute for the irrational frippery of the European customs, a liberal hospitality, and a real elegance, that should speak well for the hearts and tastes of the nation. The salary of the minister at Paris, I know it, by the experience of a house-keeper, ought to be increased by at least one half, and it would tell better for the interests of the country, were it doubled. Even in this case, however, I do not conceive that an American would be justified in mistaking the house of an Envoy for a national inn, but that the proper light to view his allowances would be to consider them as made, first as an act of justice to the functionary himself; next, as a measure of expediency, as connected with the important interests of the country. As it is, I am certain that no one but a man of fortune can accept a foreign appointment, without committing injustice to his heirs, and I believe few do accept them without sincerely regretting the step, in after years.

# Letter XII
## To James E. De Kay, Esquire.

We have not only had Mr. Canning in Paris, but Sir Walter Scott has suddenly appeared among us. The arrival of the Great Unknown, or, indeed, of any little Unknown from England, would be an event to throw all the reading clubs at home, into a state of high moral and poetical excitement. We are true village *lionizers*. As the professors of the Catholic religion are notoriously more addicted to yielding faith to miraculous interventions, in the remoter dioceses, than in Rome itself; as loyalty is always more zealous in a colony, than in a court; as fashions are more exaggerated in a province, than in a capital, and men are more prodigious to every one else, than their own valets, so do we throw the haloes of a vast ocean around the honoured heads of the celebrated men of this eastern hemisphere. This, perhaps, is the natural course of things, and is as unavoidable as that the sun shall hold the earth within the influence of its attraction, until matters shall be reversed by the earth's becoming the larger and more glorious orb of the two. Not so in Paris. Here men of every gradation of celebrity, from Napoleon down to the Psalmanazar of the day, are so very common, that one scarcely turns round in the streets, to look at them. Delicate 'and polite attentions, however, fall as much to the share of reputation, here, as in any other country, and perhaps more so, as respects literary men, though there is so little *wonder-mongering*. It would be quite impossible that the presence of Sir Walter Scott should not excite a sensation. He was frequently named in the journals, received a good deal of private, and some public notice, but, on the whole, much less of both, I think, than one would have a right to expect for him, in a place like Paris. I account for the fact, by the French distrusting the forthcoming work on Napoleon, and by a little dissatisfaction which prevails on the subject of the tone of "Paul's Letters to his Kinsfolk." This feeling may surprise you, as coming from a nation as old and as great as France, but, alas! we are all human.

The King spoke to him, in going to his chapel, Sir Walter being in waiting for that purpose, but beyond this I believe he met with no civilities from the court.

As for myself, circumstances that it is needless to recount, had brought me, to a slight degree, within the notice of Sir Walter Scott, though we had never met, nor had I ever seen him, even in public, so as to know his person. Still I was not without hopes of being more fortunate now, while I felt a delicacy about obtruding myself any further on his time and attention. Several days after his arrival went by, however, without my good luck bringing me in his way, and I began to give the matter up, though the *Princesse* [*Galitzin Souvarof*], with whom I had the advantage of being on friendly terms, flattered me with an opportunity of seeing the great writer at her house, for she had a fixed resolution of making his acquaintance before he left Paris, *coûte que coûte.*

It might have been ten days after the arrival of Sir Walter Scott, that I had ordered a carriage, one morning, with an intention of driving over to the other side of the river, and had got as far as the lower flight of steps, on my way to enter it, when, by the tramping of horses in the court, I found that another coach was driving in. It was raining, and, as my own carriage drove from the door, to make way for the new comer, I stopped where I was, until it could return. The carriage-steps rattled, and presently a large, heavy-moulded man appeared in the door of the hotel. He was gray, and limped a little, walking with a cane. His carriage immediately drove round, and was succeeded by mine, again; so I descended. We passed each other on the stairs, bowing as a matter of course. I had got to the door, and was about to enter the carriage, when it flashed on my mind that the visit might be to myself. The two lower floors of the hotel were occupied as a girls' boarding-school, the reason of our dwelling in it, for our own daughters were in the establishment; *au second*, there was nothing but our own *appartement*, and above us, again, dwelt a family whose visitors never came in carriages. The door of the boarding-school was below, and men seldom came to it, at all. Strangers, moreover, sometimes did honour me with calls. Under these impressions I paused, to see if the visitor went as far as our flight of steps. All this time, I had not the slightest suspicion of who he was, though I fancied both the face and form were known to me.

The stranger got up the large stone steps slowly, leaning, with one hand, on the iron railing, and with the other, on his cane. He was on the first landing, as I stopped, and, turning towards the next flight, our eyes met. The idea that I might be the person he wanted, seemed then to strike him for the first time. *"Est-ce Mons.* [*Cooper*], *que j'ai l'honneur de voir?"* he asked, in French and with but an indifferent accent. *"Monsieur, je m'appelle* [*Cooper*]." *"Eh bien, donc—je suis Walter Scott."*

I ran up to the landing, shook him by the hand, which he stood holding out to me cordially, and expressed my sense of the honour he was conferring. He told me, in substance, that the *Princesse* [*Galitzin Souvarof*] had been as good as her word, and having succeeded herself in getting hold of him, she had good-naturedly given him my address. By way of cutting short all ceremony he had driven from his hotel to my lodgings. All this time he was speaking French, while my answers and remarks were in English. Suddenly recollecting himself, he said— "Well, here have I been *parlez-vousing* to you, in a way to surprise you, no doubt; but these Frenchmen have got my tongue so set to their lingo, that I have half forgotten my own language." As we proceeded up the next flight of steps, he accepted my arm, and continued the conversation in English, walking with more difficulty than I had expected to see. You will excuse the vanity of my repeating the next observation he made, which I do in the hope that some of our own *exquisites* in literature may learn in what manner a man of true sentiment and sound feeling regards a trait that they have seen fit to stigmatize as unbecoming. "I'll tell you what I most like," he added, abruptly; "and it is the manner in which you maintain the ascendancy of your own country on all proper occasions, without descending to vulgar abuse of ours. You are obliged to bring the two nations in collision, and I respect your liberal hostility." This will probably be esteemed treason in our own self-constituted mentors of the press, one of whom, I observe, has quite lately had to apologize to his readers for exposing some of the sins of the English writers in reference to ourselves! But these people are not worth our attention, for they have neither the independence which belongs to masculine reason, nor manhood even to prize the quality in others. "I am afraid the mother has not always treated the daughter well," he continued, "feeling a little jealous of her growth, perhaps; for, though we hope England has not yet begun to descend on the evil side, we have a presentiment that she has got to the top of the ladder."

There were two entrances to our apartments; one, the principal, leading by an ante-chamber and *salle à manger* into the *salon*, and thence through other rooms to a terrace; and the other, by a private *corridor*, to the same spot. The door of my *cabinet* opened on this *corridor*, and though it was dark, crooked, and any thing but savoury, as it led by the kitchen, I conducted Sir Walter through it, under an impression that he walked with pain, an idea, of which I could not divest myself, in the hurry of the moment. But for this awkwardness on

my part, I believe I should have been the witness of a singular interview. General Lafayette had been with me a few minutes before, and he
had gone away by the *salon*, in order to speak to Mrs. [Cooper]. Having
a note to write, I had left him there, and I think his carriage could not
have quitted the court when that of Sir Walter Scott entered. If so, the
General must have passed out by the ante-chamber, about the time we
came through the *corridor*.

There would be an impropriety in my relating all that passed in this
interview; but we talked over a matter of business, and then the
conversation was more general. You will remember that Sir Walter was
still the *Unknown*,*and that he was believed to be in Paris, in search of
facts for the Life of Napoleon. Notwithstanding the former circumstance, he spoke of his works with great frankness and simplicity, and
without the parade of asking any promises of secrecy. In short, as he
commenced in this style, his authorship was alluded to by us both, just
as if it had never been called in question. He asked me if I had a copy of
the ———— by me, and on my confessing I did not own a single volume
of anything I had written, he laughed, and said he believed that most
authors had the same feeling on the subject: as for himself, he cared not
if he never saw a Waverley novel again, as long as he lived. Curious to
know whether a writer as great and as practised as he, felt the occasional despondency which invariably attends all my own little efforts
of this nature, I remarked that I found the mere composition of a tale a
source of pleasure; so much so, that I always invented twice as much as
was committed to paper, in my walks, or in bed, and, in my own
judgment, much the best parts of the composition never saw the light;
for, what was written was usually written at set hours, and was a good
deal a matter of chance; and that going over and over the same subject,
in proofs, disgusted me so thoroughly with the book, that I supposed
every one else would be disposed to view it with the same eyes. To this
he answered, that he was spared much of the labour of proof-reading,
Scotland, he presumed, being better off than America, in this respect;
but, still, he said he "would as soon see his dinner again, after a hearty
meal, as to read one of his own tales when he was fairly rid of it."

He sat with me nearly an hour, and he manifested, during the time
the conversation was not tied down to business, a strong propensity to
humour. Having occasion to mention our common publisher in Paris,

* He did not avow himself for several months afterwards.

he quaintly termed him, with a sort of malicious fun, "our Gosling;"*
adding, that he hoped he, at least, "laid golden eggs."

I hoped that he had found the facilities he desired, in obtaining facts
for the forth-coming history. He rather hesitated about admitting
this.—"One can hear as much as he pleases, in the way of anecdote," he
said, "but then, as a gentleman, he is not always sure how much of it he
can, with propriety, relate in a book—besides," throwing all his latent
humour into the expression of his small gray eyes, "one may even
doubt how much of what he hears is fit for history, on another account."
He paused, and his face assumed an exquisite air of confiding simplicity, as he continued with perfect *bonne foi* and strong Scottish feeling, "I
have been to see *my countryman* Macdonald, and I rather think that will
be about as much as I can do here, now." This was uttered with so much
*naïveté* that I could hardly believe it was the same man, who, a moment
before, had shown so much shrewd distrust of oral relations of facts.

I inquired when we might expect the work. "Some time in the course
of the winter," he replied, "though it is likely to prove larger than I, at
first, intended. We have got several volumes printed, but I find I must
add to the matter, considerably, in order to dispose of the subject. I
thought I should get rid of it in seven volumes, which are already
written, but it will reach, I think, to nine." "If you have two still to write,
I shall not expect to see the book before spring." "You may. Let me once
get back to Abbotsford, and I'll soon knock off those two fellows." To
this I had nothing to say, although I thought such a *tour de force* in
writing might better suit invention than history.

When he rose to go, I begged him to step into the *salon*, that I might
have the gratification of introducing my wife to him. To this he very
good naturedly assented, and entering the room, after presenting Mrs.
[Cooper] and my nephew W[illiam], he took a seat. He sat some little
time, and his fit of pleasantry returned, for he illustrated his discourse
by one or two apt anecdotes, related with a slightly Scottish accent, that
he seemed to drop and assume at will. Mrs. [Cooper] observed to him
that the *bergère* in which he was seated, had been twice honoured that
morning, for General Lafayette had not left it more than half an hour.
Sir Walter Scott looked surprised at this, and said, inquiringly, "I
thought he had gone to America, to pass the rest of his days?" On my
explaining the true state of the case, he merely observed, "he is a great
man;" and yet, I thought the remark was made coldly, or in complai-
sance to us.

*His name was *Gosselin.*

When Sir Walter left us, it was settled that I was to breakfast with him, the following day but one. I was punctual, of course, and found him in a new silk *douillette* that he had just purchased, trying "as hard as he could," as he pleasantly observed, to make a Frenchman of himself; an undertaking as little likely to be successful, I should think, in the case of his Scottish exterior, and Scottish interior, too, as any experiment well could be. There were two or three visitors present, besides Miss Ann Scott, his daughter, who was his companion in the journey. He was just answering an invitation from the *Princesse* [*Galitzin*], to an evening party, as I entered. "Here," said he, "you are a friend of the lady, and *parlez-vous* so much better than I, can you tell me whether this is for *jeudi*, or *lundi*, or *mardi*, or whether it means no day at all." I told him the day of the week intended. "You get notes occasionally from the lady, or you could not read her scrawl so readily?" "She is very kind to us, and we often have occasion to read her writing." "Well, it is worth a very good dinner to get through a page of it." "I take my revenge in kind, and I fancy she has the worst of it." "I don't know, after all, that she will get much the better of me, with this *plume d'auberge*." He was quite right, for, although Sir Walter writes a smooth even hand, and one that appears rather well than otherwise on a page, it is one of the most difficult to decipher I have ever met with. The i's, u's, m's, n's, a's, e's, t's, &c., &c., for want of dots, crossings, and being fully rounded, looking all alike, and rendering the reading slow and difficult, without great familiarity with his mode of handling the pen; at least, I have found it so.

He had sealed the note, and was about writing the direction, when he seemed at a loss. "How do you address this lady—as 'Her Highness'?" I was much surprised at this question from him, for it denoted a want of familiarity with the world, that one would not have expected in a man who had been so very much and so long courted by the great. But, after all, his life has been provincial, though, as his daughter remarked in the course of the morning, they had no occasion to quit Scotland, to see the world, all the world coming to see Scotland.

The next morning he was with me again, for near an hour, and we completed our little affair. After this, we had a conversation on the Law of Copy-Rights, in the two countries, which, as we possess a common language, is a subject of great national interest. I understood him to say that he had a double right, in England, to his works; one under a statute, and the other growing out of common law. Any one publishing a book, let it be written by whom it might, in England, duly complying with the law, can secure the right, whereas, none but a *citizen* can do the same in America. I regret to say, that I misled him on the subject of our copy-right law, which, after all, is not so much more illiberal than that of England, as I had thought it.

I told Sir Walter Scott, that, in order to secure a copy-right in America, it was necessary the book should never have been published *anywhere else*. This was said under the popular notion of the matter; or that which is entertained among the booksellers. Reflection and examination have since convinced me of my error: the publication alluded to in the law, can only mean publication in America; for, as the object of doing certain acts previously to publication is merely to forewarn the *American* public that the right is reserved, there can be no motive for having reference to any other publication. It is, moreover, in conformity with the spirit of all laws to limit the meaning of their phrases by their proper jurisdiction. Let us suppose a case. An American writes a book. He sends a copy to England, where it is published in March. Complying with the terms of our own Copy-Right Law, as to the entries and notices, the same work is published here in April. Now, will it be pretended that his right is lost, always providing that his own is the first *American* publication? I do not see how it can be so, by either the letter or the spirit of the law. The intention is to encourage the citizen to write, and to give him a just property in the fruits of his labour; and the precautionary provisions of the law are merely to prevent others from being injured for want of proper information. It is of no moment to either of these objects that the author of a work has already reaped emolument, in a foreign country. The principle is to encourage literature, by giving it all the advantages it can obtain.

If these views are correct, why may not an English writer secure a right in this country, by selling it in season, to a citizen here? An equitable trust might not, probably would not be sufficient, but a *bonâ fide* transfer for a valuable consideration, I begin to think, would. It seems to me that all the misconception which has existed on this point, has arisen from supposing that the term *publication* refers to other than a publication in the country. But, when one remembers how rare it is to get lawyers to agree on a question like this, it becomes a layman to advance his opinion with great humility. I suppose, after all, a good way of getting an accurate notion of the meaning of the law, would be to toss a dollar into the air, and cry "heads," or "tails." Sir Walter Scott seemed fully aware of the great circulation of his books in America, as well as how much he lost by not being able to secure a copy-right. Still, he admitted they produced him something. Our conversation on this subject terminated by a frank offer, on his part, of aiding me with the publishers of his own country,* but, although grateful for the kindness, I was not so circumstanced as to be able to profit by it.

He did not appear to me to be pleased with Paris. His notions of the French were pretty accurate, though clearly not free from the old-fashioned prejudices. "After all," he remarked, "I am a true Scot, never, except on this occasion, and the short visit I made to Paris in 1815, having been out of my own country, unless to visit England, and I have even done very little of the latter." I understood him to say he had never been in Ireland, at all.

I met him once more, in the evening, at the hotel of the *Princesse* [*Galitzin*]. The party had been got together in a hurry, and was not large. Our hostess contrived to assemble some exceedingly clever people, however, among whom were one or two women, who are already historical, and whom I had fancied long since dead. All the female part of the company, with the silent delicacy that the French so well understand, appeared with ribbons, hats, or ornaments of some sort or other, of a Scottish stamp. Indeed, almost the only woman in the room that did not appear to be a Caledonian was Miss Scott. She was in half-mourning, and with her black eyes and jet-black hair, might very well have passed for a French woman, but for a slight peculiarity about the cheek bones. She looked exceedingly well, and was much admired. Having two or three more places to go to, they staid but an hour. As a matter of course, all the French women were exceedingly *empressées* in their manner towards the Great Unknown, and as there were three or four that were very exaggerated on the score of romance, he was quite lucky if he escaped some absurdities. Nothing could be more patient than his manner, under it all, but as soon as he very well could, he got into a corner, where I went to speak to him. He said, laughingly, that he spoke French with so much difficulty he was embarrassed to answer the compliments. "I'm as good a lion as needs be, allowing my mane to be stroked as familiarly as they please, but I can't growl for them, in French. How is it with you?" Disclaiming the necessity of being either a good or a bad lion, being very little troubled in that way, for his amusement I related to him an anecdote. Pointing out to him a *Comtesse de* ———, who was present, I told him, this lady I had met once a week, for several months, and at every *soirée* she invariably

---

* An offer that was twice renewed, after intervals of several years.

sailed up to me to say—*"Oh, Monsieur [Cooper], quels livres!—vos charmants livres—que vos livres sont charmants!"* and I had just made up my mind that she was, at least, a woman of taste, when she approached me with the utmost *sang froid*, and cried—*"Bon soir, Monsieur [Cooper]; je viens d'acheter tous livres et je compte profiter de la première occasion pour les lire!"*

I took leave of him, in the ante-chamber, as he went away, for he was to quit Paris the following evening.

Sir Walter Scott's person and manner have been so often described, that you will not ask much of me, in this way, especially as I saw so little of him. His frame is large and muscular, his walk difficult, in appearance, though he boasted himself a vigorous mountaineer, and his action, in general, measured and heavy. His features and countenance were very Scottish, with the short thick nose, heavy lips, and massive cheeks. The superior or intellectual part of his head was neither deep nor broad, but perhaps the reverse, though singularly high. Indeed, it is quite uncommon to see a scull so round and tower-like in the formation, though I have met with them in individuals not at all distinguished for talents. I do not think a casual observer would find anything unusual in the exterior of Sir Walter Scott, beyond his physical force, which is great, without being at all extraordinary. His eye, however, is certainly remarkable. Gray, small, and without lustre, in his graver moments it appears to look inward, instead of regarding external objects, in a way, though the expression, more or less, belongs to abstraction, that I have never seen equalled. His smile is good-natured and social; and when he is in the mood, as happened to be the fact so often in our brief intercourse as to lead me to think it characteristic of the man, his eye would lighten with a great deal of latent fun. He spoke more freely of his private affairs than I had reason to expect, though our business introduced the subject naturally; and, at such times, I thought the expression changed to a sort of melancholy resolution, that was not wanting in sublimity.

The manner of Sir Walter Scott is that of a man accustomed to see much of the world without being exactly a man of the world himself. He has evidently great social tact, perfect self-possession, is quiet, and absolutely without pretension, and has much dignity; and yet it struck me that he wanted the ease and *aplomb* of one accustomed to live with his equals. The fact of his being a lion, may produce some such effect, but I am mistaken if it be not more the influence of early habits and opinions than of any thing else.

Scott has been so much the mark of society, that it has evidently changed his natural manner, which is far less restrained, than it is his habit to be in the world. I do not mean by this, the mere restraint of decorum, but a drilled simplicity or demureness, like that of girls who are curbed in their tendency to fun and light-heartedness, by the dread of observation. I have seldom known a man of his years, whose manner was so different in a *tête-à-tête*, and in the presence of a third person. In Edinburgh the circle must be small, and he probably knows every one. If strangers do go there, they do not go all at once, and, of course, the old faces form the great majority; so that he finds himself always on familiar ground. I can readily imagine that in *Auld Reekie*, and among the proper set, warmed perhaps by a glass of mountain-dew, Sir Walter Scott, in his peculiar way, is one of the pleasantest companions the world holds.

There was a certain *M. de* ——— at the *soirée* of the *Princesse* [*Galitzin*], who has obtained some notoriety as the writer of novels. I had the honour of being introduced to this person, and was much amused with one of his questions. You are to understand that the vaguest possible notions exist in France, on the subject of the United States. Empires, states, continents and islands, are blended in inextricable confusion, in the minds of a large majority of even the intelligent classes, and we sometimes hear the oddest ideas imaginable. This ignorance, quite pardonable in part, is not confined to France, by any means, but exists even in England, a country that ought to know us better. It would seem that *M. de* ———, either because I was a shade or two whiter than himself, or because he did not conceive it possible that an American could write a book, (for in this quarter of the world, there is a strong tendency to believe that every man whose name crosses the ocean from America, is merely some European who has gone there,) or, from some cause that to me is inexplicable, took it into his head that I was an Englishman who had amused a leisure year or two in the Western Hemisphere. After asking me a few questions concerning the country, he very coolly continued— *"Et, combien de temps avez-vous passé, en Amérique, Monsieur?"* Comprehending his mistake, for a little practice here makes one quick in such matters, I answered— *"Monsieur, nous y sommes, depuis deux siècles."* I question if M. de ——— has yet recovered from his surprise!

The French, when their general cleverness is considered, are singularly ignorant of the habits, institutions, and civilization of other countries. This is in part owing to their being little addicted to travelling.

Their commercial enterprize is not great; for though we occasionally see a Frenchman carrying with him into pursuits of this nature, the comprehensive views, and one might almost say, the philosophy, that distinguish the real intelligence of the country, such instances are rare, the prevailing character of their commerce being caution and close dealing. Like the people of all great nations, their attention is drawn more to themselves than to others, and then the want of a knowledge of foreign languages has greatly contributed to their ignorance. This want of knowledge of foreign languages, in a nation that has traversed Europe as conquerors, is owing to the fact that they have either carried their own language with them, or met it everywhere. It is a want, moreover, that belongs rather to the last generation, than to the present; the returned emigrants having brought back with them a taste for English, German, Italian and Spanish, which has communicated itself to all, or nearly all, the educated people of the country. English, in particular, is now very generally studied; and perhaps, relatively, more French, under thirty years of age, are to be found in Paris, who speak English, than Americans, of the same age, are to be found in New York, who speak French.

I think the limited powers of the language, and the rigid laws to which it has been subjected, contribute to render the French less acquainted with foreign nations, than they would otherwise be. In all their translations, there is an effort to render the word, however peculiar may be its meaning, into the French tongue. Thus, "township," and "city," met with in an American book, would probably be rendered by "*canton*," or "*commune*," or "*ville*;" neither of which conveys an accurate idea of the thing intended. In an English or American book, we should introduce the French word at once, which would induce the reader to inquire into the differences that exist between the minor territorial divisions of his own country, and those of the country of which he is reading. In this manner is the door opened for further information, until both writers and readers come to find it easier and more agreeable to borrow words from others, than to curtail their ideas by their national vocabularies. The French, however, are beginning to feel their poverty, in this respect, and some are already bold enough to resort to the natural cure.

The habit of thinking of other nations through their own customs, betrays the people of this country into many ridicuous mistakes. One hears, here, the queerest questions imaginable, every day; all of which, veiled by the good-breeding and delicacy that characterize the nation, betray an innocent sense of superiority, that may be smiled at, and which creates no feeling of resentment. A *savant* lately named to me the coasting tonnage of France, evidently with the expectation of exciting my admiration; and on my receiving the information coolly, he inquired, with a little sarcasm of manner — "without doubt, you have some coasting tonnage, also, in America?" "The coasting tonnage of the United States, Monsieur, is greater than the entire tonnage of France." The man looked astonished, and I was covered with questions, as to the nature of the trade that required so much shipping, among a population numerically so small. It could not possibly be the consumption of a country — he did not say it, but he evidently thought it — so insignificant and poor? I told him, that, bread, wine, and every other article of the first necessity excepted, the other consumption of America, especially in luxuries, did not fall so much short of that of France as he imagined, owing to the great abundance in which the middling and lower classes lived. Unlike Europe, articles that were imported, were mere necessaries of life, in America, such as tea, coffee, sugar, &c., &c., the lowest labourer usually indulging in them. He left me evidently impressed with new notions, for there is a desire to learn mingled with all their vanity.

But, I will relate a laughable blunder of a translator, by way of giving you a familiar example of the manner in which the French fall into error, concerning the condition of other nations, and to illustrate my meaning. In one of the recent American novels that have been circulated here, a character is made to betray confusion, by tracing lines on the table, after dinner, with some wine that had been spilt, a sort of idle occupation sufficiently common to allow the allusion to be understood by every American. The sentence was faithfully rendered; but, not satisfied with giving his original, the translator annexes a note, in which he says, "one sees by this little trait, that the use of table-cloths, at the time of the American Revolution, was unknown in America!" You will understand the train of reasoning that led him to this conclusion. In France the cover is laid, perhaps, on a coarse table of oak, or even of pine, and the cloth is never drawn; the men leaving the table with the women. In America, the table is of highly polished mahogany, the cloth is removed, and the men sit, as in England. Now the French custom was supposed to be the custom of mankind, and wine could not be traced on the wood had there been a cloth; America was a young and semi-civilized nation, and, *ergo*, in 1779, there could have been no table-cloths known in America! When men even visit a people of whom they have been accustomed to think in this way, they use their eyes through the medium of the imagination. I lately met a French traveller who affirmed that the use of carpets was hardly known among us.

# Letter XIII
## To James E. De Kay, Esquire.

I n my last, I gave you a few examples of the instances in which the French have mistaken the relative civilization of their country and America, and I shall now give you some in which we have fallen into the same error, or the other side of the question.

There has lately been an exhibition of articles of French manufacture, at Paris; one of, I believe, the triennial collections of this character, that have been established here. The court of the Louvre was filled with temporary booths, for the occasion, and vast ranges of the unfinished apartments in that magnificent palace have been thrown open for the same purpose. The court of the Louvre, of itself, is an area rather more than four hundred feet square, and I should think fully a quarter of a mile of rooms in the building itself, are to be added to the space occupied for this purpose.

The first idea, with which I was impressed, on walking through the booths and galleries, on this occasion, was the great disproportion between the objects purely of taste and luxury, and the objects of use. The former abounded, were very generally elegant and well imagined, while the latter betrayed the condition of a nation whose civilization has commenced with the summit, instead of the base of society.

In France, nearly every improvement in machinery is the result of scientific research; is unobjectionable in principles, profound in the adaptation of its parts to the end, and commonly beautiful in form. But it ends here, rarely penetrating the mass, and producing positive results. The *conservatoire des arts*, for instance, is full of beautiful and ingenious ploughs, while France is tilled with heavy, costly and cumbrous implements of this nature. One sees light mould turning up, here, under a sort of agricultural *diligences*, drawn by four, and even six heavy horses, which in America would be done quite as well, and much sooner, by two. You know I am farmer enough to understand what I say, on a point like this. In France, the cutlery, iron-ware, glass, door-fastenings, hinges, locks, fire-irons, axes, hatchets, carpenter's tools, and, in short, almost every thing that is connected with homely industry and homely comfort, is inferior to the same thing in America. It is true, many of our articles are imported, but this produces no change in the habits of the respective people; our manufactories are merely in Birmingham, instead of being in Philadelphia.

I have now been long enough in France to understand that seeing an article in an exhibition like the one I am describing, is no proof that it enters at all into the comforts and civilization of the nation, although it may be an object as homely as a harrow or a spade. The scientific part of the country has little influence, in this way, on the operative. The chasm between knowledge and ignorance is so vast in France, that it requires a long time for the simplest idea to find its way across it.

Exhibitions are every where bad guides to the average civilization of a country, as it is usual to expose only the objects that have been wrought with the greatest care. In a popular sense, they are proofs of what *can* be done, rather than of what *is* done. The cloths that I saw in the booths, for instance, are not to be met with in the shops; the specimens of fire-arms, glass, cutlery, &c. &c., too, are all much superior to any thing one finds on sale. But this is the case every where, from the boarding-school to the military parade, men invariably putting the best foot foremost, when they are to be especially inspected. This is not the difference I mean. Familiar, as every American, at all accustomed to the usages of genteel life in his own country, must be, with the better manufactures of Great Britain, I think he would be struck by the inferiority of even the best specimens of the commoner articles that were here laid before the public. But when it came to the articles of elegance and luxury, as connected with forms, taste and execution, though not always in ingenuity and extent of comfort, I should think that no Englishman, let his rank in life be what it would, could pass through this wilderness of elegancies, without wonder.

Even the manufactures in which we, or rather the English (for I now refer more to use than to production) ordinarily excel, such as carpets, rugs, porcelain, plate, and all the higher articles of personal comfort, *as exceptions*, surpass those of which we have any notion. I say, *as exceptions*, not in the sense by which we distinguish the extraordinary efforts of the ordinary manufacturer, in order to make a figure at an exhibition, but certain objects produced in certain exclusive establishments, that are chiefly the property of the crown, as they have been the offspring of regal taste and magnificence.

Of this latter character is the *Sèvres* china. There are manufactures of this name, of a quality that brings them within the reach of moderate fortunes, it is true, but one obtains no idea of the length to which luxury and taste have been pushed in this branch of art, without examining the objects made especially for the king, who is in the habit of distributing them as presents among the crowned heads and his personal favourites. After the ware has been made, with the greatest care, and of the best materials, artists of celebrity are employed to paint it. You can easily imagine the value of these articles, when you remember that each plate has a design of its own, beautifully executed in colours, and presenting a landscape or an historical subject, that is fit to be framed and suspended in a gallery. One or two of the artists employed in this manner have great reputations, and it is no uncommon thing to see miniatures, in gilded frames, which, on examination, prove to be on porcelain. Of course the painting has been subject to the action of heat, in the baking. As respects the miniatures, there is not much to be said in their favour. They are well drawn and well enough coloured, but the process and the material together, give them a glossy, unnatural appearance, which must prevent them from ever being considered as more than so many *tours de force* in the arts. But on vases, dinner setts, and all ornamental furniture of this nature, in which we look for the peculiarities of the material, they produce a magnificence of effect, that I cannot describe. Vases of the value of ten or fifteen thousand francs, or even of more money, are not uncommon, and at the exhibition there was a little table, the price of which I believe was two thousand dollars, that was a perfect treasure in its way.

Busts, and even statues, I believe, have been attempted in this branch of art. This, of course, is enlisting the statuary as well as the painter in its service. I remember to have seen, when at *Sèvres*, many busts of the late *Duc de Berri*, in the process of drying, previously to being put into the oven. Our *cicerone*, on that occasion, made us laugh, by the routine with which he went through his catalogue of wonders. He had pointed out to us the unbaked busts, in a particular room, and, on entering another apartment, where the baked busts were standing, he exclaimed—"*Ah! voilà son Altesse Royale toute cuite.*" This is just the amount of the criticism I should hazard on this branch of the *Sèvres* art, or on that which exceeds its legitimate limits—"Behold his Royal Highness, ready cooked."

The value of some of the single plates must be very considerable, and the king, frequently, in presenting a solitary vase, or ornament of the *Sèvres* porcelain, presents thousands.

The tapestry is another of the costly works, that it has suited the policy of France to keep up, while her ploughs, and axes, and carts, and other ordinary implements are still so primitive and awkward. The exhibition contained many specimens from the *Gobelins*, that greatly surpassed my expectations. They were chiefly historical subjects, with the figures larger than life, and might very well have passed, with a novice, at a little distance, for oil paintings. The dimensions of the apartment are taken, and the subject is designed, of course, on a scale suited to the room. The effect of this species of ornament is very noble and imposing, and the tapestries have the additional merit of warmth and comfort. Hangings in cloth are very common in Paris, but the tapestry of the *Gobelins* is chiefly confined to the royal palaces. Our neighbour the *duc de* ————, has some of it, however, in his hotel, a present from the king, but the colours are much faded, and the work is otherwise the worse for time. I have heard him say, that one piece he has, even in its dilapidated state, is valued at seven thousand francs. Occasionally a little of this tapestry is found, in this manner, in the great hotels; but, as a rule, its use is strictly royal.

The paper for hangings, is another article in which the French excel. We get very pretty specimens of their skill in this manufacture in America, but, with occasional exceptions, nothing that is strictly magnificent finds its way into our markets. I was much struck with some of these hangings that were made to imitate velvet. The cloth appeared to be actually incorporated with the paper, and by no ingenuity of which I was master, could I detect the means. The style of paper is common enough, every where, but this exhibition had qualities far surpassing any thing of the sort I had ever before seen. Curiosity has since led me to the paper-maker, in order to penetrate the secrets of his art, and there, like the affair of Columbus and the egg, I found the whole thing as simple as heart could wish. You will probably smile, when you learn the process by which paper is converted into velvet, which is briefly this.

Wooden moulds are used to stamp the designs, each colour being put on, by laying a separate mould on its proper place, one mould being used after another, though only one is used on any particular occasion. Thus, all the black is put on now, the green to-morrow, and the yellow next day. As to the velvets, they are produced as follows. Wool is chopped fine, and dyed the desired hue. I am not certain that cotton, or even other materials may not be used. This chopped and coloured wool is thrown into a tub; the mould is covered with some glutinous substance, and when applied it leaves on the paper the adhesive property, as types leave the ink. The paper passes immediately over the tub, and a boy throws on the wool. A light blow or two, of a rattan, tosses it about, and finally throws all back again into the tub that has not touched the glue. The *printed* part, of course, is covered with blue, or purple, or scarlet wool, and is converted, by a touch of the wand, into velvet! The process of covering a yard lasts about ten seconds, and I should think considerably more than a hundred yards of paper could be *velvetized* in an hour. We laughed at the discovery, and came away satisfied that Solomon could have known nothing about manufacturing paper-hangings, or he would not have said there was nothing "new under the sun."

But the manufacture of France that struck me as being strictly in the best taste, in which perfection and magnificence are attained without recourse to conceits, or doing violence to any of the proprieties, are the products of the *Savonnerie*, and the exquisitely designed and executed works of Beauvais. These include chair bottoms and backs, hangings for rooms, and, I believe, carpets. At all events, if the carpets do not come from these places, they are quite worthy to have that extraction. Flowers, *arabesques*, and other similar designs, exquisitely coloured and drawn, chiefly limit the efforts of the former; and the carpets were in single pieces, and made to fit the room. Nothing that you have ever seen, or probably have imagined, at all equals the magnificence of some of these princely carpets. Indeed, I know nothing that runs a closer parallel to the general civilization between France and England, and I might almost add of America, than the history of their respective carpets. In France, a vast majority of the people hardly know what a carpet is. They use mud floors, or, rising a little above the very lowest classes, coarse stone and rude tiles are substituted. The middling classes, out of the large towns, have little else besides painted tiles. The wooden *parquet* is met with, in all the better houses, and is well made and well kept. There is a finish and beauty about them, that is not misplaced even in a palace. Among all these classes, until quite lately, carpets were unknown, or at least they were confined to the very highest class of society. The great influx of English has introduced them into the public hotels, and common lodging houses, but I have visited among many French of rank and fortune, in the dead of winter, and found no carpets. A few of a very coarse quality, made of rags, adroitly tortured into laboured designs, are seen, it is true, even in indifferent houses; but the rule is, as I have told you. In short, carpets, in this country, until quite lately, have been deemed articles of high luxury; and, like nearly every thing else that is magnificent and luxurious, at the point where they have been taken up, they infinitely exceed any thing of the sort in England. The classical designs, perfect drawings, and brilliant colours, defeat every effort to surpass them,—I had almost said, all competition.

In all America, except in the new regions, with here and there, a dwelling on the frontier, there is scarcely a house to be found without carpets, the owners of which are at all above the labouring classes. Even in many of the latter they are to be found. We are carpeted, frequently, from the kitchen to the garret; the richness and rarity of the manufacture increasing as we ascend in the scale of wealth and fashion, until we reach the uttermost limits of our habits—a point where beauty and neatness verge upon elegance and magnificence. At this point, however, we stop, and the turn of the French commences. Now this is the history of the comparative civilization of the two countries, in a multitude of other matters; perhaps it would be better to say it is the general comparative history of the two countries. The English differ from us, only, in carrying their scale both higher and lower than ourselves: in being sometimes magnificent, and sometimes impoverished; but rarely, indeed, do they equal the French, in the light, classical, and elegant taste that so eminently distinguishes these people. There is something ponderous and purse-proud about the magnificence of England, that is scarcely ever visible here; though taste is evidently and rapidly on the increase in England, on the one hand, as comfort is here, on the other. The French have even partially adopted the two words "*fashionable*," and "*comfortable*."

One of the most curious things connected with the arts in France, is that of transferring old pictures from wood to canvass. A large proportion of the paintings of the sixteenth and seventeenth centuries were done on wood or copper, and many of the former are, or have been, in danger of being lost, from decay. In order to meet the evil, a process has been invented by which the painting is transferred to canvas, where it remains, to all appearance, as good as ever. I have taken some pains to ascertain in what manner this nice operation is performed. I have seen pictures in various stages of the process, though I have never watched any one through it all; and, in one instance, I saw a small Wouvermans, stripped to the shirt, if it may be so expressed, or, in other words, *when it was nothing but paint.* From what I have seen and been told, I understand the mode of effecting this delicate and almost incredible operation, to be as follows:—

A glue is rubbed over the face of the picture, which is then laid on a piece of canvas that is properly stretched and secured, to receive it. Weights are now laid on the back of the picture, and it is left for a day or two, in order that the glue may harden. The weights are then removed, and the operator commences removing the wood, first with a plane, and, when he approaches the paint, with sharp delicate chissels. The paint is kept in its place by the canvas to which it is glued, and which is itself secured to the table; and, although the entire body of the colours, hardened as it is by time, is usually not thicker than a thin wafer, the wood is commonly taken entirely from it. Should a thin fragment be left, however, or a crack made in the paint, it is considered of no great moment. The Wouvermans alluded to, was pure paint, however, and I was shown the pieces of wood, much worm-eaten, that had been removed. When the wood is away, glue is applied to the *back of the paint,* and to the canvas on which it is intended the picture shall remain. The latter is then laid on the paint. New weights are placed above it, and they are left two or three days longer, for this new glue to harden. When it is thought the adhesion between the second canvas and the paint is sufficient, the weights are removed, the picture is turned, and warm water is used in loosening the first canvas from the face of the picture, until it can be stripped off. More or less of the varnish of the picture usually comes off, with the glue, rendering the separation easier. The painting is then cleaned, retouched, and should it be necessary, varnished and framed; after which it commonly looks as well, and is really as sound and as good as ever, so far, at least, as the consistency is concerned.

Among other wonders in the exhibition, was the coronation coach of Charles X. This carriage is truly magnificent. It is quite large, as indeed are all the royal carriages, perhaps as large as an American stage-coach; the glass, pure and spotless as air, goes all round the upper compartments, so as to admit of a view of the whole interior; the pannels are beautifully painted in design; the top has gilded and well-formed angels blowing trumpets, and the crown of France surmounts the centre. The wheels, and train, and pole, are red, striped with gold. All the leather is red morocco, gilt, as is the harness. Plumes of ostrich feathers ornament the angles, and, altogether, it is a most glittering and gorgeous vehicle. The paintings, the gildings, and all the details are well executed, except the running gear, which struck me as clumsy and imperfect. The cost is said to have been about sixty thousand dollars.

Many new rooms in the Louvre were thrown open on this occasion, in order that the paintings on their ceilings might be viewed, and as I walked through this gorgeous magnificence, I felt how small were our highest pretensions to anything like elegance or splendour. The very extreme of art, of this nature, may, of itself, be of no great direct benefit, it is true, but it should be remembered, that the skill which produces these extraordinary fruits, in its road to the higher points of magnificence, produces all that embellishes life in the intermediate gradations.

In America, in the eagerness of gain, and with the contracted habits that a love of gain engenders, which by their own avidity, as is usual with the grosser passions, too often defeat their own ends, we overlook the vast importance of cultivating the fine arts, even in a pecuniary sense, to say nothing of the increased means of enjoying the very money that is so blindly pursued, which their possession entails. France is at this moment laying all christendom under contribution, simply by means of her taste. Italy, where the arts have flourished still longer, and where they have still more effectually penetrated society, would drive the English and French out of every market on earth, were the national energy at all equal to the national tastes. These things do not as exclusively belong to extreme luxury as they may at first seem. Science, skill of the nicest investigation, and great research, are all enlisted in their behalf; and, in time, implements of the most homely uses derive perfection, as by-plays, from the investigations consequent on the production of luxuries. It is true, that, by blending a certain amount of information with practice, as in the case of the American labourer, our wants find the means of furnishing their own supplies; but, apart from the fact that the man who makes a chair is not obliged to sit in it, and is therefore content to consult his profits merely, the impulses of practice are much aided by the accumulated knowledge of study. The influence that the arts of design have had on the French manufactures is incalculable. They have brought in the aid of chemistry, and mathematics, and a knowledge of antiquity; and we can trace the effects in the bronzes, the porcelain, the hangings, the chintzes, the silks, down to the very ribbands of the country. We shall in vain endeavour to compete with the great European nations, unless we make stronger efforts to cultivate the fine arts. Of what avails our beautiful glass, unless we know how to cut it; or of what great advantage, in the strife of industry, will be even the *skilful* glass-cutter, should he not also be the *tasteful* glass-cutter. It is true that classical forms and proportions are, as yet, of no great account among us, and the great mass of the American people still cling to their own uninstructed fancies, in preference to the outlines and proportions of the more approved models, and to those hues which art has demonstrated to be harmonious. This is the history of every society in its progress to perfection; and, cut off as we are from the rest of the civilized world, it is not to be expected that we are to make an extraordinary exception. But, while we may be satisfied with our own skill and taste, the happy lot of all ignorance, our customers will not have the same self-complacency, to induce them to become purchasers. We find this truth already. We beat all nations in the fabrication of common unstamped cottons. Were trade as free as some political economists pretend, we should drive all our competitors out of every market, as respects this one article. But the moment we attempt to print, or to meddle with that part of the business which requires taste, we find ourselves inferior to the Europeans, whose forms we are compelled to imitate, and of course to receive when no longer novel, and whose hues defy our art.

The wisest thing the United States could do, would be to appropriate thirty or forty millions to the formation of a marine, not to secure the coast, as our hen-roost statesmen are always preaching, but to keep, in our own hands, the control of our own fortunes, by rendering our enmity or friendship of so much account to Europe, that no power shall ever again dare trespass on our national rights:—and one of the next wisest measures, I honestly believe, would be to appropriate, at once, a million to the formation of a National Gallery, in which copies of the antique, antiques themselves, pictures, bronzes, *arabesques*, and other models of true taste, might be collected, before which the young aspirants for fame might study, and with which become imbued, as the preliminary step to an infusion of their merits into society. Without including the vast influence of such a cultivation on the manners, associations, intellects and habits of the people—an influence that can scarcely be appreciated too highly—fifty years would see the first cost returned fifty-fold, in the shape of the much beloved dollars. Will this happen? Not till men of enlightened minds—*statesmen*, instead of *political partizans*—are sent to Washington. It is the misfortune of America to lie so remote from the rest of the civilized world, as to feel little of the impulses of a noble competition, our rivalry commonly limiting itself to the vulgar exhibitions of individual vanity; and this the more to our disadvantage, as, denied access to the best models for even this humble species of contention, with the antagonists we are compelled to choose, victory is as bad as defeat.

One of the great impediments to a high class of improvement, in America, is the disposition to resent every intimation that we can be any better than we are at present. Few, perhaps no country, has ever endured so much evil-disposed and unmerited abuse as our own. It is not difficult to trace the reasons, and every American should meet it with a just and manly indignation. But, being deemed a nation of rogues, barbarous, and manifesting the vices of an ancestry of convicts, is a very different thing from standing at the head of civilization. This tendency to repel every suggestion of inferiority is one of the surest signs of provincial habits; it is exactly the feeling with which the resident of the village resents what he calls the airs of the town, and that which the inland trader brings with him among those whom he terms the "dandies" of the sea-board. In short, it is the jealousy of inferiority, on the exciting points, whatever may be the merits of its subject in other matters, and furnishes, of itself, the best possible proof that there is room for amendment. The French have a clever and pithy saying, that of—"*On peut tout dire, à un grand peuple.*" "One may tell all to a great nation."

*Note.*— Every one was telling me that I should find the country so altered, after an absence of eight years, that I should not know it. Altered, indeed, I found it; but not quite so evidently improved. It struck me that there was a vast expansion of mediocrity, that was well enough in itself, but which was so overwhelming as nearly to overshadow every thing that once stood prominent, as more excellent. This was, perhaps, no more than a natural consequence of the elasticity and growth of a young vigorous community, which, in its aggregate character, as in that of its individuals, must pass through youth to arrive at manhood. Still it was painful, and doubly so, to one coming from Europe. I saw the towns increased, more tawdry than ever, but absolutely with less real taste than they had in my youth. The art of painting alone appeared to me to have made any material advances in the right direction, if one excepts increase in wealth, and in the facilities to create wealth. The steam-boats were the only objects that approached magnificence, but while they had increased in show, they had less comfort and respectability. The taverns, as a whole, had deteriorated, though the three first I happened to enter might well compete with a very high class of European inns, viz. Head's, Barnum's, and Gadsby's.

# Letter XIV
## To James Stevenson, Esquire, Albany.

I cannot tell you whence the vulgar notions that we entertain of the French, which, with many other pernicious prejudices have made a part of our great inheritance from England, have been originally obtained. Certainly I have seen no thing, nor any person, after a long residence in the country, to serve as models to the flippant *marquis*, the overdressed courtiers, or the *petites-maîtresses* of the English dramatists. Even a French *perruquier* is quite as homely and plain a personage as an English or an American barber. But these Athenians grossly caricature themselves as well as their neighbours. Although Paris is pretty well garnished with English of all degrees, from the duke down, it has never yet been my luck to encounter an English dandy. Now and then one meets with a "*dresser*," a man who thinks more of his appearance than becomes his manhood, or than comports with good breeding; and occasionally a woman is seen who is a mere appendage to her attire, but, I am persuaded, that, as a rule, neither of these vulgar classes exists, among people of any condition, in either country. It is impossible for me to say what changes the revolution, and the wars, and the new notions, may have produced in France, but there is no sufficient reason for believing that the present cropped and fringeless, be-whiskered, and *laceless* generation of France, differs more from their be-wigged, belaced and powdered predecessors, than the men and women of any other country differ from their particular ancestors. Boys wore cock'd hats, and breeches, and swords, in America, previously to the revolution; and our immediate fathers flourished in scarlet coats, powder, ruffled fingers, and embroidered waistcoats.

The manners of the continent of Europe are more finished than those of England, and, while quiet and simplicity are the governing rules of good-breeding every where, even in unsophisticated America, this quiet and simplicity is more gracious and more graceful in France than in the neighbouring island. As yet, I see no other difference, in mere deportment, though there is abundance when one goes into the examination of character.

I have met with a good many people of the old court at Paris, and, though now and then there is a certain *roué* atmosphere about them, both men and women, as if too much time had been passed at Coblentz, they have generally, in other respects, been models of elegant demeanor. Usually they are simple, dignified, and yet extremely gracious — gracious without the appearance of affability, a quality that is almost always indicative of a consciousness of superiority. The predominant fault of manner here is too strong a hand in applying flattery, but this is as much the fault of the head as of breeding. The French are fond of hearing pleasant things. They say themselves that "a Frenchman goes into society to make himself agreeable, and an Englishman to make himself disagreeable," and the *dire* is not altogether without foundation in truth. I never met a Frenchman, in society here, who appeared to wish to enhance his importance by what are called "airs," though a coxcomb in feeling is an animal not altogether unknown to the natural history of Paris, nor is the zoological science of M. Cuvier indispensable to his discovery.

I shall probably surprise you with one of my opinions. I think the population of Paris, physically speaking, finer than that of London. Fine men and fine women are, by no means, as frequent, after allowing for the difference in whole numbers, in the French, as in the English capital, but, neither are there as many miserable, pallid and squalid objects. The French are a smaller race than the English, much smaller than the race of English gentlemen, so many of whom congregate at London; but the population of Paris has a sturdy, healthful look, that I do not think is by any means as general in London. In making this comparison, allowance must be made for the better dress of the English, and for their fogs, whose effect is to bleach the skin and to give a colour that has no necessary connexion with the springs of life, although the female portion of the population of Paris has probably as much colour as that of London. It might possibly be safer to say that the female population of Paris is finer that that of London, though I think on the whole the males may be included, also. I do not mean by this, that there is relatively as much female beauty in Paris as in London, for in this respect the latter has immeasurably the advantage, but, looks apart, that the *physique* of the French of Paris is superior to that of the English of London. The population of Paris is a favourable specimen of that of the kingdom, while that of London, Westminster expected, is not at all above the level of the entire country, if, indeed, it be as good.*

The very general notion, which exists in America, that the French are a slightly-built, airy people, and that their women, in particular, are thin and without *embonpoint*, is a most extraordinary one, for there is not a particle of foundation for it. The women of Paris are about as tall as the women of America, and could a fair sample of the two nations be placed in the scales, I have no doubt it would be found that the French women would outweigh the Americans in the proportion of six to five. Instead of being meagre, they are compactly built, with good busts, inclining to be full, and well limbed, as any one may see, who will take the trouble to walk the streets after a hard shower; for, as Falstaff told Prince Henry, "You are straight enough in the shoulders: you care not who sees your back." Indeed, I know no females to whom the opinion which we entertain of the French women may better apply than to our own, and yet I know none who are so generally well-looking.

The French are not a handsome nation. Personal beauty in either sex is rare: there is a want of simplicity, of repose, of dignity, and even of harmonious expression, what they themselves call *finesse*, in their countenances, and yet the liveliness of the eyes and the joyous character of their looks, render them agreeable. You are not to understand from this that great personal beauty does not exist in France, however, for there are so many exceptions to the rule, that they have occasionally made me hesitate about believing it a rule at all. The French quite often possess a feature in great perfection, that is very rare in England, where personal beauty is so common in both sexes. It is in the mouth, and particularly in the smile. Want of *finesse* about the mouth is a general European deficiency (the Italians have more of it than any other people I know), and it is as prevalent an advantage in America. But the races of Saxon root fail in the chin, which wants nobleness and

*This opinion remains the same in the writer, who, between the years 1806 and 1833, has been six times in London, and between the years 1826 and 1833, five times in Paris. In 1833, he left Paris for London, sailing for home from the latter place. A few days after his arrival he went to Washington, where, *during the session of Congress*, dress and air not considered, he thought he had never met so large a proportion of fine men, in any part of the world. He was particularly struck with their size, as was an American friend who was with him, and who had also passed many years abroad, having left Liverpool the same day the writer sailed from Portsmouth.

volume. Here, it is quite common to see profiles that would seem in their proper places on a Roman coin.

Although female beauty is not common in France, when it is found, it is usually of a very high order. The sweet, cherub-like, guileless expression, that belongs to the English female face, and through it, to the American, is hardly ever, perhaps never, met with here. The French countenance seldom conveys the idea of extreme, infantile, innocence. Even in the children there is a *manner*, which, while it does not absolutely convey an impression of an absence of the virtues, I think leaves less conviction of its belonging to the soul of the being, than the peculiar look I mean. One always sees *woman*; modest, amiable, *spirituel*, feminine and attractive, if you will, in a French girl; while one sometimes sees an *angel* in a young English or American face. I have no allusion now to religious education, or to religious feelings, which are quite as general in the sex, particularly the young of good families, under their characteristic distinctions, here, as anywhere else. In this particular, the great difference is, that in America it is religion, and in France it is infidelity, that is metaphysical.

There is a coquetish prettiness that is quite common in France, in which air and manner are mingled with a certain sauciness of expression, that is not easily described, but which, while it blends well enough with the style of the face, is rather pleasing than captivating. It marks the peculiar beauty of the *grisette*, who, with her little cap, hands stuck in the pockets of her apron, mincing walk, coquetish eye, and well-balanced head, is a creature perfectly *sui generis*. Such a girl is more like an actress imitating the character, than one is apt to imagine the character itself. I have met with imitators of these roguish beauties in a higher station, such as the wives and daughters of the industrious classes, as it is the fashion to call them here, and even among the banking community, but never among women of condition, whose deportment in France, whatever may be their morals, is usually marked by gentility of air, and a perfectly good tone of manner, always excepting that small taint of *rouéism* to which I have already alluded, and which certainly must have come from the camp and emigration.

The highest style of the French beauty is the classical. I cannot recall a more lovely picture, a finer union of the grand and the feminine, than the *Duchesse de* ———, in full dress, at a carnival ball, where she shone peerless among hundreds of the *élite* of Europe. I see her now, with her small, well-seated head; her large dark, brilliant eye riveted on the mazes of a *Polonaise*, danced in character; her hair, black as the raven's wing, clustering over a brow of ivory; her graceful form slightly inclining forward in delighted and graceful attention; her features just Grecian enough to be a model of delicate beauty, just Roman enough to be noble; her colour heightened to that of youth, by the heat of the room, and her costume, in which all the art of Paris was blended with a critical knowledge of the just and the becoming. And yet this woman was a grandmother!

The men of France have the same physical and the same conventional peculiarities as the women. They are short, but sturdy. Including all France, for there is a material difference in this respect between the north and the south, I should think the average stature of the French *men*, (not women) to be quite an inch and a half below the average stature of America, and possibly two inches. At home, I did not find myself greatly above the medium height, and in a crowd I was always compelled to stand on tip-toe to look over the heads of those around me; whereas, here, I am evidently *un grand*, and can see across the *Champs-Elysées*, without any difficulty. You may remember that I stand, as near as may be, to five feet ten; it follows that five feet ten is rather a tall man in France. You are not to suppose, however, that there are not occasionally men of great stature in this country. One of the largest men I have ever seen, appears daily in the garden of the *Tuileries*, and I am told he is a Frenchman of one of the north-eastern provinces. That part of the kingdom is German, rather than French, however, and the population still retain most of the peculiarities of their origin.

The army has a look of service and activity, rather than of force. I should think it more formidable by its manœuvres than its charges. Indeed, the tactics of Napoleon, who used the legs of his troops more than their muskets, aiming at concentrating masses on important points, goes to show that he depended on alertness instead of *bottom*. This is just the quality that would be most likely to prevail against your methodical, slow-thinking, and slow-moving German, and I make no question, the short, sturdy, nimble legs of the little warriors of this country have gained many a field.

A general officer, himself a six-footer, told me, lately, that they had found the tall men of very little use in the field, from their inability to endure the fatigues of a campaign. When armies shall march on rail roads, and manœuvre by steam, the grenadiers will come in play again; but, as it is, the French are admirably adapted by their *physique*, to run the career that history has given them. The Romans resembled them in this respect, Cicero admitting that many people excelled them in size, strength, beauty, and even learning, though he claimed a superiority for his countrymen, on the score of love of country and a reverence for the gods. The French are certainly patriotic enough, though their reverence for the gods may possibly be questioned.

The regiments of the guards, the heavy cavalry, and the artillery are all filled with men chosen with some care. These troops would, I think, form about an average American army, on the score of size. The battalions of the line receive the rest. As much attention is bestowed in adapting the duty to the physique, and entire corps are composed of men of as nearly as possible the same physical force, some of the regiments certainly make but an indifferent figure, as to dimensions, while others appear particularly well. Still, if not overworked, I should think these short men would do good service. I think I have seen one or two regiments, in which the average height has not exceeded five feet three inches. The chances of not being hit in such a corps are worth something, for the proportion, compared to the chances in a corps of six-footers, is as sixty-three to seventy-two, or is one-eighth in favour of the Lilliputians. I believe the rule for retreating is when one-third of the men are *hors de combat*. Now, supposing a regiment of three thousand grenadiers would be obliged to retire with a loss of one thousand men, the little fellows, under the same fire, should have, at the same time, two thousand one hundred and thirty-seven sound men left, and of course, unless bullied out of it, they ought to gain the day.

# Letter XV
## To James E. De Kay, Esquire.

I t appears to be the melancholy lot of humanity, that every institution which ingenuity can devise shall be perverted to an end
different from the legitimate. If we plan a democracy, the craven
wretch who, in a despotism, would be the parasite of a monarch, heads
us off, and gets the best of it under the pretence of extreme love for the
people; if we flatter ourselves that by throwing power into the hands of
the rich and noble, it is put beyond the temptation to abuse it, we soon
discover that rich is a term of convention, no one thinking he has
enough until he has all, and that nobility of station has no absolute
connexion with nobleness of spirit or of conduct; if we confide all to
one, indolence, favouritism, and indeed the impossibility of supervision
throw us again into the hands of the demagogue, in his new, or rather
true character, of a courtier. So it is with life; in politics, religion, arms,
arts and letters, yea, even the republic of letters, as it is called, is the
prey of schemers and parasites, and things *in fact*, are very different
from things *as they seem to be.*

"In the seventeen years that I have been a married man," said
Captain ——— of the British navy, "I have passed but seventeen
months with my wife and family." "But, now there is peace, you will
pass a few years quietly in America, to look after your affairs," said I,
by way of awkward condolence. "No, indeed; I shall return to England
as soon as possible, to make up for lost time. I have been kept so much
at sea, that they have forgotten me at home, and duty to my children requires that I should be on the spot." In the simplicity of my
heart, I thought this strange, and yet nothing could be more true.
Captain ——— was a scion of the English aristocracy, and looked to his
sword for his fortune. Storms, fagging, cruising, all were of small avail
compared to interest at the admiralty, and so it is with all things else,
whether in Europe or America. The man who really gains the victory,
is lucky, indeed, if he obtain the meed of his skill and valour. You may
be curious to know of what all this is *à propos?* To be frank with you, I
have visited the French Academy; *ces quarante qui ont l'esprit comme*

*quatre*, and, have come away fully impressed with the vanity of human things!

The occasion was the reception of two or three new members, when, according to a settled usage, the successful candidates pronounced eulogies on their predecessors. You may be curious to know what impression the assembled genius of France produced on a stranger from the western world. I can only answer, none. The academy of the sciences can scarcely ever be less than distinguished in such a nation, but when I came to look about me, and to inquire after the purely literary men, I was forcibly struck with the feebleness of the catalogue of names. Not one in five was at all known to me, and very few even of those who were, could properly be classed among the celebrated writers of the day. As France has many very clever men who were not on the list, I was desirous of knowing the reason, and then learned that intrigue, court-favour, and *"log-rolling,"* to use a quaint American term, made members of the academy as well as members of the cabinet. A moment's reflection might have told me it could not well be otherwise. It would be so in America, if we were burthened with an academy; it *is* so as respects collegiate honours; and what reason is there for supposing it should not be so in a country so notoriously addicted to intrigue as France?

One ought not to be the dupe of these things. There are a few great names, distinguished by common consent, whose claims it is necessary to respect. These men form the front of every honorary institution; if there are to be knights and nobles, and academicians, they must be of the number; not that such distinctions are necessary to them, but that they are necessary to the distinctions; after which the *oi polloi* are enrolled as they can find interest. Something very like an admission of this is contained in an inscription on the statue of *Molière*, which stands in the vestibule of the hall of the Academy, which frankly says, "though we are not necessary to your glory, you are necessary to ours." He was excluded from the forty, by intrigue, on account of his profession being that of a player. Shakspeare, himself, would have fared no better. Now, fancy a country in which there was a club of select authors, that should refuse to enrol the name of William Shakspeare on their list!

The sitting was well attended, and I dare say the addresses were not amiss, though there is something exceedingly tiresome in one of these eulogies, that is perpetrated by *malice prepense*. The audience applauded very much, after the fashion of those impromptus which are made *à loisir*, and I could not but fancy that a good portion of the assembly began to think the academy was what the cockneys call a *rum* place, before they heard the last of it. We had a poem by *Comte Daru*, to which I confess I did not listen, notwithstanding my personal respect for the distinguished writer, simply because I was most heartily wearied before he began, and because I can never make any thing of French poetry, in the academy or out of it.

It would be unjust to speak lightly of any part of the French academy, without a passing remark in honour of those sections of it, to which honour is due. In these sections may be included, I think, that of the arts, as well as that of the sciences. The number of respectable artists that exist in this country is perfectly astonishing. The *connoisseurs*, I believe, dispute the merits of the school, and ignorant as I am, in such matters, I can myself see that there is a prevalent disposition, both in statuary and painting, to sacrifice simplicity to details, and that the theatrical is sometimes mistaken for the grand; but, after admitting both these faults, and some defects in colouring, there still remains a sufficient accumulation of merit, to create wonder in one, like myself, who has not had previous opportunities of ascertaining the affluence of a great nation in this respect.

As regards the scientific attainments of the French, it is unnecessary to say anything, though I believe you will admit that they ought at least to have the effect of counteracting some of the prejudices about dancing-masters, *petits-maîtres*, and *perruquiers*, that have descended to us, through English novels and plays. Such a man as La Place, alone, is sufficient to redeem an entire people from these imputations. The very sight of one of his demonstrations will give common men, like ourselves, headaches, and you will remember that having successfully got through one of the toughest of them, he felicitated himself that there was but one other man living who could comprehend it, now it was made.

What a noble gift would it have been to his fellow-creatures, had some competent follower of La Place bestowed on them a comprehensive but popular compend of the leading astronomical facts, to be used as one of the most ordinary school books. Apart from the general usefulness of this peculiar species of knowledge, and the chances that, by thus popularizing the study, sparks might be struck from the spirit of some dormant Newton, I know no inquiry that has so strong a tendency to raise the mind from the gross and vulgar pursuits of the world, to a contemplation of the power and designs of God. It has often happened to me, when, filled with wonder and respect for the daring and art of man, I have been wandering through the gorgeous halls of some palace, or other public edifice, that an orrery or a diagram of the planetary system has met my eye, and recalled me, in a moment, from the consideration of art, and its intrinsic feebleness, to that of the sublimity of nature. At such times, this globe has appeared so insignificant, in comparison with the mighty system of which it forms so secondary a part, that I have felt a truly philosophical indifference, not to give it a better term, for all it contained. Admiration of human powers, as connected with the objects around me, has been lost in admiration of the mysterious spirit which could penetrate the remote and sublime secrets of the science; and, on no other occasions, have I felt so profound a conviction of my own isolated insignificance, or so lively a perception of the stupendous majesty of the Deity.

Passing by the common and conceded facts of the dimensions of the planets, and the extent of their orbits, what thoughts are awakened by the suggestion that the fixed stars are the centres of other solar systems, and that the eccentric comets are links to connect them all, in one great and harmonious design! The astronomers tell us, that some of these comets have no visible nucleuses, that the fixed stars are seen through their apparent densest parts, and that they can be nothing but luminous gases; while, on the other hand, others do betray dark compact bodies of more solid matter. Fixed stars unaccountably disappear, as if suddenly struck out of their places. Now, we know that ærolites are formed in the atmosphere, by a natural process, and descend in masses of pure iron. Why may not the matter of one globe, dispersed into its elements by the fusion of its consummation, reassemble, in the shape of comets, gaseous at first, and slowly increasing and condensing in the form of solid matter, varying in their course as they acquire the property of attraction, until they finally settle into new and regular planetary orbits, by the power of their own masses, thus establishing a regular reproduction of worlds to meet the waste of eternity? Were the earth dissolved into gases, by fusion, what would become of its satellite, the moon? Might not the principles of our planet, thus volatilized, yield to its nearer attraction, assemble around that orb, which, losing its governing influence, should be left to wander in infinite space, subject to a new but eccentric law of gravity, until finally reduced again within the limits of some new system? How know we that such is not the origin of comets?

Many astronomers have believed that the solar system, in company with thousands of other systems, revolves around a common centre, in orbits so vast as to defy computation, and a religious sentiment might well suggest that this centre of the universe is the throne of the Most High. Here we may fancy the Deity seated in power, and controlling, by his will, the movements of worlds, directing each to the completion of his own mysterious and benevolent designs.

It certainly might be dangerous to push our speculations too far, but there can be no risk in familiarizing men to consider the omnipotence of God, and to feel their own comparative insignificance. What ideas of vastness are obtained by a knowledge of the fact that there exist stars in the firmament, which ordinary telescopes show us only as single bodies, but which, on examination by using reflectors of a higher power, are found to be clusters of orbs—clusters of worlds—or clusters of suns! These, again, are found to be *binary* stars, or two stars revolving round each other, while they are thought, at the same time, to revolve around their central sun, and accompanied by this again, probably, to revolve around the great common centre of all!

But, in the words of the quaint old song, I must cry "Holla! my fancy, whither dost thou go?" Before taking leave of the stars altogether, however, I will add that the French, and I believe all Europe, with the exception of England, follow the natural order of time, in counting the seasons. Thus the spring commences with the vernal equinox, and the autumn with the autumnal. This division of the year leaves nearly the whole of March as a winter month, June as a spring month, and September as belonging to the summer. No general division of the seasons can suit all latitudes; but the equinoxes certainly suggest the only two great events of the year, that equally affect the entire sphere. Had the old method of computing time continued, the seasons would gradually have made the circle of the months, until their order was reversed, as they are now known to be in the northern and southern hemispheres.

Quitting the Academy, which, with its schools of the classical and the romantic, has tempted me to a higher flight than I could have believed possible, let us descend to the theatres of Paris. Talma was still playing last year, when we arrived, and as in the case of repentance, I put off a visit to the *Théâtre-Français,* with a full determination to go, because it might be made at any time. In the mean while, he fell ill and died, and it never was my good fortune to see that great actor. Mademoiselle Mars I have seen, and, certainly, in her line of characters, I have never beheld her equal. Indeed, it is scarcely possible to conceive of a purer, more severe, more faultless, and yet more poetical representation of common nature, than that which characterizes her art. Her acting has all the finish of high breeding, with just as much feeling as is necessary to keep alive the illusion. As for rant, there is not as much about her whole system, as would serve a common English, or American actress, for a single "length."

To be frank with you, so great is the superiority of the French actors, in *vaudevilles*, the light opera, and genteel comedy, that I fear I have lost my taste for the English stage. Of tragedy I say nothing, for I cannot enter into the poetry of the country at all, but, in all below it, these people, to my taste, are immeasurably our superiors; and by *ours*, you know I include the English stage. The different lines here, are divided among the different theatres, so that if you wish to laugh, you can go to the *Variétés;* to weep, to the *Théâtre-Français;* or, to gape, to the *Odéon*. At the *Porte St. Martin*, one finds vigorous touches of national character, and at the *Gymnase*, the fashionable place of resort, just at this moment, national traits polished by convention. Besides these, there are many other theatres, not one of which, in its way, can be called less than tolerable.

One can say but little in favour of the morals of too many of the pieces represented here. In this particular there is a strange obliquity of reason, arising out of habitual exaggeration of feeling, that really seems to disqualify most of the women, even, from perceiving what is monstrous, provided it be sentimental and touching. I was particularly advised, to go to the *Théâtre de Madame* to see a certain piece, by a *coterie* of very amiable women, whom I met the following night at a house where we all regularly resorted, once a week. On entering, they eagerly inquired if "I had not been charmed, fascinated; if any thing could be better played, or more touching?" Better played it could not easily be, but I had been so shocked with the moral of the piece, that I could scarcely admire the acting. "The moral! This was the first time they had heard it questioned." I was obliged to explain. A certain person had been left the protector of a friend's daughter, then an infant. He had the child educated as his sister, and she grew to be a woman, ignorant of her real origin. In the mean time, she has offers of marriage, all of which she unaccountably refuses. In fine, she was secretly cherishing a passion for her guardian *and supposed brother*; an explanation is had, they marry, and the piece closes. I objected to the probability of a well educated young woman's falling in love with a man old enough to be selected as her guardian, when she was an infant, and against whom there existed the trifling objection of his being her own brother. "But, he was *not* her brother—not even a relative." "True; but she *believed* him to be her brother." "And nature—do you count nature as nothing—a *secret sentiment* told her he was not her brother." "And use, and education, and an *open sentiment*, and all the world, told her he was. Such a woman was guilty of a revolting indelicacy and a heinous crime, and no exaggerated representation of love, a passion of great purity in itself, can ever do away with the shocking realities of such a case."

I found no one to agree with me. He was *not* her brother, and though his tongue, and all around her, told her he was, her heart, that infallible guide, told her the truth. What more could any reasonable man ask?

It was *à propos* of this play, and of my objection to this particular feature of it, that an exceedingly clever French woman laughingly told me she understood there was no such thing as love in America. That a people, of manners as artifical as the French, should suppose that others, under the influence of the cold formal exterior which the puritans have entailed on so large a portion of the republic, were without strong feeling, is not altogether as irrational as may at first appear. Art, in ordinary deportment, is both cause and effect. That which we habitually affect to be, gets, in the end, to be so incorporated with our natural propensities, as to form a part of the real man. We all know that by discipline we can get the mastery of our strongest passions, and, on the other hand, by yielding to them and encouraging them, that they soon get the mastery over us. Thus do a highly artificial people, fond of, and always seeking, high excitement, come, in time, to feel it, artificially, as it were, by natural impulses.

I have mentioned the anecdote of the play, because I think it characteristic of a tone of feeling that is quite prevalent among a large class of the French, though I am far from saying there is not a class who would, at once, see the grave sacrifice of principle that is involved, in building up the sentiments of a fiction on such a foundation of animal instinct. I find, on recollection, however, that Miss Lee, in one of her Canterbury Tales, has made the love of her plot hinge on a very similar incident. Surely, she must have been under the influence of some of the German monstrosities that were so much in vogue, about the time she wrote, for even Juvenal would scarcely have imagined any thing worse, as the subject of his satire.

You will get a better idea of the sentimentalism that more or less influences the tastes of this country, however, if I tell you that the ladies of the *coterie*, in which the the remarks on the amorous sister were made, once gravely discussed, in my presence, the question whether Madame de Stael was right or wrong, in causing *Corinne* to go through certain sentimental *experiences*, as our canters call it at home, on a clouded day, instead of choosing one on which the sun was bright; or, *vice versâ*; for I really forget whether it was on the "windy side" of sensibility, or not, that the daughter of Necker was supposed to have erred.

The first feeling is that of surprise at finding a people so artificial in their ordinary deportment, so chaste and free from exaggeration in their scenic representations of life. But reflection will show us that all finish has the effect of bringing us within the compass of severe laws, and that the high taste which results from cultivation repudiates all excess of mere manner. The simple fact is, that an educated Frenchman is a great actor all the while, and that when he goes on the stage, he has much less to do, to be perfect, than an Englishman who has drilled himself into coldness, or an American who looks upon strong expressions of feeling as affectation. When the two latter commence the business of playing assumed parts, they consider it as a new occupation, and go at it so much in earnest, that every body sees they are acting.*

You will remember, I say nothing in favour of the French tragic representations. When a great and an intellectual nation, like France, unites to applaud images and sentiments, that are communicated through their own peculiar forms of speech, it becomes a stranger to distrust his own knowledge, rather than their taste. I dare say that were I more accustomed to the language, I might enjoy Corneille and Racine, and even Voltaire, for I can now greatly enjoy Molière; but, to be honest in the matter, all reciters of heroic French poetry appear to me to depend on a pompous declamation, to compensate for the

---

* Mr. Mathews and Mr. Power were the nearest to the neat acting of France of any male English performers the writer ever saw. The first sometimes permitted himself to be led astray, by the caricatures he was required to represent, and by the tastes of his audience; but the latter, so far as the writer has seen him, appears determined to be chaste, come what, come will.

poverty of the idioms, and the want of nobleness in the expressions. I never heard any one, poet or actor, he who read his own verses, or he who repeated those of others, who did not appear to mouth, and all their tragic playing has had the air of being on stilts. Napoleon has said from the sublime to the ridiculous it is but a step. This is much truer in France than in most other countries, for the sublime is commonly so sublimated, that it will admit of no great increase. Racine, in a most touching scene, makes one of his heroic characters offer to wipe off the tears of a heroine lest they should discolour her *rouge!* I had a classmate at college, who was so very ultra courtly in his language, that he never forgot to say Mr. Julius Cæsar, and Mr. Homer.

There exists a perfect mania for letters throughout Europe, in this "piping time of peace." Statesmen, soldiers, peers, princes and kings, hardly think themselves *illustrated*, until each has produced his book. The world never before saw a tithe of the names of people of condition, figuring in the catalogues of its writers. "Some thinks he writes Cinna; he owns to Panurge," applies to half the people one meets in society. I was at dinner lately, given by the Marquis de [Marbois], when the table was filled with peers, generals, ex-ministers, ex-ambassadors, natural-ists, philosophers and statesmen of all degrees. Casting my eyes round the circle, I was struck with the singular prevalence of the *cacoëthes scribendi*, among so many men of different educations, antecedents, and pursuits. There was a soldier present who had written on taste, a politician on the art of war, a *diplomate* who had dabbled in poetry, and a jurist who pretended to enlighten the world in ethics. It was the drollest assemblage in the world, and suggested many queer associa-tions, for, I believe, the only man at table, who had not dealt in ink, was an old Lieutenant-General, who sat by me, and who, when I alluded to the circumstance, strongly felicitated himself that he had escaped the mania of the age, as it was an *illustration* of itself. Among the *convives* were Cuvier, Villemain, Daru, and several others who are almost as well known to science and letters.

Half the voluntary visits I receive, are preceded by a volume of some sort or other, as a token of my new acquaintance being a regularly initiated member of the fraternity of the quill. In two or three instances, I have been surprised at subsequently discovering that the regular profession of the writer is arms, or some other pursuit, in which one would scarcely anticipate so strong a devotion to letters. In short, such is the actual state of opinion in Europe, that one is hardly satisfied with any amount, or any quality of glory, until it is consummated by that of having written a book. Napoleon closed his career with the quill, and his successor was hardly on his throne, before he began to publish. The principal officers of the Empire, and *émigrés* without number, have fairly set to work as so many disinterested historians, and even a lady, who, by way of abbreviation, is called "The Widow of the Grand Army," is giving us regularly volumes, whose eccentricities and periodicity, as the astronomers say, can be reduced to known laws, by the use of figures.

In the middle ages golden spurs were the object of every man's ambition. Without them, neither wealth, nor birth, nor power was properly esteemed; and, at the present time, passing from the lance to the pen, from the casque and shield, to the ink-pot and fool's cap, we all seek a passport from the order of Letters. Does this augur good or evil, for the world? The public press of France is conducted with great spirit and talents, on all sides. It has few points in common with our own, beyond the mere fact of its general character. In America, a single literary man, putting the best face on it, enters into a compact with some person of practical knowledge, a printer, perhaps, and together they establish a newspaper, the mechanical part of which is confided to the care of the latter partner, and the intellectual to the former. In the country, half the time, the editor is no other than the printer himself, the division of labour not having yet reached even this important branch of industry. But looking to the papers that are published in the towns, one man of letters is a luxury about an American print. There are a few instances in which there are two, or three; but, generally, the subordinates are little more than scissors-men. Now, it must be apparent, at a glance, that no one individual can keep up the character of a daily print, of any magnitude; the drain on his knowledge and other resources being too great. This, I take it, is the simple reason why the press of America ranks no higher than it does. The business is too much divided; too much is required, and this, too, in a country where matters of grave import are of rare occurence, and in which the chief interests are centered in the vulgar concerns of mere party politics, with little or no connection with great measures, or great principles. You have only to fancy the superior importance that attaches to the views of powerful monarchs, the secret intrigues of courts, on whose results, perhaps, depend the fortunes of Christendom, and the serious and radical principles that are dependent on the great changes of systems that are silently working their way, in this part of the world, and which involve material alterations in the very structure of society, to get an idea of how much more interest a European journal, *ceteris paribus*, must be, compared to an American journal, by the nature of its facts alone. It is true that we get a portion of these facts, as light finally arrives from the remoter stars, but mutilated, and necessarily shorn of much of their interest, by their want of importance to our own country. I had been in Europe some time, before I could fully comprehend the reason why I was ignorant of so many minor points of its political history, for, from boyhood up, I had been an attentive reader of all that touched this part of the world, as it appeared in our prints. By dint of inquiry, however, I believe I have come at the fact. The winds are by no means as regular as the daily prints; and it frequently happens, especially in the winter and spring months, that five or six packets arrive nearly together, bringing with them the condensed intelligence of as many weeks. Now, newspaper finders notoriously seek the latest news, and in the hurry and confusion of reading and selecting, and bringing out, to meet the wants of the day, many of the connecting links are lost, readers get imperfect notions of men and things, and, from a want of a complete understanding of the matter, the mind gives up, without regret, the little and unsatisfactory knowledge it had so casually obtained. I take it, this is a principal cause of the many false notions that exist among us, on the subject of Europe and its events.

In France, a paper is established by a regular subscription of capital; a principal editor is selected, and he is commonly supported, in the case of a leading journal, by four or five paid assistants. In addition to this formidable corps, many of the most distinguished men of France are known to contribute freely to the columns of the prints in the interest of their cause.

The laws of France compel a journal that has admitted any statement involving facts, concerning an individual, to publish his reply, that the antidote may meet the poison. This is a regulation that we might adopt with great advantage to truth and the character of the country.

There is not, at this moment, within my knowledge, a single critical literary journal, of received authority, in all France. This is a species of literature to which the French pay but little attention, just now, although many of the leading daily prints contain articles on the principal works, as they appear.

By the little that has come under my observation, I should say the fraudulent and disgusting system of puffing and of abusing, as interest or pique dictates, is even carried to a greater length in France, than it is in either England or America. The following anecdote, which relates to myself, may give you some notion of the *modus operandi.*

All the works I had written previously to coming to Europe, had been taken from the English editions, and translated, appearing simultaneously with their originals. Having an intention to cause a new book to be printed in English, in Paris, for the sake of reading the proofs, the necessity was felt of getting some control over the translation, lest, profiting by the interval necessary to send the sheets home to be reprinted, it might appear as the original book. I knew that the sheets of previous books had been purchased in England, and I accordingly sent a proposition to the publishers, that the next bargain should be made with me. Under the impression that an author's price would be asked, they took the alarm, and made difficulties. Finding me firm, and indisposed to yield to some threats of doing as they pleased, the matter was suspended for a few days. Just at this moment, I received, through the post, a single number of an obscure newspaper, whose existence, until then, was quite unknown to me. Surprised at such an attention, I was curious to know the contents. The journal contained an article on my merits and demerits as a writer, the latter being treated with a good deal of freedom. When one gets a paper, in this manner, containing abuse of himself, he is pretty safe in believing its opinions dishonest. But I had even better evidence than common, in this particular case, for I happened to be extolled for the manner in which I had treated the character of Franklin, a personage whose name even had never appeared in anything I had written. This, of course, settled the character of the critique, and the next time I saw the individual who had acted as agent in the negotiation just mentioned, I gave him the paper, and told him I was half disposed to raise my price on account of the pitiful manœuvre it contained. We had already come to terms, the publishers finding that the price was little more than nominal, and the answer was a virtual conclusion that the article was intended to affect my estimate of the value of the intended work in France, and to bring me under subjection to the critics.*

* The writer suffers this anecdote to stand as it was written nine years since; but since his return home, he has discovered that we are in no degree behind the French in the

I apprehend that few books are brought before the public in France, dependent only on their intrinsic merits, and the system of intrigue, which predominates in every thing, is as active in this as in other interests.

In France, a book that penetrates to the provinces, may be said to be popular; and, as for a book coming *from* the provinces, it is almost unheard of. The despotism of the trade, on this point, is unyielding. Paris appears to deem itself the arbiter in all matters of taste and literature, and it is almost as unlikely that a new fashion should come from Lyons, or Bordeaux, or Marseilles, as that a new work should be received with favour, that was published in either of those towns. The approbation of Paris is indispensable, and the publishers of the capital, assisted by their paid corps of puffers and detractors, are sufficiently powerful to prevent that potent public, to whom all affect to defer, from judging for itself.

We have lately had a proof, here, of the unwillingness of the Parisians to permit others to decide for them, in any thing relating to taste, in a case that refers to us Americans. Madame Malibran arrived from America a few months since. In Europe she was unknown, but the great name of her father stood her in stead. Unluckily, it was whispered that she had met with great success in America. America! and this, too, in conjunction with music and the opera! The poor woman was compelled to appear under the disadvantage of having brought an American reputation with her, and, seriously, this single fact went nigh to destroy her fortunes. Those wretches who, as Coleridge expresses it, are "animalculæ, who live by feeding on the body of genius," affected to be displeased, and the public hesitated, at their suggestions, about accepting an artist from the "colonies," as they still have the audacity to call the great Republic. I have no means of knowing what sacrifices were made to the petty tyrants of the press, before this woman, who has the talents necessary to raise her to the summit of her profession, was enabled to gain the favour of a *"generous and discerning public"*!

---

corruption and frauds that render the pursuits of a writer one of the most humiliating and revolting in which a man of any pride of character can engage, unless he resolutely maintains his independence, a temerity that is certain to be resented by all those, who, unequal to going alone in the paths of literature, seek their ends by clinging to those who can, either as pirates or robbers.

# Letter XVI
To James Stevenson, Esquire, Albany.

W e have been the residents of a French village ever since the first of June, and it is now drawing to the close of October. We had already passed the greater part of a summer, an entire autumn, winter and spring, within the walls of Paris, and then we thought we might indulge our tastes a little, by retreating to the fields, to catch a glimpse of country life. You will smile when I add that we are only a league from the *Barrière de Clichy*. This is the reason I have not before spoken of the removal, for we are in town three or four times every week, and never miss an occasion, when there is any thing to be seen. I shall now proceed, however, to let you into the secret of our actual situation.

I passed the month of May examining the environs of the capital in quest of a house. As this was an agreeable occupation, we were in no hurry, but having set up my *cabriolet*, we killed two birds with one stone, by making ourselves familiarly acquainted with nearly every village, or hamlet, within three leagues of Paris, a distance beyond which I did not wish to go.

On the side of St. Cloud, which embraces Passy, Auteuil, and all the places that encircle the *Bois de Boulogne*, the Hyde Park of Paris, there are very many pleasant residences, but, from one cause or another, no one suited us, exactly, and we finally took a house in the village of St. Ouen, the Runnymeade of France. When Louis XVIII. came, in 1814, to his capital, in the rear of the allies, he stopped for a few days at St. Ouen, a league from the barriers, where there was a small *château* that was the property of the crown. Here he was met by M. de Talleyrand and others, and hence he issued the celebrated charter, that is to render France, forevermore, a constitutional country.

The *château* has since been razed, and a pavilion erected in its place, which has been presented to the Comtesse [du Cayla], a lady, who, reversing the ordinary lot of courtiers, is said to cause majesty to live in the sunshine of *her* smiles. What an appropriate and encouraging monument to rear on the birth-place of French liberty! At the opposite extremity of the village, is another considerable house, that was once the dwelling of M. Necker, and is now the property and country residence of M. Ternaux, or the *Baron* Ternaux, if it were polite to style him thus, the most celebrated manufacturer of France. I say polite, for the mere *fanfaronnade* of nobility is little in vogue here. The wags tell a story of some one, who was formally announced as "*Mons. le Marquis d'un tel,*" turning short round on the servant, and exclaiming with indignation, "*Marquis, toi-même!*" But this story savours of the Bonapartists, for, as the Emperor created neither *marquis* nor *vicomtes*, there was a sort of affectation of assuming these titles at the restoration, as proofs of belonging to the old *régime*.

St. Ouen is a cluster of small, mean, stone houses, stretched along the right bank of the Seine, which, after making a circuit of near twenty miles, winds round so close to the town, again, that they are actually constructing a basin, near the village, for the use of the capital; it being easier to wheel articles from this point to Paris, than to contend with the current and to thread its shoals. In addition to the two houses named, however, it has six or eight respectable abodes between the street and the river, one of which is our own.

This place became a princely residence about the year 1300, since which time it has been more or less frequented as such, down to the 4th June, 1814, the date of the memorable charter.* Madame de Pompadour possessed the *château* in 1745, so you see it has been "dust to dust" with this place, as with all that is frail.

The village of St. Ouen, small, dirty, crowded and unsavoury as it is, has a *place*, like every other French village. When we drove into it, to look at the house, I confess to having laughed outright, at the idea of inhabiting such a hole. Two large *portes cochères*, however, opened from the square, and we were admitted, through the best-looking of the two,

---

*The *château* of St. Ouen, rather less than two centuries since, passed into the possession of the *Duc de Gesvre*. Dulaure gives the following, a part of a letter from this nobleman, as a specimen of the education of a *Duc*, in the seventeenth century. "*Monsieur, me trouvant obligé de randre une bonne party de largan que mais enfant ont pris de peuis qu'il sont au campane, monsieur, cela moblige a vous suplier tres humblemant monsieur de me faire la grasse de commander monsieur quant il vous plera que lon me pay la capitenery de Monsaux monsieur vous asseurant que vous mobligeres fort sansiblement monsieur comme ausy de me croire avec toute sorte de respec, etc.*" This beats Jack Cade, out and out. The great connétable *Anne de Montmorency* could not write his name, and, as his signature became necessary, his secretary stood over his shoulder to tell him when he had made enough *pieds de mouche* to answer the purpose.

into a spacious and an extremely neat court. On one side of the gate was a lodge for a porter, and, on the other, a building to contain gardener's tools, plants, &c. The walls that separate it from the square and the adjoining gardens, are twelve or fourteen feet high, and once within them, the world is completely excluded. The width of the grounds does not exceed a hundred and fifty feet; the length, the form being that of a parallelogram, may be three hundred, or a little more; and yet in these narrow limits, which are planted *à l'Anglaise*, so well is every thing contrived, that we appear to have abundance of room. The garden terminates in a terrace that overhangs the river, and, from this point, the eye ranges over a wide extent of beautiful plain, that is bounded by fine bold hills which are teeming with gray villages and *bourgs.*

The house is of stone, and not without elegance. It may be ninety feet in length, by some forty in width. The entrance is into a vestibule, which has the offices on the right, and the great staircase on the left. The principal *salon* is in front. This is a good room, near thirty feet long, fifteen or sixteen high, and has three good windows, that open on the garden. The billiard-room communicates on one side, and the *salle à manger* on the other; next the latter come the offices again, and next the billiard-room is a very pretty little *boudoir.* Up stairs, are suites of bed-rooms and dressing-rooms; every thing is neat, and the house is in excellent order, and well furnished for a country residence. Now, all this I get at a hundred dollars a month, for the five summer months. There are also a carriage house, and stabling for three horses. The gardener and porter are paid by the proprietor. The village, however, is not in much request, and the rent is thought to be low.

One of the great advantages that is enjoyed by a residence in Europe, are the facilities of this nature. Furnished apartments, or furnished houses, can be had in almost every town of any size; and, owning your own linen and plate, nearly every other necessary is found you. It is true, that one sometimes misses comforts to which he has been accustomed in his own house; but, in France, many little things are found, it is not usual to meet with elsewhere. Thus, no principal bed-room is considered properly furnished in a good house, without a handsome secretary, and a bureau. These two articles are as much matters of course, as are the eternal two rooms and folding doors, in New York.

This, then, has been our *Tusculum* since June. M. Ternaux enlivens the scene, occasionally, by a dinner; and he has politely granted us permission to walk in his grounds, which are extensive and well laid out, for the old French style. We have a neighbour on our left, name unknown, who gives suppers in his garden, and concerts that really are worthy of the grand opera. Occasionally, we get a song, in a female voice, that rivals the best of Madame Malibran's. On our right lives a staid widow, whose establishment is as tranquil as our own.

One of our great amusements is to watch the *living* life on the river,—there is no *still* life in France. All the washerwomen of the village assemble, three days in the week, beneath our terrace, and a merrier set of *grisettes* is not to be found in the neighbourhood of Paris. They chat, and joke, and splash, and scream from morning to night, lightening the toil by never-ceasing good humour. Occasionally an enormous scow-like barge is hauled up against the current, by stout horses, loaded to the water's edge, or one, without freight, comes dropping down the stream, nearly filling the whole river as it floats broad-side to. There are three or four islands opposite, and, now and then, a small boat is seen paddling among them. We have even tried *punting* ourselves, but the amusement was soon exhausted.

Sunday is a great day with us, for then the shore is lined with Parisians, as thoroughly cockney as if Bow-bells could be heard in the *quartier Montmartre!* These good people visit us, in all sorts of ways; some on donkies, some in *cabriolets,* some in *fiacres,* and, by far the larger portion on foot. They are perfectly inoffensive and unobtrusive, being, in this respect, just as unlike an American inroad from a town, as can well be. These crowds pass vineyards on their way to us, unprotected by any fences. This point in the French character, however, about which so much has been said to our disadvantage, as well as to that of the English, is subject to some explanation. The statues, promenades, gardens, &c. &c. are, almost without exception, guarded by sentinels; and then there are agents of the police, in common clothes, scattered through the towns, in such numbers as to make depredations hazardous. In the country each *commune* has one, or more, *gardes champêtres,* whose sole business it is to detect and arrest trespassers. When to these are added the *gendarmes à pied* and *à cheval,* who are constantly in motion, one sees that the risk of breaking the laws, is attended with more hazard here, than with us. There is no doubt, on the other hand, that the training and habits, produced by such a system of watchfulness, enter so far into the character of the people, that they cease to think of doing that which is so strenuously denied them.

Some of our visitors make their appearance in a very quaint style. I

met a party the other day, among whom the following family arrangement had obtained. The man was mounted on a donkey, with his feet
just clear of the ground. The wife, a buxom brunette, was trudging
afoot in the rear, accompanied by the two younger children, a boy and
girl, between twelve and fourteen, led by a small dog, fastened to a
string, like the guide of a blind mendicant; while the eldest daughter
was mounted on the crupper, maintaining her equilibrium by a masculine disposition of her lower limbs. She was a fine, rosy cheeked *grisette*,
of about seventeen; and, as they ambled along, just fast enough to keep
the cur on a slow trot, her cap flared in the wind, her black eyes flashed
with pleasure, and her dark ringlets streamed behind her, like so many
silken pennants. She had a ready laugh for every one she met, and a
sort of malicious pleasure in asking, by her countenance, if they did
not wish they too had a donkey? As the seat was none of the most
commodious, she had contrived to make a pair of stirrups of her
petticoats. The gown was pinned up about her waist, leaving her knees
instead of her feet, as the *points d'appui.* The well-turned legs, and the
ancles, with such a *chaussure* as at once marks a *Parisienne*, were exposed
to the admiration of a *parterre* of some hundreds of idle way-farers.
Truly, it is no wonder that sculptors abound in this country, for capital
models are to be found, even in the highways. The donkey was the only
one who appeared displeased with this *monture*, and he only manifested
dissatisfaction by lifting his hinder extremities a little, as the man
occasionally touched his flanks with a nettle, that the ass would much
rather have been eating.

Not long since I passed half an hour on the terrace, an amused
witness of the perils of a voyage across the Seine, in a punt. The
adventurers were a *bourgeois,* his wife, sister, and child. Honest Pierre,
the waterman, had conditioned to take the whole party to the island
opposite, and to return them safe to the main, for the modicum of five
*sous.* The old fox invariably charged me a *franc,* for the same service.
There was much demurring and many doubts about encountering the
risks; and, more than once, the women would have receded, had not
the man treated the matter as a trifle. He affirmed *parole d'honneur* that
his father had crossed the Maine a dozen times, and no harm had come
of it! This encouraged them, and with many pretty screams, *mes fois,*
and *oh, dieus,* they finally embarked. The punt was a narrow scow, that
a ton weight would not have disturbed, the river was so low and
sluggish that it might have been forded two-thirds of the distance, and

the width was not three hundred feet. Pierre protested that the danger was certainly not worth mentioning, and away he went, as philosophical in appearance as his punt. The voyage was made in safety, and the bows of the boat had actually touched the shore on its return, before any of the passengers ventured to smile. The excursion, like most travelling, was likely to be most productive of happiness by the recollections. But the women were no sooner landed, than that rash adventurer, the husband, brother, and father, seized an oar, and began to ply it with all his force. He merely wished to tell his *confrères* of the *rue Montmartre* how a punt might be rowed. Pierre had gallantly landed to assist the ladies, and the boat, relieved of its weight, slowly yielded to the impulse of the oar, and inclined its bows from the land. "*Oh! Edouard! mon mari! mon frère!—que fais-tu?*" exclaimed the ladies. "*Ce n'est rien,*" returned the man, puffing and giving another lusty sweep, by which he succeeded in forcing the punt fully twenty feet from the shore. "*Edouard! cher Edouard!*" "*Laisse-moi m'amuser. Je m'amuse—je m'amuse,*" cried the husband, in a tone of indignant remonstrance. But *Edouard,* a tight, sleek little *épicier,* of about five and thirty, had never heard that an oar on each side was necessary in a boat, and the harder he pulled, the less likely was he to regain the shore. Of this he began to be convinced, as he whirled more into the centre of the current; and his efforts now really became frantic, for his imagination probably painted the horrors of a distant voyage, in an unknown bark, to an unknown land, and all without food or compass. The women screamed, and the louder they cried, the more strenuously he persevered in saying, "*Laisse-moi m'amuser—je m'amuse, je m'amuse.*" By this time the perspiration poured from the face of *Edouard,* and I called to the imperturbable Pierre, who stood in silent admiration of his punt while playing such antics, and desired him to tell the man to put his oar on the bottom, and to push the boat ashore. "*Oui, Monsieur,*" said the rogue, with a leer, for he remembered the francs, and we soon had our adventurer safe on *terra firma* again. Then began the tender expostulations, the affectionate reproaches, and the kind injunctions for the truant to remember that he was a husband and a father. *Edouard,* secretly cursing the punt and all rivers in his heart, made light of the matter, however, protesting to the last, that he had only been enjoying himself.

We have had a *fête,* too; for every village in the vicinity of Paris has its *fête.* The square was filled with whirligigs and flying-horses, and all the ingenious contrivances of the French to make and to spend a *sou* pleasantly. There was service in the parish church, at which our neighbours sang, in a style fit for St. Peter's; and the villagers danced *quadrilles* on the green, with an air that would be thought fine in many a country drawing-room.

I enjoy all this greatly; for, to own the truth, the crowds and mannered sameness of Paris began to weary me. Our friends occasionally come from town to see us, and we make good use of the *cabriolet*. As we are near neighbours to *St. Denis*, we have paid several visits to the tombs of the French kings, and returned, each time, less pleased with most of the unmeaning obsequies that are observed in their vaults. There was a ceremony, not long since, at which the royal family, and many of the great officers of the court assisted, and among others, M. de Talleyrand. The latter was in the body of the church, when a man rushed upon him, and actually struck him, or shoved him, to the earth, using, at the same time, language that left no doubt of the nature of the assault. There are strange rumours connected with the affair. The assailant was a *Marquis* [*d'Orsvault*], and it is reported that his wrongs, real or imaginary, are connected with a plot to rob one of the dethroned family of her jewels, or of some crown jewels, I cannot say which, at the epoch of the restoration. The journals said a good deal about it, at the time, but events occur so fast, here, that a quarrel of this sort produces little sensation. I pretend to no knowledge of the merits of this affair, and only give a general outline of what was current in the public prints, at the time.

We have also visited Enghien, and Montmorency. The latter, as you know already, stands on the side of a low mountain, in plain view of Paris. It is a town of some size, with very uneven streets, some of them being actually sharp acclivities, and a gothic church that is seen from afar, and that is well worth viewing near by. These quaint edifices afford us deep delight, by their antiquity, architecture, size, and pious histories. What matters it to us how much or how little superstition may blend with the rites, when we know and feel that we are standing in a nave that has echoed with orisons to God, for a thousand years! This of Montmorency is not quite so old, however, having been rebuilt only three centuries since.

Dulaure, a severe judge of aristocracy, denounces the pretension of the *Montmorencies* to be the *Premiers Barons Chrétiens*, affirming that they were neither the first barons, nor the first Christians, by a great many. He says, that the extravagant title has most probably been a war-cry, in the time of the crusaders. According to his account of the family, it originated, about the year 1008, in a certain Burchard, who, proving a bad neighbour to the Abbey of St. Denis, the vassals of which he was in the habit of robbing, besides, now and then, despoiling a monk, the king caused his fortress in the *isle St. Denis* to be razed; after which, by a treaty, he was put in possession of the mountain hard by, with permission to erect another hold near a fountain, at a place called in the charters, *Montmorenciacum.* Hence the name, and the family. This writer thinks that the first castle must have been built of wood!

We took a road that led us up to a bluff on the mountain, behind the town, where we obtained a new and very peculiar view of Paris and its environs. I have said that the French towns have no straggling suburbs. A few wine-houses (to save the *octroi*) are built near the gates, compactly, as in the town itself, and there the buildings cease as suddenly as if pared down by a knife. The fields touch the walls, in many places, and between St. Ouen and the *guinguettes* and wine-houses, at the *barrière de Clichy,* a distance of quite two miles, there is but a solitary building. A wide plain separates Paris, on this side, from the mountains, and of course our view extended across it. The number of villages was absolutely astounding. Although I did not attempt counting them, I should think not fewer than a hundred were in sight, all gray, picturesque, and clustering round the high nave and church tower, like chickens gathering beneath the wing. The day was clouded, and the hamlets rose from their beds of verdure, sombre but distinct, with their faces of wall, now in subdued light, and now quite shaded, resembling the glorious *darks* of Rembrandt's pictures.

# Letter XVII
## To Capt. M. Perry, U.S.N.

I am often in the saddle, since our removal to St. Ouen. I first commenced the business of exploring in the cabriolet, with my wife for a companion, during which time, several very pretty drives, of whose existence one journeying along the great roads would form no idea, were discovered. At last, as these became exhausted, I mounted, and pricked into the fields. The result has been a better knowledge of the details of ordinary rural life, in this country, than a stranger would get by a residence, after the ordinary fashion, of years.

I found the vast plain intersected by roads as intricate as the veins of the human body. The comparison is not unapt, by the way, and may be even carried out much further; for the *grandes routes* can be compared to the arteries, the *chemins vicinaux*, or cross-roads, to the veins, and the innumerable paths that intersect the fields, in all directions, to the more minute blood vessels, circulation being the object common to all.

I mount my horse and gallop into the fields at random, merely taking care not to quit the paths. By the latter, one can go in almost any direction; and, as they are very winding, there is a certain pleasure in following their sinuosities, doubtful whither they tend. Much of the plain is in vegetables, for the use of Paris, though there is occasionally a vineyard, or a field of grain. The weather has become settled and autumnal, and is equally without the chilling moisture of the winter or the fickleness of the spring. The kind-hearted peasants see me pass among them without distrust, and my salutations are answered with cheerfulness and civility. Even at this trifling distance from the capital, I miss the *brusque* ferocity that is so apt to characterize the deportment of its lower classes, who are truly the people that Voltaire has described as *"ou singes, ou tigres."* Nothing, I think, strikes an American more than the marked difference between the town and country of France. With us, the towns are less town-like, and the country less country-like, than is usually the case. Our towns are provincial from the want of tone that can only be acquired by time, while it is a fault with our country to wish to imitate the towns. I now allude to habits only, for the nature at home, owing to the great abundance of wood, is more strikingly rural than in any other country I know. The inhabitant of Paris can quit his own door in the centre of the place, and after walking an hour, he finds himself truly in the country, both as to the air of external objects, and as to the manners of the people. The influence of the capital doubtless has some little effect on the latter, but not enought to raise them above the ordinary rusticity, for the French peasants are as rustic in their appearance and habits, as the upper classes are refined.

One of my rides is through the plain that lies between St. Ouen and Montmartre, ascending the latter by its rear to the windmills, that night and day, are whirling their ragged arms over the capital of France. Thence I descend into the town, by the carriage road. A view from this height is like a glimpse into the pages of history, for every foot of land that it commands, and more than half the artificial accessories, are pregnant of the past. Looking down into the fissures between the houses, men appear the mites they are, and one gets to have a philosophical indifference to human vanities, by obtaining these bird's-eye views of them in the mass. It was a happy thought that first suggested the summits of mountains for religious contemplation; nor do I think the Father of Evil discovered his usual sagacity when he resorted to such a place for the purposes of selfish temptation; perhaps, however, it would be better to say, he betrayed the grovelling propensities of his own nature. The cathedral of Notre Dame should have been reared on this noble and isolated height, that the airs of heaven might whisper through its fane, breathing the chaunts in honour of God.

Dismounting, manfully, I have lately undertaken a far more serious enterprise—that of making the entire circuit of Paris, on foot. My companion was our old friend Capt. [Chauncey]. We met, by appointment, at eleven o'clock, just without the *barrière de Clichy*, and, ordering the carriage to come for us at five, off we started, taking the direction of the eastern side of the town. You probably know that what are commonly called the *boulevards* of Paris, are no more than a circular line of wide streets, through the very heart of the place, which obtain their common appellation from the fact that they occupy the sites of the ancient walls. Thus the street, within this circuit, is called by its name, whatever it may happen to be, and, if continued without the circuit, the term of *faubourg* or suburb is added; as in the case of the "*rue St. Honoré*," and the "*rue du faubourg St. Honoré*," the latter being strictly a continuation of the former, but lying without the site of the ancient walls. As the town has increased, it has been found necessary to enlarge its *enceinte*, and the walls are now encircled with wide avenues that are called the outer *boulevards*. There are avenues within and without the walls, and immediately beneath them; and, in many places, both are planted. Our route was on the exterior.

We began the march in good spirits, and by twelve, we had handsomely done our four miles and a half. Of course we passed the different *barrières*, and the gate of *Père La Chaise*. The captain commenced with great vigour, and for near two hours, as he expressed himself, he had me a little on his lee quarter, not more, however, he thought, than was due to his superior rank, for he had once been my senior, as a midshipman. At the *barrière du Trône* we were compelled to diverge a little from the wall, in order to get across the river by the *pont d'Austerlitz*. By this time, I had ranged up abeam of the commodore, and I proposed that we should follow the river, up as far as the wall again, in order to do our work honestly. But to this he objected that he had no wish to puzzle himself with spherical trigonometry, that plane sailing was his humour at the moment, and that he had, moreover, just discovered that one of his boots pinched his foot. Accordingly we proceeded straight from the bridge, not meeting the wall again until we were beyond the *abattoir*. These *abattoirs* are slaughter-houses, that Napoleon caused to be built, near the walls, in some places within, and in others without them, according to the different localities. There are five or six of them, that of *Montmartre* being the most considerable. They are kept in excellent order, and the regulations respecting them appear to be generally good. The butchers sell their meats, in shops, all over the town, a general custom in Europe, and one that has more advantages than disadvantages, as it enables the inhabitant to order a meal at any moment. This independence in the mode of living distinguishes all the large towns of this part of the world from our own; for I greatly question if there be any civilized people among whom the individual is as much obliged to consult the habits and tastes of *all*, in gratifying his own, as in free and independent America. A part of this uncomfortable feature in our domestic economy, is no doubt the result of circumstances unavoidably connected with the condition of a young country, but a great deal is to be ascribed to the practice of referring every thing to the public, and not a little to those religious sects who extended their supervision to all the affairs of life, that had a chief concern in settling the country, and who have entailed so much that is inconvenient and ungraceful (I might almost say, in some instances, *disgraceful*) on the nation, blended with so much that forms its purest sources of pride. Men are always an inconsistent medley of good and bad.

The captain and myself had visited the *abattoir* of *Montmartre* only a few days previously to this excursion, and we had both been much gratified with its order and neatness. But an unfortunate pile of hocks, hoofs, tallow, and nameless fragments of carcasses, had caught my companion's eye. I found him musing over this *omnium gatherum*, which he protested was worse than a bread pudding at Saratoga. By some process of reasoning, that was rather material than philosophical, he came to the conclusion that the substratum of all the extraordinary compounds he had met with at the *restaurants* was derived from this pile, and he swore, as terribly as any of "our army in Flanders," that not another mouthful would he touch, while he remained in Paris, if the dish put his knowledge of natural history at fault. He had all along suspected he had been eating cats and vermin, but his imagination had never pictured to him such a store of abominations for the *casserole*, as were to be seen in this pile. In vain I asked him if he did not find the dishes good. Cats might be good for any thing he knew, but he was too old to change his habits. On the present occasion, he made the situation of the *abattoir d'Ivry* an excuse for not turning up the river, by the wall. I do not think, however, we gained any thing in the distance, the *détour* to cross the bridge more than equaling the ground we missed.

We came under the wall again, at the *barrière de Villejuif*, and followed it, keeping on the side next the town, until we fairly reached the river, once more, beyond *Vaugirard*. Here we were compelled to walk some distance to cross the *Pont d'Iéna*, and again to make a considerable circuit through Passy, on account of the gardens, in order to do justice to our task. About this time, the commodore fairly fell astern; and he discovered that the other boot was too large. I kept talking to him over my shoulder, and cheering him on, and he felicitated me on frogs agreeing so well with my constitution. At length, we came in at the *barrière de Clichy*, just as the clocks struck three, or in four hours, to a minute, from the time we had left the same spot. We had neither stopped, eaten, nor drunk a mouthful. The distance is supposed to be about eighteen miles, but I can hardly think it is so much, for we went rather further than if we had closely followed the wall.

Our agility having greatly exceeded my calculations, we were obliged to walk two miles further, in order to find the carriage. The time expended in going this distance included, we were just four hours and a half on our feet. The captain protested that his boots had disgraced him, and forthwith commanded another pair; a subterfuge that did him no good.

One anecdote connected with the sojourn of this eccentric, but really excellent-hearted and intelligent man,* at Paris, is too good not to be told. He cannot speak a word of pure French, and of all Anglicizing of the language, I have ever heard, his attempts at it are the most droll. He calls the *Tuileries,* Tully*rees,* the *jardin des plantes* the *garden dis plants,* the *guillotine, gullyteen,* and the *garçons* of the *cafés, gassons.* Choleric, with whiskers like a bear, and a voice of thunder, if any thing goes wrong, he swears away, starboard and larboard, in French and English, in delightful discord.

He sought me out, soon after his arrival, and carried me with him, as an interpreter, in quest of lodgings. We found a very snug little apartment of four rooms, that he took. The last occupant was a lady, who in letting the rooms, conditioned that *Marie,* her servant, must be hired with them, to look after the furniture, and to be in readiness to receive her, at her return from the provinces. A few days after this arrangement I called, and was surprised, on ringing the bell, to hear the cry of an infant. After a moment's delay the door was cautiously opened, and the captain in his gruffest tone demanded, *"cur vully voo?"* An exclamation of surprize, at seeing me, followed; but instead of opening the door for my admission, he held it, for a moment, as if undecided whether to be "at home" or not. At this critical instant an infant cried again, and the thing became too ridiculous for further gravity. We both laughed outright. I entered and found the captain with a child three days old, tucked under his right arm, or that which had been concealed by the door. The explanation was very simple, and infinitely to his credit.

Marie, the *locum tenens* of the lady who had let the apartment, and the wife of a coachman who was in the country, was the mother of the infant. After its birth, she presented herself to her new master; told her story, adding, by means of an interpreter, that if he turned her away, she had no place in which to lay her head. The kind-hearted fellow made out to live abroad as well as he could, for a day or two; an easy

---

* He is since dead.

thing enough in Paris, by the way; and when I so unexpectedly entered, Marie was actually cooking the captain's breakfast in the kitchen, while he was nursing the child in the *salon!*

The dialogues between the captain and Marie, were, to the last degree, amusing. He was quite unconscious of the odd sounds he uttered in speaking French, but thought he was getting on very well, being rather minute and particular in his orders; and she felt his kindness to herself and child so sensibly, that she always fancied she understood his wishes. I was frequently compelled to interpret between them, first asking him to explain himself in English, for I could make but little of his French, myself. On one occasion, he invited me to breakfast, as we were to pass the day exploring, in company. By way of inducement, he told me that he had accidentally found some cocoa in the shell, and that he had been teaching Marie how to cook it, "ship-fashion." I would not promise, as his hour was rather early, and the distance between us so great; but before eleven I would certainly be with him. I breakfasted at home, therefore, but was punctual to the latter engagement. "I hope you have breakfasted?" cried the captain, rather fiercely, as I entered. I satisfied him on this point, and then, after a minute of demure reflection, he resumed, "you are lucky, for Marie boiled the cocoa, and, after throwing away the liquor, she buttered and peppered the shells, and served them for me to eat! I don't see how she made such a mistake, for I was very particular in my directions, and be d——d to her. I don't care so much about my own breakfast, neither, for that can be had at the next *café,* but the poor creature has lost hers, which I told her to cook out of the rest of the cocoa." I had the curiosity to inquire how he had made out to tell *Marie* to do all this. "Why, I showed her the cocoa, to be sure, and then told her to '*boily vous-même.*'" There was no laughing at this, and so I went with the captain to a *café,* after which we proceeded in quest of the "*gullyteen,*" which he was particularly anxious to see.

My rides often extend to the heights behind Malmaison and St. Cloud, where there is a fine country, and where some of the best views, in the vicinity of Paris, are to be obtained. As the court is at St. Cloud, I often meet different members of the royal family, dashing to or from town, or perhaps passing from one of their abodes to another. The style is pretty uniform, for I do not remember to have ever met the king, but once, with less than eight horses. The exception, was quite early one morning, when he was going into the country with very little *éclat,* accompanied by the Dauphine. Even on this occasion, he was in a carriage and six, followed by another with four, and attended by a dozen mounted men. These royal progresses are truly magnificent; and they serve greatly to enliven the road, as we live so near the country palace. The king has been quite lately to a camp, formed at St. Omer, and I happened to meet a portion of his equipages on their return. The carriages I saw were very neatly built post-chaises, well leathered, and contained what are here called the "officers of the mouth," alias "cooks and purveyors." They were all drawn by four horses. This was a great occasion—furniture being actually sent from the palace of Compiègne for the king's lodgings, and the court is said to have employed seventy different vehicles to transport it. I saw about a dozen.

Returning the other night from a dinner-party, given on the banks of the Seine, a few miles above us, I saw flaring lights gleaming along the high-way, which, at first, caused nearly as much conjecture as some of the adventures of Don Quixotte. My horse proving a little restive, I pulled up, placing the *cabriolet* on one side of the road, for the first impression was that the cattle émployed at some funeral procession had taken flight, and were running away. It proved to be the Dauphine dashing towards St. Cloud. This was the first time I had ever met any of the royal equipages at night, and the passage was much the most picturesque of any I had hitherto seen. Footmen, holding flaming flambeaux, rode in pairs, in front, by the side of the carriage, and in its rear; the *piqueur* scouring along the road in advance, like a rocket. By the way, a lady of the court told me lately, that Louis XVIIIth had lost some of his French by the emigration, for he did not know how to pronounce this word *piqueur*.

On witnessing all this magnificence, the mind is carried back a few generations, in the inquiry after the progress of luxury, and the usages of our fathers. Coaches were first used in England in the reign of Elizabeth. It is clear enough, by the pictures in the Louvre, that in the time of Louis XIVth the royal carriages were huge, clumsy vehicles, with at least three seats. *Mademoiselle de Montpensier*, in her Memoirs, tells us how often she took her place at the window, in order to admire the graceful attitudes of *M. de Lauzun*, who rode near it. There is still in existence, in the *Bibliothèque du Roi*, a letter of Henry IVth to Sully, in which the king explains to the grand master, the reason why he could not come to the arsenal that day: the excuse being that the queen *was using the carriage!* To-day his descendant seldom moves at a pace slower than ten miles the hour, is drawn by eight horses, and is usually accompanied by one or more empty vehicles, of equal magnificence, to receive him, in the event of an accident.

Notwithstanding all this regal splendour, the turn-outs of Paris, as a whole, are by no means remarkable. The genteelest, and the fashionable, carriage is the chariot. I like the proportions of the French carriages better than those of the English, or our own: the first being too heavy, and the last too light. The French vehicles appear to me to be, in this respect, a happy medium. But the finish is by no means equal to that of the English carriages, nor at all better than that of ours. There are, relatively, a large proportion of shabby-genteel equipages at Paris. Even the vehicles that are seen standing in the court of the *Tuileries*, on a reception day, are not at all superior to the better sort of American carriages, though the liveries are much more showy.

Few people here, own the carriages and horses they use. Even the strangers, who are obliged to have travelling vehicles, rarely use them in town, the road and the streets requiring very different sorts of equipages. There are certain job-dealers who furnish all that is required, for a stipulated sum. You select the carriage and horses, on trial, and contract at so much a month, or at so much a year. The coachman usually comes with the equipage, as does the footman sometimes, though both are paid by the person taking the coach. They will wear your livery, if you choose, and, you can have your arms put on the carriage, if desirable. I pay five hundred francs a month for a carriage and horses, and forty francs for a coachman. I believe this is the usual price. I have a right to have a pair of horses, always at my command, finding nothing but the stable, and even this would be unnecessary in Paris. If we go away from our own stable, I pay five francs a day, extra. There is a very great convenience to strangers, in particular, in this system, for one can set up, and lay down a carriage, without unnecessary trouble or expense, as it may be wanted. In every thing of this nature, we have no town that has the least the character, or the conveniences, of a capital.

The French have little to boast of in the way of horse flesh. Most of the fine coach and cabriolet cattle of Paris come from Mecklenburg, though some are imported from England. It is not common to meet with a very fine animal of the native breed. In America, land is so plenty and so cheap, that we keep a much larger proportion of brute force than is kept here. It is not uncommon with us to meet with those who live by day's work, using either oxen or horses. The consequence is, that many beasts are raised with little care, and with scarcely any attention to the breeds. We find many bad horses, therefore, in America, but still we find many good ones. In spite of bad grooming, little training, and hard work, I greatly question if even England possesses a larger proportion of good horses, comparing the population of the two countries, than America. Our animals are quicker footed, and at trotting, I suspect, we could beat the world; Christendom, certainly. The great avenue between the garden of the *Tuileries* and the *Bois de Boulogne*, with the *allées* of the latter, are the places to meet the fast goers of the French capital, and I am strongly of opinion that there is no such exhibition of speed, in either, as one meets on the Third Avenue of New York. As for the *Avenue de Neuilly*, our sulky riders would vanish like the wind from any thing I have seen on it, although one meets there, occasionally, fine animals from all parts of Europe.

The cattle of the *diligences*, of the post houses, and even of the cavalry of France, are solid, hardy and good feeders, but they are almost entirely without speed or action. The two former are very much the same, and it is a hard matter to get more than eight miles out of them, without breaking into a gallop, or more than ten, if put under the whip. Now, a short time previously to leaving home, I went eleven measured miles, in a public coach, in two minutes less than an hour, the whip untouched. I sat on the box, by the side of the driver, and know that this was done under a pull that actually disabled one of his arms, and that neither of the four animals broke its trot. It is not often our roads will admit of this, but, had we the roads of England, I make little doubt we should altogether outdo her in speed. As for the horses used here, in the public conveyances, and for the post routes, they are commonly compact, clumsy beasts, with less force than their shape would give reason to suppose. Their manes are long and shaggy, the fetlocks are rarely trimmed, the shoes are seldom corked, and, when there is a little coquetry, the tail is braided. In this trim, with a coarse harness, that is hardly ever cleaned, traces of common rope, and half the time no blinkers or reins, away they scamper, with their heads in all directions, like the classical representation of a team in an ancient car, through thick and thin, working with all their might to do two posts within an hour; one, being the legal measure. These animals appear to possess a strange *bonhomie*, being obedient, willing, and tractable, although, in the way of harness and reins, they are pretty much their own masters.

My excursions in the environs have made me acquainted with a great variety of modes of communication between the capital and its adjacent villages. Although Paris is pared down so accurately, and is almost without suburbs, the population, within a circuit of ten miles in each direction, is almost equal to that of Paris itself. St. Denis has several thousands, St. Germain the same, and Versailles is still a town of considerable importance. All these places, with villages out of number, keep up daily intercourse with the city, and in addition to the hundreds of vegetable carts that constantly pass to and fro, there are many conveyances that are exclusively devoted to passengers. The cheapest and lowest is called a *coucou*, for no reason that I can see, unless it be that a man looks very like a fool to have a seat in one of them. They are large *cabriolets*, with two and even three seats. The wheels are enormous, and there is commonly a small horse harnessed by the side of a larger, in the thills, to drag perhaps eight or nine people. One is amazed to see the living carrion that is driven about a place like Paris, in these uncouth vehicles. The river is so exceedingly crooked, that it is little used by travellers above Rouen.

The internal transportation of France, where the lines of the rivers are not followed, is carried on, almost exclusively, in enormous carts, drawn by six and even eight heavy horses, harnessed in a line. The burthen is often as large as a load of hay, not quite so high, perhaps, but generally longer, care being had to preserve the balance in such a manner as to leave no great weight on the shaft-horse. These teams are managed with great dexterity, and I have often stopped and witnessed, with admiration, the entrance of one of them into a yard, as it passed from a crowded street probably not more than thirty feet wide. But the evolutions of the *diligence*, guided as it chiefly is by the whip, and moving on a trot, are really nice affairs. I came from *La Grange*, some time since, in one, and I thought that we should dash every thing to pieces in the streets, and yet nothing was injured. At the close of the journey, our team of five horses, two on the pole and three on the lead, wheeled, without breaking its trot, into a street that was barely wide enough to receive the huge vehicle, and this too without human direction, the driver being much too drunk to be of any service. These *diligences* are uncouth objects to the eye; but, for the inside passengers, they are much more comfortable, so far as my experience extends, than either the American stage, or the English coach.

The necessity of passing the *barrière* two or three times a day, has also made me acquainted with the great amount of drunkenness that prevails in Paris. Wine can be had *outside* of the walls, for about half the price which is paid for it within the town, as it escapes the *octroi*, or city duty. The people resort to these places for indulgence, and there is quite as much low blackguardism and guzzling here, as is to be met with in any sea-port I know.

Provisions of all sorts, too, are cheaper without the gates, for the same reason; and the lower classes resort to them to celebrate their weddings, and on other eating and drinking occasions. "*Ici on fait festins et noces,*"* is a common sign, no barrier being without more or less of these houses. The *guinguettes* are low gardens, answering to the English tea-gardens of the humblest class, with a difference in the drinkables and other fare. The base of Montmartre is crowded with them.

One sometimes meets with an unpleasant adventure among these exhilarated gentry; for, though, I think, a low Frenchman is usually better natured when a little *grisé* than when perfectly sober, this is not always the case. Quite lately I had an affair that might have terminated seriously, but for our good luck. It is usual to have two sets of reins to the *cabriolets*, the horses being very spirited, and the danger from accidents in streets so narrow and crowded, being great. I had dined in town, and was coming out about nine o'clock. The horse was walking up the ascent to the *barrière de Clichy*, when I observed, by the shadow cast from a bright moon, that there was a man seated on the *cabriolet*, behind. Charles was driving, and I ordered him to tell the man to get off. Finding words of no effect, Charles gave him a slight tap with his whip. The fellow instantly sprang forward, seized the horse by the reins, and attempted to drag him to one side of the road. Failing in this, he fled up the street. Charles now called out that he had cut the reins. I seized the other pair and brought the horse up, and, as soon as he was under command, we pursued our assailant at a gallop. He was soon out of breath, and we captured him. As I felt very indignant at the supposed outrage, which might have cost, not us only, but others, their lives, I gave him in charge to two *gendarmes* at the gate, with my address, promising to call at the police office in the morning.

* Weddings and merry-makings are kept here.

Accordingly, next day I presented myself, and was surprised to find that the man had been liberated. I had discovered, in the interval, that the leather had *broken*, and had not been *cut*, which materially altered the *animus* of the offence, and I had come with an intention to ask for the release of the culprit, believing it merely a sally of temper, which a night's imprisonment sufficiently punished; but, the man being *charged* with cutting the rein, I thought the magistrate had greatly forgotten himself, in discharging him before I appeared. Indeed I made no scruple in telling him so. We had some warm words, and parted. I make no doubt I was mistaken for an Englishman, and that the old national antipathy was at work against me.

I was a good deal surprised at the termination of this, my first essay in French criminal justice. So many eulogiums have been passed on the police, that I was not prepared to find this indifference to an offence like that of wantonly cutting the reins of a spirited cabriolet horse, in the streets of Paris; for such was the charge on which the man stood committed. I mentioned the affair to a friend, and he said that the police was good only for political offences, and that the government rather leaned to the side of the rabble, in order to find support with them, in the event of any serious movement. This, you will remember, was the opinion of a Frenchman, and not mine; for I only relate the facts (one conjecture excepted,) and to do justice to all parties, it is proper to add that my friend is warmly opposed to the present *régime*.

I have uniformly found the *gendarmes* civil, and even obliging; and I have seen them show great forbearance on various occasions. As to the marvellous stories we have heard of the police of Paris, I suspect they have been gotten up for effect, such things being constantly practised here. One needs be behind the curtain, in a great many things, to get a just idea of the true state of the world. A laughable instance has just occurred, within my knowledge, of a story that has been got up for effect. The town was quite horrified, lately, with an account, in the journals, of a careless nurse permitting a child to fall into the *fossé* of the great bears, in the *jardin des plantes*, and of the bears eating up the dear little thing, to the smallest fragment, before succour could be obtained. Happening to be at the garden soon after, in the company of one connected with the establishment, I inquired into the circumstances, and was told that the nurses were very careless with the children, and that the story was published in order that the bears *should not eat up any child hereafter*, rather than because they *had eaten up* a child *heretofore*.

# Letter XVIII

## To Mrs. Pomeroy, Cooperstown.

I have said very little, in my previous letters, on the subject of our personal intercourse with the society of Paris. It is not always easy for one to be particular in these matters, and maintain the reserve that is due to others. Violating the confidence he may have received through his hospitality, is but an indifferent return from the guest to the host. Still there are men, if I may so express it, so public in their very essence, certainly in their lives, that propriety is less concerned with a repetition of their sentiments, and with delineations of their characters, than in ordinary cases; for the practice of the world has put them so much on their guard against the representations of travellers, that there is more danger of rendering a false account, by becoming their dupes, than of betraying them in their unguarded moments. I have scarcely ever been admitted to the presence of a real notoriety, that I did not find the man, or woman—sex making little difference—an actor; and this, too, much beyond the every day and perhaps justifiable little practices of conventional life. Inherent simplicity of character, is one of the rarest, as, tempered by the tone imparted by refinement, it is the loveliest of all our traits, though it is quite common to meet with those who affect it, with an address that is very apt to deceive the ordinary, and most especially the flattered, observer.

Opportunity, rather than talents, is the great requisite for circulating gossip; a very moderate degree of ability sufficing for the observation which shall render private anecdotes, more especially when they relate to persons of celebrity, of interest to the general reader. But there is another objection to being merely the medium of information of this low quality, that I should think would have great influence with every one who has the common self-respect of a gentleman. *There is a tacit admission of inferiority* in the occupation, that ought to prove too humiliating to a man accustomed to those associations, which imply equality. It is permitted to touch upon the habits and appearance of a truly great man; but to dwell upon the peculiarities of a duke, merely because he is a duke, is as much as to say he is your superior; a concession I do not feel disposed to make in favour of any *mere duke* in Christendom.

I shall not, however, be wholly silent on the general impressions left by the little I have seen of the society of Paris; and, occasionally, when it is characteristic, an anecdote may be introduced, for such things sometimes give distinctness, as well as piquancy, to a description.

During our first winter in Paris, our circle, never very large, was principally confined to foreign families, intermingled with a few French; but since our return to town, from St. Ouen, we have seen more of the people of the country. I should greatly mislead you, however, were I to leave the impression that our currency in the French capital has been at all general, for it certainly has not. Neither my health, leisure, fortune, nor opportunities, have permitted this. I believe few, perhaps no Americans, have very general access to the best society of any large European town; at all events, I have met with no one who, I have had any reason to think was much better off than myself in this respect; and, I repeat, my own familiarity with the circles of the capital, is nothing to boast of. It is in Paris, as it is every where else, as respects those who are easy of access. In all large towns there is to be found a troublesome and pushing set, who, requiring notoriety, obtrude themselves on strangers, sometimes with sounding names, and always with offensive pretensions of some sort or other; but the truly respectable and estimable class, in every country, except in cases that cannot properly be included in the rule, are to be sought. Now, one must feel that he has peculiar claims, or be better furnished with letters than happened to be my case, to get a ready admission into this set, or, having obtained it, to feel that his position enabled him to maintain the intercourse, with the ease and freedom that could alone render it agreeable. To be shown about as a lion, when circumstances offer the means; to be stuck up at a dinner table, as a piece of luxury, like strawberries in February, or peaches in April, can hardly be called association: the terms being much on a par with that which forms the *liaison*, between him who gives the entertainment, and the hired plate with which his table is garnished. With this explanation, then, you are welcome to an outline of the little I know on the subject.

One of the errors respecting the French, which has been imported into America, through England, is the impression that they are not hospitable. Since my residence here, I have often been at a loss to imagine how such a notion could have arisen, for I am acquainted with no town, in which it has struck me there is more true hospitality, than in Paris. Not only are dinners, balls, and all the minor entertainments frequent, but there is scarcely a man, or a woman, of any note in society, who does not cause his or her doors to be opened, once a fortnight at least, and, in half the cases, once a week. At these *soirées* invitations are sometimes given, it is true, but then they are general, and for the whole season; and it is not unusual, even, to consider them free to all who are on visiting terms with the family. The utmost simplicity and good taste prevail at these places, the refreshments being light and appropriate, and the forms exacting no more than what belongs to good breeding. You will, at once, conceive the great advantages that a stranger possesses in having access to such social resources. One, with a tolerable visiting list, may choose his circle for any particular evening, and, if by chance, the company should not happen to be to his mind, he has still before him the alternative of several other houses, which are certain to be open. It is not easy to say what can be more truly hospitable than this.

The *petits soupers*, once so celebrated, are entirely superseded by the new distribution of time, which is probably the most rational that can be devised for a town life. The dinner is at six, an hour that is too early to interfere with the engagements of the evening, it being usually over at eight, and too late to render food again necessary that night; an arrangement that greatly facilitates the evening intercourse, releasing it at once from all trouble and parade.

It has often been said, in favour of French society, that once within the doors of a *salon* all are equal. This is not literally so, it being impossible that such a state of things can exist; nor is it desirable that it should; since it is confounding all sentiment and feeling, overlooking the claims of age, services, merit of every sort, and setting at naught the whole construction of society. It is not absolutely true, that even rank is entirely forgotten in French society, though I think it sufficiently so to prevent any deference to it from being offensive. The social pretensions of a French peer are exceedingly well regulated, nor do I remember to have seen an instance in which a very young man has been particularly noticed on account of his having claims of this sort. Distinguished men are so very numerous in Paris, that they excite no great feeling, and the even course of society is little disturbed on their account.

Although all within the doors of a French *salon* are not perfectly equal, none are made unpleasantly to feel the difference. I dare say there are circles in Paris, in which the mere possession of money may be a source of evident distinction, but it must be in a very inferior set. The French, while they are singularly alive to the advantages of money, and extremely liable to yield to its influence in all important matters, rarely permit any manifestations of its power to escape them in their ordinary intercourse. As a people, they appear to me to be ready to yield every thing to money, but its external homage. On these points, they are the very converse of the Americans, who are hard to be bought, while they consider money the very base of all distinction. The origin of these peculiarities may be found in the respective conditions of the two countries.

In America, fortunes are easily and rapidly acquired; pressure reduces few to want; he who serves is, if any thing, more in demand than he who is to be served; and the want of temptation produces exemption from the liability to corruption. Men will, and do, daily, *corrupt themselves*, in the rapacious pursuit of gain, but comparatively few are in the market, to be bought and sold by others. Notwithstanding this, money being every man's goal, there is a secret, profound, and general deference for it; while money will do less, than in almost any other country in Christendom. Here, few young men look forward to gaining distinction by making money; they search for it, as a means; whereas, with us, it is the end. We have little need of arms in America, and the profession is in less request than that of law or merchandize. Of the arts and letters, the country possesses none, or next to none; and there is no true sympathy with either. The only career that is felt, as likely to lead, and which can lead, to distinction independently of money, is that of politics, and, as a whole, this is so much occupied by sheer adventurers, with little or no pretension to the name of statesmen, that it is scarcely reputable to belong to it. Although money has no influence in politics, or as little as well may be, even the successful politician is but a secondary man, in ordinary society, in comparison with the *millionnaire*. Now, all this is very much reversed in Paris. Money does much, while it seems to do but little. The writer of a successful comedy would be a much more important personage, in the *coteries* of Paris, than M. Rothschild; and the inventor of a new bonnet would enjoy much more *éclat* than the inventor of a clever speculation. I question if there be a community on earth, in which gambling risks in the funds, for instance, are more general than in this, and yet the subject appears to be entirely lost sight of out of the *Bourse*.

The little social notoriety that is attached to military distinction, here, has greatly surprised me. It really seems as if France has had so much military renown, as to be satiated with it. One is elbowed constantly by generals, who have gained this or that victory, and yet no one seems to care anything about them. I do not mean that the nation is indifferent to military glory, but society appears to care little or nothing about it. I have seen a good deal of fuss made with the writer of a few clever verses, but I have never seen any made with a hero. Perhaps it was because the verses were new, and the victories old.

The perfect good taste and indifference which the French manifest concerning the private affairs, and concerning the mode of living, of one who is admitted to the *salons*, has justly extorted admiration, even from the English, the people of all others who most submit to a contrary feeling. A hackney coach is not always admitted into a court-yard, but both men and women make their visits in them, without any apparent hesitation. No one seems ashamed of confessing poverty. I do not say that women of quality often use *fiacres* to make their visits, but men do, and I have seen women in them, openly, whom I have met in some of the best houses in Paris. It is better to go in a private carriage, or in a *remise*, if one can, but few hesitate, when their means are limited, about using the former. In order to appreciate this self-denial, or simplicity, or good sense, it is necessary to remember that a Paris *fiacre* is not to be confounded with any other vehicle on earth. I witnessed, a short time since, a ludicrous instance of the different degrees of feeling that exist on this point, among different people. [Susan] and myself went to the house of an English woman, of our acquaintance, who is not very choice in her French. A Mrs. ———, the wife of a colonel in the English army, sat next [Susan], as a French lady begged that her carriage might be ordered. Our hostess told her servant to order the *fiacre* of Madame ———. Now, Madame ——— kept her chariot, to my certain knowledge, but she disregarded the mistake. [Susan] soon after desired that our carriage might come next. The good woman of the house, who loved to be busy, again called for the *fiacre* of Madame [Cooper]. I saw the foot of [Susan] in motion, but catching my eye, she smiled, and the thing passed off. The *voiture de Madame* [*Cooper*], or our own carriage, was announced, just as Mrs. ——— was trying to make a servant understand she wished for hers. — "*Le fiacre de Mad-ame* ———," again put in the bustling hostess. This was too much for a colonel's lady, and, with a very pretty air of distress, she took care to explain in a way that all might hear her, that it was a *remise*.

I dare say, vulgar prejudices influence vulgar minds, here, as elsewhere, and yet I must say, that I never knew any one hesitate about giving an address, on account of the humility of the lodgings. It is to be presumed that the manner in which families that are historical, and of long-established rank, were broken down by the revolution, has had an influence in effecting this healthful state of feeling.

The great tact and careful training of the women, serve to add very much to the grace of French society. They effectually prevent all embarrassments from the question of precedency, by their own decisions. Indeed, it appears to be admitted, that when there is any doubt on these points, the mistress of the house shall settle it in her own way. I found myself lately, at a small dinner, the only stranger, and the especially invited guest, standing near *Madame la Marquise* at the moment the service was announced. A bishop made one of the trio. I could not precede a man of his years and profession, and he was too polite to precede a stranger. It was a nice point. Had it been a question between a duke and myself, as a stranger, and under the circumstances of the invitation, I should have had the *pas*, but even the lady hesitated about discrediting a father of the church. She delayed but an instant, and, smiling, she begged us to follow her to the table, avoiding the decision altogether. In America, such a thing could not have happened, for no woman, by a fiction of society, is supposed to know how to walk in company without support; but, here, a woman will not spoil her curtsey, on entering a room, by leaning on an arm, if she can well help it. The practice of tucking up a brace of females, (liver and gizzard, as the English coarsely, but not inaptly, term it,) under one's arms, in order to enter a small room that is crowded in a way to render the movements of even one person difficult, does not prevail here, it being rightly judged that a proper *tenue*, a good walk, and a graceful movement, are all impaired by it. This habit also singularly contributes to the comfort of your sex, by rendering them more independent of ours. No one thinks, except in very particular cases, of going to the door to see a lady into her carriage, a custom too provincial to prevail in a capital, anywhere. Still, there is an amusing assiduity among the men, on certain points of etiquette, that has sometimes made me laugh; though, in truth, every concession to politeness being a tribute to benevolence, is respectable, unless spoiled in the manner. As we are gossiping about trifles, I will mention a usage or two, that to you will at least be novel.

I was honoured with a letter from *le Chevalier Alexandre de Lameth,** accompanied by an offering of a book, and I took an early opportunity to pay my respects to him. I found this gentleman, who once played so conspicuous a part in the politics of France, and who is now a liberal deputy, at breakfast, in a small cabinet, at the end of a suite of four rooms. He received me politely, conversed a good deal of America, in which country he had served as a colonel, under Rochambeau, and I took my leave. That M. de Lameth should rise, and even see me into the next room, was what every one would expect, and there I again took my leave of him. But he followed me to each door, in succession, and when, with a little gentle violence, I succeeded in shutting him in the ante-chamber, he seemed to yield to my entreaties not to give himself any further trouble. I was on the landing, on my way down, when, hearing the door of M. de Lameth's apartment open, I turned and saw its master standing before it, to give and receive the last bow. Although this extreme attention to the feelings of others, and delicacy of demeanor, rather marks the Frenchman of the old school, perhaps, it is by no means uncommon here. General La Fayette, while he permits me to see him with very little ceremony, scarcely ever suffers me to leave him, without going with me as far as two or three doors. This, in my case, he does more from habit than any thing else, for he frequently does not even rise when I enter; and, sometimes, when I laughingly venture to say so much ceremony is scarcely necessary between us, he will take me at my word, and go back to his writing, with perfect simplicity.

The reception between the women, I see plainly, is graduated with an unpretending but nice regard to their respective claims. They rise, even to men, a much more becoming and graceful habit than that of America, except in evening circles, or in receiving intimates. I never saw a French woman offer her hand to a male visitor, unless a relative, though it is quite common for females to kiss each other, when the *réunion* is not an affair of ceremony. The practice of kissing among men, still exists, though it is not very common at Paris. It appears to be gradually going out with the ear-rings. I have never had an offer from a Frenchman, of my own age, to kiss me, but it has frequently occurred, with my seniors. General La Fayette practises it still, with all his intimates.

---

* Since dead.

I was seated, the other evening, in quiet conversation, with *Madame la Princesse de* ———. Several people had come and gone in the course of an hour, and all had been received in the usual manner. At length the *huissier*, walking fast through the ante-chambers, announced the wife of an ambassador. The *Princesse*, at the moment, was seated on a *divan*, with her feet raised so as not to touch the floor. I was startled with the suddenness and vehemence of her movements. She sprang to her feet, and rather ran than walked across the vast *salon* to the door, where she was met by her visitor, who, observing the *empressement* of her hostess, through the vista of rooms, had rushed forward as fast as decorum would at all allow, in order to anticipate her at the door. It was my impression, at first, that they were bosom friends, about to be restored to each other, after a long absence, and that the impetuosity of their feelings had gotten the better of their ordinary self-command. No such thing; it was merely a strife of courtesy, for the meeting was followed by an extreme attention to all the forms of society, profound curtseys, and the elaborated demeanor which marks ceremony rather than friendship.

Much has been said about the latitude of speech among the women of France, and comparisons have been made between them and our own females, to the disadvantage of the former. If the American usages are to be taken as the standard of delicacy in such matters, I know of no other people who come up to it. As to our mere feelings, habit can render any thing proper, or any thing improper, and it is not an easy matter to say where the line, in conformity with good sense and good taste, should be actually drawn. I confess a leaning to the American school, but how far I am influenced by education, it would not be easy for me to say myself. Foreigners affirm that we are squeamish, and that we wound delicacy oftener by the awkward attempts to protect it, than if we had more simplicity. There may be some truth in this, for though cherishing the notions of my youth, I never belonged to the ultra school at home, which, I believe you will agree with me, rather proves low breeding than good breeding. One sees instances of this truth, not only every day, but every hour of the day. Yesterday, in crossing the Tuileries, I was witness of a ludicrous scene that sufficiently illustrates what I mean. The statues of the garden have little or no drapery. A countryman, and two women of the same class, in passing one, were struck with this circumstance, and their bursts of laughter, running and hiding their faces, and loud giggling, left no one in ignorance of the cause of their extreme bashfulness. Thousands of both sexes pass daily beneath the same statue, without a thought of its nudity, and it is looked upon as a noble piece of sculpture.

In dismissing this subject, which is every way delicate, I shall merely say that usage tolerates a license of speech, of which you probably have no idea, but, that I think one hears very rarely, from a French woman of condition, little that would not be uttered, by an American female, under similar circumstances. So far as my experience goes, there is a marked difference, in this particular, between the women of a middle station and those of a higher rank; by rank, however, I mean hereditary rank, for the revolution has made a *pêle-mêle* in the *salons* of Paris.

Although the *petits soupers* have disappeared, the dinners are very sufficient substitutes. They are given at a better hour, and the service of a French entertainment, so quiet, so entirely free from effort, or chatter about food, is admirably adapted to rendering them agreeable. I am clearly of opinion no one ought to give any entertainment that has not the means of making it pass off as a matter-of-course thing, and without effort. I have certainly seen a few fussy dinners here, but they are surprisingly rare. At home, we have plenty of people who know that a party that has a laboured air is inherently vulgar, but how few are there that know how to treat a brilliant entertainment as a mere matter of course! Paris is full of those desirable houses in which the thing is understood.

The forms of the table vary a little, according to the set one is in. In truly French houses, until quite lately I believe, it was not the custom to change the knife, the duty of which, by the way, is not great, the cookery requiring little more than the fork. In families that mingle more with strangers, both are changed, as with us. A great dinner is served very much as at home, so far as the mere courses are concerned, though I have seen the melons follow the soup. This I believe to be in good taste, though it is not common, and it struck me, at first, as being as much out of season as the old New England custom of eating the pudding before the meat. But the French give small dinners, (small in name, though certainly very great in execution,) in which the dishes are served singly, or nearly so, the entertainment resembling those given by the Turks, and being liable to the same objection; for when there is but a single dish before one, and it is not known whether there is to be any more, it is an awkward thing to decline eating. Such dinners are generally of the best quality, but I think they should never be given except where there is sufficient intimacy to embolden the guest to say *jam satis*.

The old devotion to the sex is not so exclusively the occupation of a French *salon*, as it was, probably, half a century since. I have been in several, where the men were grouped in a corner, talking politics, while the women amused each other, as best they could, in cold, formal lines, looking like so many figures placed there to show off the latest modes of the *toilette*. I do not say this is absolutely common, but it is less rare than you might be apt to suppose.

I can tell you little of the habit of reading manuscripts, in society. Such things are certainly done, for I have been invited to be present on one or two occasions, but having a horror of such exhibitions, I make it a point to be indisposed, the choice lying between the megrims before, or after them. Once, and once only, I have heard a poet recite his verses in a well filled drawing-room, and, though I have every reason to think him clever, my ear was so little accustomed to the language, that, in the mouthing of French recitation, I lost nearly all of it.

I have had an odd pleasure in driving from one house to another, on particular evenings, in order to produce as strong contrasts as my limited visiting list will procure. Having a fair opportunity a few nights since, in consequence of two or three invitations coming in, for the evening on which several houses where I occasionally called were opened, I determined to make a night of it, in order to note the effect. As [Susan] did not know several of the people, I went alone, and you may possibly be amused with an account of my adventures: they shall be told.

In the first place I had to dress, in order to go to dinner at a house that I had never entered, and with a family of which I had never seen a soul. These are incidents which frequently come over a stranger, and, at first, were not a little awkward, but use hardens us to much greater misfortunes. At six, then, I stepped punctually into my *coupé*, and gave Charles the necessary number and street. I ought to tell you that the invitation had come a few days before, and, in a fit of curiosity, I had accepted it, and sent a card, without having the least idea who my host and hostess were, beyond their names. There was something *piquant* in this ignorance, and I had almost made up my mind to go in the same mysterious manner, leaving all to events, when happening, in an idle moment, to ask a lady of my acquaintance, and for whom I have a great respect, if she knew a *Madame* [*Dambray*], to my surprise, her answer was—"Most certainly—she is my cousin, and you are to dine there to-morrow." I said no more, though this satisfied me that my hosts were people of some standing. While driving to their hotel, it struck me, under all the circumstances, it might be well to know more of them, and I stopped at the gate of a female friend, who knows every body, and who, I was certain, would receive me even at that unseasonable hour. I was admitted, explained my errand, and inquired if she knew a *M. [Dambray]*. *"Quelle question!"* she exclaimed—*"M. [Dambray] est Chancelier de France!"* Absurd, and even awkward, as it might have proved, but for this lucky thought, I should have gone and dined with the French Lord High Chancellor, without having the smallest suspicion of who he was!

The hotel was a fine one, though the apartment was merely good, and the reception, service and general style of the house were so simple that neither would have awakened the least suspicion of the importance of my hosts. The party was small and the dinner modest. I found the *chancelier* a grave dignified man, a little curious on the subject of America, and his wife, apparently a woman of great good sense, and, I should think, of a good deal of attainment. Every thing went off in the quietest manner possible, and I was sorry when it was time to go.

From this dinner, I drove to the hotel of the *Marquis de Marbois*, to pay a visit of digestion. M. de Marbois retires so early, on account of his great age, that one is obliged to be punctual, or he will find the gate locked at nine. The company had got back into the drawing-room, and as the last week's guests were mostly there, as well as those who had just left the table, there might have been thirty people present, all of whom were men but two. One of the ladies was Madame de Souza, known in French literature as the writer of several clever novels of society. In the drawing-room, were grouped, in clusters, the Grand Referendary, M. Cuvier, M. Daru, M. Villemain, M. de Plaisance, Mr. Brown, and many others of note. There seemed to be something in the wind, as the conversation was in low confidential whispers, attended by divers ominous shrugs. This could only be politics, and watching an opportunity, I questioned an acquaintance. The fact was really so. The appointed hour had come, and the ministry of M. de Villèle was in the agony. The elections had not been favourable, and it was expedient to make an attempt to reach the *old* end, by what is called a *new* combination. It is necessary to understand the general influence of political intrigues on certain *coteries* of Paris, to appreciate the effect of this intelligence, on a drawing-room filled, like this, with men who had been actors in the principal events of France, for forty years. The name of M. Cuvier was even mentioned as one of the new ministers. Comte Roy was also named, as likely to be the new premier. I was told that this gentleman was one of the greatest landed proprietors of France, his estates being valued at four millions of dollars. The fact is curious, as showing, not on vulgar rumour, but from a respectable source, what is deemed a first rate landed property in this country. It is certainly no merit, nor do I believe it is any very great advantage; but, I think we might materially beat this, even in America. The company soon separated, and I retired.

From the *Place de la Madeleine*, I drove to a house near the *Carrousel*, where I had been invited to step in, in the course of the evening. All the buildings that remain within the intended parallelogram, which will some day make this spot one of the finest squares in the world, have been bought by the government, or nearly so, with the intent to have them pulled down, at a proper time; and the court bestows lodgings, *ad interim*, among them, on its favourites. Madame de [Mirbel] was one of these favoured persons, and she occupies a small apartment in the third story of one of these houses. The rooms were neat and well arranged, but small. Probably the largest does not exceed fifteen feet square. The approach to a Paris lodging is usually either very good, or very bad. In the new buildings may be found some of the mediocrity of the new order of things; but in all those which were erected previously to the revolution, there is nothing but extremes in this, as in most other things. Great luxury and elegance, or great meanness and discomfort. The house of Madame de [Mirbel] happens to be of the latter class, and although all the disagreeables have disappeared from her own rooms, one is compelled to climb up to them, through a dark well of a staircase, by flights of steps not much better than those we use in our stables. You have no notion of such staircases as those I had just descended in the hotels of the *Chancelier* and the *Premier Président*,* nor have we any just idea, as connected with respectable dwellings, of these I had now to clamber up. M. de [Mirbel] is a man of talents and great respectability, and his wife is exceedingly clever, but they are not rich. He is a professor, and she is an artist. After having passed so much of my youth, on top-gallant-yards, and in becketting royals, you are not to suppose, however, I had any great difficulty in getting up these stairs, narrow, steep, and winding as they were.

* M. de Marbois was the first president of the Court of Accounts.

We are now at the door, and I have rung. On whom do you imagine the curtain will rise? On a *réunion* of philosophers come to discuss questions in botany, with M. de [Mirbel], or on artists, assembled to talk over the troubles of their profession, with his wife? The door opens, and I enter.

The little drawing-room is crowded; chiefly with men. Two card tables are set, and at one I recognize a party, in which are three dukes of the *vieille cour*, with M. de Duras at their head! The rest of the company was a little more mixed, but, on the whole, it savoured strongly of Coblentz and the *émigration*. This was more truly French than any thing I had yet stumbled on. One or two of the grandees looked at me as if, better informed than Scott, they knew that General La Fayette had not gone to America to live. Some of these gentlemen certainly do not love us; but I had cut out too much work for the night to stay and return the big looks of even dukes, and, watching an opportunity, when the eyes of Madame de [Mirbel] were another way, I stole out of the room.

Charles now took his orders, and we drove down into the heart of the town, somewhere near the general post-office, or into those mazes of streets that, near two years of practice, have not yet taught me to thread. We entered the court of a large hotel, that was brilliantly lighted, and I ascended, by a noble flight ·of steps, to the first floor. Ante-chambers communicated with a magnificent saloon, which appeared to be near forty feet square. The ceilings were lofty, and the walls were ornamented with military trophies, beautifully designed, and which had the air of being embossed and gilded. I had got into the hotel of one of Napoleon's marshals, you will say, or at least into one of a marshal of the old *régime*. The latter conjecture may be true, but the house is now inhabited by a great woollen manufacturer, whom the events of the day have thrown into the presence of all these military emblems. I found the worthy *industriel* surrounded by a groupe, composed of men of his own stamp, eagerly discussing the recent changes in the government. The women, of whom there might have been a dozen, were ranged, like a neglected parterre, along the opposite side of the room. I paid my compliments, staid a few minutes, and stole away to the next engagement.

We had now to go to a little, retired, house on the *Champs-Elysées*. There were only three or four carriages before the door, and on ascending to a small, but very neat apartment, I found some twenty people collected. The mistress of the house was an English lady, single, of a certain age, and a daughter of the Earl of [Dunmore], who was once governor of New York. Here was a very different set. One or two ladies of the old court, women of elegant manners, and seemingly of good information, several English women, pretty, quiet and clever, besides a dozen men of different nations. This was one of those little *réunions* that are so common in Paris, among the foreigners, in which a small infusion of French serves to leaven a considerable batch of human beings from other parts of the world. As it is always a relief to me to speak my own language, after being a good while among foreigners, I staid an hour at this house. In the course of the evening an Irishman of great wit and of exquisite humour, one of the paragons of the age in his way, came in. In the course of conversation, this gentleman, who is the proprietor of an Irish estate, and a Catholic, told me of an atrocity in the laws of his country, of which until then I was ignorant. It seems that any younger brother, or next heir, might claim the estate by turning Protestant, or drive the incumbent to the same act. I was rejoiced to hear that there was hardly an instance of such profligacy known.* To what baseness will not the struggle for political ascendancy urge us!

In the course of the evening, Mr. ———, the Irish gentleman, gravely introduced me to a Sir James [De Bathe], adding, with perfect gravity, "a gentleman whose father humbugged the Pope—humbugged infallibility." One could not but be amused with such an introduction, urged in a way so infinitely droll, and I ventured, at a proper moment, to ask an explanation, which, unless I was also humbugged, was as follows.

Among the *détenus* in 1804, was Sir [James Michael De Bathe], the father of Sir James [Wynne De Bathe], the person in question. Taking advantage of the presence of the Pope at Paris, he is said to have called on the good-hearted Pius, with great concern of manner, to state his case. He had left his sons in England, and through his absence they had fallen under the care of two Presbyterian aunts; as a father he was naturally anxious to rescue them from this perilous situation. "Now Pius," continued my merry informant, "quite naturally supposed that all this solicitude was in behalf of two orthodox Catholic souls, and he got permission from Napoleon for the return of so good a father, to his own country, never dreaming that the conversion of the boys, if it ever

* I believe this infamous law, however, has been repealed.

took place, would only be from the Protestant Episcopal Church of England, to that of Calvin; or a rescue from one of the devil's furnaces, to pop them into another." I laughed at this story, I suppose with a little incredulity, but my Irish friend insisted on its truth, ending the conversation with a significant nod, Catholic as he was, and saying— "humbugged infallibility!"

By this time it was eleven o'clock, and as I am obliged to keep reasonable hours, it was time to go *the* party of the evening. Count [Pozzo di Borgo], of the [Russian] Legation, gave a great ball. My carriage entered the line at the distance of near a quarter of a mile from the *hôtel; gendarmes* being actively employed in keeping us all in our places. It was half an hour before I was set down, and the *quadrilles* were in full motion when I entered. It was a brilliant affair, much the most so I have ever yet witnessed in a private house. Some said there were fifteen hundred people present. The number seems incredible, and yet, when one comes to calculate, it may be so. As I got into my carriage to go away, Charles informed me that the people at the gates affirmed that more than six hundred carriages had entered the court that evening. By allowing an average of little more than two to each vehicle, we get the number mentioned.

I do not know exactly how many rooms were opened on this occasion, but I should think there were fully a dozen. Two or three were very large *salons*, and the one in the centre, which was almost at fever heat, had crimson hangings, by way of cooling one. I have never witnessed dancing at all comparable to that of the quadrilles of this evening. Usually there is either too much or too little of the dancing master, but on this occasion every one seemed inspired with a love of the art. It was a beautiful sight to see a hundred charming young women, of the first families of Europe, for they were there of all nations, dressed with the simple elegance that is so becoming to the young of the sex, and which is never departed from here until after marriage, moving in perfect time to delightful music, as if animated by a common soul. The men, too, did better than usual, being less lugubrious and mournful than our sex is apt to be in dancing. I do not know how it is in private, but in the world, at Paris, every young woman seems to have a good mother; or, at least, one capable of giving her both a good tone, and good taste.

At this party I met the ———, an intimate friend of the ambassador, and one who also honours me with a portion of her friendship. In talking over the appearance of things, she told me that some hundreds of *applications for invitations* to this ball had been made. "Applications! I cannot conceive of such meanness. In what manner?" "Directly; by note, by personal intercession—almost by tears. Be certain of it, many hundreds have been refused." In America we hear of refusals to go to balls, but we have not yet reached the pass of sending refusals to invite! "Do you see Mademoiselle———, dancing in the set before you?" She pointed to a beautiful French girl, whom I had often seen at her house, but whose family was in a much lower station in society than herself. Certainly—pray how came *she* here?" "I brought her. Her mother was dying to come, too, and she begged me to get an invitation for her and her daughter; but it would not do to bring the mother to such a place, and I was obliged to say no more tickets could be issued. I wished, however, to bring the daughter, she is so pretty, and we compromised the affair in that way." "And to this the mother assented!" "Assented! How can you doubt it—what funny American notions you have brought with you to France!"

I got some droll anecdotes from my companion, concerning the ingredients of the company on this occasion, for she could be as sarcastic as she was elegant. A young woman near us attracted attention by a loud and vulgar manner of laughing. "Do you know that lady?" demanded my neighbour. "I have seen her before, but scarcely know her name." "She is the daughter of your acquaintance, the *Marquise de* ———." "Then she is, or was, a *Mademoiselle de* ———." "She is not, nor properly ever was, a *Mademoiselle de* ———. In the revolution the *Marquis* was imprisoned by you wicked republicans, and the *Marquise* fled to England, whence she returned, after an absence of three years, bringing with her this young lady, then an infant a few months old." "And *Monsieur le Marquis?*" "He never saw his daughter, having been beheaded in Paris, about a year before her birth." "*Quelle contretemps!*" "*N'est-ce pas?*"

It is a melancholy admission, but it is no less true, that good breeding is sometimes quite as active a virtue, as good principles. How many more of the company present were born about a year after their fathers were beheaded, I have no means of knowing; but had it been the case with all of them, the company would have been of as elegant demeanor, and of much more *retenue* of deportment, than we are accustomed to see, I will not say in *good*, but certainly in *general* society, at home. One of the consequences of good breeding is also a disinclination, positively a distaste, to pry into the private affairs of others. The little specimen to the contrary, just named, was rather an exception, owing to the character of the individual, and to the indiscretion of the young lady in laughing too loud, and then the affair of a birth so *very* posthumous was rather too *patent* to escape all criticism.

My friend was in a gossiping mood this evening, and as she was well turned of fifty, I ventured to continue the conversation. As some of the *liaisons* which exist here must be novel to you, I shall mention one or two more.

A *Madame de J*—— passed us, leaning on the arm of *M. de C*——. I knew the former, who was a widow; had frequently visited her, and had been surprised at the intimacy which existed between her and *M. de C*——, who always appeared quite at home, in her house. I ventured to ask my neighbour if the gentleman were the brother of the lady. "Her brother! It is to be hoped not, as he is her husband." "Why does she not bear his name, if that be the case?" "Because her first husband is of a more illustrious family than her second; and then there are some difficulties on the score of fortune. No, no. These people are *bonâ fide* married. *Tenez*— do you see that gentleman who is standing so assiduously near the chair of *Madame de S*——? He who is all attention and smiles to the lady?" "Certainly— his politeness is even affectionate." "Well it ought to be, for it is *M. de S*——, her husband." "They are a happy couple, then." "*Hors de doute*— he meets her at *soirées* and balls; is the pink of politeness; puts on her shawl; sees her safe into her carriage, and—" "Then they drive home together, as loving as Darby and Joan." "And then he jumps into his *cabriolet*, and drives to the lodgings of——. *Bon soir, Monsieur* [*Cooper*], you are making me fall into the vulgar crime of scandal."

Now, as much as all this may sound like invention, it is quite true, that I repeat no more to you than was said to me, and no more than what I believe to be exact. As respects the latter couple, I have been elsewhere told that they literally never see each other, except in public, where they constantly meet, as the best friends in the world.

I was lately in some English society, when Lady G —— bet a pair of gloves with Lord R—— that he had not seen Lady R—— in a fortnight. The bet was won by the gentleman, who proved satisfactorily that he had met his wife at a dinner party, only ten days before.

After all I have told you, and all that you may have heard from others, I am nevertheless inclined to believe, that the high society of

Paris is quite as exemplary as that of any other large European town. If we are any better ourselves, is it not more owing to the absence of temptation, than to any other cause? Put large garrisons into our towns, fill the streets with idlers, who have nothing to do but to render themselves agreeable, and with women with whom dress and pleasure are the principal occupations, and then let us see what protestantism and liberty will avail us, in this particular. The intelligent French say that their society is improving in morals. I can believe this, of which I think there is sufficient proof by comparing the present with the past, as the latter has been described to us. By the past, I do not mean the period of the revolution, when vulgarity assisted to render vice still more odious—a happy union, perhaps, for those who were to follow—but the days of the old *régime*. Chance has thrown me in the way of three or four old dowagers of that period, women of high rank, and still in the first circles, who, amid all their *finesse* of breeding, and ease of manner, have had a most desperate *rouée* air about them. Their very laugh, at times, has seemed replete with a bold levity, that was as disgusting as it was unfeminine. I have never, in any other part of the world, seen loose sentiments *affichés*, with more effrontery. These women are the complete antipodes of the quiet, elegant *Princesse de* ———, who was at Lady [Virginia Murray]'s, this evening; though some of them write *Princesses* on their cards, too.

The influence of a court must be great on the morals of those who live in its purlieus. Conversing with the Duc de ———, a man who has had general currency in the best society of Europe, on this subject, he said,—"England has long decried our manners. Previously to the revolution, I admit they were bad; perhaps worse than her own; but I know nothing in our history as bad as what I lately witnessed in England. You know I was there, quite recently. The king invited me to dine at Windsor. I found every one in the drawing-room, but His Majesty and Lady [Conyngham]. She entered but a minute before him, like a queen. Her reception was that of a queen; young, unmarried females kissed her hand. Now, all this might happen in France, even now; but Louis XV., the most dissolute of our monarchs, went no farther. At Windsor, I saw the husband, sons, and daughters of the favourite, in the circle! *Le Parc-aux-Cerfs* was not as bad as this."

"And yet, M. de ———, since we are conversing frankly, listen to what I witnessed, but the other day, in France. You know the situation of things at St. Ouen, and the rumours that are so rife. We had the *fête*

*Dieu*, during my residence there. You, who are a Catholic, need not be told that your sect believe in the doctrine of the 'real presence.' There was a *reposoir* erected in the garden of the *château*, and God, in person, was carried, with religious pomp, to rest in the bowers of the ex-favourite. It is true, the husband was not present: he was only in the provinces!"

"The influence of a throne makes sad parasites and hypocrites," said M. de ———, shrugging his shoulders.

"And the influence of the people, too, though in a different way. A courtier is merely a well-dressed demagogue."

"It follows, then, that man is just a poor devil."

But I am gossiping away with you, when my Asmodean career is ended, and it is time I went to bed. Good night.

v.    The Palace of Versailles, from the Park

VI.    The Castle of Pierre Fonds

VII. The Abattoir of Montmartre

VIII.   The Palace of the Tuilleries, from the Garden

# Letter XIX
### To Jacob Sutherland, Esquire, New York.

The Chambers have been opened with the customary ceremonies and parade. It is usual for the King, attended by a brilliant *cortège*, to go, on these occasions, from the Tuileries to the Palais Bourbon, through lines of troops, under a salute of guns. The French love *spectacles*, and their monarch, if he would be popular, is compelled to make himself one, at every plausible opportunity.

The garden of the Tuileries is a parallelogram, of, I should think, fifty acres, of which one end is bounded by the palace. It has a high vaulted terrace on the side next the river, as well as at the opposite end, and one a little lower, next the *rue de Rivoli*. There is also a very low broad terrace, immediately beneath the windows of the palace, which separates the buildings from the *parterres*. You will understand that the effect of this arrangement, is to shut out the world from the persons in the garden, by means of the terraces, and, indeed, to enable them, by taking refuge in the woods that fill quite half the area, to bury themselves almost in a forest. The public has free access to this place, from an early hour in the morning, to eight or nine at night, according to the season. When it is required to clear them, a party of troops marches, by beat of drum, from the *château*, through the great *allée*, to the lower end of the garden. This is always taken as the signal to disperse, and the world begins to go out, at the different gates. It is understood that the place is frequently used as a promenade, by the royal family, after this hour, especially in the fine season; but, as it would be quite easy for any one, evilly disposed, to conceal himself among the trees, statues and shrubs, the troops are extended in very open order, and march slowly back to the palace, of course driving every one before them. Each gate is locked, as the line passes it.

The only parts of the garden, which appear, on the exterior, to be on a level with the street, though such is actually the fact with the whole of the interior, are the great gate opposite the palace, and a side gate near its southern end; the latter being the way by which one passes out, to cross the Pont Royal.

In attempting to pass in at this gate the other morning, for the first time, at that hour, I found it closed. A party of ladies and gentlemen were walking on the low terrace, beneath the palace windows, and a hundred people might have been looking at them from without. A second glance showed me, that among some children, were the heir presumptive, and his sister Mademoiselle d'Artois. The exhibition could merely be an attempt to feel the public pulse, for the country house of *la Bagatelle*, to which the children go two or three times a week, is much better suited to taking the air. I could not believe in the indifference that was manifested, had I not seen it. The children are both engaging, particularly the daughter, and yet, these innocent and perfectly inoffensive beings were evidently regarded more with aversion, than with affection.

The display of the opening of the session produced no more effect on the public mind, than the appearance on the terrace of *les Enfants de France*. The Parisians are the least loyal of Charles's subjects, and though the troops, and a portion of the crowd, cried *vive le roi*, it was easy to see that the disaffected were more numerous than the well-affected.

I have attended some of the sittings since the opening, and shall now say a word on the subject of the French parliamentary proceedings. The hall is an amphitheatre, like our own; the disposition of the seats and speaker's chair being much the same as at Washington. The members sit on benches, however, that rise one behind the other, and through which they ascend and descend, by aisles. These aisles separate the different shades of opinion, for those who think alike sit together. Thus the *gauche* or left is occupied by the extreme liberals; the *centre gauche*, by those who are a shade nearer the Bourbons. The *centre droit*, or right centre, by the true Bourbonists, and so on, to the farthest point of the semicircle. Some of the members affect even to manifest the minuter shades of their opinions, by their relative positions in their own sections, and I believe it is usual for each one to occupy his proper place.

You probably know that the French members speak from a stand, immediately beneath the chair of the president, called a tribune. Absurd as this may seem, I believe it to be a very useful regulation, the vivacity of the national character rendering some such check on loquacity quite necessary. Without it, a dozen would often be on their feet at once; as it is, even, this sometimes happens. No disorder that ever occurs in our legislative bodies, will give you any just notion of that which frequently occurs here. The president rings a bell as a summons to keep order, and as a last resource he puts on his hat, a signal that the sitting is suspended.

The speaking of both chambers is generally bad. Two-thirds of the members read their speeches, which gives the sitting a dull, monotonous character, and as you may suppose, the greater part of their lectures are very little attended to. The most parliamentary speaker is M. Royer Collard, who is, just now, so popular that he has been returned for seven different places at the recent election.

M. Constant is an exceedingly animated speaker, resembling in this particular Mr. McDuffie. M. Constant, however, has a different motion from the last gentleman, his movement being a constant oscillation over the edge of the tribune, about as fast, and almost as regular, as that of the pendulum of a large clock. It resembles that of a sawyer in the Mississippi. General La Fayette speaks with the steadiness and calm, that you would expect from his character, and is always listened to with respect. Many professional men speak well, and exercise considerable influence in the house, for here, as elsewhere, the habit of public and extemporaneous speaking gives an immediate ascendancy in deliberative bodies.

Some of the scenes one witnesses in the Chamber of Deputies are amusing by their exceeding vivacity. The habit of crying *écoutez* prevails, as in the English parliament, though the different intonations of that cry are not well understood. I have seen members run at the tribune, like children playing puss in a corner; and, on one occasion, I saw five different persons on its steps, in waiting for the descent of the member in possession. When a great question is to be solemnly argued, the members inscribe their names for the discussion, and are called on to speak in the order in which they stand on the list.

The French never sit in committee of the whole, but they have adopted in its place an expedient, that gives power more control over the proceedings of the two houses. At the commencement of the session, the members draw for their numbers in the *bureaux*, as they are called. Of these *bureaux*, there are ten or twelve, and, as a matter of course, they include all the members. As soon as the numbers are drawn, the members assemble in their respective rooms, and choose their officers; a president and secretary. These elections are always supposed to be indicative of the political tendency of each *bureau*;

those which have a majority of liberals, choosing officers of their own opinions, and *vice versâ*. These *bureaux* are remodelled, periodically, by drawing anew; the term of duration being a month or six weeks. I believe the chamber retains the power to refer questions, or not, to these *bureaux*; their institution being no more than a matter of internal regulation, and not of constitutional law. It is, however, usual to send all important laws to them, where they are discussed and voted on: the approbation of a majority of the *bureaux* being, in such cases, necessary for their reception in the chambers.

The great evil of the present system is the *initiative* of the king. By this reservation in the charter, the crown possesses more than a veto, all laws actually emanating from the sovereign. The tendency of such a regulation is either to convert the chambers into the old *lits de justice*, or to overthrow the throne, an event which will certainly accompany any serious change here. As might have been, and as *would* have been anticipated, by any one familiar with the action of legislative bodies, in our time, this right is already so vigorously assailed, as to give rise to constant contentions between the great powers of the state. All parties are agreed that no law can be presented, that does not come originally from the throne; but the liberals are for putting so wide a construction on the right to amend, as already to threaten to pervert the regulation. This has driven some of the Bourbonists to maintain that the chambers have no right, at all, to amend a royal proposition. Any one may foresee, that this is a state of things which cannot peaceably endure for any great length of time. The ministry are compelled to pack the chambers, and in order to effect their objects, they resort to all the expedients of power that offer. As those who drew up the charter had neither the fore-thought, nor the experience, to anticipate all the embarrassments of a parliamentary government, they unwittingly committed themselves, and illegal acts are constantly resorted to, in order that the system may be upheld. The charter was bestowed *ad captandum*, and is a contradictory *mélange* of inexpedient concessions and wily reservations. The conscription undermined the popularity of Napoleon, and Louis XVIII., in his charter says, "The conscription is abolished; the *recruiting* for the army and navy shall be settled by a law." Now the conscription *is not* abolished; but, if pushed on this point, a French jurist would perhaps tell you it is *now* established by law. The feudal exclusiveness, on the subject of taxation, is done away with, all men being equally liable to taxation. The nett pay of the army is about two sous a day; *this* is settled by law, passed by the representatives of those who pay two hundred francs a year, in direct taxation. The conscription, in appearance, is general and fair enough; but he who has money can always hire a substitute, at a price quite within his power. It is only the poor man, who is never in possession of one or two thousand francs, that is obliged to serve seven years at two sous a day, nett.

France has gained, beyond estimate, by the changes from the old to the present system, but it is in a manner to render further violent changes necessary. I say *violent*, for political changes are everywhere unavoidable, since questions of polity are, after all, no other than questions of facts, and these are interests that will regulate themselves, directly or indirectly. The great desideratum of a government, after settling its principles in conformity with controlling facts, is to secure to itself the means of progressive change, without the apprehension of convulsion. Such is not the case with France, and further revolutions are inevitable. The mongrel government which exists, neither can stand, nor does it deserve to stand. It contains the seeds of its own destruction. Here, you will be told, that the King is a Jesuit, that he desires to return to the ancient *régime*, and that the opposition wishes merely to keep him within the limits of the charter. My own observations lead to a very different conclusion. The difficulty is in the charter itself, which leaves the government neither free, nor despotic; in short, without any distinctive character.

This defect is so much felt, that, in carrying out the details of the system, much that properly belongs to it has been studiously omitted. The King can do no wrong, here, as in England, but the ministers are responsible. By way of making a parade of this responsibility, every official act of the king is countersigned by the minister of the proper department, and, by the theory of the government, that particular minister is responsible for that particular act. Now, by the charter, the peers are the judges of political crimes. By the charter, also, it is stipulated that no one can be proceeded against except in cases expressly provided for by law, and in the *forms* prescribed by the law. You will remember that, all the previous constitutions being declared illegal, Louis XVIII. dates his reign from the supposed death of Louis XVII., and that there are no fundamental precedents that may be drawn in to aid the constructions, but that the charter must be interpreted by its own provisions. It follows, then, as a consequence, that no minister can be legally punished until a law is enacted to dictate the punishment, explain the offences, and point out the forms of procedure. Now, no such law has ever been proposed, and although the chambers may *recommend* laws to the king, they must await his pleasure in order even to discuss them openly, and enlist the public feeling in their behalf. The responsibility of the ministers was proposed *ad captandum*, like the abolition of the conscription, but neither has been found convenient in practice.*

The electors of France are said to be between eighty and one hundred thousand. The qualifications of a deputy being much higher than those of an elector, it is computed that the four hundred and fifty members must be elected from among some four or five thousand available candidates. It is not pretended that France does not contain more than this number of individuals who pay a thousand francs a year in direct taxes, for taxation is so great that this sum is soon made up; but a deputy must be forty years old, a regulation which at once excludes fully one half the men, of itself; and then it will be recollected that many are superannuated, several hundreds are peers, others cannot quit their employments, &c., &c. I have seen the number of available candidates estimated as low, even, as three thousand.

The elections in France are conducted in a mode peculiar to the nation. The electors of the highest class have two votes, or for representatives of two descriptions. This plan was an after-thought of the king, for the original charter contains no such regulation, but the munificent father of the national liberties saw fit, subsequently, to qualify his gift. Had Louis XVIII. lived a little longer, he would most probably have been dethroned before this; the hopes and expectations which usually accompany a new reign, having, most probably, deferred the crisis for a few years. The electors form themselves into colleges, into which no one who is not privileged to vote is admitted. This is a good regulation, and might be copied to advantage at home. A law prescribing certain limits around each poll, and rendering it penal for any but those authorized to vote at that particular poll, to cross it, would greatly purify our elections. The government, here, appoints the presiding officer of each electoral college, and the selection is always carefully made of one in the interests of the ministry, though in

---

* When the ministers of Charles X. were tried, it was without law, and they would probably have escaped punishment altogether, on this plea, had not the condition of the public mind required a concession.

what manner such a functionary can influence the result, is more than I can tell you. It is, however, thought to be favourable to an individual's own election to get this nomination. The vote is by ballot, though the charter secures no such privilege. Indeed that instrument is little more than a declaration of rights, fortified by a few general constituent laws.

The same latitude exists here, in the constructions of the charter, as exists at home, in the constructions of the constitution. The French have, however, one great advantage over us, in daring to think for themselves elevated into, as La Fayette expresses, so many "little imitate England, too, it is neither a numerous nor a strong party. These *doctrinaires*, as the name implies, are men who wish to defer to theories, rather than facts; a class, that is to be found all over the world. For obvious reasons, the English system has admirers throughout Europe, as well as in America, since nothing can be more agreeable, for those who are in a situation to look forward to such an advantage, than to see themselves elevated into, as La Fayette expresses, so many "little legitimacies." The peerage, with its exclusive and hereditary benefits, is the aim of all the nobility of Europe, and wishes of this sort make easy converts to any philosophy that may favour the desire.

One meets, here, with droll evidences of the truth of what I have just told you. I have made the acquaintance of a Russian of very illustrious family, and he has always been loud and constant in his eulogiums of America and her liberty. Alluding to the subject, the other day, he amused me by *naïvely* observing, "Ah, you are a happy people — you are *free* — and so are the *English*. Now, in Russia, all rank depends on the commission one bears in the army, or on the will of the Emperor. I am a Prince; my father was a Prince; my grandfather, too; but it is of no avail. I get no privileges by my birth; whereas, in England, where I have been, it is *so* different — and I dare say it is different in America, too?" I told him it was, indeed, "very different in America." He sighed, and seemed to envy me.

The party of the *doctrinaires* is the one that menaces the most serious evil to France. It is inherently the party of aristocracy; and, in a country as far advanced as France, it is the combinations of the few, that, after all, are most to be apprehended. The worst of it is, that, in countries where abuses have so long existed, the people get to be so disqualified for entertaining free institutions, that even the disinterested and well-meaning are often induced to side with the rapacious and selfish, to prevent the evils of reaction.

In a country so much inclined to speculate, to philosophize, and to reason on every thing, it is not surprising that a fundamental law, as vaguely expressed as the charter, should leave ample room for discussion. We find that our own long experience in these written instruments, does not protect us from violent differences of opinion, some of which are quite as extravagant as any that exist here, though possibly less apt to lead to as grave consequences.*

* The discussion which grew out of the law to protect American industry, affords a singular instance of the manner in which clever men can persuade themselves and others, into any notion, however extravagant. The uncouth doctrine of nullification turned on the construction that might be put on the intimacy of the relations created by the Union, and on the nature of the sovereignties of the states.

Because the constitution commences with a declaration, that it is formed and adopted by "we the people of the United States," overlooking, not only all the facts of the case, but misconceiving the very meaning of the words they quote, one party virtually contended, that the instrument was formed by a consolidated nation. On this point their argument, certainly sustained in part by unanswerable truth, mainly depends.

The word "people" has notoriously several significations. It means a "population;" it means the "vulgar;" it means any particular portion of a population, as "rich people," "poor people," "mercantile people," &c. &c. In a political sense, it has always been understood to mean that portion of the population of a country, which is possessed of *political rights*. On this sense, then, it means a *constituency* in a representative government, and so it has always been understood in England, and is understood to-day in France. When a question is referred to the "people" at an election in England, it is not referred to a tithe of the population, but to a particular portion of it. In South Carolina and Louisiana, in the popular sense of Mr. Webster, there is no "people" to refer to, a majority of the men of both states possessing no civil rights, and scarcely having a civil existence. Besides "people," in its broad signification, includes men, women and children, and no one will contend, that the two latter had any thing to do with the formation of our constitution. It follows, then, that the term has been used in a limited sense, and we must look to incidental facts to discover its meaning.

The convention was chosen not by any common constituency, but by the constituencies of the several states, which, at that time, embraced every gradation between a democratical and an aristocratical polity. Thirteen states existed in 1787, and yet the constitution was to go into effect when it was adopted by any nine of them. It will not be pretended that this decision would be binding on the other four, and yet it is possible that these four dissenting states should contain more than half of all the population of the confederation. It would be very easy to put a proposition, in which it might be demonstrated arithmetically, that the constitution could have been adopted against a considerable majority of whole numbers. In the face of such a fact, it is folly to suppose the term "people" is used in any other than a conventional sense. It is well known, in addition to the mode of its adoption, that every provision of the constitution can be altered, with a single exception, by three-fourths of the states. Perhaps more than half of the entire population, (excluding the Territories and the District,) is in six of the largest states, at this moment. But whether this be so or not, such a combination could easily be made, as would demonstrate that less than a third of the population of the country, can at any time alter the constitution.

It is probable that the term "we the people," was used in a sort of contra-distinction to the old implied right of the sovereignty of the king, just as we idly substituted the words "God save the people," at the end of a proclamation, for "God save the king." It was a form. But, if it is desirable to affix to them any more precise signification, it will not do to generalize, according to the argument of one party; but we are to take the words, in their limited and appropriate meaning, and with their accompanying facts. They can only allude to the constituencies, and these constituencies existed only *through* the states, and were as varied as their several systems. If the meaning of the term "we the people" was misconceived, it follows that the argument which was drawn from the error was worthless. The constitution of the United States was not formed by the *people* of the United States, but by such a portion of them as it suited the several states to invest with political powers, and under such combinations as gave the decision to any thing but a majority of the nation. In other words, the constitution was certainly formed by the *states* as *political bodies*, and without any necessary connection with any general or uniform system of polity.

Any theory based on the separate sovereignties of the states, has, on the other hand, a frail support. The question was not *who* formed the constitution, but *what* was formed. All the great powers of sovereignty, such as foreign relations, the right to treat, make war and peace, to control commerce, to coin money, &c. &c. are expressly ceded. But these are not, after all, the greatest blows that are given to the doctrine of reserved sovereignty. A power to *alter* the constitution, as has just been remarked, has been granted, by which even the *dissenting states* have become bound. The only right reserved, is that of the equal representation in the senate, and it would follow, perhaps, as a legitimate consequence, the preservation of the confederated polity; but South Carolina could, under the theory of the constitution, be stripped of her right to control nearly every social interest; every man, woman and child in the state dissenting. It is scarcely worth while to construct a sublimated theory, on the sovereignty of a community so situated by the legitimate theory of the government, under which it actually exists!

No means can be devised, that will always protect the weak from the aggressions of the strong, under the forms of law; and nature has pointed out the remedy, when the preponderance of good is against submission; but one cannot suppress his expression of astonishment, at finding any respectable portion of a reasoning community, losing sight of this simple and self-evident truth, to uphold a doctrine as weak as that of nullification, viewed as a legal remedy.

If the American statesmen, (*quasi* and real,) would imitate, the good curate and the bachelor of Don Quixote, by burning all the political heresies, with which their libraries, not to say their brains, are now crammed, and set seriously about studying the terms, and the nature of the national compact, without reference to the notions of men who had no connection with the country, the public would be the gainers, and occasionally one of them might stand a chance of descending to posterity in some other light than that of the mere leader of a faction.

# Letter XX

## To R. Cooper, Esq., Cooperstown.

I have said nothing to you of La Grange, though I have now been there no less than three times. Shortly after our arrival in Paris, Gen. La Fayette had the kindness to send us an invitation, but we were deterred from going, for some time, by the indisposition of one of the family. In the autumn of 1826 I went, however, alone; in the spring I went again, carrying Mrs. [Cooper] with me; and I have now just returned from a third visit, in which I went with my wife, accompanied by one or two more of the family.

It is about twenty-seven miles from Paris to Rosay, a small town that is a league from the castle. This is not a post-route, the great road ending at Rosay, and we were obliged to go the whole distance with the same horses. Paris is left by the *Boulevard de la Bastille*, the *Barrière du Trône*, and the *château* and woods of Vincennes. The second time I went into *Brie*, it was with the general himself, and in his own carriage. He showed me a small pavilion, that is still standing in a garden near the old site of the Bastile, and which he told me once belonged to the hotel that *Beaumarchais* inhabited, when in his glory, and in which pavilion this witty writer was accustomed to work. The roof was topped by a vane, to show which way the wind.blew, and in pure *fanfaronnade*, or to manifest his contempt for principles, the author of Figaro had caused a large copper *pen* to do the duty of a weather-cock, and there it stands to this day, a curious memorial equally of his wit and of his audacity.

At the *Barrière du Trône* the general pointed out to me the spot where two of his female connexions suffered under the *guillotine*, during the reign of terror. On one occasion, in passing, we entered the castle of Vincennes, which is a sort of citadel for Paris, and which has served for a state prison since the destruction of the Bastile. Almost all of these strong old places were formerly the residences of the kings, or of great nobles, the times requiring that they should live constantly protected by ditches and walls.

Vincennes, like the tower of London, is a collection of old buildings, enclosed within a wall, and surrounded by a ditch. The latter, however, is dry. The most curious of the structures, and the one which gives the place its picturesque appearance, in the distance, is a cluster of exceedingly slender, tall, round towers, in which the prisoners are usually confined, and which is the *donjon* of the hold. This building, which contains many vaulted rooms piled on each other, was formerly the royal abode, and it has even now a ditch of its own, though it stands within the outer walls of the place. There are many other high towers on the walls, and until the reign of Napoleon there were still more, but he caused them to be razed to the level of the walls, which of themselves are sufficiently high.

The chapel is a fine building, being Gothic. It was constructed in the time of Charles V. There are also two or three vast *corps de bâtiments*, which are almost palaces in extent and design, though they are now used only as quarters for officers, &c. &c. The *donjon* dates from the same reign. The first room in this building is called the *salle de la question*, a name which sufficiently denotes its infernal use. That of the upper story is the room in which the kings of France formerly held their councils. The walls are sixteen feet thick, and the rooms are thirty feet high. As there are five stories, this *donjon* cannot be less than a hundred and forty or fifty feet in elevation. The view from the summit is very extensive, though it is said that, in the time of Napoleon, a screen was built around the battlement, to prevent the prisoners, when they took the air, from enjoying it. As this conqueror was cruel from policy alone, it is probable this was merely a precaution against signals; for it is quite apparent, if he desired to torment his captives, France has places better adapted to the object than even the *donjon* of Vincennes. I am not his apologist, however; for, while I shall not go quite as far as the Englishman who maintained, in a laboured treatise, that Napoleon was the beast of the Revelations, I believe he was any thing but a god.

Vincennes was a favourite residence of St. Louis, and there is a tradition that he used to take his seat under a particular oak, in the adjoining forest, where all who pleased were permitted to come before him, and receive justice from himself. Henry V. of England died in the *donjon of Vincennes*, and I believe his successor, Henry VI., was born in the same building. One gets a better notion of the state of things, in the ages of feudality, by passing an hour in examining such a hold, than in a week's reading. After going through this habitation, and studying its barbarous magnificence, I feel much more disposed to believe that

Shakspeare has not outraged probability in his dialogue between Henry and Catharine, than if I had never seen it, bad as that celebrated love scene is.

Shortly after quitting Vincennes, the road crosses the Marne, and stretches away across a broad bottom. There is little of interest between Paris and Rosay. The principal house is that of Gros Bois, which once belonged to Moreau, I believe, but is now the property of the Prince de Wagram, the young son of Berthier. The grounds are extensive, and the house is large, though I think neither in very good taste, at least so far as one could judge in passing.

There are two or three ruins on this road, of some historical interest, but not of much beauty. There is usually a nakedness, unrelieved by trees or other picturesque accessories, about the French ruins, which robs them of half their beauty, and dirty, squalid hamlets and villages, half the time, come in to render the picture still less interesting.

At Rosay another route is taken, and La Grange is approached by the rear, after turning a small bit of wood. It is possible to see the tops of the towers, for an instant, on the great road before reaching the town.

It is not certainly known in what age the *château* was built, but, from its form, and a few facts connected with its origin, whose dates *are* ascertained, it is thought to be about five hundred years old. It never was more than a second-rate building of its class, though it was clearly intended for a baronial hold. Originally, the name was *La Grange en Brie*, but by passing into a new family it got the appellation of La Grange Bléneau, by which it is known at present. You are sufficiently familiar with French to understand that *grange* means barn or granary, and that a liberal translation would make it Bleneau-farm.

In 1399, a marriage took place between the son of the lord of La Grange en Brie, with a daughter of a branch of the very ancient and great family of *Courtenay*, which had extensive possessions, at that time, in Brie. It was this marriage which gave the new name to the castle, the estate in consequence passing into the line of *Courtenay-Bléneau*. In 1595 the property, by another marriage with an heiress, passed into the well-known family *d'Aubussons, Comtes de la Feuillade*. The first proprietor of this name was the grandfather of the *Maréchal de la Feuillade*, the courtier who caused the *Place des Victoires* to be constructed at Paris, and he appropriated the revenues of the estate, which, in 1686, were valued at nine thousand francs, to the support and completion of his work of flattery. The property at that time was, however, much more extensive than it is at present. The son of this courtier dying without issue in 1725, the estate was purchased by M. Dupré, one of the judges of France.

With this magistrate commences, I believe, the connexion of the ancestors of the La Fayettes with the property. The only daughter married M. d'Aguesseau; and her daughter again, married the duc de Noailles-d'Ayen, carrying with her, as a marriage portion, the lands of Fontenay, La Grange, &c. &c., or in other words, the ancient possessions of M. de la Feuillade. The Marquis de La Fayette married one of the Mesdemoiselles de Noailles, while he was still a youth, and when the estate, after a short sequestration, was restored to the family, General La Fayette received the *château* of La Grange, with some six or eight hundred acres of land around it, as his wife's portion.*

Although the house is not very spacious for a *château* of the region in which it stands, it is a considerable edifice, and one of the most picturesque I have seen in this country. The buildings stand on three sides of an irregular square. The fourth side must have been either a high wall, or a range of low offices formerly, to complete the court and the defences, but every vestige of them has long since been removed. The ditch, too, which originally encircled the whole castle, has been filled in, on two sides, though still remaining on the two others, and greatly contributing to the beauty of the place, as the water is living, and is made to serve the purposes of a fish-pond. We had carp from it, for breakfast, the day after our arrival.

La Grange is constructed of hewn stone, of a good greyish colour, and in parts of it there are some respectable pretensions to architecture. I think it probable that one of its fronts has been rebuilt, the style being so much better than the rest of the structure. There are five towers, all of which are round, and have the plain, high, pyramidal roof, so common in France. They are without cornices, battlements of any sort, or, indeed, any relief to the circular masonry. One, however, has a roof of a square form, though the exterior of the tower itself is, at least, in part, round. All the roofs are of slate.

The approach to the castle is circuitous, until quite near it, when the road enters a little thicket of evergreens, crosses a bridge, and passes

---

* Mr. Adams, in his Eulogy on La Fayette, has called the duc de Noailles, the first peer of France. The fact is of no great moment, but accuracy is always better than error. I believe the duc de Noailles was the youngest of the old *ducs et pairs* of France. The duc d'Uzès, I have always understood was the oldest.

beneath an arch to the court, which is paved. The bridge is now permanent, though there was once a draw, and the grooves of a port-cullis are still visible beneath the arch. The shortest side of the square is next the bridge, the building offering here but little more than the two towers, and the room above the gate-way. One of these towers forms the end of this front of the castle, and the other is of course, at an angle. On the exterior, they are both buried in ivy, as well as the building which connects them. This ivy was planted by Charles Fox, who, in company with General Fitzpatrick visited La Grange, after the peace of Amiens. The windows, which are small and irregular on this side, open beautifully through the thick foliage, and as this is the part of the structure that is occupied by the children of the family, their blooming faces thrust through the leafy apertures have a singularly pleasing effect. The other three towers stand, one near the centre of the principal *corps de bâtiment*, one at the other angle, and the third at the end of the wing opposite that of the gate. The towers vary in size, and are all more or less buried in the walls, though still so distinct as greatly to relieve the latter, and every where to rise above them. On the open side of the court there is no ditch, but the ground, which is altogether park-like, and beautifully arranged, falls away, dotted with trees and copses, towards a distant thicket.

Besides the *rez de chaussée*, which is but little above the ground, there are two good stories all round the building, and even more in the towers. The dining-room and offices are below, and there is also a small oratory, or chapel, though I believe none of the family live there. The entrance to the principal apartments is opposite the gate, and there is also here, an exterior door which communicates directly with the lawn, the ditch running behind the other wing, and in front of the gate only. The great stair-case is quite good, being spacious, easy of ascent, and of marble, with a handsome iron railing. It was put there by the mother of Madame La Fayette, I believe, and the general told me, it was nearly the only thing of value, that he found among the fixtures, on taking possession. It had escaped injury.

I should think the length of the house on the side of the square which contains the stair-case, might be ninety feet, including the tower at the end, and the tower at the angle; and perhaps the side which contains the offices, may be even a little longer; though this will also include the same tower in the same angle, as well as the one at the opposite corner; while the side in which is the gate-way can scarcely exceed sixty feet. If my estimates, which are merely made by the eye, are correct, including the towers, this would give an outside wall of two hundred and fifty feet, in circuit. Like most French buildings, the depth is comparatively much less. I question if the outer drawing-room is more than eighteen feet wide, though it is near thirty long. This room has windows on the court and on the lawn, and is the first apartment one enters after ascending the stairs. It communicates with the inner drawing-room, which is in the end tower of this side of the *château*, is quite round, of course, and may be twenty feet in diameter.

The General's apartments are on the second floor. They consist of his bed-room, a large cabinet, and the library. The latter is in the tower at the angle, on the side of the stair-case. It is circular, and from its windows overlooks the moat, which is beautifully shaded by willows and other trees. It contains a respectable collection of books, besides divers curiosities.

The only bed-rooms I have occupied are, one in the tower, immediately beneath the library, and the other in the side tower, or the only one which does not stand at an angle, or at an end of the building. I believe, however, that the entire edifice, with the exception of the oratory, the offices, the dining-room, which is a large apartment on the *rez de chaussée*, the two drawing-rooms, two or three cabinets, and the library, and perhaps a family-room or two, such as a school-room, painting-room, &c., is subdivided into sleeping apartments, with the necessary cabinets and dressing-rooms. Including the family, I have known thirty people to be lodged in the house, besides servants, and I should think it might even lodge more. Indeed its hospitality seems to know no limits, for every new comer appears to be just as welcome as all the others.

The cabinet of La Fayette communicates with the library, and I passed much of the time during our visit, alone with him, in these two rooms. I may say that this was the commencement of a confidence with which he has since continued to treat me, and of a more intimate knowledge of the amiable features and simple integrity of his character, that has greatly added to my respect. No one can be pleasanter in private, and he is full of historical anecdotes, that he tells with great simplicity, and frequently with great humour. The cabinet contains many portraits, and, among others, one of Mad. de Stael, and one of his own father. The former I am assured is exceedingly like; it is not the resemblance of a very fascinating woman. In the latter I find more resemblance to some of the grandchildren than to the son, although there is something about the shape of the head that is not unlike that of La Fayette's.

Gen. La Fayette never knew his father, who was killed, when he was quite an infant, at the battle of Minden. I believe the general was an only child, for I have never heard him speak of any brother or sister, nor indeed of any relative at all, as I can remember, on his own side, though he often alludes to the connexions he made by his marriage. I asked him how his father happened to be styled the *Comte* de La Fayette, and he to be called the *Marquis*. He could not tell me: his grandfather was the *Marquis* de La Fayette, his father the *Comte*, and he again was termed the *Marquis*. "I know very little about it," said he, "beyond this. I found myself a little *Marquis*, as I grew to know any thing, and boys trouble themselves very little about such matters; and then I soon got tired of the name, after I went to America. I cannot explain all the foolish distinctions of the feudal times, but I very well remember that when I was quite a boy, I had the honour to go through the ceremony of appointing the *curé* of a very considerable town in *Auvergne*, of which I was the *Seigneur*. My conscience has been quite easy about the nomination, however, as my guardians must answer for the sin, if there be any."

I was at a small dinner given by the *Comte de Ségur*, just before we went to La Grange, and at which Gen. La Fayette and M. Alexander de Lameth were also guests. The three had served in America, all of them having been colonels while little more than boys. In the course of the conversation, M. de Lameth jokingly observed that the Americans paid the greater deference to Gen. La Fayette because he was a *Marquis*. For a long time there had been but one Marquis in England, (Lord Rockingham) and the colonists appreciating all other Marquises by this standard, had at once thought they would do no less than make the *Marquis* de La Fayette a general. "As for myself, though I was the senior colonel, and (as I understood him to say) his superior in personal rank, I passed for nobody, because I was only a *chevalier*." This sally was laughed at, at the time, though there is something very unsettled in the use of those arbitrary personal distinctions on which the French formerly laid so much stress. I shall not attempt to explain them. I contented myself by whispering to M. de Lameth, that we certainly knew very little of such matters in America, but I questioned if we were ever so ignorant as to suppose there was only *one Marquis* in France. On the contrary, we are a little too apt to fancy every Frenchman a *Marquis*.

There was formerly a regular parish church attached to the *château*, which is still standing. It is very small, and is within a short distance of the gate-way. The congregation was composed solely of the inhabitants of the *château*, and the people of the farm. The church contains epitaphs and inscriptions in memory of three of the *d'Aubussons*, whose hearts were buried here, viz. Leon, Comte de la Feuillade, a lieutenant-general; Gabriel, Marquis de Montargis; and Paul d'Aubusson, a knight of Malta; all of whom were killed young, in battle.

The general has about three hundred and fifty acres in cultivation, and more than two in wood, pasture and meadow. The place is in very excellent condition, and seems to be well attended to. I have galloped all over it, on a little filly belonging to one of the young gentlemen, and have found beauty and utility as nicely blended, as is often to be met with, even in England, the true country of *fermes ornées*, though the name is imported.

The third day of our visit, we all drove three or four leagues across the country, to see an old ruin of a royal castle called Vivier. This name implies a pond, and sure enough we found the remains of the buildings in the midst of two or three pools of water. This has been a considerable house, the ruins being still quite extensive and rather pretty. It was originally the property of a great noble, but the kings of France were in possession of it, as early as the year 1300. Charles V. had a great affection for Vivier, and very materially increased its establishment. His son, Charles VI., who was at times deranged, was often confined here, and it was after his reign, and by means of the long wars that ravaged France, that the place came to be finally abandoned as a royal abode. Indeed it is not easy to see why a king should ever have chosen this spot at all for his residence, unless it might be for the purpose of hunting, for even now it is in a retired, tame, and far from pleasant part of the country.

There are the ruins of a fine chapel and of two towers of considerable interest, beside extensive fragments of more vulgar buildings. One of these towers, being very high and very slender, is a striking object; but, from its form and position, it was one of those narrow wells that were attached to larger towers, and which contained nothing but the stairs. They are commonly to be seen in the ruins of edifices built in the thirteenth and fourteenth centuries, in France; and, what is worthy of remark, in several instances, notwithstanding their slender forms, I have met with them standing, although their principals have nearly disappeared. I can only account for it, by supposing that their use and delicacy of form have required more than ordinary care in the construction.

The ruins of Vivier, belong to M. Parquin, a distinguished lawyer of Paris. This gentleman has a small country house near by, and General La Fayette took us all to see him. We found him at home, and met, quite as a matter of course, with a polite reception. M. Parquin gave us much curious information about the ruin, and took us to see some of the subterraneous passages that he has caused to be opened.

It is thought that some of these artificial caverns were prisons, and that others were intended merely as places for depositing stores. The one we entered was of beautiful masonry, vaulted with the nicest art, and seemed to communicate with the ruins, although the outlet was in the open field and some distance from the walls. It might have been intended for the double purpose of a store-house and an outlet; for it is rare to meet with a palace, or a castle, that has not, more or less, of these private means of entrance and retreat. The Tulieries is said to abound with them, and I have been shown the line of an under-ground passage, between that palace and one of the public hotels, which must be fully a quarter of a mile in length.

Dulaure gives an extract from a report of the state of the *château* of Vivier, made about the year 1700, with a view to know whether its condition were such as to entitle the place to preserve certain of its privileges. In this document, the castle is described as standing in the centre of a marsh, surrounded by forest, and as so remote from all civilization, as to be nearly forgotten. This, it will be remembered, is the account of a royal abode, that stands within thirty miles of Paris!

In the very heart of the French capital, are the remains of an extensive palace of one of the Roman Emperors, and yet it may be questioned if one in a thousand, of those who live within a mile of the spot, have the least idea of the origin of the buildings. I have inquired about it, in its immediate neighbourhood, and it was with considerable difficulty, I could discover any one who even knew that there was such a ruin at all, in the street. The great number of similar objects, and the habit of seeing them daily, has some such effect on one, as the movement of a crowd in a public thorough-fare, where images pass so incessantly before the eye, as to leave no impression of their peculiarities. Were a solitary bison to scamper through the *rue St. Honoré*, the worthy Parisians would transmit an account of his exploits to their children's children, while the way-farer on the prairies takes little heed of the flight of a herd. As we went to La Grange, we stopped at a tavern, opposite to which was the iron gate of a small *château*. I asked the girl who was preparing our *goûter*, to whom the house belonged. "I am sorry I cannot tell you, sir," she answered; and then seeing suspicion in my face, she promptly added—"for do you see, sir, I have only been here *six weeks*." Figure to yourself an American girl, set down opposite an iron gate, in the country, and how long do you imagine she would be ignorant of the owner's name? If the blood of those pious inquisitors, the puritans, were in her veins, she would know more, not only of the gate, but of its owner, his wife, his children, his means, his hopes, wishes, intentions and thoughts, than he ever knew himself, or would be likely to know. But if this prominent love of meddling in its very nature must of necessity lead to what is worse than contented ignorance, gossipping error, and a wrong estimate of our fellow creatures, it has, at least, the advantage of keeping a people from falling asleep over their every day facts. There is no question that the vulgar and low bred propensity of conjecturing, meddling, combining, with their unavoidable companion, *inventing*, exists to a vice, among a portion of our people; but, on the other hand, it is extremely inconvenient when one is travelling, and wishes to know the points of the compass, as has happened to myself, if he should ask a full grown woman whereabouts the sun rises in that neighbourhood, he is repulsed with the answer, that—"Monsieur ought to know that better than a poor garden-woman like me!"

We returned to Paris, after a pleasant visit of three days at La Grange, during which we had delightful weather, and altogether a most agreeable time. The habits of the family are very regular and simple, but the intercourse has the freedom and independence of a country-house. We were all in the circular drawing-room, a little before ten, breakfast being served between ten and eleven. The table was French, the morning repast consisting of light dishes of meat, *compotes*, fruits, and sometimes *soupe au lait*; one of the simplest and best things for such a meal, that can be imagined. As a compliment to us Americans, we had fish fried and broiled, but I rather think this was an innovation. Wine, to drink with water, as a matter of course, was on the table. The whole ended with a cup of *café au lait*. The morning then passed as each one saw fit. The young men went shooting, the ladies drove out, or read, or had a little music, while the general and myself were either walking about the farm, or were conversing in the library.

We dined at six, as at Paris, and tea was made in the drawing-room about nine.

I was glad to hear from General La Fayette, that the reports of Americans making demands on his purse, like so many other silly rumours that are circulated, merely because some one has fancied such a thing might be so, are untrue. On the contrary, he assures me that applications of this nature are very seldom made, and most of those that have been made have proved to come from Englishmen, who have thought they might swindle him in this form. I have had at least a dozen such applications myself, but I take it nothing is easier, in general, than to distinguish between an American, and a native of Great Britain. It was agreed between us, that in future, all applications of this nature, should be sent to me for investigation.*

* Under this arrangement, two or three years later, an applicant was sent for examination, under very peculiar circumstances. The man represented himself to be a shopkeeper of Baltimore, who had come to England with his wife and child, to purchase goods. He had been robbed of all he had, according to his account of the matter, about a thousand pounds in sovereigns, and was reduced to want, in a strange country. After trying all other means, in vain, he bethought him of coming to Paris, to apply to General La Fayette, for succour. He had just money enough to do this, having left his wife in Liverpool. He appeared with an English passport, looked like an Englishman, and had even caught some of the low English idioms, such as, "I am agreeable," for "it is agreeable to me," or, "I agree to do so," &c. &c. The writer was exceedingly puzzled to decide as to this man's nationality. At length, in describing his journey to Paris, he said, "they took my passport from me, when we got *to the lines.*" This settled the matter, as no one but an American would call a *frontier*, the *lines*. He proved, in the end, to be an American, and a great rogue.

IX.  The Palace of the Legislative Body (Palais Bourbon)

x.    The Castle of Vincennes

XI.  The Chateau of La Grange-Bléneau

XII.   The Ruins of the Royal Castle

# Letter XXI
## To R. Cooper, Esq., Cooperstown.

W e all went to bed, a night or two since, as usual, and awoke to learn that there had been a fight in the capital. One of the countless under-plots had got so near the surface, that it threw up smoke. It is said, that about fifty were killed and wounded, chiefly on the part of the populace.

The insecurity of the Bourbons is little understood in America. It is little understood even by those Americans, who pass a few months in the country, and in virtue of frequenting the *cafés*, and visiting the theatres, fancy they know the people. Louis XVIII. was more than once on the point of flying, again, between the year 1815 and his death; for since the removal of the allied troops, there is really no force for a monarch to depend on, more especially in and around the capital, the army being quite as likely to take sides against them, as for them.

The government has determined on exhibiting vigour, and there was a great show of troops the night succeeding the combat. Curious to see the effect of all this, two or three of us got into a carriage and drove through the streets, about nine o'clock. We found some two or three thousand men on the *boulevards*, and the *rue St. Denis*, in particular, which had been the scene of the late disorder, was watched with jealous caution. In all, there might have been four or five thousand men under arms. They were merely in readiness, leaving a free passage for carriages, though in some of the narrow streets, we found the bayonets pretty near our faces.

An American being supposed *ex officio*, as it were, to be a well-wisher to the popular cause, there is, perhaps, a slight disposition to look at us with distrust. The opinion of our *travellers'* generally favouring liberty is, in my judgment, singularly erroneous, the feelings of a majority being, on the whole, just the other way, for, at least, the first year or two of their European experience; though, I think, it is to be noticed, by the end of that time, that they begin to lose sight of the personal interests which, at home, have made them any thing but philosophers on such subjects, and to see and appreciate the immense advantages of freedom over exclusion, although the predominance of the former may not always favour their own particular views. Such, at least, has been the result of my own observations, and so far from considering a fresh arrival from home, as being likely to be an accession to our little circle of liberal principles, I have generally deemed all such individuals as being more likely to join the side of the aristocrats, or the exclusionists in politics. This is not the moment to enter into an examination of the causes that have led to so singular a contradiction between opinions and facts, though I think the circumstance is not to be denied, for it is now my intention to give you an account of the manner in which matters are managed here, rather than enter into long investigations of the state of society at home.

Not long after my arrival in France, a visit was announced, from a person who was entirely unknown to me, but who called himself a *littérateur*. The first interview passed off, as such interviews usually do, and circumstances not requiring any return on my part, it was soon forgotten. Within a fortnight, however, I received visit the second, when the conversation took a political turn, my guest freely abusing the Bourbons, the aristocrats, and the present state of things in France. I did little more than listen. When the way was thus opened, I was asked if I admired Sir Walter Scott, and particularly what I thought of Ivanhoe, or, rather, if I did not think it an indifferent book. A little surprised at such a question, I told my *littérateur*, that Ivanhoe appeared to me to be very unequal, the first half being incomparably the best, but that, as a whole, I thought it stood quite at the head of the particular sort of romances to which it belonged. The Antiquary, and Guy Mannering, for instance, were both much nearer perfection, and, on the whole, I thought both better books; but Ivanhoe, especially its commencement, was a noble poem. But did I not condemn the want of historical truth in its pictures? I did not consider Ivanhoe as intended to be history; it was a work of the imagination, in which all the fidelity that was requisite, was enough to be probable and natural, and that requisite I thought it possessed in an eminent degree. It is true, antiquarians accused the author of having committed some anachronisms, by confounding the usages of different centuries, which was perhaps a greater fault, in such a work, than to confound mere individual characters; but of this I did not pretend to judge, not being the least of an antiquarian myself. Did I not think he had done gross injustice to the noble and useful order of the Templars? On this point I could say no more than on the preceding, having but a very superficial knowledge of the Templars, though I thought the probabilities seemed to be perfectly well respected. Nothing could *seem* to be more true, than Scott's pictures. My guest then went into a long vindication of the Templars, stating that Scott had done them gross injustice, and concluding with an exaggerated compliment, in which it was attempted to persuade me that I was the man to vindicate the truth, and to do justice to a subject that was so peculiarly connected with liberal principles. I disclaimed the ability to undertake such a task, at all; confessed that I did not wish to disturb the images which Sir Walter Scott had left, had I the ability; and declared I did not see the connection between his accusation, admitting it to be true, and liberal principles. My visitor soon after went away, and I saw no more of him for a week, when he came again. On this occasion, he commenced by relating several *piquant* anecdotes of the *Bourbons* and their friends, gradually and ingeniously leading the conversation, again, round to his favourite Templars. After pushing me, for half an hour, on this point, always insisting on my being the man to vindicate the order, and harping on its connection with liberty, he took advantage of one of my often-repeated protestations of ignorance of the whole matter, suddenly to say — "well, then, *Monsieur, go and see for yourself*, and you will soon be satisfied that my account of the order is true." "Go and see what?" "The Templars." "There are no longer any." "They exist still." "Where?" "Here, in Paris." "This is new to me; I do not understand it." "The Templars exist; they possess documents to prove how much Scott has misrepresented them, and — but, you will remember that the actual government has so much jealousy, of every thing it does not control, that secrecy is necessary — and, to be frank with you, M. [Cooper], I am commissioned by the Grand Master, to invite you to be present, at a secret meeting, this very week."

Of course, I immediately conjectured that some of the political agitators of the day had assumed this taking guise, in order to combine their means, and carry out their plans.* The proposition was gotten rid of, by my stating, in terms that could not be misunderstood, that I was a traveller, and did not wish to meddle with any thing that required secrecy, in a foreign government; that I certainly had my own political

---

* Since the revolution of 1830, these Templars have made public, but abortive efforts, to bring themselves into notice, by instituting some ceremonies, in which they appeared openly in their robes.

notions, and if pushed, should not hesitate to avow them anywhere; that the proper place for a writer to declare his sentiments, was in his books, unless under circumstances which authorized him to act; that I did not conceive foreigners were justifiable in going beyond this; that I never had meddled with the affairs of foreign countries, and that I never would; and that the fact of this society's being secret, was sufficient to deter me from visiting it. With this answer, my guest departed, and he never came again.

Now, the first impression was, as I have told you, and I supposed my visitor, although a man of fifty, was one of those who innocently lent himself to these silly exaggerations; either as a dupe, or to dupe others. I saw reason, however, to change this opinion.

At the time these visits occurred, I scarcely knew any one in Paris, and was living in absolute retirement—being, as you know already, quite without letters. About ten days after I saw the last of my *littérateur*, I got a letter from a high functionary of the government, sending me a set of valuable medals. The following day, these were succeeded by his card, and an invitation to dinner. Soon after, another person, notoriously connected with court intrigues, sought me out, and overwhelmed me with civilities. In a conversation that shortly after occurred between us, this person gave a pretty direct intimation, that by pushing a little, a certain decoration that is usually conferred on literary men, was to be had, if it were desired. I got rid of all these things, in the straightforward manner, that is the best for upsetting intrigues; and having really nothing to conceal, I was shortly permitted to take my own course.

I have now little doubt that the *littérateur* was a *spy*, sent, either to sound me on some point connected with La Fayette and the republicans, or possibly to lead me into some difficulty, though I admit that this is no more than conjecture. I give you the facts, which, at the time, struck me as, at least, odd, and you may draw your own conclusions. This, however, is but one of a dozen adventures, more or less similar, that have occurred, and I think it well to mention it, by way of giving you an insight into what sometimes happens here.*

My rule has been, whenever I am pushed on the subject of politics, to deal honestly and sincerely with all with whom I am brought in contact, and in no manner to leave the impression, that I think the

---

* A conversation, which took place *after* the revolution of 1830, with one of the parties named, leaves little doubt as to the truth of the original conjecture.

popular form of government an unavoidable evil, to which America is obliged to submit. I do not shut my eyes to the defects of our own system, or to the bad consequences that flow from it, and from it alone; but, the more I see of other countries, the more I am persuaded, that, under circumstances which admit but of a choice of evils, we are greatly the gainers by having adopted it. Although I do not believe every other nation is precisely fitted to imitate us, I think it is their misfortune they are not so. If the inhabitants of other countries do not like to hear such opinions, they should avoid the subject with Americans.

It is very much the custom here, whenever the example of America is quoted in favour of the practicability of republican institutions, to attribute our success to the fact of society's being so simple, and the people so virtuous. I presume I speak within bounds, when I say that I have heard the latter argument urged a hundred times, during the last eighteen months. One lady, in particular, who is exceedingly clever, but who has a dread of all republics, on account of having lost a near friend during the reign of terror, was especially in the practice of resorting to this argument, whenever, in our frequent playful discussions of the subject, I have succeeded in disturbing her inferences, by citing American facts. "*Mais, Monsieur, l'Amérique est si jeune, et vous avez les vertus que nous manquons,*" &c., &c., has always been thought a sufficient answer. Now, I happen to be one of those who do not entertain such extravagant notions of the exclusive and peculiar virtues of our own country. Nor, have I been so much struck with the profound respect of the Europeans, in general, for those very qualities that, nevertheless, are always quoted as the reason of the success of what is called the "American experiment." Quite the contrary: I have found myself called on, more than once, to repel accusations against our morality of a very serious nature; accusations that we do *not* deserve; and my impression certainly is, that the American people, so far as they are at all the subjects of observation, enjoy any thing but a good name, in Europe. Struck by this flagrant contradiction, I determined to practice on my female friend, a little; a plan that was successfully carried out, as follows.

Avoiding all allusion to politics, so as to throw her completely off her guard, I took care to introduce such subjects, as should provoke comparisons on other points, between France and America; or rather, between the latter and Europe generally. As our discussions had a tinge of philosophy, neither being very bigoted, and both preserving perfect good humour, the plot succeeded admirably. After a little time, I took occasion to fortify one of my arguments by a slight allusion to the *peculiar virtues* of the American people. She was too well-bred to controvert this sort of reasoning at first, until, pushing the point, little by little, she was so far provoked as to exclaim, "you lay great stress on the exclusive virtues of your countrymen, Monsieur, but I have yet to learn that they are so much better than the rest of the world!" "I beg a thousand pardons, Madame, if I have been led into an indiscretion on this delicate subject; but you must ascribe my error to your own eloquence, which, contrary to my previous convictions, had persuaded me into the belief that we have some peculiar unction of this nature, that is unknown in Europe. I now begin to see the mistake, and to understand *que nous autres Américains*, are to be considered *virtuous*, only where there is question of the practicability of maintaining a republican form of government, and, as great rogues on all other occasions." Madame de ——— was wise enough, and good tempered enough, to laugh at the artifice, and the allusion to *"nous autres vertueux,"* has got to be a *mot d'ordre* with us. The truth is, that the question of politics is exclusively one of personal advantages, with a vast majority of the people of Europe; one set selfishly struggling to maintain their present superiority, while the other is as selfishly, and in some respects as blindly, striving to overturn all that is established, in order to be benefited by the scramble that will follow; and religion, justice, philosophy, and practical good, are almost equally remote from the motives of both parties.

From reflecting on such subjects, I have been led into a consideration of the influence of political institutions on the more ordinary relations of society. If the conclusions are generally in favour of popular rights, and what is called freedom, there can be little question that there are one or two weak spots, on our side of the question, that it were better did they not exist. Let us, for the humour of the thing, look a little into these points.

It is a common remark of all foreigners, that there is less social freedom in America than in most other countries of Christendom. By social freedom, I do not mean as relates to the mere forms of society, for in these we are loose rather than rigid; but that one is less a master of his own acts, his own mode of living, his own time, being more rigidly amenable to public opinion, on all these points, than elsewhere. The fact, I believe, out of all question, is true; at least it appears to be true, so far as my knowledge of our own, and of other countries extends. Admitting then the fact to be so, it is worth while to throw away a moment in inquiring into the consequent good and evil of such a state of things, as well as in looking for the causes. It is always a great assistant in our study of others, to have some tolerable notions of ourselves.

The control of public opinion has, beyond question, a salutary influence on the moral *exterior* of a country. The great indifference which the French, and indeed the higher classes of most European countries, manifest to the manner of living of the members of their different circles, so long as certain appearances are respected, may do no affirmative good to society, though at the same time it does less positive harm than you may be disposed to imagine. But this is not the point to which I now allude. Europeans maintain that, in things, *innocent in themselves*, but which are closely connected with the independence of action and tastes of men, the American is less his own master than the inhabitant of this part of the world; and this is the fact I, for one, feel it necessary to concede to them. There can be no doubt that society meddles much more with the private affairs of individuals, and affairs too, over which it properly has no control, in America than in Europe. I will illustrate what I mean, by an example.

About twenty years since there lived in one of our shire-towns a family, which, in its different branches, had numerous female descendants, then all children. A member of this family, one day, went to a respectable clergyman, his friend, and told him that he and his connections had so many female children, whom it was time to think of educating, that they had hit upon the plan of engaging some suitable instructress, with the intention of educating their girls all together, both for economy's sake and for convenience, as well as that such near connections might be brought up in a way to strengthen the family tie. The clergyman warmly remonstrated against the scheme, assuring his friend, *that the community would not bear it, and that it would infallibly make enemies!* This was the feeling of a very sensible man, and of an experienced divine, and I was myself the person making the application. This is religiously true, and I have often thought of the circumstance since, equally with astonishment and horror.

There are doubtless many parts of America, even, where such an interference with the private arrangement of a family would not be dreamt of; but there is a large portion of the country in which the feeling described, by my clerical friend, does prevail. Most observers would refer all this to democracy, but I do not. The interference would not proceed from the humblest classes of society at all, but from those nearer one's own level. It would proceed from a determination to bring all within the jurisdiction of a common opinion, or to be revenged on delinquents, by envy, hatred, and all uncharitableness. There is no disposition in America, to let one live as he or she may happen to please to live; the public choosing, though always in its proper circle, to interfere, and say *how* you must live. It is folly to call this by terms as sounding as republicanism or democracy, which inculcate the doctrine of as much personal freedom as at all comports with the public good. He is, indeed, a most sneaking democrat, who finds it necessary to consult a neighbourhood before he can indulge his innocent habits and tastes. It is sheer *meddling*, and no casuistry can fitly give it any other name.

A portion of this troublesome quality is owing, beyond question, to our provincial habits, which are always the most exacting; but I think a large portion, perhaps I ought to say the largest, is inherited from those pious but exaggerated religionists who first peopled the country. These sectaries extended the discipline of the church to all the concerns of life. Nothing was too minute to escape their cognizance, and a parish sat in judgment on the affairs of all who belonged to it. One may easily live so long in the condition of society that such an origin has entailed on us, as to be quite unconscious of its peculiarities, but I think they can hardly escape one who has lived much beyond its influence.

Here, perhaps, the fault is to be found in the opposite extreme, though there are so many virtues consequent on independence of thought and independence of habits, that I am not sure the good does not equal the evil. There is no canting, and very little hypocrisy, in mere matters of habits, in France; and this, at once, is abridging two of our own most besetting vices. Still the French can hardly be called a very original people. Convention ties them down mercilessly in a great many things. They are less under the influence of mere fashion, in their intercourse, it is true, than some of their neighbours, reason and taste exercising more influence over such matters, in France, than almost any where else; but they are mannerists in the fine arts, in their literature, and in all their *feelings*, if one can use such an expression.

The gross exaggerations of the romantic school that is, just now, attracting so much attention, are merely an effort to liberate themselves. But, after allowing for the extreme ignorance of the substratum of society, which, in France, although it forms so large a portion of the whole, should no more be taken into the account in speaking of the national qualities, than the slaves of Carolina should be included in an estimate of the character of the Carolinians, there is, notwithstanding this mannerism, a personal independence here, that certainly does not exist with us. The American goes and comes when he pleases, and no one asks for a passport; he has his political rights; talks of his liberty; swaggers of his advantages, and yet does less as he pleases, even in innocent things, than the Frenchman. His neighbours form a police, and a most troublesome and impertinent one it sometimes proves to be. It is also unjust, for having no legal means of arriving at facts, it half the time condemns on conjecture.

The truth is, our institutions are the result of facts and accidents, and, being necessarily an imitative people, there are often gross inconsistencies between our professions and our practice; whereas the French have had to struggle through their apprenticeship in political rights, by the force of discussions and appeals to reason, and theory is still too important to be entirely overlooked. Perhaps no people understand the *true* private characters of their public men so little as the Americans, or any people so well as the French. I have never known a distinguished American, in whom it did not appear to me that his popular character was a false one; or a distinguished Frenchman whom the public did not appear to estimate very nearly as he deserved to be. Even Napoleon, necessary as he is to the national pride, and dazzling as is all military renown, seems to me to be much more justly appreciated at Paris, than any where else. The practice of meddling can lead to no other result. They who wish to stand particularly fair before the public, resort to deception, and I have heard a man of considerable notoriety in America confess that he was so much afraid of popular comments, that he always acted as if an enemy were looking over his shoulder. With us, no one scruples to believe that he knows all about a public man, even to the nicest traits of his character; all talk of him, as none should talk but those who are in his intimacy, and, what between hypocrisy on his part—an hypocrisy to which he is in some measure driven by the officious interference with his most private interests—and exaggerations and inventions, that ingenious tyrant, public opinion, comes as near the truth as a fortune teller who is venturing his prediction in behalf of a stranger.*

In France the right of the citizen to discuss all public matters is not only allowed but *felt*. In America it is not *felt*, though it is allowed. A homage must be paid to the public, by assuming the disguise of acting as a public agent, in America; wherereas, in France, individuals address their countrymen, daily, under their own signatures. The impersonality of *we*, and the character of public journalists, is almost indispensable, with us, to impunity, although the mask can deceive no one, the journalists notoriously making their prints subservient to their private passions and private interests, and being *impersonal* only in the use of the imperial pronoun. The *representative*, too, in America, is privileged to teach, in virtue of his collective character, by the very men who hold the extreme and untenable doctrine of instruction! It is the fashion to say in America, *that the people will rule*; it would be nearer the truth, however, to say, *the people will seem to rule*.

I think that these distinctions are facts, and they certainly lead to odd reflections. We are so peculiarly situated as a nation, that one is not to venture on conclusions too hastily. A great deal is to be imputed to our provincial habits; much to the circumstance of the disproportion between surface and population, which, by scattering the well-bred and intelligent, a class at all times relatively small, serves greatly to lessen their influence in imparting a tone to society; something to the inquisitorial habits of our pious forefathers, who appear to have thought that the charities were nought, and, in the very teeth of revelation, that Heaven was to be stormed by impertinences; while a good deal is to be conceded to the nature of a popular government whose essential spirit is to create a predominant opinion, before which,

---

* I can give no better illustration of the state of dependence to which men are reduced in America, by this spirit of meddling, than by the following anecdote. A friend was about to build a new town house, and letting me know the situation, he asked my advice as to the mode of construction. The inconveniences of an ordinary American town house were pointed out to him,—its unfitness for the general state of society, the climate, the other domestic arrangements, and its ugliness. All were admitted, and the plan proposed in place of the old style of building was liked, but still my friend hesitated about adopting it. "It will be a genteeler and a better looking house than the other." "Agreed." "It will be really more convenient." "I think so, too." "It will be cheaper." "Of that there is no question." "Then why not adopt it?" "To own the truth, I *dare not build differently from my neighbours!*"

right or wrong, all must bow until its *cycle* shall be completed. Thus it is, that we are always, more or less, under one of two false influences, the blow or its rebound; action that is seldom quite right, or reaction that is always wrong; sinning heedlessly, or repenting to fanaticism. The surest process in the world, of "riding on to fortune" in America, is to get seated astride a lively "reaction," which is rather more likely to carry with it a unanimous sentiment, than even the error to which it owes its birth.

As much of this weakness as is inseparable from humanity exists here, but it exists under so many modifying circumstances, as, in this particular, to render France as unlike America as well may be. Liberty is not always pure philosophy nor strict justice, and yet, as a whole, it is favourable to both. These are the spots on the political sun. To the eye which seeks only the radiance and warmth of the orb, they are lost, but he who studies it, with calmness and impartiality, sees them, too plainly, to be in any doubt of their existence.

# Letter XXII
## To James E. De Kay, M. D.

A lthough we have not been without our metaphysical hallucinations in America, I do not remember to have heard that "animal magnetism" was ever in vogue among us. A people who are not very quick to feel the poetry of sentiment, may well be supposed exempt from the delusions of a doctrine which comprehends the very poetry of physics. Still, as the subject is not without interest, and as chance has put me in the way of personally inquiring into this fanciful system, I intend, in this letter, to give you an account of what I have both heard and seen.

I shall premise by saying that I rank "animal magnetism" among the "arts" rather than among the "sciences." Of its theory I have no very clear notion, nor do I believe that I am at all peculiar in my ignorance; but until we can say what is that other "magnetism" to which the world is indisputably so much indebted for its knowledge and comforts, I do not know that we are to repudiate this, merely because we do not understand it. Magnetism is an unseen and inexplicable influence, and that is "metallic" while this is "animal;" *voilà tout.* On the whole, it may be fairly mooted which most controls the world, the animal or the metallic influence.

To deal gravely with a subject that, at least, baffles our comprehension, there are certainly very extraordinary things related of animal magnetism, and apparently on pretty good testimony. Take, for instance, a single fact. M. *Jules Cloquet* is one of the cleverest practitioners of Paris, and is in extensive business. This gentleman publicly makes the following statement. I write it from memory, but have heard it and read it so often, that I do not think my account will contain any essential error.

A woman, who was subject to the magnetic influence, or who was what is commonly called a *somnambule*, had a cancer in the breast. M. [Chapelain], one of the principal magnetisers of Paris, and from whom, among others, I have had an account of the whole affair, was engaged to magnetise this woman, while M. Cloquet operated on the diseased part. The patient was put asleep, or rather into the magnetic trance, for it can scarcely be called sleep, and the cancer was extracted, without the woman's *manifesting the least terror, or the slightest sense of pain!* To the truth of the substance of this account, M. Cloquet, who does not pretend to explain the reason, nor profess to belong, in any way, to the school, simply testifies. He says that he had such a patient, and that she was operated on, virtually, as I have told you. Such a statement, coming from so high a source, induced the Academy, which is certainly not altogether composed of magnetisers, but many of whose members are quite animal enough to comprehend the matter, to refer the subject to a special committee, which committee, I believe, was comprised of very clever men. The substance of their report was pretty much what might have been anticipated. They said that the subject was inexplicable, and that "animal magnetism" could not be brought within the limits of any known laws of nature. They might have said the same thing of the comets! In both cases we have facts, with a few established consequences, but are totally without elementary causes.

Animal magnetism is clearly one of three things: it is what it pretends to be, an unexplained and as yet incomprehensible physical influence; it is delusion; or it is absolute fraud.

A young countryman of ours, having made the acquaintance of M. C[hapelain], professionally, and being full of the subject, I have so far listened to his entreaties as to inquire personally into the facts, a step I might not have otherwise been induced to take.

I shall now proceed to the history of my own experience in this inexplicable mystery. We found M. C[hapelain] buried in the heart of Paris, in one of those vast old hotels, which give to this town the air of generations of houses, commencing with the quaint and noble of the sixteenth century, and ending with the more fashionable pavilion of our own times. His cabinet looked upon a small garden, a pleasant transition from the animal within to the vegetable without. But one meets with gardens, with their verdure and shrubbery and trees, in the most unexpected manner, in this crowded town.

M. C[hapelain] received us politely, and we found with him one of his *somnambules,* but as she had just come out of a trance, we were told she could not be put asleep again that morning. Our first visit therefore went no farther than some discourse on the subject of "animal magnetism," and a little practical by-play, that shall be related in its place.

M. C[hapelain] did not attempt ascending to first principles, in his explanations. Animal magnetism was animal magnetism—it was a fact, and not a theory. Its effects were not to be doubted; they depended on testimony of sufficient validity to dispose of any mere question of authenticity. All that he attempted was hypothesis, which he invited us to controvert. He might as well have desired me to demonstrate that the sun is not a carbuncle. On the *modus operandi*, and the powers of his art, the doctor was more explicit. There were a great many gradations in quality in his *somnambules*, some being better and some worse; and there was also a good deal of difference in the *intensity* of the *magnetisers*. It appears to be settled that the best *somnambules* are females, and the best *magnetisers* males, though the law is not absolute. I was flattered with being, by nature, a first-rate magnetiser, and the doctor had not the smallest doubt of his ability to put me to sleep; an ability, so far as his theory went, I thought it was likely enough he might possess, though I greatly questioned his physical means.

I suppose it is *primâ facie* evidence of credulity, to take the trouble to inquire into the subject at all; at any rate, it was quite evident I was set down as a good subject, from the moment of my appearance.Even the *somnambule* testified to this, though she would not then consent to be put into a trance in order to give her opinion its mystical sanction.

The powers of a really good *somnambule* are certainly of a very respectable class. If a lock of hair be cut from the head of an invalid, and sent a hundred leagues from the provinces, such a *somnambule*, properly magnetised, becomes gifted with the faculty to discover the seat of the disease, however latent; and, by practice, she may even prescribe the remedy, though this is usually done by a physician, like M. C[hapelain], who is regularly graduated. The *somnambule* is, properly, only versed in pathology, any other skill she may discover being either a consequence of this knowledge, or the effects of observation and experience. The powers of a somnambule extend equally to the *morale* as well as to the *physique*. In this respect a phrenologist is a pure quack in comparison with a lady in a trance. The latter has no dependence on bumps and organs, but she looks right through you, at a glance, and pronounces *ex cathedrâ* whether you are a rogue, or an honest man; a well disposed, or an evil disposed child of Adam. In this particular, it is an invaluable science, and it is a thousand pities all young women were not magnetised before they pronounce the fatal vows, as not a few of them would probably wake up, and cheat the parson of his fee. Our sex is difficult to be put asleep, and are so obstinate, that I doubt if they would be satisfied with a shadowy glimpse of the temper and dispositions of their mistresses.

You may possibly think I am trifling with you, and that I invent as I write. On the contrary, I have not related one half of the miraculous powers which being magnetised imparts to the thoroughly good *somnambule*, as they were related to me by M. C[hapelain], and vouched for by four or five of his patients who were present, as well as by my own companion, a firm believer in the doctrine. M. C[hapelain] added that *somnambules* improve by practice, as well as *magnetisers*, and that he has such command over one of his somnambules that he can put her to sleep, by a simple effort of the will, although she may be in her own apartment, in an adjoining street. He related the story of M. Cloquet and the cancer, with great unction, and asked me what I thought of that? Upon my word, I did not very well know what I did think of it, unless it was to think it very queer. It appeared to me to be altogether extraordinary, especially as I knew M. Cloquet to be a man of talents, and believe him to be honest.

By this time I was nearly magnetised with second-hand facts; and I became a little urgent for one or two that were visible to my own senses. I was promised more testimony, and a sight of the process of magnetising some water that a patient was to drink. This patient was present; the very type of credulity. He listened to every thing that fell from M. C[hapelain] with a *gusto* and a faith that might have worked miracles truly, had it been of the right sort, now and then turning his good-humoured marvel-eating eyes on me, as much as to say, "what do you think of that, now?" My companion told me, in English, he was a man of good estate, and of proved philanthropy, who had no more doubt of the efficacy of animal magnetism than I had of my being in the room. He had brought with him two bottles of water, and these M. C[hapelain] *magnetised*, by pointing his fingers at their orifices, rubbing their sides, and ringing his hands about them, as if washing them, in order to disengage the subtle fluid that was to impart to them their healing properties, for the patient drank no other water.

Presently a young man came in, of a good countenance, and certainly of a very respectable exterior. As the *somnambule* had left us, and this person could not consult her, which was his avowed intention in coming, M. C[hapelain] proposed to let me see his own power as a magnetiser, in an experiment on this patient. The young man consenting, the parties were soon prepared. M. C[hapelain] began by telling me, that he would, *by a transfusion of his will*, into the body of the patient, compel him to sit still, although his own desire should be to rise. In order to achieve this, he placed himself before the young man, and threw off the fluid from his fingers' ends, which he kept in a cluster, by constant forward gestures of the arms. Sometimes he held the fingers pointed at some particular part of the body, the heart in preference, though the brain would have been more poetical. The young man certainly did not rise; neither did I, nor any one else in the room. As this experiment appeared so satisfactory to every body else, I was almost ashamed to distrust it, easy as it really seemed to sit still, with a man flourishing his fingers before one's eyes.

I proposed that the doctor should see if he could pin me down, in this invisible fashion, but this he frankly admitted he did not think he could do *so soon*, though he foresaw I would become a firm believer in the existence of animal magnetism, ere long, and a public supporter of its wonders. In time, he did not doubt his power to work the same miracle on me. He then varied the experiment, by making the young man raise his arm *contrary* to his wishes. The same process was repeated, all the fluid being directed at the arm, which, after a severe trial, was slowly raised, until it pointed forward like a finger-board. After this, he was made to stand up, in spite of himself. This was the hardest affair of all, the doctor throwing off the fluid in handsful; the magnetized refusing for some time to budge an inch. At length he suddenly stood up, and seemed to draw his breath like one who finally yields after a strong trial of his physical force.

Nothing, certainly, is easier than for a young man to sit still and to stand up, pretending that he strives internally to resist the desire to do either. Still if you ask me, if I think this was simple collusion, I hardly know what to answer. It is the easiest solution, and yet it did not strike me as being the true one. I never saw less of the appearance of deception than in the air of this young man; his face, deportment, and acts being those of a person in sober earnest. He made no professions, was extremely modest, and really seemed anxious not to have the experiments tried. To my question, if he resisted the will of M. C[hapelain], he answered, as much as he could, and said, that when he rose, he did it because he could not help himself. I confess myself disposed to believe in his sincerity and good faith.

I had somewhat of a reputation, when a boy, of effecting my objects, by pure dint of teasing. Many is the shilling I have abstracted, in this way, from my mother's purse, who, constantly affirmed, that it was sore against her will. Now, it seems to me, that M. C[hapelain], may, very easily, have acquired so much command over a credulous youth, as to cause him to do things of this nature, as he may fancy, against his own will. Signs are the substitutes of words, which of themselves are purely conventional, and, in his case, the flourishing of the fingers are merely so many continued solicitations to get up. When the confirmation of a theory that is already received, and which is doubly attractive by its mysticisms, depends, in some measure, on the result, the experiment becomes still less likely to fail. It is stripping me of all pretensions to be a physiognomist, to believe that this young man was not honest; and I prefer getting over the difficulty in this way. As to the operator himself, he might, or might not be the dupe of his own powers. If the former, I think it would, on the whole, render him the more likely to succeed with his subject.

After a visit or two, I was considered sufficiently advanced to be scientifically examined. One of the very best of the *somnambules* was employed on the occasion, and every thing being in readiness, she was put to sleep. There was a faith-shaking brevity in this process, which, to say the least, if not fraudulent, was ill-judged. The doctor merely pointed his fingers at her once or twice, looking her intently in the eye, and the woman gaped; this success was followed up by a flourish or two of the hand, and the woman slept; or was magnetised. Now this was hardly sufficient even for my theory of the influence of the imagination. One could have wished the *somnambule* had not been so drowsy. But there she was, with her eyes shut, giving an occasional, hearty gape and the doctor declared her perfectly fit for service. She retained her seat, however, moved her body, laughed, talked, and, in all other respects, seemed to be precisely the woman she was before he pointed his fingers at her. At first, I felt a disposition to manifest that more parade was indispensable to humbugging me (who am not the Pope, you will remember,) but reflection said, the wisest way was to affect a little faith, as the surest means of securing more experiments. Moreover, I am not certain, on the whole, that the simplicity of the operation is not in favour of the sincerity of the parties, for, were deception deliberately planned, it would be apt to call in the aid of more mummery, and this, particularly, in a case in which there was probably a stronger desire than usual to make a convert.

I gave the *somnambule* my hand, and the examination was commenced, forthwith. I was first physically inspected, and the report was
highly favourable to the condition of the animal. I had the satisfaction
of hearing from this high authority, that the whole machinery of the
mere material man was in perfect order, every thing working well and
in its proper place. This was a little contrary to my own experience, it is
true, but as I had no means of seeing the interior clock-work of my own
frame, like the *somnambule*, had I ventured to raise a doubt, it would
have been overturned by the evidence of one who had ocular proofs of
what she said, and should, beyond question, have incurred the ridicule
of being accounted a *malade imaginaire*.

Modesty must prevent my recording all that this obliging *somnambule*
testified to, on the subject of my *morale*. Her account of the matter was
highly satisfactory, and I must have been made of stone, not to credit
her and her mysticisms. M. C[hapelain] looked at me, again and again,
with an air of triumph, as much as to say, "what do you think of all that
now; are you not *really* the noble, honest, virtuous, disinterested, brave
creature, she has described you to be?" I can assure you, it required no
little self-denial to abstain from becoming a convert to the whole
system. As it is very unusual to find a man with a good head, who has
not a secret inclination to believe in phrenology, so does he, who is thus
purified by the scrutiny of animal magnetism, feel disposed to credit
its mysterious influence. Certainly, I might have gaped, in my turn,
and commenced the moral and physical dissection of the *somnambule*,
whose hand I held, and no one could have given me the lie, for nothing
is easier than to speak *ex cathedrâ*, when one has a monopoly of
knowledge.

Encouraged by this flattering account of my own condition, I begged
hard for some more indisputable evidence of the truth of the theory. I
carried a stop-watch, and as I had taken an opportunity to push the stop
on entering the room, I was particularly desirous that the *somnambule*
should tell me the time indicated by its hands, a common test of their
powers I had been told; but to this M. C[hapelain] objected, referring
every thing of this tangible nature to future occasions. In fine, I could
get nothing during three or four visits, but pretty positive assertions,
expressions of wonder that I should affect to doubt what had been so
often and so triumphantly proved to others, accounts physical and
moral, like the one of which I had been the subject myself, and which
did not admit of either confirmation or refutation, and often repeated

declarations, that the time was not distant when, in my own unworthy person, I was to become one of the most powerful magnetisers of the age. All this did very well to amuse, but very little towards convincing; and I was finally promised, that at my next visit, the *somnambule* would be prepared to show her powers, in a way that would not admit of cavil.

I went to the appointed meeting with a good deal of curiosity to learn the issue, and a resolution not to be easily duped. When I presented myself, (I believe it was the fourth visit,) M. C[hapelain] gave me a sealed paper, that was not to be opened for several weeks, and which, he said, contained the prediction of an event that was to occur to myself, between the present time and the day set for the opening of the letter, and which the *somnambule* had been enabled to foresee, in consequence of the interest she took in me and mine. With this sealed revelation, then, I was obliged to depart, to await the allotted hour.

M. C[hapelain] had promised to be present at the opening of the seal, but he did not appear. I dealt fairly by him, and the cover was first formally removed, on the evening of the day endorsed on its back, as the one when it would be permitted. The *somnambule* had foretold that, in the intervening time, one of my children would be seriously ill, that I should magnetise it, and that the child would recover. Nothing of the sort had occurred. No one of the family had been ill, I had not attempted to magnetise any one, or even dreamed of it, and of course, the whole prediction was a complete failure.

To do M. C[hapelain] justice, when he heard the result, he manifested surprise rather than any less confident feeling. I was closely questioned, first, as to whether either of the family had not been ill, and secondly, whether I had not felt a secret desire to magnetise any one of them. To all these interrogatories, truth compelled me to give unqualified negatives. I had hardly thought of the subject during the whole time. As this interview took place at my own house, politeness compelled me to pass the matter off as lightly as possible. There happened to be several ladies present, however, the evening M. C[hapelain] called, and, thinking the occasion a good one for him to try his powers on some one besides his regular *somnambules*, I invited him to magnetise any one of the party who might be disposed to submit to the process. To this he made no difficulty, choosing an English female friend as the subject of the experiment. The lady in question raised no objection, and the doctor commenced with great zeal, and with every appearance of faith in his own powers. No effect, however, was produced on this lady, or on one or two more of the party, all of whom obstinately refused even to gape. M. C[hapelain] gave the matter up, and soon after took his leave, and thus closed my personal connection with animal magnetism.

If you ask me for the conclusions I have drawn from these facts, I shall be obliged to tell you, that I am in doubt how far the parties concerned deceived others, and how far they deceived themselves. It is difficult to discredit entirely all the testimony that has been adduced in behalf of this power; and one is consequently obliged to refer all the established facts to the influence of the imagination. Then testimony itself is but a precarious thing, different eyes seeing the same objects in very different lights.

Let us take ventriloquism as a parallel case to that of animal magnetism. Ventriloquism is neither more nor less than imitation; and yet, aided by the imagination, perhaps a majority of those who know any thing about it, are inclined to believe there is really such a faculty as that which is vulgarly attributed to ventriloquism. The whole art of the ventriloquist consists in making such sounds as would be produced by a person, or thing, that should be actually in the circumstances that he wishes to represent. Let there be, for instance, five or six sitting around a table, in a room with a single door; a ventriloquist among them, wishes to mislead his companions, by making them believe that another is applying for admission. All he has to do is to make a sound similar to that which a person on the outside would make, in applying for admission. "Open the door, and let me in," uttered in such a manner, would deceive any one who was not prepared for the experiment, simply because men do not ordinarily make such sounds when sitting near each other, because the words themselves would draw the attention to the door, and because the sounds would be suited to the fictitious application. If there were *two* doors, the person first moving his head towards one of them, would probably give a direction to the imaginations of all the others; unless, indeed, the ventriloquist himself, by his words, or his own movements, as is usually the case, should assume the *initiative*. Every ventriloquist takes especial care to *direct* the imagination of his listener to the desired point, either by what he says, by some gesture, or by some movement. Such, undeniably, is the fact in regard to ventriloquism; for we know enough of the philosophy of sound, to be certain it can be nothing else. One of the best ventriloquists of this age, after affecting to resist this explanation of his mystery, candidly admitted to me, on finding that I stuck to the principles of reason, that all his art consisted of no more than a power to control the imagination by imitation, supported occasionally by acting. And, yet I once saw this man literally turn a whole family out of doors, in a storm, by an exercise of his art. On that occasion, so complete was the delusion, that the good people of the house actually fancied sounds which came from the ventriloquist, came from a point considerably beyond the place where they stood, and on the side *opposite* to that occupied by the speaker, although they stood at the top of a flight of steps, and he stood at the bottom. All this time, the sounds appeared to me to come from the place whence, by the laws of sound, except in cases of reverberation, and of the influence of the imagination, they only could appear to come; or, in other words, from the mouth of the ventriloquist himself. Now, if the imagination can effect so much, even in crowded assemblies, composed of people of all degrees of credulity, intelligence, and strength of mind, and when all are prepared, in part at least, for the delusion, what may it not be expected to produce on minds peculiarly suited to yield to its influence, and this, too, when the prodigy take the captivating form of mysticism and miracles.

In the case of the patient of M. Cloquet, we are reduced to the alternatives of denying the testimony, of believing that recourse was had to drugs, of referring all to the force of the imagination, or of admitting the truth of the doctrine of animal magnetism. The character of M. Cloquet, and the motiveless folly of such a course, compel us to reject the first; the second can hardly be believed, as the patient had not the appearance of being drugged, and the possession of such a secret would be almost as valuable as the art in question itself. The doctrine of animal magnetism we cannot receive, on account of the want of uniformity and exactitude in the experiments, and I think, we are fairly driven to take refuge in the force of the imagination. Before doing this, however, we ought to make considerable allowances for exaggerations, colouring, and the different manner in which men are apt to regard the same thing. My young American friend, who *did* believe in animal magnetism, viewed several of the facts I have related with eyes more favourable than mine, although even he was compelled to allow that M. C[hapelain] had much greater success with himself, than with your humble servant!

# Letter XXIII

## To Richard Cooper, Esquire, Cooperstown.

W e entered France in July, 1826, and having remained in and about the French capital, until February, 1828, we thought it time to change the scene. Paris is effectually the centre of Europe, and a residence in it, is the best training an American can have, previously to visiting the other parts of that quarter of the world. Its civilization, usages, and facilities, take the edge off of our provincial admiration, remove prejudices, and prepare the mind to receive new impressions, with more discrimination and tact. I would advise all our travellers to make this their first stage, and then to visit the north of Europe, before crossing the Alps, or the Pyrenees. Most people, however, hurry into the south, with a view to obtain the best as soon as possible, but it is with this, as in most of our enjoyments, a too eager indulgence defeats its own aim.

We had decided to visit London, where the season, *or winter*, would soon commence. The necessary arrangements were made, and we sent round our cards of p. p. c., and obtained passports. On the very day we were to quit Paris, an American friend wrote me a note to say that a young connexion of his was desirous of going to London, and begged a place for her in my carriage. It is, I believe, a peculiar and a respectable trait, in the national character, that we so seldom hesitate about asking, or acceding to, favours of this sort. Whenever woman is concerned, our own sex yield, and usually without murmuring. At all events, it was so with W[illiam], who cheerfully gave up his seat in the carriage to Miss [Wiggin], in order to take one in the *coupé* of the *diligence*. The notice was so short, and the hour so late, that there was no time to get a passport for him, and, as he was included in mine, I was compelled to run the risk of sending him to the frontiers without one. I was a consul at the time: a titular one, as to duties, but, in reality as much of a consul, as if I had ever visited my consulate.* The only official paper I pos-

---

* There being so strong a propensity to cavil at American facts, lest this book might fall into European hands, it may be well to explain a little. The consulate of the writer was given to him solely to avoid the appearance of going over to the enemy, during his residence abroad. The situation conferred neither honour nor profit, there being no

sessed, in connection with the office, the commission and *exequatur* excepted, was a letter from the *Préfet* of the Rhone, acknowledging the receipt of the latter. As this was strictly a French document, I gave it to W[illiam], as proof of my identity, accompanied by a brief statement of the reasons why he was without a passport, begging the authorities, at need, to let him pass as far as the frontier, where I should be in season to prove his character. This statement I signed as consul, instructing W[illiam] to show it, if applied to for a passport, and if the *gendarmes* disavowed me, to show the letter, by way of proving who I was. The expedient was clumsy enough, but it was the best that offered.

This arrangement settled, we got into the carriage and took our leave of Paris. Before quitting the town, however, I drove round to the *rue d'Anjou*, to take my leave of General La Fayette. This illustrious man had been seriously ill, for some weeks, and I had many doubts of my ever seeing him again. He did not conceive himself to be in any danger, however, but spoke of his speedy recovery as a matter of course, and made an engagement with me for the ensuing summer. I bade him adieu, with a melancholy apprehension that I should never see him again.

We drove through the gates of Paris, amid the dreariness of a winter's evening. You are to understand that every body quits London and Paris just as night sets in. I cannot tell you whether this is caprice, or whether it is a usage that has arisen from a wish to have the day in town, and a desire to relieve the monotony of roads so often travelled, by sleep; but so it is. We did not fall into the fashion, simply because it is a fashion, but the days are so short in February, in these high latitudes, that we could not make our preparations earlier.

I have little agreeable to say concerning the first forty miles of the journey. It rained, and the roads were, as usual, slippery with mud, and full of holes. The old *pavés* are beginning to give way, however, and we actually got a bit of *terre* within six posts of Paris. This may be considered a triumph of modern civilization; for, whatever may be said and sung in favour of Appian ways and Roman magnificence, a more

---

salary, and, in his case, not fees enough to meet the expense of the office opened by a deputy. The writer suspects he was much too true to the character and principles of his native country, to be voluntarily selected by its government as the object of its honours or rewards, and it is certain he never solicited either. There are favours, it would seem, that are reserved, in America, for those who most serve the interests of her enemies! A day of retribution will come.

cruel invention for travellers and carriage wheels, than these *pavés*, was never invented. A real Paris winter's day is the most uncomfortable of all weather. If you walk, no device of leather will prevent the moisture from penetrating to your heart; if you ride, it is but an affair of mud and *gras de Paris*. We enjoyed all this until nine at night, by which time we had got enough of it, and in Beauvais, instead of giving the order *à la poste*, the postilion was told to go to an inn. A warm supper and good beds put us all in good humour, again.

In putting into the mouth of Falstaff, the words "shall I not take mine ease, in mine inn," Shakspeare may have meant no more than the drowsy indolence of a glutton, but they recur to me with peculiar satisfaction, whenever I get unbooted and with a full stomach, before the warm fire of a hotel, after a fatiguing and chilling day's work. If any man doubt whether Providence has not dealt justly by all of us, in rendering our enjoyments dependent on comparative rather than on positive benefits, let him travel through a dreary day, and take his comfort at night, in a house where every thing is far below his usual habits, and learn to appreciate the truth. The sweetest sleep I have ever had, has been caught on deck, in the middle watch, under a wet pee-jacket, and with a coil of rope for a pillow.

Our next day's work carried us as far as Abbeville, in Picardy. Here we had a capital supper of game, in a room that set us all shivering with good honest cold. The beds, as usual, were excellent. The country throughout all this part of France is tame and monotonous, with wide reaches of grain-lands, that are now brown and dreary, here and there a wood, and the usual villages of dirty stone houses. We passed a few hamlets, however, that were more than commonly rustic and pictur-esque, and in which the dwellings seemed to be of mud, and were thatched. As they were mostly very irregular in form, the street winding through them quite prettily, they would have been good in their way, had there been any of the simple expedients of taste to relieve their poverty. But the French peasants of this province appear to think of little else but their wants. There was occasionally a venerable and generous old vine, clinging about the door, however, to raise some faint impressions of happiness.

We passed through, or near, the field of Cressy. By the aid of the books, we fancied we could trace the positions of the two armies, but it was little more than very vague conjecture. There was a mead, a breadth of field well adapted to cavalry, and a wood. The river is a mere brook, and could have offered but little protection, or resistance to the passage of any species of troops. I saw no village, and we may not have been within a mile of the real field, after all. Quite likely no one knows where it is. It is very natural that the precise sites of great events should be lost, though our own history is so fresh and full, that to us it is apt to appear extraordinary. In a conversation with a gentleman of the Stanley family, lately, I asked him if Lathom-house, so celebrated for its siege in the civil wars, was still in the possession of its ancient proprietors. I was told it no longer existed, and that, until quite recently, its positive site was a disputed point, and one which had only been settled by the discovery of a hole in a rock, in which shot had been cast during the siege, and which hole was known to have formerly been in a court. It is no wonder that doubts exist as to the identity of Homer, or the position of Troy.

We have anglicized the word Cressy, which the French term *Crécy*, or, to give it a true Picard orthography, *Créci*. Most of the names that have this termination are said to be derived from this province. Many of them have become English, and have undergone several changes in the spelling. Tracy, or Tracey; de Courcy, or de Courcey; Montmorency, and Lacy or Lacey, were once *Traci, Courci, Montmorenci* and *Laci*.* The French get over the disgrace of their ancient defeats, very ingeniously, by asserting that the English armies of old were principally composed of Norman soldiers, and that the chivalrous nobility which performed such wonders were of purely Norman blood. The latter was probably more true than the former.

As we drew nearer to the coast, the country became more varied. Montreuil and Samer are both fortified, and one of these places, standing on an abrupt, rocky eminence, is quite picturesque and quaint. But we did not stop to look at any thing very minutely, pushing forward, as fast as three horses could draw us, for the end of our journey. A league or two from Boulogne, we were met by a half dozen mounted runners from the different inns, each inviting us to give our custom to his particular employer. These fellows reminded me of the

---

* The celebrated Sir William Draper was once present when the subject turned on the descent of families, and the changes that names underwent. "Now my own is a proof of what I say," he continued, with the intention to put an end to a discourse that was getting to savour of family pride — "my family being directly derived from King Pepin." "How do you make that out, Sir William?" "By self evident orthographical testimony — as you may see — Pepin, Pipkin, Napkin, Diaper, Draper."

wheat-runners on the hill at Albany, though they were as much more clamorous and earnest, as a noisy protestation-making Frenchman is more obtrusive than a shrewd, quiet calculating Yankee. We did not stop in Boulogne, to try how true were the voluble representations of these gentry, but, changing horses at the post, went our way. The town seemed full of English, and we gazed about us, with some curiosity, at a place that has become so celebrated by the great demonstration of Napoleon. There is a high monument standing at no great distance from the town, to commemorate one of his military parades. The port is small and crowded, like most of the harbours on both sides of the channel.

We had rain, and chills and darkness, for the three or four posts that succeeded. The country grew more and more tame, until after crossing an extensive plain of moist meadow land, we passed through the gate of Calais. I know no place that will give you a more accurate notion of this celebrated port than Powles Hook. It is, however, necessary to enlarge the scale greatly, for Calais is a town of some size, and the hommock on which it stands, and the low land by which it is environed, are much more considerable in extent than the spot just named.

We drove to the inn that Sterne has immortalized, or, one at least that bears the same name, and found English comfort united with French cookery and French taste. After all, I do not know why I may not say French comforts, too; for in many respects they surpass their island neighbours even in this feature of domestic comfort. It is a comfort to have a napkin even when eating a muffin; to see one's self entire in a mirror, instead of *edging* the form into it, or out of it, sideways; to drink good coffee; to eat good *côtelettes*, and to be able to wear the same linen for a day, without having it soiled. The Bible says, "comfort me with flaggons or apples," I really forget which, — and if either of these is to be taken as authority, a *côtelette* may surely be admitted into the *carte de conforts*.

We found Calais a clean town, and possessing a certain medium aspect, that was as much English as French. The position is strong, though I was not much struck with the strength of the works. England has no motive to wish to possess it, now that conquest on the continent is neither expedient nor possible. The port is good for nothing, in a warlike sense, except to protect a privateer or two; though the use of steam will probably make it of more importance in any future war, than it has been for the last two centuries.

We found W[illiam] safely arrived. At one of the frontier towns he had been asked for his passport, and, in his fright, he gave the letter of the Prefet of the Rhone, instead of the explanation I had so cleverly devised. This letter commenced with the words "Monsieur le Consul" in large letters, and occupying, according to French etiquette, nearly half of the first page. The *gendarme*, a *vieux moustache*, held his lantern up to read it, and seeing this ominous title, it would seem that Napoleon and Marengo, and all the glories of the Consulate arose in his imagination. He got no further than those three words, which he pronounced aloud, and, then folding the letter, he returned it with a profound bow, asking no further questions. As the *diligence* drove on, W[illiam] heard him say — *"apparemment vous avez un homme très considérable, là dedans, Monsieur le Conducteur."* So much for our fears, for passports, and for *gendarmes*!

We went to bed, with the intention of embarking for England in the morning.

# Explanatory Notes

1.30-31 "by fear, favour, or the hope of reward": adapted from a formula used in the oath administered in the nineteenth century to the foreman of a grand jury.

3.2 CAPTAIN SHUBRICK, U. S. N.: William Branford Shubrick (1790-1874), with whom the novelist served as a midshipman in 1809-10 and to whom he dedicated *The Pilot* and *The Red Rover*, was Cooper's closest friend. Shubrick's distinguished naval career ended with his retirement as a rear-admiral in 1862.

3.5 White Hall wharf: off South Street, next to the Battery.

3.19-20 the town house . . . hotel: The Coopers had lived at 345 Greenwich Street since 1824; during their last weeks before sailing, they stayed at the City Hotel.

3.30 the Lexington: a new eighteen-gun sloop, of which Shubrick took command in 1826.

4.13-14 an Italian family of high rank: probably Napoleon Louis Bonaparte (1804-1831) and his wife, the Princess Charlotte (1802-1839), whom Cooper met in Florence in 1830. Charlotte was a daughter of Joseph Bonaparte and lived with him in Philadelphia and Bordentown, New Jersey, until her marriage in 1827.

5.10 Our ship: A vessel of 368 tons, the *Hudson* was launched in 1822 and belonged to the Black X line of London packets. She inaugurated regular service between New York and London in 1824 and plied that route until 1832, when she began a thirty-year career as a whaler.

5.33 The little Don Quixote: one of the four vessels belonging to the second line of Havre packets. At 260 tons, she was approximately two-thirds the size of the *Hudson*.

7.14-15 an experiment that has since failed: A lightship that was stationed off Sandy Hook in 1823 was removed in 1829 when the twin Navesink lights on the Highlands above the Hook went into operation.

7.19-20 send it an-end: hoist it up all the way.

7.40-8.1 the master: Henry L. Champlin commanded the *Hudson* from 1824 to 1829.

9.10  The Crisis: A packet belonging to the Black X Line, she sailed from London in early January 1826 and was last seen near the ice fields on 18 March.

10.12-13  the Insurgente . . . the Hornet: United States naval vessels that were lost at sea with all hands between 1800 and 1829.

10.22  two young officers: Acting Lieutenant Stephen Decatur McKnight and James Lyman, a master's mate.

14.17  an Indiaman: The *Halsewell,* commanded by Richard Pierce, was wrecked on the coast of Dorset on 6 January 1786 with the loss of more than 150 lives.

15.21  another little castle: probably Hurst Castle, at the entrance to the Solent.

17.2  MRS. POMEROY: Cooper's sister Anne (1784-1870), who married George Pomeroy, a Cooperstown pharmacist, in 1803. She is named also as the recipient of Letters VI and XVIII.

17.5-6  Mr. and Mrs. [Pedersen]: Peder Pedersen (1774-1851), Danish minister to the United States, and his wife, the former Anna Caroline Loughton Smith (1791-1878) of Philadelphia.

17.19  The consul at Cowes: Robert R. Hunter, who served as consul there from 1823 to 1842.

18.3  I had twice visited England: as a foremast-hand aboard the merchantman *Stirling* in 1806-07.

19.2  Mrs. [Cooper]: the former Susan Augusta De Lancey (1792-1852), whom Cooper married in 1811.

19.21  a book of travels: Godfrey T. Vigne's *Six Months in America,* published in two volumes in London by Whittaker, Treacher, and Company in 1832 and in one volume in Philadelphia by T. T. Ash in 1833. The passage to which Cooper refers appears in the London edition on II, 272.

20.16-17  the Duke of Norfolk: Bernard Edward Howard (1765-1842), twelfth Duke of Norfolk.

20.18  another castle: Cowes Castle, built in 1540.

20.20  the Marquis of Anglesey: Henry William Paget (1768-1854), first Marquis of Anglesey.

21.28  one of the King's architects: John Nash (1752-1835), who built East Cowes Castle in 1798.

22.1-2  A near relation of [Susan]'s: John Peter De Lancey (1753-1828), Mrs. Cooper's father. He served as a major with the Pennsylvania Loyalists in the Revolution and afterwards as a captain in the Royal Irish Regiment.

22.34  coachee: a long, lightweight horse-carriage.

23.30  a fine old village church: St. Mary's, the earliest portions of which

date from the twelfth century. For a condensed account of this
visit to Carisbrooke, see Cooper's letter to Mrs. Pomeroy of 24 July
1826 (*Letters and Journals,* I, 147-48).

23.34  a ruined priory: Carisbrooke Priory, founded in 1156 and dissolved
by Henry V in 1415.

24.24  "unhonoured dead": Thomas Gray, "Elegy Written in a Country
Churchyard," 1. 93.

26.26  two more of Henry VIIIth's forts: probably Calshot Castle on the
west bank of Southampton Water and Netley Castle on the east
bank.

28.2  Mrs. R[omaine]: Mary Watts Romaine (or Romayne), distantly related
to Mrs. Cooper.

28.6  Mrs. L[aight]: Elizabeth Watts Laight (1784?-1866), wife of Henry
Laight, a New York attorney. Her mother was Mrs. Cooper's aunt.

28.7  Mrs. McA[dam]: Anne Charlotte De Lancey (1786-1852), who in fact
did not marry John Louden McAdam until more than a year after
the Cooper's visit to Southampton.

28.27  two of the co-labourers: John Adams and Thomas Jefferson.

28.35  one . . . of an architecture much more ancient: probably the Manor
House at Bitterne, across the Itchen from Southampton.

29.20  a little battery: at Netley Castle.

30.2  R. COOPER, ESQ.: Richard Cooper (1808-1862), the son of Cooper's
brother Richard Fenimore. A practicing lawyer, Richard Cooper
assisted the novelist in most of his legal cases and in 1850 married
Maria Frances, the youngest Cooper daughter. He is named also as
the recipient of Letters IV, V, X, XX, XXI, and XXIII.

30.27  a house: Kempshott House near Basingstoke in Hampshire, where
the Prince of Wales occasionally resided in the early 1790's.

32.26  Virginia Water: an artificial lake in Windsor Great Park, a favorite
fishing spot of George IV.

33.13  one whose great name: the Duke of Wellington, to whom Apsley
House was presented by the government in 1820.

33.17-18  Brooks', White's, the Thatched House: political clubs on St.
James's Street.

33.19-20  Buckingham-house . . . ruins: Buckingham House, built in 1705,
was altered and enlarged in 1825 to become Buckingham Palace.

33.20  *"palazzo-non-finito"*: the then unfinished mansion that was later vari-
ously known as York House, Stafford House, Sutherland House, and
Lancaster House and for a time housed the London Museum.

33.25  Crockford's: a private club and gambling house on St. James's Street.

34.2  The respectable woman: Mrs. Wright, with whom Cooper again
stayed during his visit to London in 1828.

34.7  Somerset-house: an office building which housed the Royal Society and the Royal Academy of Arts, as well as a number of governmental departments.

34.35-36  the business . . . capital: negotiations concerning the English publication of *The Prairie.*

37.34-35  I shall refer . . . description: See *Gleanings in Europe: England,* Letter IV.

38.29  Mr. L[ynch]: Dominick Lynch, a fashionable importer of French wines in New York City.

38.36  Madame Pasta played *Semiramide:* The Italian soprano Giudetta Negri Pasta (1798-1865) was then at the height of her popularity. Rossini's opera *Semiramide* was first performed in 1823.

39.1-2  Madame Malibran: The Spanish mezzo-contralto Maria Felicita Garcia Malibran (1808-1836) sang in New York from 1825 to 1827.

39.14  Stephen Price: (1782-1840), manager of the Park Theater in New York, who leased the Drury Lane Theatre for the season of 1826-27.

39.39  Mr. M———: probably John Miller, a London bookseller, publisher, and literary agent who had published *The Pilot, Lionel Lincoln,* and *The Last of the Mohicans* in England and was bargaining for *The Prairie.*

41.4  the White Horse Cellar, in Piccadilly: a coaching inn on Fetter Lane, not Piccadilly.

43.36  Roman remains: probably the site of the Roman station of Clausentum, on the grounds of Bitterne Manor.

45.15  fear and trembling: Philippians ii.12.

45.28-30  Mrs. Opie . . . a passion: In the concluding dialogue of Amelia Opie's novel *Temper* (1816), the heroine observes that "there is nothing so like a commoner in a passion as a lord in one."

46.29-30  tradition attributes to . . . Caesar: The tower was in fact built under Francis I in the early sixteenth century.

48.12  the consul: Reuben G. Beasley, who was appointed from Virginia in 1817 and died in office in 1847.

54.14  one of William's barons . . . Tankerville: Cooper is incorrect in tracing the earls of Tankerville to a Norman ancestor who came from Tancarville. They descend from John Grey (d. 1421), who was created the first Earl of Tankerville for his services in the campaign of Henry V in Normandy, 1417-19.

55.38-39  Carroll Place: Upon his return to New York, Cooper rented a house at 4 Bleeker Street, Carroll Place.

56.10  the cathedral: For a parallel account of Cooper's impressions of the cathedral of Notre-Dame at Rouen, see his letter of 24 July 1826 to Mrs. Pomeroy (*Letters and Journals,* I, 149-151).

59.23 a considerable *bourg:* Pont-de-l'Arche, principal town of the canton of Eure.

60.32 the church: Notre-Dame, begun in the thirteenth century.

60.39 Sir Francis Burdett: (1770-1844), prominent spokesman in Parliament for liberal causes and supporter of the Reform Bill.

61.5 "silent fingers pointing to the skies": Cf. Coleridge's "spire-steeples, which . . . point as with a silent finger to the sky and stars" (*The Friend,* 23 November 1809, and *Biographia Literaria,* Satyrane's Letter I).

61.23 a village: probably Moussel, the first village on the road running east from Vernon.

62.4-5 "The wisest, greatest, *meanest,* of mankind": "The wisest, brightest, meanest of mankind" (*An Essay on Man,* iv.282).

62.8 The church: Notre-Dame, begun in the twelfth century.

64.3 two little palaces: the Ministère de la Marine and the Hôtel de Crillon, on opposite sides of the Rue Royale.

65.13-14 Our own minister: James Brown (1766-1835), United States minister to France from 1823 to 1829.

69.10 one of those silly ceremonies: The ritual was performed on 15 October 1826.

69.13-14 Madame la Vicomtesse de Gontaut-Biron: Marie Joséphine de Montaut-Navailles, Duchesse de Gontaut (1772-1857), was appointed governess of the royal children in 1819.

69.15 Baron de Damas: Ange Hyacinthe Maxence, Baron de Damas (1785-1862), minister of foreign affairs from 1824 to 1828, took charge of the education of the young Duc de Bourdeaux in April 1828 after the death of his first male governor, the Duc de Rivière. It was Rivière who in fact received the child from the hands of Madame de Gontaut in the ceremony that Cooper describes.

70.15 this occasion: on 10 September 1826. For a similar account of this day at the races, see Cooper's letter of 1-15? October 1826 to Mrs. Peter Augustus Jay (*Letters and Journals,* I, 162-63).

70.26 a young American friend: probably Dr. George Wilkes (1801?-1876), the son of Cooper's friend Charles Wilkes. In a letter of mid-August 1826 to Luther Bradish, the novelist reported that "George Wilkes is here, and quite well—I see a good deal of him" (*Letters and Journals,* I, 155).

70.36 *Mademoiselle d'Artois:* Louise Marie Thérèse de Bourbon (1819-1864).

71.15 the *Dauphine:* Marie Thérèse Charlotte, Duchesse d'Angoulême (1778-1851), daughter of Louis XVI.

72.13 Dutch collars: horse collars that encircle the breast of the animal rather than the neck; now commonly called "breastplates."

75.21 a friend: Luther Bradish (1783-1863), an old acquaintance of Cooper, had been sent abroad on an unofficial diplomatic mission in 1820 by John Quincy Adams. In early 1826, shortly after Bradish returned to New York, Cooper asked him to write letters of introduction for use during his own forthcoming visit to Europe.

78.4-5 Mr. Canning . . . came to Paris: on 16 September 1826.

78.13 the entertainment at St. Cloud: on 19 October 1826.

78.16 a great diplomatic dinner: given on 30 September 1826. For a less restrained account of the affair, see Cooper's letter of 1-15? October 1826 to Mrs. Jay (*Letters and Journals*, I, 158-62).

78.19 the regular Secretary: Daniel Sheldon of Connecticut served as Secretary of Legation in Paris from 1816 to 1828.

80.7 a former French minister: probably Joseph Alexandre Jacques Durant de Mareuil (1769-1835), who was Envoy Extraordinary and Minister Plenipotentiary from France when Cooper visited Washington in March 1826 to secure a consular appointment in anticipation of his trip to Europe.

82.26 the *Hôtel Monaco:* better known as the Hôtel de Matignon, 57 Rue de Varenne. The mansion was acquired by Honoré Camille, Prince of Monaco and Duc de Valentinois, in 1751.

82.36 Prince of Salm: Frederick III (1746-1794), Prince of Salm-Kyrburg, who built the Hôtel Salm on the Rue de Lille in 1786. In 1804, the government bought the mansion for the grand chancellery of the Legion of Honor.

83.9-10 our own . . . justice": spoliation claims by the United States for damages done to American shipping by the French during the Napoleonic wars.

83.27 Madame Adelaide of Orleans: Eugénie Adélaïde Louise d'Orléans (1777-1847), sister of Louis Philippe.

83.36-37 the Swiss *Chargé d'Affaires:* Cooper identifies the Swiss chargé as a M. de Ischann in his letter to Mrs. Jay (see the note for 78.16).

83.39 the Prussian: Baron Heinrich von Werther (1772-1859).

85.24-25 a clergyman and his wife: Dr. Samuel Farmar Jarvis (1786-1851), who had resigned the rectorate of St. Paul's Church in Boston in 1826 in order to travel and study in Europe. His wife was the former Sarah McCurdy of Saybrook, Connecticut. Cooper's letter to Mrs. Jay (see the note for 78.16) identifies Dr. and Mrs. Jarvis as guests at the Browns' party.

85.33-34 the Duke of Villa Hermosa: Jose Antonio de Aragon (d. 1852), diplomat and general.

85.37 the Golden Fleece: a secular chivalric order founded in 1429 and conferred upon members of the nobility and heads of state for service to the Catholic Church.

85.39 Lord and Lady Granville: Granville Leveson Gower (1773-1846), first Earl of Granville, and the former Harriet Elizabeth Cavendish.

86.5-6 The Austrian ambassador and ambassadress: Antal Rudolf, Count Apponyi (1782-1852), served as ambassador to France from 1826 to 1848. His wife was the former Teresa di Nogarola.

86.28 the Nuncio: Vincenzo Macchi (1770-1860), who became nuncio to France in 1820 and was appointed to the college of cardinals on 2 October 1826.

86.35 Lord Clanricarde: Ulick John De Burgh (1802-1874), who had married Canning's daughter Harriet.

87.38-39 some of us . . . West Jersey: The novelist's ancestor William Cooper immigrated to West Jersey in 1679 and there founded an extensive family.

88.21 one of his followers: Godert de Ginkel (1630-1703), created Earl of Athlone in 1692.

88.28-29 Mad. de [Reede-Ginckel]: the former Henrietta Dorothea Maria Hope (1790-1830), widow of the seventh Earl of Athlone.

89.10 "bite their thumbs" at me: Cf. *Romeo and Juliet*, I.i.42-43, "I will bite my thumb at them, which is a disgrace to them if they bear it."

90.14 O[gde]n: James De Peyster Ogden (1790?-1870), Cooper's friend and business associate.

93.7 an Archbishop of Paris: either Christophe de Beaumont (1703-1781) or his successor, Antoine Leclerc de Juigné (1728-1811). Cooper's anecdote is a version of one told by Jeanne Louise Henriette Campan in her *Memoirs of the Private Life of Marie Antoinette,* first published in Paris, London, and Philadelphia in 1823. According to Madame Campan, Princess Victoire, daughter of Louis XV and aunt of Louis XVI, was told by a bishop that she could eat her favorite waterfowl during Lent if the gravy of the bird did not congeal within a quarter of an hour after being drained into a very cold silver dish.

94.10 *chasse-café:* a liqueur taken to remove the taste of coffee or tobacco.

94.20 a recent negotiation: involving the competing claims of the United States and Great Britain to Oregon.

94.23-24 two individuals of high station: apparently a reference to John Evelyn Denison (1800-1873), who later became Viscount Ossington, and Lady Charlotte Cavendish Bentinck, a daughter of William, fourth Duke of Portland, and related to Canning by marriage. Cooper had met Denison in America in 1824 and would seem to have said something in his favor in this conversation with Canning.

In any event, Denison was appointed to an office in Canning's administration on 2 May 1827 and married Lady Charlotte on 14 July 1827. The Coopers encountered the couple in Switzerland in the summer of 1828.

96.2  JACOB SUTHERLAND, ESQ.: (1787?-1845), a boyhood friend of Cooper and a justice of the New York State Supreme Court from 1823 to 1835. He is named also as the recipient of Letter XIX.

99.28-29  three or four . . . young Englishmen: Edward Geoffrey Smith Stanley (1779-1869), later fourteenth Earl of Derby; John Stuart-Wortley (1801-1855), later second Baron Wharncliffe; Henry Labouchere (1798-1869), later created Baron Taunton; and Evelyn Denison (see the note for 94.23-24). Cooper met them in 1824, when they were touring the United States.

102.2  COL. BANKHEAD: James Bankhead (1783-1856) of Virginia, a career military officer. Cooper's acquaintance with Bankhead may have begun during his naval service at Oswego in 1808-09, for the Fifth Infantry Regiment, in which Bankhead was appointed captain on 18 June 1808, was then stationed on the Great Lakes.

102.31  a *petite guerre,* on the plains of Issy: No such military exercise is reported in the Paris newspapers for the summer of 1826, the period assigned to it by the chronology of *France.* On 26 October 1827, however, Charles X and the men of the royal family attended a mock battle on the Plain of Issy identical to the one that Cooper describes.

102.32  The sudden disbandment . . . in 1830: Cooper refers to the royal guards, not the National Guard.

104.36-37  the *fête* of the Trocadero: The elaborate re-enactment was staged on 31 August 1826, the third anniversary of the taking of the Spanish fortress.

104.38  the *Dauphin:* Louis Antoine, Duc d'Angoulême (1775-1844).

105.24  a great review: on 29 April 1827.

108.13-14  "the king's name is a tower of strength": *Richard III,* V.iii.12.

109.33  *à la Robinson:* in the manner of Robinson Crusoe.

110.8  an old, English general: Sir John Ormsby Vandeleur (1763-1849).

111.15  the charter: the document promulgated in 1814 by which the parliamentary government of the Bourbon Restoration was established.

112.24  the present king of Sweden: Charles XIV (1763-1843), who, as Jean Baptiste Jules Bernadotte, had served brilliantly as a marshal under Napoleon.

113.5  *Maréchal Molitor:* Gabriel Jean Joseph, Comte Molitor (1770-1849).

113.6-7  *Maréchal Mortier:* Édouard Adolphe Casimir Joseph Mortier (1768-1835), Duc de Trévise.

113.8 *Lamarque:* Maximilien, Comte Lamarque (1770-1832), a general under Napoleon.

113.25-26 I have seen Marshal Soult in company: together with Marshals Marmont, Mortier, and Lauriston at a dinner party given by Mrs. James Brown in March 1827; see Cooper's letter of 26 March 1827 to Mrs. Jay (*Letters and Journals*, I, 202).

115.2 MRS. SAMUEL W. BEALL: Cooper's niece Elizabeth Fenimore Cooper (1809-1879), the daughter of his brother Isaac, married Samuel Wootton Beall in 1829. Beall served as receiver for the sale of public lands in Green Bay, Wisconsin, from 1827 to 1834.

115.3 a ceremony: The Coopers attended the *grand couvert* of Charles X on 1 January 1827. For a slightly different account of the affair, see the novelist's letter to William Leete Stone, published in the *New-York Commercial Advertiser* for 24 March 1827 and reprinted in *Letters and Journals*, I, 189-98.

115.7 the *fête* of the king: celebrated on 4 November.

117.33 a duel: fought on 19 March 1778. According to some accounts, Artois wrung the nose of the Duchesse de Bourbon after she raised his mask at a ball.

119.1 *Suckers:* natives of Illinois.

119.8-10 The last independent Dauphin . . . the Black Prince: The last dauphin, Umbert II, sold Dauphiné in 1349 to Philip VI of France, not to his son John II. John, who succeeded to the throne in 1350, was captured by Edward, Prince of Wales, at Poitiers in 1356 and held for ransom until his death in 1364.

119.23 The Boar of Ardennes: Guillaume, Comte de la Marck, beheaded in 1485. He figures importantly in Scott's *Quentin Durward.*

120.10-11 "If Coke . . . *I'll Knight him":* According to A.M.W. Stirling's *Coke of Norfolk and His Friends* (London: John Lane, 1912), pp. 347-48, the Prince Regent, offended by an address to him that Coke delivered on 21 April 1817, declared, " 'If Coke of Norfolk enters my presence, by God, I'll knight him!' The speech was repeated to Coke. 'If he dares,' was the rejoinder, 'by God, I'll break his sword.' "

121.35 Baron Louis, not the financier, but the king's physician: The financier was Baron Joseph Dominique Louis (1755-1837), three times minister of finance during the Restoration and the July Monarchy, but the *premier médecin* of Charles X was Baron Antoine Portal (1742-1832). Cooper's memory evidently failed him here, for in his letter to Stone (see the note for 115.3), he identifies the royal physician as "the baron Pertal."

121.36 Sancho's tormentor: in *Don Quixote,* Part II, Chapter xlvii, where the physician altogether prevents Sancho from eating his gubernatorial dinner.

125.8 *Monsieur Tonsons:* a reference to the apparently ubiquitous but actually non-existent title character of William T. Moncrieff's *Monsieur Tonson!* (1821). The farce was first produced in New York in 1822 and was performed there many times before the Coopers sailed for Europe.

125.16-18 Commodore . . . anchored: In Smollett's *Peregrine Pickle*, Chapter viii, Trunnion exclaims, "O damn ye! you are safe at an anchor."

125.39 *M. Louis:* See the note for 121.35.

130.31-32 "to visit the sins of the fathers on the children": Cooper's wording of this phrase from the Second Commandment is that of *The Book of Common Prayer* rather than of the King James Version of the Bible.

133.21 The balcony, in which La Fayette appeared: On the morning of 6 October 1789, Lafayette, as commander of the National Guard, saved Marie Antoinette from the mob that had invaded Versailles the night before by appearing with her on the balcony and kneeling and kissing her hand.

134.18 the celebrated dinner was given to the officers: At a banquet held on 1 October 1789, the officers pledged their loyalty to the royal family. Viewed by the starving people of Paris as a display of contempt for their own sufferings, the feast incited the mob to invade Versailles a few days later.

136.10 leaguers: members of the Holy League, an organization of French Catholics which aimed at the suppression of Protestantism and which, with the aid of Philip II of Spain, opposed the rule of Henry IV after his accession in 1589.

136.11 Marshal Biron: Armand de Gontaut, Baron de Biron (1524-1592).

138.2 JAMES STEVENSON: (1789?-1852), a boyhood friend of Cooper and mayor of Albany from 1826 to 1828. He is named also as the recipient of Letters XIV and XVI.

142.28 P. P. C.: *pour prendre congé.*

146.30-31 the protracted negotiation for indemnity: See the note for 83.9-10. The breakdown of the negotiations in late 1834 brought France and the United States to the brink of war and formed one of the principal topics of the series of political letters that Cooper, using the signature "A. B. C.," wrote for the New York *Evening Post* from 1834 to 1836.

148.2 JAMES E. DE KAY: (1792-1851), zoologist, botanist, and a leading member of Cooper's Bread and Cheese Club in New York. He is named also as the recipient of Letters XIII, XV, and XXII.

148.4-5 The arrival of the Great Unknown: Scott reached Paris on 29 October 1826 and took lodgings at the Hôtel de Windsor on the

Rue de Rivoli. Cooper's letter of 7-13? November to Mrs. Jay (*Letters and Journals*, I, 169-70) parallels *France* in its account of his meetings with Scott in Paris.

148.29-30  the forthcoming work on Napoleon: Scott's *Life of Napoleon Buonaparte* was published in July 1827.

149.2  the notice of Sir Walter Scott: Soon after Scott's arrival in Paris, Cooper wrote to him proposing that his forthcoming *Napoleon* be copyrighted in the United States as the property of an American citizen, a scheme intended to assure Scott a return from American reprints of the work.

149.8  *Princesse [Galitzin Souvarof]*: daughter-in-law of the Princess Galitzin and granddaughter of General Souvarof. So intent was she on meeting Scott that she assured him that "Elle vouloit traverser des mers pour aller vois S. W. S."; see Edgar Johnson, *Sir Walter Scott: The Great Unknown* (New York: Macmillan Company, 1970), II, 1001.

149.13  ten days after the arrival of Sir Walter Scott: Scott's *Journal* gives the date of his first meeting with Cooper as 3 November 1826.

151.9  a matter of business: In the course of this discussion, Scott rejected the plan that Cooper had proposed in his letter and enlisted Cooper's support in securing the agreement of Carey or some other American publisher to share half the profits of *Napoleon* and the future works of Scott in return for exclusive right of publication. Cooper's prompt effort to interest Carey in such an agreement met with no success.

152.40  *Gosselin:* Charles Gosselin (1792-1859), a Parisian bookseller and publisher, published Cooper's works in French translation. During the years of the novelist's residence in Europe, Gosselin paid him for the privilege.

153.2  the following day but one: Scott's *Journal* gives 4 November, a day earlier, as the date of his second meeting with Cooper.

153.34  The next morning: According to Scott's *Journal*, his meeting with Cooper on 6 November, the day of the Princess Galitzin's party, was at breakfast at his own lodgings, not Cooper's. After the publication of the *Journal* entries in Lockhart's *Memoirs of the Life of Sir Walter Scott* in 1837, however, Cooper insisted on the accuracy of his own version of their encounters in Paris: "The diary is incorrect, to my certain knowldege, in a variety of things, as well as in its dates. I did not breakfast with Sir Walter Scott on the day that I met him at the soirée of the Princess Galitzin, for instance, but the day before." See Cooper's letter to the *Knickerbocker*, 11 (1838), 380-86, reprinted in *Letters and Journals*, III, 317-23.

155.15  one or two women: Scott's *Journal* mentions an elderly Madame de Bouffleurs as one of the guests at the party. She was in fact the

former Comtesse de Sabran (1750-1827), the widow of the Chevalier
Stanislas Jean de Bouffleurs, but Cooper, like Scott, may have
confused her with the Comtesse de Bouffleurs (1725-1800), the friend
of Hume and Rousseau.

155.21 half-mourning: worn in commemoration of her mother, Lady Charlotte Carpenter Scott, who died on 14 May 1826.

159.22 a laughable blunder of a translator: Cooper refers to the note which
A. J. B. Defauconpret appended to his translation of *The Spy*, first
published in 1822, as a gloss on the scene in Chapter xiii in which
Colonel Wellmere draws figures on the table with spilled wine: "On
comprend bien que l'on avait oublié de mettre la nappe, ou plutôt,
à cette époque, c'était un luxe de table fort rare en Amérique"
(*L'Espion* [Paris: Charles Gosselin, 1827], II, 33, n. 1).

161.7 an exhibition: Cooper attended the great industrial exhibition of 1
August-2 October 1827. Such exhibitions during the Restoration
were not triennial but quadrennial, previous ones having been held
in 1819 and 1823.

165.12 nothing "new under the sun": Ecclesiastes i.9.

165.16 the *Savonnerie:* a royal carpet and tapestry factory that was established in the early seventeenth century on the site of a soap works.
It merged with the Gobelins factory in 1826.

170.39-40 Head's, Barnum's, and Gadsby's: hotels in Philadelphia, Baltimore,
and Washington, D. C., respectively.

172.3 Coblentz: In June 1791, the brothers of Louis XVI established a large
colony of *émigrés* in Coblenz, formed a government in exile, and
raised an army. The threat of invasion by the forces of the French
revolutionary government scattered the exiles in late 1792.

173.12-14 as Falstaff . . . your back": *Henry IV*, Part I, II.iv.148-50.

173.36 an American friend: James De Peyster Ogden (see the note for
90.14), who, having just returned from service as American consul
at Liverpool, accompanied Cooper on his visit to Washington in
December 1833.

176.2 Cicero admitting: in his speech *De haruspicum responso,* ix.19.

177.34-178.1 *ces quarante . . . quatre:* The quip is the invention of the
French playwright Alexis Piron (1689-1773).

178.3 the reception of two or three new members: probably the reception
of Charles Fourier and Charles Marie de Feletz on 17 April 1827.

181.38 he fell ill and died: Talma died on 19 October 1826.

181.39-40 Mademoiselle Mars: Anne Françoise Hippolyte Mars (1779-1847)
performed at the Théâtre-Français, where she was best known for
her roles in Molière's comedies.

182.7 "length": theatrical slang for a portion of an actor's part consisting
of forty-two lines.

182.26 *Théâtre de Madame:* The Théâtre du Gymnase was renamed the Théâtre de Madame in 1824, when the Duchesse de Berri became its special patroness.

182.26 a certain piece: Eugène Scribe's *Rodolphe, ou Frère et sœur,* a one-act play first performed at the Théâtre du Gymnase on 20 November 1823. It was incorporated in the repertory of the theater and received twenty-seven performances during Cooper's first residence in Paris.

183.36-37 Miss Lee, in one of her Canterbury Tales: *The Canterbury Tales* (1797) were written by the sisters Harriet and Sophia Lee. Cooper's reference is to Sophia's story "The Clergyman's Tale—Henry, or, Pembroke," in which the hero and heroine fall in love, though they have been taught to believe that he is her illegitimate half-brother.

184.10 the "windy side" of sensibility: Cf. "the windy side of the law" (*Twelfth Night,* III.iv.164) and "the windy side of care" (*Much Ado About Nothing,* II.i.315).

184.35 Mr. Power: Tyrone Power (1795-1841), whose first stunning success in comic Irish roles came in London in 1826. His American debut was at the Park Theater in New York in 1833.

185.4-5 Napoleon . . . a step: The famous saying was first reported in the Abbé de Pradt's *Historie de l'ambassade dans le grand duché de Varsovie en 1812* (Paris: Pillet, 1815), p. 219.

185.7-8 Racine, in a most touching scene: apparently a reference to *Bérénice,* IV.ii.10, where Phénice offers to help the distraught heroine to prepare herself for an interview with Titus: "Souffrez que de vos pleurs je répare l'outrage."

185.13 "piping time of peace": *Richard III,* I.i.24.

185.16-17 "Some thinks he writes Cinna; he owns to Panurge": Oliver Goldsmith, "The Haunch of Venison," 1. 78.

185.18 Marquis de [Marbois]: François Barbé de Marbois (1745-1837), consul general to the United States in the 1780's.

186.3 his successor . . . to publish: Louis XVIII, who took pride in his literary talents and scholarly accomplishments, was the author of *Relation d'un voyage à Bruxelles et à Coblentz, en 1791* (1823), as well as of volumes of poetry and letters.

188.10-14 Having an intention . . . the original book: After some delays, Gosselin agreed on 4 October 1826 to pay 2,000 francs for the right to publish an authorized translation of *The Prairie.*

189.20 her father: Manuel Garcia (1775-1832), the Spanish tenor and composer, was reputed to be the greatest teacher of singing of his day.

189.26 "animalculæ, who live by feeding on the body of genius": Coleridge's expression has not been found in any of his writings or the numerous reports of his conversation that were published by the time of the composition of *France.*

190.31  Comtesse [du Cayla]: the former Zoé Talon (1785-1852), favorite of Louis XVIII.

191.2  M. Ternaux: Baron Guillaume Louis Ternaux (1763-1833), a political ally of Lafayette and owner of the house that Cooper rented in Saint-Ouen, as well as of the large country house which he himself occupied there.

191.36  Jack Cade: leader of the rebel mob in *Henry VI,* Part II.

196.10-24  There was a ceremony . . . at the time: Marie Armand Guerri de Maubreuil (1782-1855), Marquis d'Orsvault, struck down the seventy-three-year-old Talleyrand as he left Saint-Denis at the conclusion of a memorial service for Louis XVI on 20 January 1827. Maubreuil had been sentenced to five years in prison for attempting to steal the jewels of Queen Catherine of Westphalia in 1814. In his defense, he charged Talleyrand with hiring him not only to rob Queen Catherine but to assassinate Napoleon, and he now sought to disgrace Talleyrand publicly.

198.2  CAPT. M. PERRY, U. S. N.: Matthew Calbraith Perry (1794-1858), one of Cooper's many naval friends and brother of Oliver Hazard Perry. He is best remembered as the negotiator of the treaty which opened Japan to trade with the West.

198.28-29  the people . . . *tigres":* In his letter of 21 November 1766 to Madame du Deffand, Voltaire writes, "Vôtre nation est partagée en deux espèces, l'une de singes oisifs qui moquent de tout, et l'autre de Tigres qui déchirent"; see *Voltaire's Correspondence,* ed. Theodore Besterman (Geneva: Institut et Musée Voltaire, 1961), LXIII, 116.

199.28  Capt. [Chauncey]: Ichabod Wolcott Chauncey (1784-1835), who had served with Cooper as a midshipman in 1809-10 and had arrived in Paris in the summer or early fall of 1827. The two old friends made their circuit of the city in mid-November. See Thomas Philbrick, "Cooper's Naval Friend in Paris," *American Literature,* 52 (1981), 634-638.

201.14  he swore . . . Flanders": a reference to one of Uncle Toby's speeches in Sterne's *Tristram Shandy,* Book II, Chapter xi.

204.5-6  The king . . . St. Omer: The royal encampment was from 9 to 16 September 1827.

216.1  *le Chevalier Alexandre de Lameth:* After playing an important role in the early phases of the French Revolution and serving in several civil posts under Napoleon, Lameth (1760-1829) became a staunch ally of Lafayette in promoting the liberal cause during the Restoration.

219.23 I determined to make a night of it: In constructing this account of his evening of visits, Cooper apparently conflated several social affairs that actually took place on separate dates; see the notes for 221.17 and 224.8.

220.7-8 *M. [Dambray]*: Charles Henri Dambray (1760-1829).

220.13 The hotel: the Hôtel du Chancelier, 11 Place Vendôme.

220.27 Madame de Souza: the Marquise de Souza-Botelho (1761-1836), the former Adèle Marie Émilie Filleul and, by her first marriage, Comtesse Flahaut. Her first novel, *Adèle de Senanges,* appeared in 1794 and was followed by a succession of other tales of the fashionable world in which she herself moved.

220.29 the Grand Referendary: Charles Louis Huguet (1759-1839), Marquis de Sémonville. As *grand référendaire,* Sémonville administered the funds allocated to the Chamber of Peers.

220.30 M. de Plaisance: Anne Charles Lebrun (1775-1859), Duc de Plaisance, had a distinguished career as a general in the Napoleonic wars and served repeatedly as aide-de-camp to the Emperor. He was the son-in-law of Marbois.

220.34-35 The appointed hour had come: As a consequence of the victory of the liberals in the elections of November 1827, Villèle resigned his office on 3 January 1828.

221.2-3 Comte Roy: Comte Antoine Roy (1764-1847), a royalist lawyer and politician, served for a second time as minister of finance in 1828-29 but did not become premier.

221.17 Madame de [Mirbel]: Dame Lizinska Rue de Mirbel (1796-1849), wife of the botanist Charles François Brisseau de Mirbel (1776-1854), painted the portraits of both Scott and Cooper while they were in Paris at this time. She was court painter to Louis XVIII and Charles X, a position which may account for the royalist flavor of her soiree. Cooper's account of the affair is based upon his visit to her on 25 March 1827; see his letter to Mrs. Jay of 26 March 1827 (*Letters and Journals,* I, 202).

222.8 M. de Duras: Amédée de Durfort (1771-1838), Duc de Duras, first gentleman of the royal chamber to Louis XVIII.

222.19 the general post-office: on the Rue Jean-Jacques-Rousseau at the site of the present Hôtel des Postes.

222.29 a great woolen manufacturer: probably Baron Ternaux (see the note for 191.2), called *"le prince des mérinos"* for his extensive sheep farms and textile factories. His salon in the magnificent Hôtel de Massiac, fronting on the Place des Victoires, was a gathering place for the more moderate members of the political left.

223.1 an English lady: Lady Virginia Murray, the youngest daughter of

John Murray, fourth Earl of Dunmore, who was governor of New
York in 1770-71.

223.11-12  an Irishman of great wit and of exquisite humor: probably
Patrick Lattin of County Kildare and the Chausée d'Antin, a member
of Lady Murray's circle. According to Lady Morgan's *France, in
1829-30* (New York: J. & J. Harper, 1830), I, 53, his wit combined "all
that is best in French or Irish peculiarity."

223.20-23  In the course . . . infallibility: One of the more than 700 British
civilians detained in France after the renewal of the conflict with
England in the spring of 1803, Sir James Michael De Bathe (d. 1808)
succeeded in enlisting the aid of Pius VII, who had come to Paris
in November 1804 to consecrate Napoleon as emperor. The objects
of the Pope's solicitude were De Bathe's two sons, James Wynne
(1792-1828) and William Plunkett (1793-1870).

224.8  *the* party of the evening: Cooper's account of this great ball tallies
with his description in his letter to Mrs. Jay of 26 March 1827
(*Letters and Journals*, II, 203-205 and 210) of a ball given by Pozzo di
Borgo "a week or two since."

224.38  the _____, an intimate friend of the ambassador: The details point
to the Princess Galitzin, whom Cooper accompanied to Pozzo's ball.

225.18  some droll anecdotes: The story of the exiled marquise that follows
is an altered version of an anecdote that Cooper heard about one
of the guests at Pozzo's ball and repeated in his letter of 26 March
1827 to Mrs. Jay (*Letters and Journals*, I, 205). According to his informant, the lady in question, "a Madame d'Aguesseau," had gone
alone to England during the Revolution and had returned fifteen
years later with a daughter whose father was an English nobleman.
The gossip concerns the Marquise d'Aguesseau (1759-1849), who,
leaving her husband in France, fled to England at the time of the
Terror and returned in 1800 with a four-year old girl called Georgina
Howard, reputedly her illegitimate daughter.

227.31  Lady [Conyngham]: the former Elizabeth Denison (d. 1861), the
wife of Henry, first Marquis Conyngham. She became the favorite
of George IV in 1820.

227.36  *Le Parc-aux-Cerfs:* a private brothel established for Louis XV in an
inconspicuous quarter of the town of Versailles.

227.39-228.1  the *fête Dieu:* the festival of Corpus Christi, observed in 1827
on 17 June.

229.3  The Chambers have opened: on 5 February 1828.

230.8  *la Bagatelle:* an elaborate retreat of the French royal family in the
Bois de Boulogne.

231.9  M. Royer Collard: Pierre Paul Royer-Collard (1763-1845), leader of
the Doctrinaires.

231.15 a sawyer: a fallen tree trunk that bobs up and down in the current.

234.37 When the ministers of Charles X. were tried: by the Court of Peers, 15-21 December 1830.

236.8 the law to protect American industry: the "Tariff of Abominations" of 1828, which induced Calhoun to formulate his doctrine of nullification.

237.39-40 the good curate and the Bachelor of Don Quixote: In *Don Quixote*, Part I, Chapter vi, the barber Master Nicholas, not the bachelor Samson Carrasco, assists the curate in burning Quixote's books.

238.11 Rosay: now commonly spelled Rozoy or Rozay.

238.26 two his female connexions: There were three, not two, for the grandmother, mother, and sister of Lafayette's wife were guillotined in the Place du Trône on 22 July 1794, five days before the Reign of Terror ended.

239.28-29 the Englishman . . . the Revelations: Several demonstrations of Bonaparte's identity with the beast were published in England during the Napoleonic era. See John Ashton, *English Caricature and Satire on Napoleon I* (London: Chatto and Windus, 1888), pp. 9-10.

239.35-36 Henry VI., was born in the same building: Henry VI was born at Windsor eight months before his father's death at Vincennes.

240.1-2 his dialogue between Henry and Catharine: in *Henry V,* V.ii.

240.7-8 the Prince de Wagram: Napoléon Alexandre Louis Joseph Berthier (1810-1887).

240.35-36 *Maréchal de la Feuillade:* François d'Aubusson (d. 1691).

241.10 one of the Mesdemoiselles de Noailles: Marie Adrienne Françoise de Noailles (1759-1807), whom Lafayette married in 1774.

241.11 a short sequestration: in 1794-95, when La Grange was considered still to belong to the estate of the Duchesse d'Ayen, Lafayette's mother-in-law.

241.14-243.28 Although the house . . . all the others: Most of the details of Cooper's physical description of La Grange parallel those given in his letter of 26 March 1827 to Mrs. Jay (*Letters and Journals,* I, 206-08).

241.36 Mr. Adams in his Eulogy on La Fayette: John Quincy Adams delivered the eulogy before both houses of Congress on 31 December 1834; it was published in New York in 1835.

242.9 General Fitzpatrick: Richard Fitzpatrick (1747-1813), Fox's most intimate friend.

243.38 his own father: Michel Louis Christophe Roch Gilbert du Motier (1732-1759).

244.10-11 his grandfather: Edouard de Lafayette (d. 1740).

245.14 *fermes ornées:* gentlemen's farms.

246.3 M. Parquin: an Orleanist lawyer best known for his fervent and successful defense of his brother Charles, who was tried for his participation in Louis Napoleon's abortive coup at Strasbourg in 1836.

246.27-28  an extensive palace of one of the Roman emperors: the Palais des Thermes, once thought to have been the residence of Julian the Apostate (331-363), but now known to have been a public bath.

249.4  a fight in the capital: Rioting occurred on 19 and 20 November 1827 following the news of the victory of the liberals in the elections.

251.24-25  The Templars exist: The ancient name was adopted by an order of Free Masons established in France in the early nineteenth century. Like other Masonic orders, it was regarded by the government during the Restoration as a source of subversive liberal thought and activity.

252.16  a high functionary: Comte Gilbert Joseph Gaspard de Chabrol (1773-1843), prefect of the Seine, who, on 20 December 1826, sent Cooper a medal commemorating the opening of the Bourse. The novelist declined Chabrol's subsequent dinner invitation because of illness.

255.24-25  a respectable clergyman: Daniel Nash (1763-1836), rector of Christ Church in Cooperstown. In this anecdote of "twenty years since," Cooper adopts a chronology appropriate to the actual composition of *France* rather than to the supposed date of the letter, for the incident must have taken place during his residence in Cooperstown from 1813 to 1817.

260.25  *M. Jules Cloquet:* Jules Germain Cloquet (1790-1883), a prominent surgeon and a friend and memorialist of Lafayette. He and the hypnotist Chapelain performed the experiment which Cooper describes on 12 April 1829. The patient was a Madame Plantin.

261.11  a special committee: The Académie des Sciences in fact appointed a commission to examine the question of animal magnetism in 1826, three years before Cloquet's operation. Its report, finally issued in 1831, did include the operation among the evidence it had gathered to substantiate its generally favorable judgment of the claims of the magnetizers.

261.21  A young countryman of ours: Albert Brisbane (1809-90), later well known as a socialist reformer.

268.39-269.1  One of the best ventriloquists of this age: probably Alexandre, whom the Coopers had seen in Paris at the home of the Countess Terzi.

271.2  the *Préfet* of the Rhone: Comte René de Brosses (1771-1834), to whom Cooper had sent the exequatur on 26 September 1826.

272.9-10  "shall I not take mine ease, in mine inn": *Henry IV,* Part I, III.iii.80-81.

273.6-7  a gentlemen of the Stanley family: probably Edward Stanley; see the note for 99.28-29.

273.27  one of these places: Montreuil, which rises from a marshy valley.

273.34  Sir William Draper: Lieutenant-General Sir William Draper (1721-1787) was related by marriage to Mrs. Cooper, the apparent source of this anecdote.

274.7-8  the great demonstration of Napoleon: Napoleon assembled a huge army and flotilla of transports intended for the invasion of England at Boulogne. He abandoned the project in August 1805.

274.8  a high monument: the Colonne Napoléon, the first stone of which was laid by Marshal Soult in 1804. At the time of Cooper's visit, the column had been altered so as to commemorate the restoration of the Bourbons.

274.16  Powles Hook: Cooper uses the common early nineteenth-century spelling of Paulus Hook, now a part of Jersey City, New Jersey.

274.20  the inn that Sterne has immortalized: the Hotel Dessein at Calais, in which the opening chapters of *A Sentimental Journey* are set.

274.28-29  The Bible . . . forget which: "Stay me with flagons, comfort me with apples" (Song of Solomon ii.5).

# Appendix A
Bentley's Analytical Table of Contents

de Talleyrand. Charles X. Panoramic Procession. Droll Effect.
The Dinner. M. de Talleyrand's Office. The Duchesse de Berri.
The Catastrophe. An Aristocratic Quarrel.

# Appendix B
## Cooper's Manuscript Letter on France

Cooper's undated, untitled holograph manuscript of this unpublished chapter is deposited in the Cooper Family Papers and is printed here with the permission of Paul Fenimore Cooper, Jr. It contains two folio sheets measuring 15¼″ x 12⅞″ folded in half to make eight sides measuring 7⅝″ x 12⅞″. All rectos and versos are filled with Cooper's script in black ink; the alterations are in the same hand and ink. The paper is heavy-weight, cream-colored, and woven, with no chain-lines or watermarks.

In the present transcription of the manuscript, angled brackets (< >) enclose words, letters, or punctuation marks that Cooper deleted by crossing out. Arrows (↑ ↓) enclose words that he inserted above the line of script. A question mark following a word or letter enclosed within brackets indicates a conjectural reading. Punctuation missing at the end of sentences is supplied within square brackets. On four occasions, Cooper wrote words that he obviously did not intend. On each of those occasions, the correct word is supplied in the body of the text, and the word that Cooper wrote is given in an accompanying footnote.


To ———

Some of the ↑common↓ usages of France are so different from our own as to deserve a short notice. My attention has been <recalled> ↑attracted↓ to the subject of a <marriage> ↑nuptial ceremony↓ in the La Fayette family, <his gr> ↑the eldest↓ daughter of M. George La Fayette having married M. Adolphe Perier, the nephew of the celebrated deputy of that name.+ ↑+(Note (Who died in 1832, Prime Minister of France.)↓

Marriage, by law, is <purely> a civil contract in France, and must be contracted before the civil authorities, though all the catholics defer to the usages of their church. Some abortive attempts have been made to reestablish divorces, but there seems to be such a horror of the former abuse of the privilege, that the proposition is not received with much favor.

When the parties go before the magistrate, which usually occurs a few days previously to the nuptial benediction, though sometimes they go from the office of the *maire* to the church, it is usual for a number of their chosen friends to accompany them, in which case the contract sets forth the fact of their presence. I was invited to be present at both ceremonies on the occasion of the marriage of Mademoiselle La Fayette, but receiving the notice too late, at the General's request I went to the *bureau du maire* to sign the contract. The paper was so full of names, that the secretary could barely find room for mine on the margin of a sheet. I believe this signing of the contract is deemed an act of attention, and it is so regulated at Court, that the King ↑regularily↓ signs these documents, for the favored few, at the *grand* or *petit lever,* according to the rank of the parties, and the degree of honor he wishes to confer. I cannot tell you the precise difference between these two *levers* but, judging from the names, I take it one is ↑at↓ his ordinary *toilette,* and that the other has more of the state of royalty about it. Scarcely a week passes that we do not see in the journals that "His <m> ↑Majesty↓ signed the contract of marriage between *M. le comte d'un tel,* <with> ↑and↓ Mademoiselle d'une telle,<"> at the *grand lever,* this morning &c &c." This is a thing to talk of hereafter, you will understand, as our women, <before the revolution,> used to talk of their having danced, before the revolution, with some younger son of a Lord, or stray Baronet.

After the civil marriage has taken place printed letters, called *faire parts+* ↑+Note (To make acquainted with)↓ are sent to all the friends and acquaintances. As neither marriages, births nor deaths are inserted in the journals, unless in particular cases, this is an attention necessary to apprise those who visit them of the occurrence. As you may not have seen any of these missives I shall translate one or two of them, taken at random from a pile of a hundred.

"M. George La Fayette, Member of the Chamber of Deputies, and Madame George La Fayette, have the honour to apprise you (*de vous faire part)* of the marriage of <their> of Mademoiselle Mathilde La Fayette, their daughter, with M. Maurice Bureaux de Pusy, the Prefect of Vaucluse."

"You are invited to be present at the nuptial benediction, which will be given Thursday next, in the church of the Assumption[.]"

The mother of the bridegroom, with whom I had not the honor of an acquaintance sent me a similar notice and invitation, on her part, it being etiquette for [*written over* to] ↑the nearest friends of↓ both the parties in the

Some of the usages of France are so different from our own as to merit a short notice. My attention has been attracted to the subject of a nuptial ceremony marriage in the La Fayette family, the eldest daughter of Mr George La Fayette having married Mr Adolfe Perier, the nephew of the celebrated deputy of that name & state (who died in 1832, Prime Minister of France).

Marriage, by law, is purely a civil contract in France, and must be contracted before the civil authorities, though all the catholics defer to the usages of their church. Some abortive attempts have been made to reestablish divorces, but there seems to be such a horror of the former abuse of the privilege, that the proposition is not received with much favor.

When the parties go before the magistrate, which usually occurs a few days previously to the nuptial benediction, though sometimes they go from the office of the maire to the church, it is usual for a number of their chosen friends to accompany them, in which case the contract sets forth the fact of their presence. I was invited to be present at both ceremonies on the occasion of the marriage of Mademoiselle La Fayette, but receiving the notice too late, at the General's request I went to the bureau du maire to sign the contract. The paper was so full of names, that the secretary could barely find room for mine on the margin of a sheet. I believe this signing of the contract is deemed an act of attention, and it is so regulated at Court, that His King signs these documents, for the favored few, at the grand or petit lever, according to the rank of the parties, and the degree of honor he wishes to confer. I cannot tell you the precise difference between these two levers but, judging from the names, I take it one is his ordinary toilette, and that the other has more of the state of royalty about it. Scarcely a week passes that we do not see in the journals that "His Majesty signed the contract of marriage between Mr le comte d'un tel, and with Mademoiselle d'une telle, at the grand lever, this morning &c." This is a thing to talk of hereafter, you will understand, as our women, before the revolution, used to talk of their having danced, before the revolution, with some younger son of a Lord, or some stingy Baronet.

After the civil marriage has taken place printed letters, called faire parts (notes to make acquainted with) are sent to all the friends and acquaintances. As neither marriages, births nor deaths are inserted in the journals, unless in particular cases, this is an attention necessary to apprise those who visit them of the occurrence. As you may not have seen any of these missives I shall translate one or two of them, taken at random from a pile of hundreds.

"Mr George La Fayette, Member of the Chamber of Deputies and Madame George La Fayette, have the honor to apprise you (de vous faire part) of the marriage of their of Mademoiselle Mathilde La Fayette, their daughter, with Mr Maurice Bureau de Puy, the Prefect of Vaucluse."

"You are invited to be present at the nuptial benediction, which will be given Thursday night, in the church of the Assumption."

The mother of the bridegroom, with whom I had not the honor of an acquaintance, sent me a similar notice and invitation, on her part, it being etiquette for both the parties the married friends of

case of ↑a↓ marriage to pay this compliment. The notice too, always come from the parents or guardians of the bride and bridegroom. ↑David the sculptor is the only person who ever sent me such a notice in his own name[.]↓

The *faire parts,* in the case of deaths are much more elaborate. Take one as a sample.

"*Monsieur le Prince et Madame la Princesse Aldobrandini, Messieurs Marc Antoine, Camille, Scipion Borghese Aldobrandini, Monsieur le Vicomte et Madame la Vicomtesse de Mortemart* have the honor to apprise you of the <loss> afflicting loss they have sustained in the person of His Excellency the Prince Camille Borghese, who died in his palace at Florence, the 9th May last."

This note has the simplicity that almost always <denotes> accompanies high rank at Paris. The relatives named were the nearest of kin only, though two of them were mere boys. But, in such cases, <the> children of a year old, or of a day old, I believe, are always included. I presume if a woman died in child birth, the innocent cause of her death would join in the *faire part,* provided it had a name. At least I have received many from <child> boys in their petticoats, and I presume the rule is absolute.

I find ↑among my papers↓ a *faire part* headed with a figure of Time, with his scythe and glass, apprising ↑me↓ of the death of the mother of an acquaintance, and signed by fourteen <names> ↑persons↓, wh<ich>↑o↓ conclude by styling themselves the "Son, Brother, Sister, ↑and↓ the Nephews and Neices of the deceased." This is the only communication of the sort, that was printed in this form. I translate another as a curiosity omitting the names.

M. A_____ Mademoiselle Stephanie A_____ Messieurs George, Henri, Ferdinand, Thomas Alphonse A_____; Madame *Veuve* B_____, Messieurs Jean and Etienne B_____ and Madame Frederic B_____ and her children; M. Cæsar A_____ and his children, Mademoiselle Virginie A_____, Madame Veuve Auguste A_____ and her two sons Auguste and Pierre; Madame C_____ born A_____, and her daughters and sons in law, Messieurs and Mesdames D_____ and F_____, and their children and Monsieur and Madame G_____, have the honor to apprise you of the afflicting loss they have just sustained in the person of Madame A_____ (Nathalie-Caroline-Marthe) born B_____, their wife, mother daughter, sister, sister in law, niece, aunt, and cousin, who died at Paris &c &c." This is verbatim, as a translation, the names excepted. You will perceive it is a little *bourgeois.*

A birth is always announced by the father. These communications are usually lithographied, and all but those of persons of high rank have been sent to me through ↑the↓ post-office. When a person dies notice is sent to a<n> ↑public↓ officer, and a physician is sent to examine the body. This form is observed in order to make sure that the deceased died fairly, as well as to make the proper registrations. I believe most of these usages, if not all of them, prevail in a great measure <all> over the ↑entire↓ continent of Europe.

The <matter> ↑ceremonies↓ of funerals are done by the job, and in a very unceremonious manner. The style is subdivided into a certain number of prices, and can have a three thousand franc-funeral, a two-thousand-franc-funeral, or, a one-thousand-franc-funeral. I am not sure of having got the scale exactly right, but I <do> know that a friend of mine assured me that he paid the first sum for a very shabby genteel sort of a ceremony. The mourning coaches are of a very coarse description, and there is the usual amount of black cloth, black horses and black feathers; I say usual, for, though we have no such customs, every one knows that the customs ↑did↓ prevail among our English forefathers.

I have attended many funerals at Paris, and, in a few instances, when American clergymen have been present. The French who were present on the latter occasions, have almost always spoke to me, with pleasure, of the touching simplicity and solemn character of our offices, and well they might, for the contrast between one of our[1] enterments and one of their own, noth-withstanding the black cloth and black horses is too much in our favor to be overlooked. I much question if any people have the same decent solemnities as the Americans, though we too, are getting to be a little indifferent in the towns.

The masses in a catholic church are always striking, though the matter of fact ↑and irreverent↓ manner of the performers almost destroys the feeling of devotion. I have frequently stood behind a pillar or a pier in a cathedral listening to the chants, and some exquisite moments have I thus been enabled to procure, but the illusion has always vanished wherever the eye got too much behind the scene. The catholics jumble their ceremonies together, too, in a way to give them the appearance of nothing but prescribed observances. We were present at a <f> ↑marriage↓ <here>, not long since, in one of the large churches of Paris, when a funeral service was going on in the body of the building. The body was not thirty feet from the railing of the altar, before which the bridal party was arrayed. The contrast was frightful. One groupe was all in deep black, the pall swept over the pavement, and the deep-mouthed chant rung in the arches of the church like <thunder> awful warnings against the vanities of the world. Our priest was scarcely audible, and once or twice we stole looks behind us, as if we thought the mourners were forbidding the bans. The pretty bride looked doubly alarmed, and truly the whole scene was suited to inspire a dread of evil omens.

An American is apt to be astonished at the mode in which marriages are brought about in France. Nothing is more common than to see advertisements that one is in quest of a wife or a husband. There are, I am told,

[1]Cooper wrote "their."

regular marriage-brokers, who, in such cases, settle the preliminaries, and bring the parties together. The advertisements usually run in some such manner as this—Viz—"A gentleman of a respectable profession, aged two and thirty, with an income of four thousand francs independently of his occupation desires to form a matrimonial connection with a *demoiselle*, of reputable family and corresponding means &c." Some times, "a widow will not be objected to," closes the notice. The reference is usually·to some well known agent. "The friends of a young lady, under nineteen, with a fortune of one hundred and fifty thousand francs desire &c &c."

Now, all this is serious, for the practice is <too> ↑so↓ common as to disarm a joke. I am told that very many marriages are made yearly, precisely in this manner. The parties meet, like each other, strike a bargain, <and> go <to,> ↑before↓ the maire and thence to church. Such marriages, however, are usually made when the lady is not very well provided with friends.

Nothing is more common, when a girl reaches the proper age, which is from nineteen to one or two and[2] twenty, for her female friends to set on foot a proper inquiry for a <bon> ↑*bon*↓ *parti,* or a good match, as we should term it. I have several times heard elderly <ladies> ↑women↓ <in> say that they had been requested to look out for a husband for a young friend, and beg their acquaintances to let them know if any good thing of the sort should come under their notice. The same thing is done, on the part of young men.

Among people of condition a little more *ménagement* is observed, perhaps, though marriages are made essentially in the same manner. The girl is no longer brought out of her convent at seventeen, and told "Mademoiselle, voilà votre mari," but usages have given way, a little, before the influence of the revolution. Talking one day with an old lady, of the *ancien régime,* on this subject, she said that her fortune had been some or thirty or forty thousand dollars a year, that she was put into a convent a mere child, brought out of it at sixteen, shown a gentleman near twice her own age, and told she was to marry him, in a forthnight. "I would as soon have thought of committing murder, as to have dreamed of disobedience." "And of course you were married<?"> Madame?" "*Certainement;* it was M. de_____."
"And you have reason to felicitate yourself, on the prudence of your friends, Madame; the marriage has been so happy." "Ma fois—surement oui. Tenez Monsieur_____; I believe the <mode> ↑mode↓ a good one, and I should never have thought of an infidelity to M. de_____, had he not first set the example." The exquisite *naiveté* with which the old lady gave this account of the matter was irresistibly droll, and I had some difficulty to keep from betraying my sympathy <by downright laughter> ↑in a manner that would have↓ done a scandal to my breeding. It would be unfair to quote this

[2]Cooper wrote "in."

woman as a sample of high toned French morals, below which she certainly falls very far, but, notwithstaning, she is received, is welcome at court, and has a place in general society.

Accident has thrown us in the way of witnessing the process of match-making in its details. The subject of it was a very charming girl with a very good fortune, of, from a hundred and fifty to two hundred thousand dol-lars. She is of the mercantile class, or rather her father is a *gros bourgeois.*

Some three or four and twenty proposals were made to this young lady. In every case she was permitted to decide for herself. Some of the men she never saw, and ↑with↓ neither of them, had she the least intimacy, before her selection was made. When matters got so far as to render an interview desirable, it was arranged that the parties should meet at the house of some mutual friend, where they might see each other, or dance together. Con-versing with a young unmarried French girl is, even now, rather a serious affair, and it is considered under bred to show them too much attention in society. They are rarely spoken to, by the men at all, and not much by their own sex. Their communications with each other are extremely modest and reserved, in public, where they are seen as pretty ornaments of a salon rather than as part of the society. The rigid laws of the old *régime* are, however, giving way a little, and it is one of the concessions to allow young lady now to say "no." Violence is seldom done their inclinations, I believe, though it is still the theory to commence, not "with a little aversion" per-haps, but with nothing more than its absence.

The suitors of our young acquaintance, during a twelvemonth, would form a curious list. Nobles, wealthy *roturiers,* avocats, *agents de change,* sol-diers and *savans* were of the number. One was too tall, another too short; this was too ugly, and that too handsome. One was too noble, an[3] odd objection for Europe, and I was <comb?> ↑compelled↓ to laugh at her objection to a particular suitor, whom she rejected incontinently for being *trop musqué.* The remark was a good one, however, and showed good sense on her part, for though it is possible to be a fop and have good qualities, yet one who is not permitted to examine very closely does well in taking it as evidence against much character of any sort. The natural propensity to dandyism is almost conclusive evidence of a frivolous mind, though men sometimes become puppies by accident or caprice. It is fair to suppose that a young creature of warm affections and great humour, with a good deal of character, chose to suspend her decision until she found a stronger bias than common, in favor of some particular candidate for her smile. She finally selected the son of a judge, and they were married accordingly.

*On* <cherche un> *s'occupe de trouver un mari pour M_____."* said <the> an intimate female friend to me, one day, alluding to *Mademoiselle_____,* a young lady of our acquaintance, if I can call that an acquaintance which

[3]Cooper wrote "and."

went no farther than a salutation on entering the drawing room of the mother, or a bow in an assembly. This young <lady> ↑girl↓ was of one of the first families of Europe, and yet they busied themselves in finding a *bon parti* for her, <only> so much the more for that fact. <It> It was the only manner in which a young woman so situated could ever be married with decorum.

These things shock us at first, but I can assure you, not half as much as our mode of procedure shocks them. They would deem it madness to cast a young and inexperienced girl on the world, to seek her fortune, as it were, and to trust all her future hopes to the caprices and impulses of her tender years. It would be madness in France, whatever it may be in America[.]

If <our> ↑their↓ usages seem strange, <many are> ↑ours appear to be↓ an infatuatration. A young Frenchman, who had passed many years in America, not long since returned home. He had not been in Paris before he proposed to a young female friend that they should take a walk in the *Bois de Boulogne.* I was informed of the fact, by an elderly person, who laughed immoderately at the idea, and repeated the strange request, at least <a dozen> ↑three↓ times. In his eyes it was like asking the lady to jump off of the *Pont Neuf.* A proposition of this nature would be a little extraordinary in <well bred> ↑the better sort of↓ society in America but, nineteen <and> ↑in↓ twenty would see no harm in it. Our ↑young↓ women ought to be told plainly that the innocent freedom of their manners is liable to great misconstructions by foreigners, and if they had heard one half of the calumnious reports concerning themselves that have reached my ears in Europe, they would learn how to distinguish between those who do, and those who do not understand the usages of the country.

If you ask me which of two modes of educating girls, that are so very opposite to each other I prefer, it would not be easy to answer. I certainly do not admire the French system, and one sees certain extreme cases at home, which are very much like running *amuck*[.] Something between the two would be in better taste, more prudent and more just, than either the French or the American mode, for if our girls need more control and *retenue* in company, these need more liberty. In the way of respectability, there is little difference between a *managing mother,* with her frowns, and hints, and smiles, and manoeuves, and one that cooly sits down to make a close bargain for the disposal of her daughter. The latter is incomparably the most honest. We have as few *manoeuvreers,* perhaps, as can well be expected, and the best argument we can use, is to urge this fact, while in France every marriage, <above> ↑contracted↓ out of the laboring classes, is, more or less, a matter of trade. "Voilà mes *deux enfants avec leurs beaux maris!"* said the old Princesse_____ to me, one evening, pointing with pride to her handsome sons in law—"Both of those marriages were love matches—*n'est ce pas drôle?*"

Singular enough it was, for girls of their rank, although I suspect the mother considered a very incipient inclination, taken in through the eyes, as love.

The manner in which the family ties endure in France, is a beautiful trait in the national character, and says a great deal in favor of their matrimonial code. I have never heard a French child utter a disrespectful word, or betray a disrespectful look to a parent. Such things must happen, but judging from my own knowledge, I should think much more rarely than with us. Several generations frequently live in the same house, and relatives seldom meet, after the shortest absences, without embraces. Much of this, as well as of our coldness, is mere manner, but when manner quickens the affections and increases the honest blandishments of life, it becomes a virtue. I remember to have been lectured, when a boy in an eastern college, for ↑the indecency of↓ walking arm in arm with a friend, and, in my boyhood, it was deemed indecorous, in that section of the country, for the religious part of the community to give their arms to their wives in walking to church. The clergyman used even to preceed his family a few paces, by way of example. We know that there formerly existed a law against a man's caressing even his children on the sabbath, and to kiss his wife was misprision of Faith. All this has left a <lasting> ↑deep↓ impression on the manners of a ↑large↓ portion of our people, and is the cause of so much of the ↑cold and↓ repulsive manner for which they are noted. Still, <the> after making every proper allowance for exterior, and including all sections of the country, I think in the beautiful harmony of the family tie, and in deference to years and paternity, the French have much the advantage of us.

By the laws of France, no one can contract a marriage without the consent of the parents, or guardians before an age tolerably advanced. I believe it is also necessary to obtain the consent of the grandfather should he be alive. At a certain age, twenty five or thirty, a man may marry without this consent, but not until he has cited his father formally to appear and give a valid reason for his opposition, and the father's neglecting to appear, or being unprovided with a proper objection. I am not acquainted with the minor provisions of this law, but such, I believe, is its principle.

To elope with a girl under sixteen, is an offence punishable by the gallies. No marriage under such circumstances is valid. Should a priest celebrate a marriage contrary to any of these provisions, he is liable to severe punishment, and, though the Roman church considers marriage a sacrament and indissoluble, without the consent of the Pope, the French laws are also inexorable. I presume this difficulty is one of the contested points, for, if I remember right, the attempt at a *concordat* failed. But the Gallican church has always shown some independence of the <Conclave> ↑Holy See↓.

This you will remember is peculiarily a pious reign. Among his other indiscretions, the King allows the Jesuits to exist in France, contrary it is affirmed to unrepealed law, by which they were formerly expelled, and to the other sources of discontent, is added the constant and deep-rooted apprehension of their intrigues and power. On the occasion of the *Fête Dieu* last summer, the whole court, the royal family included, walked in procession, from their parish church, the celebrated St. Germain l'Auxerrois, through the Carrousel to the palace. I saw them, the ladies and all with the honest-looking and zealous old king at their head, without his hat, following in the train of the sacred elements, accompanied by a goodly company of devotees. It created as much scandal among the Parisians, that Marshall Soult should be seen carrying a candle in such ranks, as if he had been cashiered and sent back to carry a musket in those ranks from which he rose by his valor and talents.

The introduction of the name of this veteran reminds me of a<n> ↑recent↓ occurrence which, though foreign to the other subjects of this letter, is too much illustrative of French character to be omitted altogether, and which may nevertheless be forgotten unless inserted here. You know that Napoleon was in the habit of bestowing titles on his generals, and diplomates, taken from the scenes of their exploits. Thus Paris is full of nobles who bear names derived from foreign countries. M. Soult is *Duc de Dalmatie*, M. Savary, *Duc de Rovigo*, M. Lannes, *Duc de Montebello*, M. Le Brun *Duc de Plaisance*, M. Fouché *Duc d'Otrante*, M. Mouton, *Comte de Lobau*, &c &c, with a hundred others. Now all the places I have named, with the exception of Otranto,+ +Note (The Italians pronounce this word *Otranto*, saying the emphasis on the first syllable, and not *Otranto*.) and in the territories of the House of Austria, and the Emperor took exceptions at strangers appropriating to themselves names that he probably thought justly belonged to him. The Count d'Appony his Ambassador gave an entertainment lately, and you will judge of the amusement ↑and surprise↓ of the company when the groom of the chamber announced *Monsieur, le Marèchal Duc Soult*, instead of le Marèchal Duc de Dalmatie! The old warrior is said to have retired indignantly, the papers have been in a fury, the *salons* agitated, and the army ready to march on Vienna at a minute's warning.

The opposition accused the government of a willingness to compromise the national honor, with a view to oblige the Holy Alliance and to obliterate the impression left by the glory of the Empire, while the government itself maintained what the French pithily term *un mime silence*. It is understood, however, that the affair has been amicably arranged, and that the old Marshall keeps his beloved and well earned Dalmatia, in name at least. What would be thought in England if the servant of the Spaniard should announce Lord St. Vincent as Viscount Jervis? Are you aware that[4] the King of England granted to the widow, and I presume descendants if there are any, of Gen. Ross, the right to bear the appellation of Ross of Bladensburg? I have seen the card of the lady thus written, and so far from grudging her

[4]Cooper wrote "the."

this empty reward, the feeling was that of pity, that it had been so hardly earned. We ought to retaliate in kind and have our Scott of Chippewa, Brown of Bridgewater, Gaines of Erie, McComb-Prevost and Jackson-Packenham. I remember a negro <of> ↑in the service of↓ my father<'s> reproving me gravely, ↑when a boy,↓ for saying Lord *Corn*wallis. "What should I call him then, Joe?" "Lord *Cob*wallis; dont you know, sir, that General Washington shelld him of all his grain?" The black merely carried out the idea of his betters. Notwithstanding all the noise that was made on this occasion, the French generals are better known in the world, by their family names, than by their titles, one hearing the term of Marshall Soult ten times, where he hears that of the Duc de Dalmatie once. There appears to be a sort of silent convention, which has established that the military rank should always go with the family name, or that under which most of the glory was earned. It is no easy matter violently to supplant opinion.

M. Soult is the owner of the best gallery of Spanish paintings in Paris. Understanding that he was kind enough to let it be seen on application, I ventured to address a note to him to that effect, and received an immediate and exceedingly polite permission. Here it will be no more than just to say that the liberality of all the French institutions, in this respect, and, in particular, their delicacy towards strangers, are such as to excite admiration and respect. The latter are often admitted to places of this sort, when the natives are excluded, on the ground that their time is limited. You will recollect that Paris has frequently <forty> ↑thirty↓ or <fifty> ↑forty↓ thousand strangers within its walls, and that many of them remain years, in order properly to appreciate this liberality.

There are so many <more> ↑<other>↓ travellers better qualified than myself, to give their opinions of pictures, that I purposely abstain from saying much about them, but this I may remark, *en passant,* that ↑, as a rule,↓ it is hazardous to judge of any great artist, without having visited the country in which he worked. Were one to see nothing of Rubens, but his pictures in the Louvre, however he might be disposed to admire the richness of his colouring, he would carry away a very erroneous impression of his true merits. The same might be said of Raphael and of nearly all the Italian painters, while the French school would obtain higher relative rank than it is, perhaps, entitled to assume.

The Hotel óf *M. de Dalmatie* is in Spain, by a fiction of the arts. Most of his pictures were obtained in the country itself, and under circumstances that set little limits to the selection. They are chiefly altar pieces found in churches and convents, and the works of Murillo and Velasquez are, of course, prominent among them. The former artist is a marvel of extremes, delighting equally in some of the sublimest subjects of divinity and the

lowest of man. He gives to his Madonnas a peculiar ideal beauty and innocence, and to his beggar boys the very perfection of animal enjoyment and
animal characteristics. This is a high proof of talent, for, I take it, in the
possession of the requisite knowledge, a man of true genius is as capable of
treating one thing or nothing, although his tastes or accident may give him
a particular bias.

I was looking at a *Madonna* in one of Murillo's Assumption's, (a subject
he often painted) when a connoisseur desired me to examine if the picture
showed any thing out of the usual way. After a close scrutiny, I thought the face
↑of the virgin↓ had been retouched. I was then told the following anecdote,
which I repeat nearly verbatim, leaving you to judge of its truth. I presume, however, there is no reason to doubt it.

The advance of the French army, under Marshall Soult, reached a small
town in Spain, that contained a convent. An ↑inferior↓ officer entered the
chapel of the Monastery, where he found this Assumption, as an altar piece.
He had it taken down, and was about to roll it up, as a prize, when an order
arrived, for the advance to move on, and he had barely time to cut out
the <face> ↑head↓ with his knife leaving the remainder of the picture
on the pavement of the chapel. Here it was found and presented to the
Marshall, who sent it into France.

At the peace, when there was leisure to set up and admire pictures, an
inquiry was instituted for the lucky possessor of the <fac> head of Madonna.
He was soon found, but his price was sixty thousand francs. A small sum
was given for permission to copy it, and the part which I supposed had
been retouched, was this copy neatly fitted to the original. The Emperor
Alexandre is said to have bought the original, which is now at St. Petersburg.
There is nothing very marvellous in this story, but the price.

## NOTES

301.22 a nuptial ceremony: Natalie Lafayette (1803-1878) married Casimir Périer's nephew Adolphe, a wealthy manufacturer and political liberal, on 9 January 1828.

302.35-36 the marriage of . . . Mathilde La Fayette: Mathilde (1805-1886), the second daughter of George Lafayette, married Maurice Poivre Bureaux de Pusy, a young political ally of her grandfather, in 1832.

303.10-11 Prince Camille Borghese: Cooper first met Camillo Borghese (1775-1832), a "short, fat good-humoured and well-looking man" who was "once brother in law of Bonaparte and the richest subject of the Pope," at Pozzo di Borgo's ball in March 1827; see his letter of 26 March 1827 to Mrs. Jay (*Letters and Journals,* I, 210). Borghese's family and that of his brother, Prince Francesco Aldobrandini (1776-1839), were friendly to the Coopers during their residence in Florence in 1828-29. The others named in the announcement are Aldobrandini's three sons, his daughter, Maria, and his son-in-law, Anne Victurnien Henri, Vicomte de Mortemart.

306.22 "with a little aversion": In Sheridan's *The Rivals* (1775), I.ii, Mrs. Malaprop observes that "'Tis safest in matrimony to begin with a little aversion."

308.12 an eastern college: Yale, which Cooper attended in 1803-05.

308.40 the attempt at a *concordat* failed: Efforts to reach a new agreement between Rome and the Gallican Church began in 1814 but were abandoned after years of negotiation, leaving the Napoleonic Concordat of 1801 still in effect.

309.3-4 the *Fête Dieu* last summer: on 17 June 1827.

309.20-21 M. LeBrun: See the Explanatory Note for *France,* 220.30.

309.21 M. Mouton: Georges Mouton, Comte de Lobau (1770-1838), who, as a general in Napoleon's army, won his title in the Austrian campaign of 1809.

309.27 The Count d'Appony: See the Explanatory Note for *France,* 85.5-6. In January 1827, Appony, acting on instructions from his government, pointedly refused to acknowledge the Napoleonic military titles of Marshals Marmont and Oudinot. On 1 February, Soult received an invitation from Appony addressed to "M. le maréchal Soult" (rather than "M. le maréchal duc de Dalmatie") and sent back a stinging refusal, patently designed to provoke a duel.

310.3 McComb-Prevost: Cooper's reference is to General Alexander Macomb (1782-1841).

310.4 a negro: probably Joseph Stewart, who was butler and body servant in Judge Cooper's household for thirty years.

310.37 The Hotel of *M. de Dalmatie:* the Hôtel du Périgord, 69 Rue de l'Université.

# TEXTUAL APPARATUS

# Textual Commentary

The copy-text of *Gleanings in Europe: France* is the first American edition, a single impression of 2,000 copies published by Carey, Lea and Blanchard in two volumes in Philadelphia on 4 March 1837.[1] It is the only available authorial form of *France*, for neither the manuscript from which it was set nor the proof sheets which Cooper corrected have survived. Conceivably, the many variants in the first English edition—entitled *Recollections of Europe* and published in two volumes in a printing of 1,250 copies by Richard Bentley in London on 24 January 1837,[2] more than a month before the American edition appeared—could be the result of Cooper's intervention, but a knowledge of the circumstances of the two publications and an analysis of the differences in their texts argue strongly against that possibility.

Cooper's correspondence indicates that with *France* he followed the procedures that he had used with his two previous travel books. Immediately after seeing the new work through the press in Philadelphia, he wrote to Bentley from New York on 19 November 1836 that "By the London Ship of the 20th I send an entire copy of Gleanings in Europe—France, in two volumes. Care of John Miller, Henrietta Street, London, and by the Liverpool Ship of the 24th duplicates, care of Roskell, Ogden & co."[3] From those copies, presumably corrected sheets or revises pulled from Carey's formes, Bentley promptly styled, printed, and published the book, thereby establishing the priority of publication that assured him the British quasi-copyright.

Collation makes it clear that Bentley's edition of *France* did indeed derive from Carey's.[4] Most of the 3,817 Bentley variants are in accidentals—principally in punctuation, spelling, capitalization, and the use of italics[5]—and are characteristic of nineteenth-century British reprints of American books. Of the eighty-nine substantive variants in the Bentley text, thirty-nine are corrections of obvious errors in the Carey edition,[6] while twelve introduce new errors.[7] The remaining thirty-eight substantive variants—all fewer than six words in length—are stylistic in nature, many of them designed to refine Cooper's occasional conversational informality.[8] In no instance do the variants in the Bentley text exhibit the freedom and boldness that are characteristic of Cooper's revisions elsewhere, nor do they give any indication that the

British compositors set their text from the author's manuscript and thereby recovered readings which the Carey text had lost. On the contrary, it is apparent that the Bentley variants represent the work of a competent copy editor engaged in the improvement of the often carelessly printed Carey text. Like the topical summaries that the British publisher inserted at the beginnings of chapters and gathered as a helpful analytical Table of Contents at the front of each volume,[9] the variants reflect the high editorial standards of the Bentley house rather than the intrusion of the author's hand.

The other contemporaneous printings of *France* or of parts of it similarly derive—immediately or ultimately—from the Carey text.[10] A lengthy extract that appeared in the *National Gazette and Literary Register* for 15 February 1837, more than two weeks before the American publication of *France*, clearly follows the published Carey text.[11] A French edition in one volume, printed by J. Smith and published in Paris as *Recollections of Europe* under the separate imprints of Baudry's European Library and A. and W. Galignani on 18 March 1837, derives from the British edition, as its reproduction of nearly all of the Bentley substantive variants indicates.[12] The British publisher himself reissued the book as two volumes in one with the title *Cooper's Travels: Europe* stamped on the spine. Although the title page carries no date and no record of the publication appears in the Bentley Papers, the fact that the letterpress is virtually identical to that of the Bentley edition of 1837 supports the conclusion that the volume is a reissue of the original sheets rather than a new impression.[13]

Hence the copy-text—the Carey, Lea and Blanchard edition—is the only available authorial text of *Gleanings in Europe: France*. That it is a less than perfect text is acknowledged by the errata slip which is tipped into the Carey edition between the verso of the title page and the first page of the Preface:

## ERRATA.

The peculiar circumstances under which this book, and the second part of Switzerland have been printed, are the cause of many errors that exist in both. Such French as *"Je n'en sais n'en,"* "bonhomie," "Leurres des moiselles," &c. &c., for *"Je n'en sais rien," "bonhommie,"* and *"Leurs desmoiselles,"* will be understood by most readers. Some of the English errors are less obvious. "The *wants* of the last twenty years," for instance, will not easily be seen to mean "the *events* of the," &c. A few sentences are rendered unintelligible by the mistakes. One error in Switzerland is owing to the author himself, who admitted it into a note, by confounding the title assumed by one of the northern kings when at Paris, with that of the alleged favourite of Marie Antoinette. "Count Koningsmarke" should have been "Count Fersen."

Joan of Arc was not *"buried"* in the square of Rouen, but "burned." "Cerulean chair" should read "Curule chair," &c. &c. &c.[14]

Although three of the seven specified errors belong to the second part of *Switzerland* (entitled *Gleanings in Europe: The Rhine* in the Cooper Edition), the errata slip amply testifies to Cooper's dissatisfaction with the inaccuracy of the Carey edition of *France* and to his desire to present a correct and readable text.[15] In keeping with that desire, the Cooper Edition emends all errors in wording and punctuation wherever they are detected. The emendation of substantive errors is illustrated by the following examples:

*Nonsense words:* at 126.10, the phrase "the place were I stood" is emended to "the place where I stood";

*Doubled words:* at 19.22-23; "a a . . . man" is emended to "a . . . man";

*Confused Homonyms:* at 150.38, "lead" is emended to "led";

*Disagreement of Subject and Verb or Noun and Pronoun:* at 41.32-34, "the English gentlemen . . . stands" is emended to "the English gentleman . . . stands";

*Inappropriate Verb Forms:* at 24.6-7, "had not Carisbrooke . . . lay" is emended to "had not Carisbrooke . . . lain";

*Faulty French Constructions:* at 133.30-31, *"salle de gardes"* is emended to *"salle des gardes."*

The Textual Notes comment on substantive emendations that do not fall within these categories or that involve special problems.

Most of the emendations by the Cooper Edition correct errors in accidentals. Here a double standard has been applied in an effort to fulfill Cooper's intentions by observing the distinction that he evidently meant to maintain by his use of roman type and italics. When French words and phrases are italicized in the copy-text, they tend to follow French practice in spelling and accentuation. When those same words are printed in roman type, their form tends to follow contemporaneous British and American practice. Thus the copy-text prints "hotel" at 222.21 and *"hôtel"* at 224.11, and *"Villèle"* at 86.10 and "Villele" at 87.4. Accordingly, the Cooper Edition corrects the spelling, accentuation, and hyphenation of words in roman type, whether French or English, only if they violate the standards of nineteenth-century British and American practice as determined by Webster's *Dictionary* of 1828, the report of accepted nineteenth-century usage in the *Oxford English Dictionary,* and, for the names of people and places, the forms employed in contemporaneous issues of the London *Times.* The copy-text forms of italicized French words, however, are emended if they violate contemporaneous French practice as it is recorded in Laveux's *Nouveau dictionnaire de la langue française* (Paris, 1820) and, for proper nouns, contemporaneous issues of the *Journal des Débats,*

Michaud's *Biographie universelle* and its revision (Paris, 1811-1828 and 1853-1866), or Dulaure's *Histoire . . . des environs de Paris* (Paris, 1825-1828) and *Histoire . . . de Paris* (1825).

The Cooper Edition corrects the following categories of errors in accidentals:

*Misspellings:* for example, at 62.6, "ettiquette" is emended to "etiquette";

*Misleading Punctuation:* at 7.33, "heavens; in" is emended to "heavens, in";

*Incorrect accentuation:* at 121.33, *"jèune"* is emended to *"jeune";*

*Incorrect hyphenation:* at 17.28, *"passe partout"* is emended to *"passe-partout";*

*Uncapitalized Titles before Names:* at 86.35, "lord Clanricarde" is emended to "Lord Clanricarde."

The Cooper Edition makes no attempt to regularize inconsistent forms that are sanctioned by contemporaneous practice, nor does it emend idiosyncratic punctuation that does not distort or obscure Cooper's meanings. All corrections are reported in the list of Emendations.

The two remaining categories of emendation consist of modifications or augmentations of the copy-text rather than corrections of it. The letter numbers in the second volume of the copy-text have been changed to make them sequential with those in the first volume. And, wherever possible, the Cooper Edition supplies within square brackets the names of people and places which are represented in the copy-text by a letter followed by a three- or four-em dash or by the dash alone. Thus "L_____" becomes "L[ynch]" at 38.29, and "Mrs._____" becomes "Mrs. [Jarvis]" at 90.2.[16] Like the corrections, these changes are reported in the list of Emendations.

The present edition of *Gleanings in Europe: France* is thus an unmodernized critical text, no portion of which has been silently emended. In conformity with the design of the Cooper Edition as a whole, however, the visual appurtenances of the copy-text, such as general typestyling and the styling of chapter openings, have not been retained.

## NOTES

1. *The Cost Book of Carey & Lea, 1825-1838,* ed. David Kaser (Philadelphia: University of Pennsylvania Press, 1963), p. 213; Robert E. Spiller and Philip C. Blackburn, *A Descriptive Bibliography of the Writings of James Fenimore Cooper* (New York: R. R. Bowker Company, 1934), p. 89.

2. *The Letters and Journals of James Fenimore Cooper,* ed. James Franklin Beard, 6 vols. (Cambridge: Harvard University Press, Belknap Press, 1960-1968), III, 149, n. 2, and 222, n. 3. The publication date is furnished by *The Lists of the Publications of Richard Bentley & Son, 1829-1898* (Bishops Stortford: Chadwyck-Healey, 1975), microfiche 5, folio 207.

3. *Letters and Journals,* III, 249. See also JFC to Mrs. Cooper, 4 November 1836 (*Letters and Journals,* III, 248).
4. James F. Beard's copy #1 of the Carey edition was collated with his copy of the Bentley edition.
5. These variants fall into nineteen categories:

| | |
|---|---:|
| *Internal Punctuation.* | 2,269 instances |
| *Hyphenation of Compound Words* | |
| Two words changed to one hyphenated word (e.g., long remembered→long-remembered) | 144 instances |
| Hyphenated word changed to two words (e.g., ship-channel→ship channel) | 37 instances |
| Hyphenated word changed to one word (e.g., re-appeared →reappeared) | 59 instances |
| One word changed to hyphenated word (e.g., churchyard →church-yard) | 1 instance |
| *Italicization* | |
| Words and phrases changed from roman to italic (e.g., somnambule→*somnambule*) | 5 instances |
| Words and phrases changed from italic to roman (e.g., *Princesse*→Princesse) | 445 instances |
| *Spelling* | |
| Correct American spellings changed to British preferences (e.g., favor→favour) | 147 instances |
| Corrections of incorrect spellings (e.g., Compèigne→Compiègne) | 83 instances |
| *Capitalization* | |
| Lower case capitalized (e.g., christendom→Christendom) | 145 instances |
| Capitals made lower case (e.g., Queen→queen) | 93 instances |
| *Treatment of accent marks* (e.g., *epicier*→*épicier*) | 96 instances |
| *Compression of two words into one word* (e.g., every thing→everything) | 124 instances |
| *Terminal sentence punctuation* (e.g., public."!→*public!"*) | 50 instances |
| *Treatment of apostrophes* (e.g., squire→'squire) | 6 instances |
| *Paragraphing* (e.g., brother. "But→brother. ¶ "But) | 4 instances |
| *Treatment of numerals* | |
| Numerals written out (e.g., 11→eleven) | 2 instances |
| Written numbers changed to numerals (e.g., first→1st) | 4 instances |
| *Expansion of abbreviations* (e.g., Gen.→General) | 14 instances |

6. Substantive corrections of errors in the Carey edition: 10.35, enemies' [in the Carey]→enemy's [in the Bentley]; 18.18, Thames'→Thames; 19.22, a a well-disposed→a well-disposed; 19.35, lead→leads; 24.7, lay→lain; 41.32, gentlemen→gentleman; 45.15, boats'→boat's; 50.21, that→than; 56.8, de l'Angleterre→d'Angleterre; 57.14, buried→burned; 67.10, commences→commence;

67.11, encloses→enclose; 76.36, event he→even the; 81.21, *leurres des moiselles*
→leurs desmoiselles; 98.21, put→put it; 98.24, de ———," that→de —, "that;
101.7-8, are or have been lawyers→is, or has been, a lawyer; 137.19, andof→and
of; 141.9, servant's→servants'; 150.38, lead→led; 157.12, that Sir→Sir; 186.27,
scissor's men→scissors-men; 193.14, waters→water's; 194.10, strot→trot; 199.38,
*fauxbourg*→du Faubourg; 204.35, tell→tells; 220.9, *la France*→France; 222.27,
of→or; 224.17, affirm→affirmed; 225.31, *Ne c'est-ce*→*N'est-ce;* 240.36, *de la
Victoire*→des Victoires; 241.19, have→has; 247.12, which in its very nature
must of necessity→must of necessity in its very nature; 253.20, *jeunes*→jeune;
265.5, many→may; 267.27, neither→either; 270.8, takes→take; 270.9, re-
moves→remove; 270.9, prepares→prepare.

7. Substantive errors initiated in the Bentley edition: 5.37, vessel [in the Carey]
→pessel [in the Bentley]; 11.7, Charleston→Charlestown; 59.22, not but→not;
120.4, Coucy."*→Coucy."; 157.26, two→too; 201.37, we→me; 218.12, *petits*→
*petit;* 226.27, monsieur ———, you→Monsieur;— you; 237.31, sovereignty→cov-
ereignty; 258.38, It→I; 271.38, enemies→enemie; 273.3, likely no→likely; no.

8. Substantive stylistic changes in the Bentley edition: 1.16, almost success [in the
Carey]→success [in the Bentley]; 1.25, a very small, pretension→very small
pretensions; 3.20, a hotel→an hotel; 12.15, soon→as soon; 17.11, neighbours'→
neighbour's; 21.34, or→and; 28.22, XIVth→the Fourteenth; 28.25, drunk→
drank; 32.26, run→ran; 35.5, an American→American; 36.28, VIIth's→the
Seventh's; 37.32, uniformity to→uniformity in; 41.34-35, stands as a rule→
stands; 56.20, VIIth's→the Seventh's; 58.4, out→out of; 78.34, a hotel→an
hotel; 79.23, &c. &c.→&c.; 93.8, XVIth's→the Sixteenth's; 104.15, displayed→
deployed; 125.20, eat→ate; 136.34, have→had; 155.32, I'm→I am; 155.37, this
lady I had met→I had met this lady; 158.31, opened→open; 173.24-25, quite
often→often; 176.4-5, a reverence→reverence; 176.22, would be→were; 181.2,
around→round; 189.20, her in stead→in her stead; 192.2, gardener's→gar-
deners'; 192.28, One of the great advantages that is→Among the great
advantages; 197.17, quite two→two; 198.34, the nature→nature; 218.16,
opinion→opinion that; 220.10, gone and dined→dined; 236.27, a civil→civil;
250.38, antiquarian→antiquary; 270.8, off of→off; 272.13, a hotel→an hotel.

9. The Bentley Table of Contents is reproduced for the reader's convenience in Appendix A, pp. 296-300.

10. Hinman collation of five copies of the Carey edition itself reveals no evidence
of authorial intervention during the printing of that edition. The collation
included two copies owned by James F. Beard (designated #1 and #2), two
copies owned by the New York Public Library (DW and *KL), and the copy
owned by the American Antiquarian Society.

11. Of the six substantive variants in the extract, which corresponds to 77.38-95.30
of the present edition, four are deletions made for the sake of abridgement
and the remaining two are obvious misprints. A second extract, corresponding to 260.3-269.38, was printed in the *National Gazette* for 3 March 1837, the
day before American publication of *France*; it contains no substantive variants
from the Carey text.

12. *Bibliographie de la France* (Paris: Pillet Ainé, 1837), XXVI, 130, entries 1422 and 1423. Examination of a copy of the Baudry edition owned by the University of North Carolina Library (914.2 C777e) reveals that it retains eighty-one of the eighty-nine Bentley substantive variants. All of the eight exceptions correct obvious errors in the Bentley edition.

13. The copy examined is owned by the Holy Cross College Library (DC27 C7). Bentley also reissued the book as *Travels and Excursions in Various Parts of the World: France,* Volumes X and XI of an undated eleven-volume set of Cooper's travel works.

14. At 123.33 and 207.1, the Cooper Edition retains the correct copy-text spelling *"bonhomie,"* though the errata slip in the Carey, Lea and Blanchard edition calls for *"bonhommie."*

15. Cooper complained to Bentley in his letter of 17 October 1837 that "all the travels contain outrageous blunders" (*Letters and Journals,* III, 298). In a letter bearing the oddly appropriate date 31 June 1838, he warned his friend and reader Horatio Greenough that "none of the travels have been printed even decently, with the exception of the first part of Switzerland. Indeed the verbal mistakes are terrific." Citing a glaring error in the Bentley edition of *Italy,* he said that he could point out "a hundred similar blunders, in nearly all the books" (*Letters and Journals,* III, 329).

16. One such identification requires special mention. When Cooper refers to his wife by her first name in the copy-text, he writes "A_____." The Cooper Edition emends that form to "[Susan]" in keeping with the writer's practice in his correspondence with family members.

# Textual Notes

6.26-27  The Cooper Edition here supplies the missing definite article in keeping with Cooper's idiom elsewhere; cf. 6.30, "the lower bay."

7.8  Here and at 205.29, the copy-text divides a word at the end of a line and leaves a space where the hyphen should appear. Accordingly, the Cooper Edition prints it as one word.

52.30  Robert E. Spiller suggests in his edition of *Gleanings in Europe: France* (New York: Oxford University Press, 1928), p. 71, n. 4, that a pun on *"roche"* ("rock") and *"rouche"* ("mud") is intended in the copy-text form, but other contemporaneous quotations of the saying indicate that the distinction on which the supposed word-play depends is the result of a spelling error. Thus Lady Morgan writes in her *France in 1829-30*, 2 vols. (New York: J. and J. Harper, 1830), II, 179, "Still a name is but a name; there are de la Rochefoucaulds, and de la Rochefoucaulds." Cooper himself in a letter of 2 April 1833 to Samuel F. B. Morse quotes "the French saying—'Il y a de la Rochefaucauld et de la Rochefaucauld'" (*Letters and Journals*, II, 381).

57.14  The Cooper Edition reading "burned" is supplied by the errata slip.

67.3  This edition emends the phrase "in a clouded day" as uncharacteristic of Cooper's style; cf. 68.2-3, "on a day like that." In a letter of 7 March 1849 to John Fagan, Cooper observes that compositors working from his manuscripts "often mistake an 'on' for 'in,' my o resembling an i" (*Letters and Journals*, VI, 15).

81.21  The errata slip calls for the faulty reading *"leurs desmoiselles."*

92.17  An alternative emendation would seem to be "servants out of livery help to serve the different *plats*," but the context requires the reading adopted by the Cooper Edition.

93.21  The copy-text reading suggests that Cooper originally intended to address this letter not to Mrs. Pomeroy but to his nephew Richard Cooper, as are Letters III, IV, V, X, XX, XXI, and XXIII, or, more likely, to his niece Mrs. Samuel W. Beall, as is Letter IX.

115.2  Cooper's error in the name of his niece's husband is inexplicable. In *The Chronicles of Cooperstown* (1838), he uses the correct name.

121.25 The errata slip supplies the correct word, "curule."

171.12 The capitalization of "Duke" in the copy-text is misleading. Cooper's reference is to the rank, not to a specific individual, and hence this edition adopts the lower-case spelling.

196.11 There is a space in the copy-text for the missing letter.

205.29 See the textual note for 7.8.

212.39 The word "indifference" in the copy-text clearly contradicts Cooper's meaning and, accordingly, is emended to "difference."

247.12 The Cooper Edition deletes the word "which" and the preceding comma as the syntax of the sentence requires.

271.6 There is no such place as "Need" along William's route. In keeping with Cooper's evident meaning, this edition adopts the lower-case spelling of the word.

# Emendations

The following list records all changes in substantives and accidentals introduced into the copy-text. The reading of the present edition appears to the left of the square bracket; the authority for that reading, followed by a semicolon, the copy-text reading, and the copy-text symbol appear to the right of the bracket. In emendations of punctuation, a curved dash ( ∼ ) to the right of the bracket represents the same word as the one to the left of the bracket, and a caret ( ∧ ) indicates the absence of a punctuation mark from the copy-text. An asterisk (*) to the left of an entry indicates that a textual note comments on the emendation. When identical emendations occur three or more times, they are listed in a single entry located at the initial occurrence. The Cooper Edition, designated CE, is the authority for all emendations.

The following text is referred to:

A   *Gleanings in Europe.* Philadelphia: Carey, Lea and Blanchard, 1837.

| | |
|---|---|
| 3.19 | Manhattanese]CE; Manhattenese A |
| 5.2 | Apennines]CE; Appenines A |
| 5.39 | Mr. [Cooper]]CE; Mr._____ A |
| *6.26-27 | the lower]CE; lower A |
| *7.8 | settling]CE; set tling A |
| 7.20 | an-end]CE; an end A |
| 7.33 | heavens,]CE; ∼ ; A |
| 10.35 | enemy's]CE; enemies' A |
| 10.35 | Castilian]CE; Castillian A |
| 11.11 | degree]CE; ∼ , A |
| 15.18 | angles]CE; angels A |
| 17.6 | Mrs. [Pedersen]]CE; Mrs._____ A |
| 17.28 | *passe-partout*]CE; *passe partout* A |
| 18.18 | Thames]CE; ∼ ' A |
| 19.2 | Mrs. [Cooper]]CE; Mrs._____ A *Also emended at* 85.25, 151.3, 152.28-29, 152.32, *and* 238.8. |

| | |
|---|---|
| 19.16 | C[ooperstown]]CE; C_____ A |
| 19.22 | a well-disposed]CE; a a well-disposed A |
| 19.35 | leads]CE; lead A |
| 22.2 | [Susan]'s]CE; A_____'s A |
| 22.26-27 | Mrs. [Pedersen]]CE; Mrs._____ A |
| 22.30 | Hudson,]CE; ∼ ʌ A |
| 23.5 | McAdam]CE; M'Adam A |
| 23.13 | McAdamized]CE; M'Adamized A |
| 23.16 | McAdam]CE; M'Adam A |
| 23.21 | [Susan]]CE; A_____ A *Also emended at* 25.24, 28.20, 45.19, 53.35, 53.38, 214.24, 214.27, 214.30, 214.33, *and* 219.24. |
| 24.7 | lain]CE; lay A |
| 24.21 | C[ooperstown]]CE; C_____ A |
| 25.22 | poor,]CE; ∼ ; A |
| 28.2 | R[omaine]]CE; R_____ A |
| 28.6 | L[aight]]CE; L_____ A |
| 28.7 | McA[dam]]CE; M'A_____ A |
| 28.7 | [Susan]'s]CE; A_____'s A |
| 28.32 | Southampton]CE; Southamptom A |
| 29.16 | cockneys]CE; cocknies A |
| 29.17 | cockneys]CE; cocknies A |
| 32.35 | C[ooperstow]n]CE; C_____n A |
| 33.17 | Brooks']CE; Brookes' A |
| 34.7-8 | Clement's-le-Dane]CE; Clements-le-Dane A |
| 35.32 | Margaret's]CE; Magaret's A |
| 36.28 | VIIth's]CE; VIIth's. A |
| 37.16 | "land-fall,"]CE; 'land-fall,' A |
| 37.31 | banqueting]CE; banquetting A |
| 38.29 | L[ynch]]CE; L_____ A *Also emended at* 38.37, 39.3, 39.7, *and* 39.24. |
| 40.23 | us;]CE; ∼ , A |
| 40.33 | Atalanta]CE; Atalantis A |
| 41.18 | Runnymeade]CE; Runny Meade A |
| 41.32 | gentleman]CE; gentlemen A |
| 45.15 | boat's]CE; boats' A |
| 45.29 | passion,]CE; ∼ ; A |
| 46.39 | *gendarmes*]CE; *gensd'armes* A *Also corrected at* 208.37, 209.24, 271.8, *and* 275.14. |
| 46.39 | *commissionnaires*]CE; *commissionaires* A |
| 47.21 | P[aul]]CE; P_____ A |
| 47.27 | *Hôtel*]CE; *Hotel* A |
| 47.27 | *d'Angleterre*]CE; *de l'Angleterre* A *Also corrected at* 47.28 *and* 52.34. |

| | |
|---|---|
| 47.28 | *Savez-vous,*]CE; *Savez-vous* ʌ A |
| 47.28 | *où* ]CE; *ou* A |
| 47.28 | *foi*]CE; *fois* A |
| 47.29 | *foi*]CE; *fois* A |
| 47.29 | *près*]CE; *pres* A |
| 48.20 | *côtelettes*]CE; *cotelettes* A |
| 48.35 | *commissionnaire*]CE; *commissionaire* A |
| 49.3 | W[illiam]]CE; W_____ A *Also emended at* 55.1, 58.23, 152.29, 270.25, 271.4, 271.8, 275.1, *and* 275.12. |
| 49.5 | C[ooperstow]n]CE; C_____n A |
| 49.13 | *où* ]CE; *ou* A |
| 49.15 | *viséd*]CE; *visèd* A |
| 49.29 | gets]CE; get A |
| 49.34 | H[unte]r]CE; H_____r A |
| 50.13 | relic]CE; relick A |
| 50.21 | than]CE; that A |
| *52.30 | *Rochefoucauld, et de la Rochefoucauld*]CE; *Rochefoucald, et de la Rouchefoucald* A |
| 52.34 | *Hôtel*]CE; *Hotel* A |
| 54.11 | *Quillebeuf*]CE; *Quilleboeuf* A |
| 54.17 | *Quillebeuf*]CE; *Quilleboeuf* A |
| 55.9 | being:]CE; ~ ʌ A |
| 55.30 | *contretemps*]CE; *contre tems* A *Also corrected at* 94.37, 127.7, 143.2, *and* 225.30. |
| 55.38 | valises]CE; velises A |
| 56.8 | d'Angleterre]CE; de l'Angleterre A |
| *57.14 | burned]CE; buried A |
| 57.29 | *présenter*]CE; *presenter* A |
| 59.25 | *parce que*]CE; *parceque* A |
| 59.26 | *pays-là* ]CE; *pays là* A |
| 61.1 | which]CE; ~, A |
| 61.8 | unpleasantly,]CE; ~ ; A |
| 61.21 | excitements]CE; ~, A |
| 62.6 | etiquette]CE; ettiquette A |
| 62.18 | pavilions]CE; pavillions A *Also corrected at* 63.31-32 *and* 70.19. |
| 63.9 | *l'Etoile*]CE; *L'Etoile* A |
| 63.19-20 | abortions,]CE; ~ ʌ A |
| 63.25 | *Champs-Elysées*]CE; *Champs Elysées* A *Also corrected at* 64.2, 175.18, *and* 222.37. |
| 63.25-26 | verdure]CE; verdue A |
| 63.32 | *Tuileries.*]CE; ~, A |

| | |
|---|---|
| 63.37 | *Tuile*]CE; *Tuil* A |
| 65.4 | *Faubourg*]CE; *Fauxbourg* A |
| 65.17 | Montmartre]CE; Monmartre A |
| 66.2 | *Faubourgs*]CE; *Fauxbourgs* A |
| 66.19 | balloons]CE; baloons A |
| 66.23 | pavilion-tops]CE; pavillion-tops A |
| 66.36 | atmosphere]CE; amosphere A |
| *67.3 | on]CE; in A |
| 67.10 | commence]CE; commences A |
| 67.11 | enclose]CE; encloses A |
| 69.13 | Vicomtesse]CE; Viscomtesse A |
| 69.20 | *Marie-Antoinette*]CE; *Marie Antoinette* A *Also corrected at* 130.11. 130.25, 132.33, *and* 133.4-5. |
| 70.2 | *émigrés*]CE; *emigrés* A |
| 70.5 | *Champ*]CE; *Champs* A *Also corrected at* 105.18 *and* 105.26. |
| 70.11 | Pavilions]CE; Pavillions A |
| 70.29 | pavilion]CE; pavillion A *Also corrected at* 70.33, 71.10, *and* 71.35. |
| 71.4 | balustrade]CE; ballustrade A |
| 75.6 | destroyed]CE; distroyed A |
| 76.36 | even the]CE; event he A |
| 78.8-9 | hail-fellow]CE; hale-fellow A |
| 79.5-6 | *gendarme*]CE; *gensd'arme* A |
| 79.7 | *basse-cour*]CE; *basse cour* A |
| 79.22 | Lansdowne-house]CE; Lansdown-house A |
| 79.34 | you]CE; your A |
| 80.21 | *rez*]CE; *rèz* A |
| 81.6 | *maître*]CE; *maitre* A *Also corrected at* 85.18, 93.1, *and* 125.36. |
| *81.21 | *leurs demoiselles*]CE; *leurres des moiselles* A |
| 82.36 | Salm]CE; Salms A |
| 83.2 | Sheldon]CE; Shelden A |
| 86.35 | Lord]CE; lord A |
| 86.37 | *aplomb*]CE; *àplomb* A |
| 87.6 | fidgety]CE; fidgetty A |
| 87.15 | fidgety]CE; fidgetty A |
| 88.23 | de [Reede-Ginckel]]CE; de _____ A |
| 88.28-29 | de [Reede-Ginckel]]CE; de _____ A |
| 89.32 | Damas,]CE; ~ ∧ A |
| 90.2 | Mrs. [Jarvis]]CE; Mrs. _____ A |
| 90.11 | Mrs. [Jarvis]]CE; Mrs. _____ A |
| 90.14 | O[gde]n]CE; O_____n A |
| 90.16 | Alas!]CE; ~ ? A |

| | |
|---|---|
| 91.15 | *soufflés*]CE; *souflés* A |
| 91.16 | *vol-au-vent*]CE; *vol au vent* A |
| *92.17 | help the guests]CE; help A |
| 93.13 | bigoted]CE; bigotted A |
| *93.21 | sister-in-law]CE; aunt A |
| 93.26 | *maigre*]CE; *maïgre* A |
| 93.33 | *rafraîchissante*]CE; *refraichissante* A |
| 93.39 | *côtelette*]CE; *côtellette* A |
| 94.10 | *chasse-café*]CE; *chasse café* A |
| 98.21 | put it]CE; put A |
| 98.21 | *boîte*]CE; *boite* A |
| 98.24 | de ——, "that]CE; ~ ____," ~ A |
| 98.25 | Mad.]CE; ~ ∧ A |
| 99.38 | devise),]CE; ~ ) ∧ A |
| 100.29 | debaters]CE; debators A |
| 101.7-8 | is or has been a lawyer]CE; are or have been lawyers A |
| 105.8-9 | abject spirit]CE; abject-spirit A |
| 107.16 | *Etat-Major*]CE; *Etat Major* A |
| 107.24 | *gendarmes*]CE; *gens-d'armes* A |
| 108.6 | *gendarmes*]CE; *gens-d'armes* A |
| 108.13 | that "the]CE; " ~ ∧ ~ A |
| 108.17 | *gendarme*]CE; *gens-d'arme* A |
| 112.24 | *Masséna*]CE; *Massena* A |
| 113.5 | *Maréchal*]CE; *Marêchal* A |
| *115.2 | Samuel]CE; Singleton A |
| 115.6 | viz.]CE; ~ ∧ A |
| 115.9 | *gentilhomme*]CE; *gentil'homme* A |
| 116.27 | five-and-twenty]CE; five-and twenty A |
| 117.13 | children]CE; chlldren A |
| 117.18 | *d'Orléans*]CE; *d'Orleans* A |
| 117.20 | *d'Enghien*]CE; *d'Enghein* A |
| 118.33 | crown;]CE; ~, A |
| *121.25 | curule]CE; cerulean A |
| 121.33 | *jeune*]CE; *jèune* A |
| 123.14 | *jeunes*]CE; *jèunes* A |
| 123.16 | *huissier*]CE; *hussier* A |
| 124.21 | *épiciers*]CE; *epiciers* A |
| 125.36 | *Cambacérès*]CE; *Cambaceres* A |
| 126.7 | *pieds*]CE; *pièds* A |
| 126.10 | where]CE; were A |
| 126.34 | your [aunt]]CE; your ____ A |
| 127.4 | your [aunt]]CE; your ____ A |

| | |
|---|---|
| 127.14-15 | *à outrance*]CE; *à l'outrance* A |
| 128.11 | Compiègne]CE; Compèigne A *Also corrected at* 128.31-32, 135.36, 136.36, *and* 204.11. |
| 130.30 | XV.,]CE; ~. ∧ A |
| 130.35 | *Garde-Chasse*]CE; *Garde de Chasse* A |
| 130.36 | *Seigneur*]CE; *Seignieur* A |
| 131.2 | *Seigneur*]CE; *Seignieur* A |
| 131.6 | *Garde-Chasse*]CE; *Garde de Chasse* A |
| 132.7 | windows]CE; ~, A |
| 133.27 | *gentilshommes*]CE; *gentilhommes* A |
| 133.30-31 | *des gardes*]CE; *de gardes* A |
| 133.36 | *œil de bœuf*]CE; *oeil de boeuf* A |
| 135.13 | transferred]CE; transfered A |
| 135.32 | *Jacques*]CE; *Jaques* A |
| 135.33 | *Faubourg*]CE; *Fauxbourg* A |
| 136.3 | *Pierre-fond*]CE; *Pierre Fond* A |
| 136.14 | XIII.,]CE; ~. ∧ A |
| 137.19 | and of]CE; andof A |
| 141.9 | servants']CE; servant's A |
| 142.7 | immerged]CE; emerged A |
| 143.6 | connexion]CE; connexon A |
| 148.1 | XII]CE; I A |
| 149.8 | *Princesse* [*Galitzin Souvarof*]]CE; *Princesse* _____ A |
| 149.11-12 | *coûte que coûte*]CE; *coute qui coute* A |
| 149.26 | girls']CE; girl's A |
| 149.26 | boarding-school,]CE; boarding-school; A |
| 149.28 | *second*]CE; *seconde* A |
| 149.39 | *Mons.* [*Cooper*]]CE; *Mons.* _____ A |
| 149.41 | *m'appelle* [*Cooper*]]CE; *m'appele* _____ A |
| 150.3-4 | *Princesse* [*Galitzin Souvarof*]]CE; *Princesse* _____ A |
| 150.38 | led]CE; lead A |
| 151.20 | Waverley]CE; Waverly A |
| 152.12 | Macdonald]CE; M'Donald A |
| 153.3 | *douillette*]CE; *douilliette* A |
| 153.9 | *Princesse* [*Galitzin*]]CE; *Princesse* _____ A *Also emended at* 155.12-13 *and* 157.15-16. |
| 156.1 | *Monsieur* [*Cooper*]]CE; *Monsieur* _____ A |
| 156.1 | *quels*]CE; *quelles* A |
| 156.4 | *Monsieur* [*Cooper*]]CE; *Monsieur* _____ A |
| 156.5 | *première*]CE; *premiere* A |
| 156.34 | himself.]CE; ~.. A |
| 156.37 | *aplomb*]CE; *àplomb* A |

| | |
|---|---|
| 157.12 | Sir]CE; that Sir A |
| 157.33 | *temps*]CE; *tems* A |
| 157.36 | *depuis*]CE; *dépuis* A |
| 157.36 | *siècles*]CE; *siécles* A |
| 159.3 | *savant*]CE; *savan* A |
| 161.1 | XIII]CE; II A |
| 162.39 | *Sèvres*]CE; *Sêvres* A *Also corrected at* 163.27, 163.34, *and* 163.39. |
| 163.33 | *Royale toute cuite*]CE; *Royal tout cuit* A |
| 166.11 | carpeted]CE; carpetted A |
| 170.13 | rogues,]CE; ∼ ; A |
| 171.1 | XIV]CE; III A |
| 171.8 | *petites-maîtresses*]CE; *petites maitresses* A |
| *171.12 | duke]CE; Duke A |
| 175.1 | *Polonaise*]CE; *Polognnaise* A |
| 177.1 | XV]CE; IV A |
| 177.14 | throw]CE; throws A |
| 178.29 | *Molière*]CE; *Moliere* A |
| 178.30-31 | "though we]CE; ∧ ∼ "∼ A |
| 179.12 | *connoisseurs*]CE; *connisseurs* A |
| 179.24 | *petits-maîtres*]CE; *petits maîtres* A |
| 181.37 | *Théâtre-Français*]CE; *Théâtre Français* A |
| 182.15 | *Théâtre-Français*]CE; *Théâtre Français* A |
| 182.16 | *Odéon*]CE; *Odeon* A |
| 182.26 | *Théâtre de Madame*]CE; *Théâtre Madame* A |
| 182.27 | *coterie*]CE; *côterie* A |
| 184.5 | *coterie*]CE; *côterie* A |
| 184.11 | Necker]CE; Neckar A |
| 185.18 | de [Marbois]]CE; de _____ A |
| 185.21 | *cacoëthes*]CE; *cacœthes* A |
| 186.4 | *émigrés*]CE; *emigrés* A |
| 186.27 | scissors-men]CE; scissor's men A |
| 189.32 | *public"!*]CE; ∼ ."! A |
| 190.1 | XVI]CE; V A |
| 190.31 | [du Cayla]]CE; de _____ A |
| 191.1 | Necker]CE; Neckar A |
| 191.4 | *fanfaronnade*]CE; *fanfaronade* A |
| 191.10 | *régime*]CE; *règime* A |
| 191.27 | *portes cochères*]CE; *porte-cochères* A |
| 191.36 | *respec,*]CE; ∼ . A |
| 191.37 | connêtable]CE; connêtable A |
| 191.39 | *pieds*]CE; *piés* A |

| | |
|---|---|
| 193.14 | water's]CE; waters A |
| 193.32 | *champêtres*]CE; *champêtre* A |
| 193.34 | *gendarmes*]CE; *gensdarmes* A |
| 193.34 | *pied*]CE; *pié* A |
| 194.10 | trot]CE; strot A |
| 195.9 | *confrères*]CE; *confreres* A |
| 195.13 | *frère*]CE; *frere* A |
| 195.13 | *fais-tu*]CE; *fais tu* A |
| 195.18 | *épicier*]CE; *epicier* A |
| 195.39 | *sou*]CE; *sous* A |
| *196.11 | since]CE; ince A |
| 196.17 | [*d'Orsvault*]]CE; *de* _____ A |
| 196.37 | *Chrétiens*]CE; *Chretiens* A |
| 197.13 | *octroi*]CE; *ortroi* A |
| 198.1 | XVII]CE; VI A |
| 199.28 | Capt. [Chauncey]]CE; Capt. _____ A |
| 199.37 | *faubourg*]CE; *fauxbourg* A |
| 199.38 | *du faubourg*]CE; *fauxbourg* A |
| 200.8 | *La Chaise*]CE; *la Chaise* A |
| 200.12 | *Trône*]CE; *trone* A |
| 200.14 | *d'Austerlitz*]CE; *d'Austerlitz* A |
| 201.22 | *d'Ivry*]CE; *d'Ivry* A |
| 201.25 | *Villejuif*]CE; *Ville Juif* A |
| 201.28 | *d'Iéna*]CE; *de Jéne* A |
| 202.10 | *jardin*]CE; *jardins* A |
| 202.11 | Choleric]CE; Cholerick A |
| 203.28-29 | '*boily vous-même.*' "]CE; "*boily vous-même.* ᴧ" A |
| 204.35 | tells]CE; tell A |
| 204.37 | *Bibliothèque*]CE; *Bibliotheque* A |
| *205.29 | unnecessary]CE; un necessary A |
| 205.34 | capital.]CE; ~ ᴧ A |
| 208.7 | *octroi*]CE; *ortroi* A |
| 208.19 | exhilarated]CE; exhilirated A |
| 209.33 | *jardin*]CE; *jardins* A |
| 210.1 | XVIII]CE; VII A |
| 210.24 | ability]CE; ~ , A |
| *212.39 | difference]CE; indifference A |
| 213.31 | *millionnaire*]CE; *milionaire* A |
| 213.34 | *coteries*]CE; *côteries* A |
| 214.32-33 | Madame [Cooper]]CE; Madame _____ A |
| 214.34 | *Madame [Cooper]*]CE; *Madame* _____ A |
| 215.24 | curtsey]CE; curtesy A |

| | |
|---|---|
| 216.18 | La Fayette]CE; la Fayette A |
| 216.36 | La Fayette]CE; la Fayette A |
| 218.11 | *pêle-mêle*]CE; *pèle mèle* A |
| 219.39 | [*Dambray*]]CE; *de* _____ A *Also emended at* 220.8 *and* 220.8. |
| 220.9 | *de France*]CE; *de la France* A |
| 220.39 | *coteries*]CE; *côteries* A |
| 221.17 | de [Mirbel]]CE; de _____ A *Also emended at* 221.26, 221.33, 222.3, *and* 222.16. |
| 221.31 | *Président*]CE; *President* A |
| 222.8 | *vieille*]CE; *veille* A |
| 222.10 | *émigration*]CE; *emigration* A |
| 222.27 | or at]CE; of at A |
| 222.30 | have]CE; has A |
| 223.2 | of [Dunmore]]CE; of _____ A |
| 223.21 | Sir James [De Bathe]]CE; Sir James _____ A |
| 223.27 | Sir [James Michael De Bathe]]CE; Sir William _____ A |
| 223.28 | Sir James [Wynne De Bathe]]CE; Sir James _____ A |
| 224.9 | Count [Pozzo di Borgo]]CE; Count _____ A |
| 224.9 | [Russian] Legation]CE; _____ Legation A |
| 224.11 | *gendarmes*]CE; *gensdarmes* A |
| 224.17 | affirmed]CE; affirm A |
| 225.31 | *N'est-ce*]CE; *Ne c'est-ce* A |
| 226.27 | *Monsieur* [*Cooper*]]CE; *monsieur* _____ A |
| 227.21 | Lady [Virginia Murray]'s]CE; Lady _____ _____'s A |
| 227.31 | Lady [Conyngham]]CE; Lady _____ A |
| 227.36 | *Parc-aux-Cerfs*]CE; *parc des Cerfs* A |
| 228.2 | 'real presence.']CE; " ~ ~." A |
| 228.3 | *reposoir*]CE; *reposior* A |
| 229.1 | XIX]CE; VIII A |
| 231.12 | McDuffie]CE; M'Duffie A |
| 233.25 | carrying]CE; carying A |
| 238.1 | XX]CE; IX A |
| 238.14 | *Bastille*]CE; *Bastile* A |
| 238.15 | *Trône*]CE; *Trone* A |
| 238.21 | *fanfaronnade*]CE; *fanfaronade* A |
| 238.25 | *Trône*]CE; *Trone* A |
| 239.12 | *bâtiments*]CE; *batiments* A |
| 239.35 | VI.,]CE; ~. ʌ A |
| 240.14 | squalid]CE; ~, A |
| 240.35 | *Maréchal*]CE; *Marèschal* A |
| 240.36 | *des Victoires*]CE; *de la Victoire* A |

| | |
|---|---|
| 241.19 | has]CE; have A |
| 241.29 | pyramidal]CE; pyrimidal A |
| 241.39 | d'Uzès]CE; d'Uzés A |
| 244.1 | grandchildren]CE; grand children A |
| 246.7 | information]CE; imformation A |
| 246.20 | Dulaure]CE; Du Laure A |
| 247.3 | *goûter*]CE; *gouter* A |
| 247.10 | owner,]CE; ~ ; A |
| *247.12 | meddling in]CE; meddling, which in A |
| 247.32 | *compotes*]CE; *compôtes* A |
| 249.1 | XXI]CE; X A |
| 251.28 | M. [Cooper]]CE; M. _____ A |
| 253.20 | *jeune*]CE; *jeunes* A |
| 253.21 | *vertus*]CE; *vertues* A |
| 260.1 | XXII]CE; XI A |
| 260.32 | M. [Chapelain]]]CE; M. _____ A |
| 261.22 | C[hapelain]]]CE; C _____ A *Also emended at* 261.26, 261.34, 262.1, 262.28, 263.7, 263.9, 263.24, 263.31. 263.38, 264.1, 264.36, 265.3, 266.15, 266.33, 267.8, 267.16, 267.25, 267.33, 268.3, *and* 269.37. |
| 265.5 | may]CE; many A |
| 267.27 | either]CE; neither A |
| 269.30 | uniformity]CE; unifornity A |
| 270.1 | XXIII]CE; XII A |
| 270.8 | take]CE; takes A |
| 270.9 | remove]CE; removes A |
| 270.9 | prepare]CE; prepares A |
| 270.26 | Miss [Wiggin]]]CE; Miss _____ A |
| *271.6 | need]CE; Need A |
| 273.7 | Lathom-house]CE; Latham-house A |
| 273.27 | Samer]CE; Saumer A |
| 275.6 | *gendarme*]CE; *gensdarme* A |
| 275.12 | *très*]CE; *tres* A |

# Word-Division

List A records compounds or possible compounds which are hyphenated at the end of the line in the copy-text and which must be editorially resolved as hyphenated or unhyphenated. The resolution in the Cooper Edition is indicated by the form in which the word appears in the list. The forms adopted are those that Cooper employs most frequently elsewhere in the copy-text, or, in those instances in which the word appears only once, the forms are derived from his treatment of those words in manuscripts or first editions of works of this period. List B records compounds which are hyphenated at the end of the line in the Cooper Edition. Words divided at the end of the line and not listed here should be transcribed as unhyphenated words.

## LIST A

| | | | |
|---|---|---|---|
| 3.35 | household | 38.32 | Opera-house |
| 5.3 | Highlands | 45.5 | steam-boat |
| 7.9 | seaward | 45.17 | bachelor-looking |
| 9.21 | eastward | 51.3 | outer-harbour |
| 11.23 | seaman | 53.2 | seamen |
| 12.3 | Eddystone | 55.39 | thirty-seven |
| 12.6 | Ninety-seven | 56.4 | straight-forward |
| 12.20 | in-shore | 58.21 | twenty-five |
| 13.6 | ship-owners | 63.3 | *Marly-la-* |
| 14.19 | ill-fated | 63.27 | well-dressed |
| 15.33 | seamen | 66.26 | twelvemonth |
| 21.24 | Anglo-Saxon | 70.8 | overlook |
| 24.38 | good-looking | 71.13 | hard-featured |
| 27.18 | Below-bar | 71.20 | gentlemen |
| 28.5 | drawing-room | 71.21 | Frenchman |
| 28.15 | -great-grand- | 79.22 | Sutherland-house |
| 33.6 | mail-coaches | 79.39 | bed-rooms |
| 33.20 | *-non-finito* | 80.14 | bed-room |
| 37.25 | commonwealth | 81.8 | drawing-room |

| | | | |
|---|---|---|---|
| 84.35 | foresee | 206.28 | outdo |
| 85.7 | statesmen | 208.10 | sea-port |
| 86.36 | -in-law | 209.21 | Frenchman |
| 89.38 | clergyman | 210.29 | self-respect |
| 93.21 | fast-days | 212.4 | fortnight |
| 96.35 | hardship | 217.4 | ante-chambers |
| 102.8 | Frenchmen | 221.30 | staircases |
| 114.24 | mock-fights | 221.36 | top-gallant- |
| 115.29 | ante-chamber | 223.30 | good-hearted |
| 116.27 | five-and- | 224.6 | humbugged |
| 119.7 | Dolphinstown | 235.27 | grandfather |
| 121.9 | *embonpoint* | 243.24 | dressing-rooms |
| 124.26 | sunflowers | 244.40 | Frenchman |
| 128.27 | upland | 246.14 | store-house |
| 130.35 | Dairy-Woman | 246.35 | thorough-fare |
| 133.13 | drawing-room | 248.15-16 | shop-keeper |
| 136.5 | high-way | 249.5 | under-plots |
| 137.2-3 | roebucks | 257.10 | passport |
| 145.19 | countryman | 263.26 | good-humoured |
| 154.40 | copy-right | 265.20 | faith-shaking |
| 156.17 | tower-like | 266.7 | clock-work |
| 161.32 | iron-ware | 266.30 | stop-watch |
| 164.27 | paper-maker | 271.5 | passport |
| 166.24 | purse-proud | 272.25 | grain-lands |
| 167.16 | worm-eaten | 274.1 | wheat-runners |
| 169.39 | *statesmen* | | |
| 170.28 | overwhelming | | |
| 171.8 | overdressed | | |
| 172.11 | Englishman | **LIST B** | |
| 178.15 | *log-rolling* | | |
| 185.13 | Statesmen | 1.18 | self-distrust |
| 186.13 | ink-pot | 5.13 | -of-war's |
| 190.34 | birth-place | 5.39 | well-wisher |
| 194.19 | way-farers | 11.4 | main-topsail |
| 194.39 | two-thirds | 11.27 | south-west |
| 195.25-26 | *Laisse-moi* | 13.20 | top-mast |
| 202.4 | forthwith | 27.9 | twenty-eight |
| 202.28 | outright | 27.35 | bed-rooms |
| 203.28-29 | *vous-même* | 31.13 | -ck-bud |
| 204.7 | post-chaises | 33.25 | Adam-street |
| 204.16 | high-way | 33.27 | blubber-cheeks |
| 205.12 | shabby-genteel | 34.7 | -le-Dane |

| | | | | |
|---|---|---|---|---|
| 63.2 | semi-barbarous | | 155.6 | old-fashioned |
| 69.13 | Gontaut-Biron | | 156.25 | good-natured |
| 76.29 | eating-houses | | 169.13 | self-complacency |
| 78.8 | hail-fellow | | 171.21 | be-whiskered |
| 79.39 | eating-rooms | | 174.24 | well-balanced |
| 80.22 | *ante-chamber* | | 195.25 | *Laisse-moi* |
| 80.29 | New-York | | 203.14 | ship-fashion |
| 81.4 | carriage-boxes | | 203.28 | *vous-même* |
| 84.15 | heart-burning | | 214.13 | court-yard |
| 84.17 | dinner-table | | 228.4 | ex-favourite |
| 85.16 | ill-bred | | 240.32 | *Courtenay-Bléneau* |
| 85.32 | well-built | | 245.6 | lieutenant-general |
| 113.12 | side-walk | | 248.15 | shop-keeper |
| 113.36 | guard-house | | 251.19 | often-repeated |
| 133.4 | *Marie-Antoinette* | | 252.23 | straight-forward |

# Index

This index includes persons, places, things, and topics of concern that are mentioned or alluded to in Cooper's text, including his own footnotes. Subjects that are glossed in the Explanatory Notes of this edition are indicated by an asterisk (*) placed before the appropriate page number. The letter "n" following a numeral indicates a reference to a note in Cooper's text.